A SYSTEMS APPROACH
TO SMALL GROUP
INTERACTION

A SYSTEMS APPROACH TO SMALL GROUP INTERACTION

FOURTH EDITION

STEWART L. TUBBS

Dean, College of Business

Eastern Michigan University

McGRAW-HILL, INC.

New York St. Louis San Francisco Auckland Bogotá
Caracas Lisbon London Madrid Mexico City Milan
Montreal New Delhi San Juan Singapore
Sydney Tokyo Toronto

A Systems Approach to Small Group Interaction

Copyright © 1992, 1988, 1984, 1978 by McGraw-Hill, Inc. All rights reserved.
Printed in the United States of America. Except as permitted under the United
States Copyright Act of 1976, no part of this publication may be reproduced or
distributed in any form or by any means, or stored in a data base or retrieval
system, without the prior written permission of the publisher.

6 7 8 9   DOH DOH 9 0 9 8 7 6 5 4

ISBN 0-07-065407-7

This book was set in Plantin by General Graphic Services, Inc.
The editors were Hilary Jackson, Lyn Beamesderfer, and James R. Belser;
the production supervisor was Friederich W. Schulte.
The cover was designed by David Romanoff.
R. R. Donnelley & Sons Company was printer and binder.

This book is printed on acid-free paper.

Library of Congress Cataloging-in-Publication Data

Tubbs, Stewart L., (date).
    A systems approach to small group interaction / Stewart L. Tubbs.
    —4th ed.
        p.   cm.
    Includes bibliographical references and index.
    ISBN 0-07-065407-7
    1. Work groups.   2. Small groups.   3. Organizational behavior.
    I. Title
    HD66.T82   1992
    302.3′4—dc20   91-14550

ABOUT THE AUTHOR

Stewart L. Tubbs is dean of the College of Business and professor of management at Eastern Michigan University. He received his doctorate in communication and organizational behavior from the University of Kansas. His master's degree in communication and his bachelor's degree in science are from Bowling Green State University. He has completed postdoctoral work in management at Michigan State University, the University of Michigan, and Harvard Business School.

Dr. Tubbs has also taught at General Motors Institute and at Boise State University, where he was chairman of the Management Department and later associate dean of the College of Business.

He has been named an Outstanding Teacher three times, has consulted extensively for Fortune 500 companies, and is past chairman of the Organizational Communication division of the Academy of Management. Dr. Tubbs is the co-author, with Sylvia Moss, of *Interpersonal Communication* and *Human Communication*. He is also listed in *American Men and Women of Science, Contemporary Authors, Directory of American Scholars,* the *International Who's Who in Education,* and *Outstanding Young Men of America.*

To the memory of
my father and mother

CONTENTS

ix

3   Group Circumstances and Structure   96

4   Leadership and Social Influence Processes   148

5   Communication Processes   208

6   Conflict Resolution and Decision-Making Processes   265

7   Consequences   325

PREFACE

This book is intended as a primary text for courses in group communication. Since it was first published, it has been used by over thirty thousand students. While I am very pleased with the book's success, I feel an increased responsibility to improve it wherever possible. As a result, this is the most extensive revision and updating of any edition thus far.

In the fourth edition, I have retained the general systems approach, which is unique to this book. This approach views the small group as an open system of simultaneously interacting forces. This conceptual framework originally evolved out of my desire to organize and synthesize the small group literature for my own teaching. For this edition, new material has been added from over one hundred sources, the vast majority of which have appeared in print since the third edition of this book was published in 1988.

FEATURES

The book's format—text with readings—continues to be unique among small group texts. This edition has a much expanded table of contents. Also new in this edition are a preview and glossary of key terms at the beginning of each chapter.

Following each glossary is a real-life case study that illustrates the principles discussed in the chapter. Three out of the seven cases are new for this edition. Following each case is the text of the chapter itself.

At the end of each chapter are exercises designed for student involvement and skill development. Following each set of exercises are two carefully chosen reading selections for each chapter. The readings elaborate on one or more of the topics discussed in the chapter. Four of the reading selections are new for this edition.

PLAN OF THE BOOK

Chapter 1, entitled "What Is Small Group Interaction?" offers key definitions and reviews the classic models for analyzing small group behavior. It also explains the conceptual overview of the remainder of the book. New in this edition are:

- The case study on the Saturn Corporation.
- The section entitled "Why Study Small Groups?"
- Expanded treatment of general systems theory.

Chapter 2, "Relevant Background Factors," discusses six characteristics of individual group members that will influence the group's functioning. They are personality, sex, age, health, attitudes, and values. New in this edition are:

- Personality factors illustrated in the lives of such notables as Jessica Savitch and Sammy Davis, Jr.

- Material on sex in the workplace as well as the role of gender in career success.

- Information on certain values that are associated with career advancement.

- A revised reading selection that demonstrates the applications of attitude change theory for leaders.

Chapter 3, "Group Circumstances and Structure," discusses the group's physical environment, group size and structure, and different types of groups. New in this edition are:

- Material on the family group.

- Material on social groups (including street gangs).

- Information on educational groups.

- Discussion of the Nominal Group Technique (NGT).

- A reading selection applying contemporary leadership concepts to educational groups.

Chapter 4, "Leadership and Social Influence Processes," discusses status, power, leadership, group norms, and conformity pressures. New in this edition are:

- The opening case study.

- Information on the relationship between status and group acceptance of an individual.

- Research findings on the relationship of physical size and shape to starting job salary.

- Information on leadership styles.

- Research findings on the characteristics of highly effective college presidents.

- Research findings on peer pressure and its relation to academic achievement among students.

- Material on peer pressure and its effect on teenage sexual practices.

- A new case study in the student exercises section.

Chapter 5, "Communication Processes," deals with the unique aspects of communication in the small group setting. It covers language behavior, self-disclosure, and interaction roles. New in this edition are:

- Research on group structure and communication.

- Information on the use of "strategic ambiguity."

- Research findings on nonverbal communication.

- Information on how to effectively use criticism.

- Expanded coverage of the topic of confirming versus disconfirming communication behaviors.

- Contemporary examples of language behaviors related to an airline crash, the renaming of manholes in California, and the banning of the 2 Live Crew album "As Nasty As They Wanna Be."

- A reading selection that shows the tremendous improvement in a General Motors factory resulting from improved supervisory communication and the effective use of groups.

Chapter 6, "Conflict Resolution and Decision-Making Processes," examines the various methods for organizing group problem solving as well as the topic of conflict resolution. New in this edition are:

- Expanded coverage of left brain and right brain functioning.

- Material on the uses of decision-making methods in the multibillion-dollar Superconducting Super Collider decision.

- Contemporary applications of brainstorming.

- Expanded coverage of "principled negotiation" as a method of conflict management.

- Expanded coverage of conflict-reducing techniques.

- A reading selection on conflict resolution.

Chapter 7, "Consequences," is devoted to the outcomes of group activity. It covers solutions to problems, changes in interpersonal relations, improved information flow, increased risk taking, interpersonal growth, and organizational change. New in this edition are:

- Descriptions of the use of group techniques to create a major organizational turnaround that resulted in the best American car quality at Buick.

- An entirely new section on team building that includes dramatic new research findings linking the successes of such varied teams as the McDonald's Chicken McNuggets team, the Mt. Everest climbing team, and the cardiac surgical teams of Dr. Michael Debakey and Dr. Denton Cooley.

- The identification of the ten most common pitfalls of teambuilding.

- Examples of organizational change at Xerox and Fernco.

Much of the new material shows the applications of group dynamics to job settings, thus continuing the book's strong integration of research and theory with life and career applications.

INSTRUCTOR'S MANUAL

The instructor's manual that accompanies the text has sample syllabi, additional class exercises, suggested films, and a variety of test questions that cover each chapter. The goal, as in the previous editions, is to make the book as usable as possible for the instructor.

ACKNOWLEDGMENTS

I would like to thank the reviewers whose valuable suggestions helped guide this latest revision. They are Terry Chmielewski, University of Wisconsin, Eu Claire; Robert Cocetti, Kearney State College; Dan Curtis, Central Missouri State University; Tim Harper, San Jose City College; William Harpine, University of Akron; James Hasenauer, California State University, Northridge; Lisa Newman, University of Cincinnati; and David Walker, Middle Tennessee State University. Finally, I would especially like to thank Heidi Welser for her research assistance, Mary Schmaltz for her excellent help in various stages of the manuscript preparation, and Bridgette Darby for her assistance.

Stewart L. Tubbs

A SYSTEMS APPROACH TO SMALL GROUP INTERACTION

What Is Small Group Interaction?

PREVIEW

Chapter 1 is dedicated to laying the groundwork for the rest of the book. It begins with a definition of small group interaction. *It describes and explains Mills's six models for studying and analyzing small groups. Chapter 1 also introduces systems theory along with a general systems model. The Tubbs Model of Small Group Interaction identifies three categories of variables: relevant background factors, internal influences, and consequences. Ten general systems concepts that apply to the model are explained briefly.*

GLOSSARY

Input: Input is the raw material of small group interaction. It includes the six relevant background factors: personality, sex, age, health, attitudes, and values. It also includes information the group receives from outside the group.

Throughput: Throughput refers to all the actual verbal and nonverbal behaviors that occur in the course of a group discussion.

Output: Output is often referred to as encompassing solutions, interpersonal relations, improved information flow, risk taking, interpersonal growth, and organizational change. It is sometimes called the end result of group interaction.

Cycles: A cycle is characterized by the results of group interaction being fed back to the group and becoming input for future interactions. For example, a team's success adds strength to the group's cohesion in future activities.

Negative Entropy: Entropy is characterized by all systems moving toward disorganization or death. Negative entropies are the forces that maintain the organization of a system.

Feedback: Feedback is the receiving of information by groups in order to modify themselves.

Dynamic Equilibrium: Dynamic equilibrium is reached at a point at which the forces to change and the forces to resist change are equal.

Differentiation: Differentiation is the specialization that occurs among people in small group communication.

Integration: Integration in small group communication is synonymous with organization. It is the coordination of the various parts of the group.

Equifinality: Equifinality is the potential for adaptation that groups possess. This allows for various possible approaches to achieve a goal.

CASE STUDY: Saturn Corporation

Spring Hill, Tenn.

If you had visited the General Motors assembly plant in Lordstown, Ohio, in the early 1970s, you would have found wall-to-wall arguments. You might find workers arguing at the Saturn Corporation car manufacturing complex near Nashville, but don't get the idea that there is any real resemblance between the two plants.

There are those who say that GM never does anything different, that Saturn is nothing more than an update of the Chevrolet Vega built at Lordstown in the 1970s, which was a new and improved version of the Chevrolet Corvair of the 1960s. Saturn really does have something new here—so different that tradition-minded visitors find it difficult to comprehend. The assembly line worker really, really has been given a decisive voice in the workplace. In fact, they must have their say, or nothing gets done. That's been true nearly since the inception of Saturn eight years ago, and the big plant in Tennessee is partly their handiwork.

The Vega started out as a cleansheet approach to small car production. Engineers and manufacturing experts mustered the latest technology, drew blueprints showing that cars could be assembled at the then unheard of rate of 100 per hour, and hustled them down to the plant floor without consulting workers.

It just didn't work. Lordstown in the 1970s became an industrial battleground, a daily class struggle between management and labor. And its memory was fresh in the minds of GM and UAW officials who set up Saturn as a people-oriented shop.

The sin of earlier GM cars was that workers were excluded from the planning process and simply ordered to do what management thought best. The sin of Saturn may be that GM went too far in the opposite direction, making workers directly responsible for important details of the production process. But Saturn people don't think so.

Opportunity Beats Risk

The basic unit of organization at Saturn is the work team, about a dozen people in charge of a segment of the production process. Everyone at Saturn is on salary, which eliminates, at the team level, one distinction between management and labor. At Saturn, there are the represented (by the United Auto Workers) and the nonrepresented. Both are present at every level of decision making, and both must sign off on decisions.

Indeed, the Saturn Bible—guidelines that specify thirty work unit functions—starts with the requirement that decisions be made by consensus, with "no formal leader apparent in the process." Everyone in the team must agree on a step before it can be taken, and all team members "must be at least 70 percent comfortable with the decision, and 100 percent committed to its implementation," the document says.

This leads to a lot of what Michael E. Bennett, president of UAW Local 1853 at Saturn and a top-level production planning coordinator, describes as "constructive conflict," which apparently gets down at times to some good old-fashioned yelling. "Can you imagine in the old world—General Motors or Ford or Chrysler or a Japanese plant—where the union, in effect, could hold up a decision for a year and a half because we couldn't come to consensus on it?" Bennett asked. "That's what happened here. It took us a year and a half to make a decision on the production system in general assembly, to get that technology and those people issues all melded together."

Concept Can Be 'Confusing'

No other car plant in the world puts so much authority so close to the actual work, and it often becomes troublesome. "There can be ambiguity around here in terms of newness, in terms of responsibility and authority, and you can find yourself somewhat confused and frustrated." Then why bother with teams, you wonder.

First, the auto industry has discovered that teamwork is the most effective way to focus on continuous improvement of the production process. But Charles J. Stridde, Saturn's chief personnel coordinator, says there's a more important reason—it's a means of getting people more actively involved in and more committed to their jobs.

"Ownership" is Saturn's magic word. It is used here in two senses. People should feel they have a personal stake in the success of the enterprise, and at Saturn that is literally true; a majority of Saturn workers left GM jobs elsewhere, burning their bridges behind them. "There's no going back," Stridde said.

Pay Tied to Sales Goals

Second, 20 percent of every Saturn worker's paycheck is at risk. In the most practical way possible, their success will be tied to that of the firm. Saturn workers now are paid the same amount as comparable hourly workers elsewhere at GM. But when the plant is fully operational, 80 percent of the standard rate will be paid, and the rest will depend on meeting sales goals.

This new role for the worker, coming after a century of occasionally blood-soaked labor strife, doesn't sit too well with some observers. Michael Parker, a former autoworker and author, describes modern work teams as "conceptual chain gangs" and says their installation at other plants has been stressful because many people naturally dislike them. He concedes, however, that they boost productivity.

But Saturn people say the focus on teamwork is what sets them apart from other operations—especially Japanese auto plants, where teams are mere problem-solving units. "If we do what the Japanese have done, we won't be any better than the Japanese," says Saturn manufacturing engineer Ed Raby.

1. What does this case study tell you about working in groups versus working in teams? What are the advantages and disadvantages of each?

2. Would you recommend setting up an organizational structure similar to that of the Saturn plant? Why, or why not?

3. In your own work experience, how have teams been used? What were the results? What changes would you recommend?

From James V. Higgins, "Line Workers Really Do Help Make Decisions," *The Detroit News*, May 13, 1990, pp. 1D, 3D.

A DEFINITION

If you were going to define the term "small group interaction," how would you do it? First, you would probably want to consider size. Would two people constitute a group? How about fifty people? Most (although not all) experts agree that a group consists of at least three people. Because this book is about small groups, we can arbitrarily consider "small" to range from three to about twenty people.

But size is only one consideration. Shaw (1976) has proposed six different considerations in identifying a group. They are (1) perceptions (do members make an impression on others?); (2) motivation (is the group rewarding?); (3) goals (working together for a purpose); (4) organization (each person has some organized role to play, such as moderator, note taker, etc.); (5) interdependence (each person is somewhat dependent on the others); and (6) interaction (the group is small enough to allow face-to-face communication among members). A group may be defined in any of the above ways.

What do we mean by interaction? Interaction simply means communication. This includes talking and listening, headnods, gestures, glances, pats on the back, smiles, frowns, and any other behavior to which people assign meaning. Because communication occurs in an ever-changing context, we refer to this as the *process* of communication. The analogy that is often used is that of a movie or a videotape as opposed to a snapshot of group behavior. To summarize, small group interaction is the process by which three or more members of a group exchange verbal and nonverbal messages in an attempt to influence one another.

What is the difference between a group and a team? The term "group" is more general. A team is a type of group. Larson and LaFasto (1989) define a team as having "two or more people; it has a specific . . . goal to be attained; and coordination of activity among the members . . . is required for the attainment of the . . . goal" (p. 19). Notice how similar that definition is to Dyer's (1987) definition, which states that: "all teams represent a collection of people who must collaborate, to some degree, to achieve common goals . . ." (p. 24). The word "team" also has come to connote closer cooperation and cohesiveness than the term "group." So when we use the word "team," it implies closeness as well as cooperation.

Perhaps you noticed the extensive use of the word "team" in the Saturn case. This is simply one of many ways the company promotes closer, more cooperative employee relationships.

Why Study Small Groups?

As we saw in the Saturn Corporation case, modern organizations are undergoing a radical transformation designed to better utilize human potential, primarily through the increased use of small groups. In fact, Fortune magazine calls effective work groups "the productivity breakthrough of the 1990's" (Dumaine, 1990, p. 52). For example, Saturn Corporation was created with a revolutionary new organizational structure that uses groups as the basic leadership unit. In fact, the name Saturn was chosen to reflect the concentric rings of decision-making teams that run the

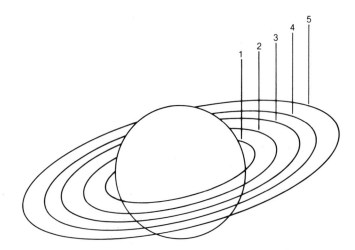

organization. Experts argue that this is the prototype of the organizational structure of the future.

In your lifetime, and in your career, you will undoubtedly be very much affected by these organizational changes. The exciting thing about all this is that the world of work will be more enriching and interesting than it was for your parents' generation. However, the challenge is for you to improve your proficiency in small group situations. This book is dedicated to that end.

In over twenty years of college teaching, the one question that students have asked me the most is "How can I become a success?" Students are often surprised by the answers. The effective use of small groups has been found to be essential to career success. After extensive examination of successful people, Whetton and Cameron (1984, p. 6) have identified what they consider the nine most important skills required for career success. They are:

1. Development of Self-Awareness;

2. Managing Personal Stress;

3. Solving Problems Creatively;

4. Establishing Supportive Communication;

5. Gaining Power and Influence;

6. Improving Employee Performance Through Motivation;

7. Delegating and Decision Making;

8. Managing Conflict;

9. Conducting Effective Group Meetings.

Of these nine, only the second (managing personal stress) is not a part of the material covered in this book. In other words, this book is devoted to improving your understanding of the major action skills required for your career success. However, the important thing to remember is that we are talking about behavioral skills, not just knowing about those skills. Like all skills, development begins with new information and proceeds with practice, practice, and more practice, with continual modification and improvement based on feedback from previous performance.

Small groups can help you in college as well as in your career. For example, Fiske (1990) reported a Harvard University study conducted at twenty-one universities that showed that students who study in small groups learn more effectively than those who don't. Also, small group study experiences correlate with overall satisfaction in college (p. A1). For years Harvard Business School has required that their students form study groups and remain in those groups throughout the course (Kelly and Kelly, 1986). Furthermore, Sorenson, Savage, and Orem (1990) surveyed 440 business schools in the United States, Canada, and South America and found that an increasing number were adding small group communication courses to their required curriculum because of the increasing relevance to student needs. For example, Connecticut General Life Insurance Company (1975) found that the average executive spends over 700 hours a year in meetings, or almost two out of every five working days totally spent in small group meetings.

Learning to work effectively in small groups can save you time and money. The chart on page 8 shows the value of people's time as their salary increases. If we can learn to improve our meeting effectiveness and thus cut the number and length of meetings, it can yield a measurable savings. Westinghouse reportedly installed electronic numerical key pads in meeting rooms and had each group member enter his or her salary into the computer as he or she came into the room. Then the computer was started as the meeting began and gave a continuous readout of the cost of the meeting as time went on. Over a few months' time, corporatewide, Westinghouse cut its meeting times in half by simply making participants aware of the cost of each meeting and the cost of each person's comments. Evidently, this important feedback made people more consciously weigh the real value of their comments and encouraged them to waste less time.

Leaders are increasingly learning to improve their use of small groups to effectively accomplish organizational goals. Few leaders in today's complex society can succeed on their own without the help of competent and committed team members.

Bradford and Cohen (1984, pp. 10–11) have argued persuasively in their best-selling book, *Managing for Excellence,* that the Manager as Hero style, which worked well in the past, has given way to the Manager as Developer, which is the style for today and for the future. They identify four myths of the heroic management style:

1. The good manager knows at all times what is going on in the department;

2. The good manager should have more technical expertise than any subordinate;

3. The good manager should be able to solve any problem that comes up (or at least solve it before the subordinate can);

4. The good manager should be the primary (if not the only) person responsible for how the department is working.

They go on to say that:

> The solution that worked yesterday is only slightly appropriate today and will be irrelevant tomorrow. Task complexity virtually assures that no one person can have all the necessary knowledge which forces a heightened degree of interdependence among subordinates (and a much greater demand for coordination) if work is to be successfully accomplished, especially at an excellent level. . . . Heroism may be motivating for the superior but it has the opposite effect on subordinates. . . . Today there are far more subordinates who want to be challenged by work; they place "challenging jobs" and "a change to grow and develop" ahead of such rewards as pay, status, and job security. (pp. 12, 15)

In this book we will explore the working mechanism of the Manager as Developer— namely, the small group.

THE VALUE OF PEOPLE'S TIME

Salary Year	Salary Week	Benefits = 40% Total Salary	Total Week	Value Per Hour	Value Per Minute
$ 1,000	$ 19.23	$ 7.69	$ 26.92	$ .67	$ .01
2,000	38.46	15.38	53.84	1.35	.02
3,000	57.69	23.08	80.77	2.02	.03
4,000	76.92	30.77	107.69	2.69	.04
5,000	96.15	38.46	134.61	3.37	.06
6,000	115.38	46.15	161.53	4.04	.07
7,000	134.62	53.85	188.47	4.71	.08
8,000	153.85	61.54	215.39	5.38	.09
9,000	173.08	69.23	242.31	6.06	.10
10,000	192.31	76.92	269.23	6.73	0.11
20,000	384.62	153.85	538.47	13.46	0.22
30,000	576.92	230.77	807.69	20.19	0.34
40,000	769.23	307.69	1076.92	26.92	0.45
50,000	961.54	384.62	1346.16	33.65	0.56
60,000	1153.85	461.54	1615.39	40.38	0.67
70,000	1346.15	538.46	1884.61	47.12	0.79
80,000	1538.46	615.38	2153.84	53.85	0.90
90,000	1730.77	692.31	2423.08	60.58	1.01
100,000	1923.08	769.23	2692.31	67.31	1.12

See the article by Bradford and Cohen at the end of this chapter.

John Gardner (1990), in his best-selling book, *On Leadership,* emphasized the same point of view when he wrote, "when I use the word leader, I am in fact referring to the leadership team. No individual has all the skills—and certainly not the time— to carry out all the complex tasks of contemporary leadership" (p. 10). Similarly, Manz and Sims (1990), in their book entitled *Super-Leadership,* write, "SuperLeaders marshal the strength of many, for their strength does not lie solely in their own abilities, but in the vast, multiple talents of those that surround them" (p. xvi). On a broader scale, anthropologist Walter Goldschmidt argues that every person in every human society needs group affiliation. He has observed this need in such diverse groups as street gangs, yuppies in corporate America, and the Tlingit Indians in Alaska (Hendrix 1990, p. B5).

As you read further in this book you will find that a strong understanding of group dynamics and the skills to use that understanding will be among the most important factors in your success as a leader and as a person. Although this book is primarily about problem-solving groups, its focus is broader than that. The lessons contained herein also apply to your friendship groups, your family, and your classroom groups. A good example of the broad application of group dynamics is illustrated in the following example.

In 1990 the Detroit Pistons won the National Basketball Association championship for the second straight year. Greenberg (1990) wrote an article emphasizing the strong role that teamwork played in their success. He stated:

> When the NBA picked its official All-Star team at season's end, no Piston made the first or second team. Joe Dumars made third team.
>
> No surprises. The Pistons didn't have a player among the NBA's Top 20 scorers this season. They didn't have a player among the Top 10 in field-goal percentage or three-point percentage. They didn't have a player in the Top 10 in rebounding. Or steals. Or blocked shots.
>
> All they did was win their second consecutive NBA championship. And nobody anywhere doubts the validity of their title. They might not shine in the individual stats, but the Pistons shine in the only one that really matters. They are simply the best. . . .
>
> The Pistons rely on everyone and no one. You don't know who's going to kill you because on a given night, they all can. Individually, the Pistons have some nice parts. Together, they have an awesome team. For now, the only thing that can stop them is the off-season.

CONCEPTUAL ORIENTATIONS FOR SMALL GROUPS

Small group interaction is very complicated and involves a large number of factors that act and interact simultaneously. In addition, these factors are in a continual state of flux. Think of the difficulty of trying to describe and analyze all the behaviors that occur at just one party! We have all been to parties that generate far more reactions than we would have thought. One entire book (Pettinger 1964) was devoted to the *first five minutes* of interaction in one communication situation. This prompted one friend to speculate that, at that rate, a *one-hour* discussion would require a twelve-volume series! The point is that any attempt to provide a conceptual orientation for small group interaction or any social process must be highly simplified.

Mills's Models

Mills (1967) identified six models for studying and analyzing small groups. They are:

- the quasi-mechanical model
- the organismic model
- the conflict model
- the equilibrium model
- the structural-functional model
- the cybernetic-growth model

Each of these models offers a different perspective from which to view small group processes. Each model is based upon certain assumptions that affect the questions we ask about group behavior as well as the answers we are likely to obtain.

The *quasi-mechanical model* assumes that a group is like a machine. All behavioral acts in a group are seen as functions that can be categorized. Each functional act (e.g., a question) calls for a reaction (e.g., an answer). All actions and reactions are quantifiable and may be added, subtracted, multiplied, or divided in such a way to represent the dynamics of the group mathematically. Bales's (1950, 1970) work, as described in Chapter 4, is an example of such an approach. Group behavior is considered to follow universal and unchanging laws. This model also assumes that people are merely interchangeable parts in the system and that all problem-solving groups will exhibit many of the same behaviors. Mills (1967) criticizes the quasi-mechanical model for not telling us much about group discussion and for not being very relevant in its application.

The *organismic model* assumes that groups are like biological organisms. That is, they have a period of formation (birth), a life cycle, and, eventually, a death. Different people in the group become differentiated in their behaviors (e.g., task leader, recorder, social leader) just as bodily systems carry on different functions (e.g., digestive, respiratory, muscular). The emphasis is upon the group's *natural* evolution and development. Thus natural, ongoing, real-life groups are more often the object of study than artificial, zero-history groups created for the purpose of a laboratory study.

The *conflict model* assumes that the small group is a context for an endless series of conflicts. All members of groups have to face the conflict of being truly independent versus conforming to some extent to the group norms and expectations. Also, because there are many groups to affiliate with, individuals feel conflict in deciding which group to join. The person with several bids from fraternities is a classic example; the choice is difficult to make. Within the group, differences of opinion are a continual source of potential conflict. Conflicts arise between groups as well. Mills (1967) argues that this model is too limited in that it tends to overlook all the socially binding (cohesive) factors in favor of the socially divisive factors. It is too one-sided.

The ***equilibrium model*** assumes that groups and group members have a need to maintain some sort of balance or equilibrium—for example, that conflicts among group members tend to be followed by attempts to smooth over hard feelings and return to a state of interpersonal harmony. Several equilibrium models have been developed. The first was Heider's balance theory, which is described in Chapter 2. Although the equilibrium models give us insight into a relatively simple level of analysis, when all the important elements are considered, the model is too limited to be able to explain much. For example, if I have an attitude toward a friend (positive), and he says something I don't like (negative), I can resolve this by agreeing with him or disliking him. But what if I forgive his comment, even though I still disagree with him on that issue, and continue to like him and agree with him on lots of other issues?

The ***structural-functional model*** assumes that the group is a goal-seeking system that is constantly adapting to meet new demands. It assumes that goal attainment is the primary source of satisfaction to its members. It also assumes that some members will take on the function of keeping the group functioning. These so-called group-maintenance functions serve to keep interpersonal relations from breaking down so that the group ceases to function. The model is one of the better ones available, because it includes the role of learning, by which groups survive by adapting to the demand for new behaviors.

The ***cybernetic-growth model*** shifts the emphasis from group survival to group growth. This model assumes the existence of agents that help the group adapt to new information (or feedback). Thus growth and development are attained by the group's responding to feedback from its earlier performance. Three types of feedback, (1) goal seeking, (2) group restructuring, and (3) self-awareness, are required to help the group grow and develop. Mills (1967, p. 20) uses the example of the quarterback of a football team to illustrate the three types of feedback:

He reads the weakness in other teams' defenses and tries to capitalize on them (goal seeking); due to unforeseen circumstances, he may have to revise the pre-game strategy, trying out one modification after the other (internal re-arrangement); and on each play he assesses the developing weaknesses or strengths in his team, and, in general, the present state and condition of his team (consciousness). Since he can act on his ideas—observe the effects of his action and therefore test them—he is in a position to learn to direct his team. Through self-monitoring, self-steering, and testing these processes, he is able to increase his capabilities for self-determination.

Mills argues convincingly that this model is strong in that it helps us identify the important factors or variables that lead to growth on the part of the group as well as on the part of the individual members. A partial list of potential end results of group growth for individual members includes the following (Mills 1967, p. 22):

Indicators of a Person's Capacity to Grow

1. *Adaptation*

    a. Receptivity to a wider range of information about himself, others, his groups, his and other societies, and the physical environment

    b. Receptivity to new freedoms, responsibilities, and obligations—to new roles

    c. Flexibility in modifying his ideas, beliefs, personal norms, and emotional attachments without loss of intellectual or moral integrity

2. *Goal-attainment*

    a. Capacity to postpone immediate gratification, and to conceive of and evaluate an increasing number of avenues for gratification

    b. Capacity to decommit himself from one goal, and to recommit himself to new and additional goals, and to learn how to attain them

3. *Integration*

    a. Capacity to perform in an expanded repertoire of roles and variety of social relations without suffering diffusion of his identity

4. *Pattern-maintenance and extension*

    a. Capacity for deeper emotional involvement with others without surrendering his self

    b. Increasing ability to convey his experience, learning, and capabilities to others

GENERAL SYSTEMS PERSPECTIVE

Although the six models described here have a number of worthwhile characteristics, a seventh model, which synthesizes elements of the first six, seems to be even more appropriate for conceptualizing small group interaction. The remainder of this book is organized around the idea that small group interaction can most adequately be thought of as occurring in a system of interdependent forces, each of which can be analyzed and set in the perspective of other forces. This idea represents a so-called general systems theory of thinking about small groups.

The general systems theory originated with Ludwig Von Bertelanffy, a theoretical biologist, as a way to think about and study the constant, dynamic adjustments of living phenomena. An open system such as a group is defined as an organized set of interrelated and interacting parts that attempts to maintain its own balance amid the influences from its surrounding environment. Cushman and Cahn (1985, p. 10) describe it as follows:

> Communication in general and interpersonal communication in particular can best be understood by describing the systems in which communication takes place. The concept *system* refers to a set of components which influence each other and which constitute a whole or unity for the purpose of analysis. To call a set of components a system implies that the components are organized in some way and that we are interested in the principles of organization or interdependence that make the whole work, rather than in the parts in their own right.

Let us look at a contemporary example. In July of 1990, there was an unusually high number of babies born in and around San Francisco. It took officials only a short while to count back nine months to October 17, 1989, when the same area suffered a large earthquake. The 1990 babies then were referred to as "quake babies." One hospital official was quoted as saying, "We had a blackout situation, but not a lot of devastation from the quake in our area. And people had a lot of time on their hands" (Associated Press, July 12, 1990, p. A1). This is an example of systems theory. Elements in a system are interrelated, and a change in one part of the system (blackouts in the early evening) can cause changes in another part of the system (the birth rate nine months later).

Kilmann (1989, p. 5) explains it this way:

> The first worldview, a simple machine, argues for single efforts at change, much like replacing one defective part in some mechanical apparatus: The one defective part can be replaced without affecting any other part. This single approach works only for fixing a physical, nonliving system. The quick fix cannot hope to heal a human being, much less a living, breathing organization. The simple machine view represents one-dimensional thinking—much like studying the world as a collection of isolated cities.
>
> The second worldview, the open system, argues for a more integrated approach in which several parts must be balanced simultaneously in order to manage the whole organization. Here a dynamic equilibrium exists between an organization and its changing environment. The organization consists of systems, such as strategies, structures, and rewards. The environment contains its own systems, too, such as the government, suppliers, competitors, and consumers.

Norman Cousins, a writer, stumbled upon the interrelationship of psychological systems and physiological health through his own serious illness. His discoveries have led to a renewed interest in a systems approach to health called holistic medicine. He writes:

> Emotional states have long been known to affect the secretion of certain hormones—for example, those of the thyroid and adrenal glands. It has been recently discovered that the brain and the pituitary gland contain a heretofore unknown class of hormones which are chemically related and which go by the collective name endorphins. The physiological activity of some endorphins presents great similarity to that of morphine, heroin, and

other opiate substances which relieve pain, not only by acting on the mechanisms of pain itself, but also by inhibiting the emotional response to pain and therefore suffering. (Cousins 1980, p. 20)

Finally, as suggested by the open systems model, the consequences, or outputs, of the group are fed back into the system through the feedback loop. Katz and Kahn (1978, p. 17) describe an open system this way: "Activities can be examined in relation to the *energic input* into the system, the *transformation of energies within the system,* and the *resulting product or energic output*" (italics added). They also say (p. 16) that "our theoretical model for the understanding of [social] organizations is that of an input-output system in which the energic return from the output reactivates the system."

Let's look at it in less theoretical terms. A highly successful baseball team develops a renewed sense of energy from having a winning season. This energy is reinvested in the team by new attitudes of becoming even more successful, admiring each other more, and so forth. This new energy and motivation level may allow team members to enjoy a higher level of status, a new and more democratic style of leadership, and a more luxurious physical environment within which to work or live. (This entire process of multiple causation is indicated by the two-headed arrows in the model; see Figure 1.1.) Keep in mind that the model appears to be static, like a photograph. But in reality, small group behaviors should be modeled by a movie, with each of the parts *moving* in relation to the others.

Different levels of systems analysis and the type of system studied include:

- Astronomy—universal systems

- Ecology—planetary systems

- Political science—political systems

- Sociology—social systems

- Psychology—human systems

- Physiology—organ systems

- Molecular biology—microscopic systems

General systems theory has been applied to many different fields of study, including biology, engineering, mathematics, and psychiatry. Systems analysis has become a particularly popular way of analyzing human behavior in organizations and has been written about in several sources (Katz and Kahn 1978, Seiler 1967, Kast and Rosenzweig 1970, Huse and Bowditch 1973.)

More recently, Ancona (1990) has written emphatically that teams or groups should be analyzed from an "open systems" framework identical to that described throughout this book.

FIGURE 1.1   THE TUBBS MODEL OF SMALL GROUP INTERACTION.

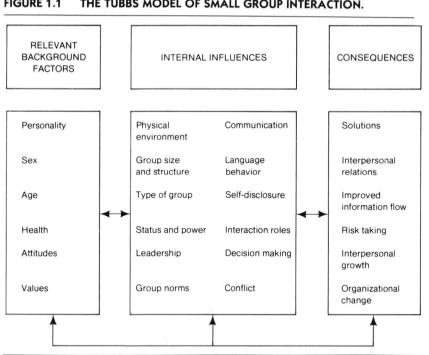

GENERAL SYSTEMS CONCEPTS

With some of this background in mind, let us look briefly at ten general systems concepts that apply to small group communication and are suggested by our general systems model (Katz and Kahn 1978, pp. 23–30).

INPUT   Input refers to the raw material of small group interaction. It includes all six of the relevant background factors depicted in the model. It also includes information the group receives from outside the group. For example, problem-solving group members in the midst of a discussion may notice that they are running short on time. This new information will probably influence the group to change procedures (e.g., stop talking about side issues) and focus more directly or efficiently on solving the problem at hand.

A system that has inputs from outside is called an *open system*. An open system is said to interact with its environment, in contrast to remaining isolated. Gross (1964, p. 113) identifies four phenomena characteristic of open systems:

1. Entries and exits, which transform outsiders into members and members into outsiders.

2. Multiple membership, which results in members' loyalties to outside groups.

3. Resource exchange, which involves the absorption of inputs in the production process and in the delivery of output produced.

4. Mutual or reciprocal influence on the part of both members and outsiders.

Anyone who has ever felt torn between two different groups will be able to understand the relevance of Gross's four points.

THROUGHPUT   Throughput refers to the internal influences depicted in our model. It means all of the actual verbal and nonverbal behaviors that occur in the course of a group discussion. It includes the process of creating and modifying ideas in the course of a discussion. Throughput is the heart and in some cases the entirety of what most small group communication books discuss. Chapters 3 through 6 will discuss these variables in detail.

OUTPUT   Output is referred to in the consequences section of our model. These are sometimes called the end results of group interaction. However, as we shall soon see, end results imply a beginning and an end, which is somewhat misleading, because groups often have an ongoing life history, during which these outputs, or consequences, are continually being modified on the basis of continuing interaction. Chapter 7 is devoted to discussing the consequences, or outputs, of small group interaction.

CYCLES   Often the outputs of group interaction are fed back to the group and become inputs for future interactions. For example, a severe personality conflict in one meeting (of a group) may reduce the level of cohesiveness or interpersonal closeness of group members. As a result some members may refuse to attend future meetings, some may attend but will not participate as openly, or some may try harder the next time to be more diplomatic in their remarks in order to avoid a recurrence of the conflict. The arrows at the bottom of our model (Figure 1.1) indicate what is commonly called a feedback loop. This loop represents the cyclical and ongoing nature of group processes and also implies that the process does not begin and end anew with each group meeting, but rather builds on all the past experiences of each group member.

NEGATIVE ENTROPY   The entropic process is a universal law of nature in which all systems eventually move toward disorganization or death. Recently, we have seen the entropic process overtake Frontier Airlines, several hundred banks, Osborn Computers, Addressograph-Multigraph, and many others. To combat the process of disorganization and/or death, a system must employ negative entropy. If you have ever been in a meeting that seemed to be completely out of control and was a total waste of time, you know how easily entropy can overtake a group.

Max DePree, chairman of the board of Herman Miller Furniture Company, writes:

> Some months ago, I was on what is known in the financial industry as a "dog and pony show." Our team was in Boston making a presentation to some sophisticated financial analysts. After the presentation and during the question-and-answer period, one of the analysts said to me, "What is one of the most difficult things that you personally need to work on?" He seemed very surprised when I said, "The interception of entropy."
>
> I am using the word "entropy" in a loose way, because technically it has to do with the second law of thermodynamics. From a corporate management point of view, I choose to define it as meaning that everything has a tendency to deteriorate. One of the important things leaders need to learn is to recognize the signals of impending deterioration. (DePree 1989, p. 98)

FEEDBACK   All systems must receive feedback to modify themselves. Think of a bowling game in which you saw the ball go down the lane and through a black cover and you never saw which pins you hit and never heard the sound of the ball striking the pins. You would never play a second game. Or imagine going to school year after year and never gettting an assignment back and never getting any grades or comments from an instructor. We all want feedback on our performance. In a rather funny example of feedback modifying a group's behavior, the City Council of Boise, Idaho, decided to change its meetings from Monday night to Tuesday night because of Monday night football. The council had been meeting on Monday nights since 1929. However, because the public turnout was so poor, the council decided to modify its meeting time in response to the feedback that the televised football games were just too much competition (Popkey 1986).

DYNAMIC EQUILIBRIUM   Management and labor have reached an unspoken agreement in virtually every organization of what constitutes "a fair day's work for a fair day's pay." This is an example of an equilibrium. Similarly, students and teachers often negotiate throughout the course of a term. However, should students fail to read their assignments, teachers will often react by throwing "pop" quizzes, thus upsetting the equilibrium. Once the students change their performance, equilibrium returns. Similarly, when an organization finds itself losing market share or profit margins, it often has to upset the fair day's work for a fair day's pay equilibrium. In 1985 General Motors decided to eliminate the Cost of Living Allowance (COLA) for its salaried workers. This seemed to change the "fair day's pay" side of the equation. Salaried employees decided not to work so hard, thus restoring their feeling of equilibrium. In groups, we each decide if membership is worth what we are putting into it. If not, we slack off and may even eventually quit the group to find one that more nearly meets our sense of equilibrium.

DIFFERENTIATION   Ever since the Industrial Revolution began, organizations have become increasingly more specialized. It is no longer adequate to have generalists; organizations must now have specialists in production, inspection, materials handling, transportation, legal affairs, accounting, payroll, sales, engineering, plant layout, maintenance, management information systems, distribution, service, real estate, finance, public relations, and labor relations, for example. In groups we also see different people gravitating toward certain roles. In addition, it is a rare group in which each member's attitudes are the same toward any topic.

INTEGRATION   As groups and organizations become more complex and differentiated, the need for integration and coordination of the various parts increases. Without integration, the group or organization becomes chaotic. Imagine being in a hospital in which the lab results or X rays couldn't be communicated to the physician for interpretation or the pharmacy couldn't get your prescription in order to obtain your medication. Or worse yet, imagine a scenario in which the emergency room wasn't accessible because the driveways were blocked for repair. In groups, if too many subgroups talk at once, coordination soon breaks down, as it does if each person is trying to follow a different agenda (or no agenda). Integration, then, is synonymous with organizing.

Drucker (1990, p. 101) wrote in the *Harvard Business Review* that all manufacturing plants in the future will need to be set up using a "systems approach." He offered the following contemporary example:

> When Honda decided six or seven years ago to make a new, upscale car for the U.S. market, the most heated strategic debate was not about design, performance, or price. It was about whether to distribute the Acura through Honda's well-established dealer network or to create a new market segment by building separate Acura dealerships at high cost and risk. This was a marketing issue, of course. But the decision was made by a team of design, engineering, manufacturing, and marketing people.

EQUIFINALITY   You have undoubtedly heard the expression, "There is more than one way to skin a cat." This expression captures part of what is meant by the term "equifinality." This concept means that, although two groups may have different members, leadership styles, decision-making methods, and so on, they may still arrive at the same solution to a given problem. There is an incredibly large number of combinations of all the variables in our small group model. These combinations may in some cases interact in such a way as to produce the same group consequences, but from dramatically different processes. Conversely, two groups may attempt to use the same procedures but end up with different outcomes. Thus, equifinality refers to the unpredictability and potential for adaptation groups possess.

For readers who are familiar with small group literature, a synthesis of different small group models is offered in Figure 1.2. You will note the considerable similarity of conceptual approaches that span more than thirty years of writing. Note, however,

FIGURE 1.2   SYNTHESIS OF GROUP MODELS

Homans (1950)	External system		Internal system	
Stogdill (1959)	Member inputs	Mediating variables	Resultant variables	
Thibaut and Kelley (1959)	Exogenous variables	Endogenous variables	Resultant variables	
McGrath and Altman (1966)	Properties of group members	Conditions imposed on group	Interaction process	Performance
Kibler and Barker (1969)	Antecedents	Messages	Consequences	
Fisher (1971)	Inputs	Mediating variables	Outputs	
Gouran (1973)	Context of communication	Communication behaviors	Group outcomes	
Tubbs (1992)	Relevant background factors	Internal influences	Consequences	

that the present model is the only one that explicitly emphasizes the dynamic and simultaneous interaction of all the component parts. (See also Orton and Weick 1990.)

Mosca (1990, p. 10) argues that the twenty-first century will require more and more of a systems approach. He writes:

> Future managers will have to know how to create a working environment which considers shared values and direction. Responsibilities and initiatives will have to be passed down to the operational level. Employees will have to be made aware of the organization's overall mission. This is an indication that the levels of management will be compressed and employees will have more interaction with managers at all levels.
>
> Tomorrow's manager will not be encumbered with the manual processing data and will have the ability to interact through a keyboard and video screen. Therefore, the 21st century employee will be a component of the systems concept. The systems concept is gathering all of the interrelated operational and management functions together to achieve a common goal. What is being advocated here is that the systems concept is the creation of synergy which represents one of managements challenges and combining all of its components with the organization to function as a whole to maximize efficiency.

THE SYSTEMS PERSPECTIVE: THE TUBBS MODEL

As an undergraduate and then as a graduate student, I took a total of nine courses in group dynamics. In each course I always felt a certain sense of discomfort with my inability to get an overall "feel" for the big picture of small group interaction. Each textbook took a different approach, and each approach seemed to somewhat contradict the other. Few if any of the books had a conceptual model which explained the relationships of all the important variables related to small groups.

As a result, when I began to teach my first small groups course, I had difficulty in picking out a textbook. As I studied various group communication texts, I found that all of them covered many of the same topics such as leadership, communication, problem-solving, etc. I found, however, that the topics were like so many playing cards which could be shuffled and reshuffled to form a book's table of contents. There was no conceptual model which integrated the topics in a meaningful way. It was only when I studied advanced theoretical books on groups that I found conceptual theories and models that did a better job of tying all the important topics together. These books, however, were not intended for beginning undergraduate students. When I tried using them as texts, students were very unhappy with the choices.

At about the same time, I began to study more and more of the literature on organizational behavior. I read the late Rensis Likert's (1967) now classic text which organized the variables in that discipline into three categories: (1) causal variables, (2) intervening variables, and (3) end-result variables. This was the closest I had come to find the conceptualization which made sense. Likert's model seemed to be lacking, too, as it implied a beginning and an end (e.g., causal, intervening, and end-result variables).

Finally, I found the missing link in the general systems literature, which at that time had never been applied in a small group text. The systems approach advanced the idea that all the various component parts of the model are interrelated and that a change in one often creates changes in other parts of the system. In addition, in an open system, so-called "end results" are fed back into the beginning of the group and become causal variables for future behaviors.

Over time, I began to develop my own materials and eventually developed an open systems model of small group interaction (Figure 1.1) which seemed to provide what I had been looking for. My model conceptualized the small group field and could be adapted for a text written for the introductory student. This systems model grew out of the conceptual groundwork which had been laid by several other authors. Figure 1.2 summarizes those authors' models.

The Tubbs Model organizes the important small group variables into three major categories, (1) relevant background factors, (2) internal influences, and (3) consequences. This model offers several advantages over previous introductory small group books. First, it helps students grasp the conceptual overview which I had not found in books when I was a student. Second, this model shows the dynamic interactive nature of all the variables in the model, and avoids the cause and effect thinking of earlier models. Third, it explicitly shows how consequences, or outputs, of one small group experience can become background factors or inputs to the next group experience.

This model is reinforced throughout the text with real-life case studies, student exercises, and carefully selected readings. I hope that this book's combination of theory and application will be useful to you.

Relevant Background Factors

"Relevant background factors" refers to attributes within the individual participants that existed prior to the group's formation and that will endure in some modified form after the group no longer exists. These background factors influence the group's functioning; in turn, the group process affects the group's outcomes, or results.

Let us look at a few of these factors. Each of us has a distinct personality. The mix of personalities will undoubtedly have some influence on the "chemistry" or working relationships within the group. For example, when filming *The Godfather III*, Al Pacino and Diane Keaton broke off their long-running relationship, which caused severe setbacks in filming the movie. This illustrates both personality conflict as well as the influence of sex or gender on the group's functioning. Obviously, any group membership that includes both sexes involves a very volatile element. In fact, many companies have policies that do not allow husbands and wives to work in the same department. Obviously, any time the two sexes interact, there is the potential for romantic relationships to influence the group's functioning.

Age is certainly a factor important to group activities. Age itself is probably not as important as the different attitudes that tend to accompany different age groups. Therefore, groups containing members of a similar age group tend also to be somewhat more similar or homogamous with regard to attitudes. For example, how different would a group discussion concerning Madonna be if your parents were in the group?

Health also plays a role in influencing groups. If individuals are suffering from health problems, their energy level and the stamina with which they address problems are often reduced. In one work group, a member who had chronic pneumonia was consistently the most outstanding contributor at each meeting of the group that she was able to attend. However, her frequent health-related absences handicapped the group.

Values also exert a powerful influence in groups. Think about a discussion on the subject of abortion, gun control, or racism. Think how quickly the values of the group members will rapidly come into play and how they will most likely affect both the group's processes and its outcomes. Keep in mind that all six of these relevant background factors are constantly interacting with one another. For example, values and attitudes are closely related, as are age and health, and sex and personality. And all of these factors (except sex) are constantly changing over the course of our human experiences. The relevant background factors are the subject of Chapter 2.

Internal Influences

The second set of variables in the model is referred to as *internal influences*. These factors influence the actual functioning of the group. Imagine how physical environment plays a role when the group meets in a quiet conference room with comfortable furniture compared to meeting in a noisy corner of a room with poor ventilation, heavy cigarette smoke, poor lighting, and a hot temperature. Similarly, imagine the way a group interacts when there are only four or five compared to fifteen to twenty. Typically, the smaller the group, the higher the individual satisfaction of group members with the discussion.

The *type of group* refers to an educational group compared, let's say, to a social group or a work group. Obviously, each of these would perform differently. Chapter 3 discusses in greater depth the factors of physical environment, group size and structure, and group type.

Chapter 4 is devoted to three very important topics: (1) status and power, (2) leadership, and (3) group norms. Status and power strongly influence group outcomes. If a group such as the President's cabinet is meeting to discuss a problem, obviously, the President has the highest status and resulting power. Similarly, if the Chicago Bulls are meeting, Michael Jordan would have an especially high level of status within the group, and his opinions would most likely be more powerful than any other member of the group.

Leadership is probably one of the two most important *internal influences*. Thus, we have devoted quite a bit of attention to it. As mentioned earlier in this chapter, many people learn how to increase their own leadership by studying small group interaction. The trend of the present and most definitely of the future is for greater participative leadership, which heavily utilizes group interaction.

The third topic in Chapter 4 is group norms. These are unwritten rules that strongly influence our behaviors. Usually norms are so much a part of our thinking that we only become aware of them when someone violates them. For example, if someone dresses (or undresses) in a fashion that is completely out of place, it violates our sense of what is comfortable (or NORMal). Conformity pressure to adhere to group norms is a powerful influence on every small group.

Chapter 5 discusses (1) communication, (2) language behavior, (3) self-disclosure, and (4) interaction roles. Communication is the other most important *internal influence*. Thus, we have dedicated a significant amount of coverage to it. Virtually every human behavior has the potential to communicate, and so it permeates all aspects of group behavior.

Language behavior focuses on the verbal part of communication and the intimate relationship between words and thoughts. This body of knowledge is often referred to as *semantics*. Several language-related communication difficulties are discussed, and practical methods for improvement are included.

Self-disclosure refers to the amount we reveal about ourselves to others. Too little self-disclosure results in an isolation from others. On the other hand, too much self-disclosure with virtual strangers is inappropriate. The contexts of appropriate self-disclosure as a method for personal growth and development are discussed.

Chapter 6 covers two important topics—decision making and conflict. Many traditional small group books have been exclusively devoted to the topic of decision making. The skills covered in this section will serve you throughout your entire lifetime as you solve literally thousands of problems.

Conflict is something all of us experience. This section discusses the dynamics of conflict and attempts to better equip you for managing conflicts in your life, especially in group situations.

Consequences

Finally, Chapter 7 looks at the reasons why we engage in group activities in the first place—that is, the results that can be obtained from groups. They are the raison d'etre of a group, the reason the group is formed. These are (1) solutions to problems, (2) improvements in interpersonal relations, (3) improvements in the flow of information between and among people, (4) improvements in the level of risk taking, (5) interpersonal growth through group methods, and (6) organizational change. Each of these end results, or consequences, of group interaction is a worthwhile goal.

As you read this book, keep in mind the consequences that are possible. As you focus on what is often referred to as "the bottom line," you will better understand how the systems approach ties all these variables together.

SUMMARY

We opened this chapter with a look at a real-life example of a small groups team. The Saturn Case illustrated both the challenge and potential of effective small group management. The case study is reinforced with key definitions of the language and terms unique to the study of small groups. The section on "Why Study Small Groups" highlights the many advantages of this area of study.

Having laid this initial groundwork, we examined several conceptual orientations of the small group, and discussed six theoretical models for analyzing the small group process. The "General Systems Perspective" examined the many theories presented that help categorize the elements of group communications. Drawing from these general philosophies, this textbook is based upon a *new* theory of small group interaction: The Tubbs Model—A Systems Perspective. The Tubbs Model is a conceptual model that illustrates and defines the relationships of all the important variables of the small group.

In the next six chapters and the accompanying readings, each part of the model will be discussed in greater detail: Chapter 2 covers *relevant background factors;* Chapters 3–6 are devoted to *internal influences,* and Chapter 7 deals with the *consequences* of small group interaction.

EXERCISES

1. First Impressions

Each person in the class should introduce himself or herself. Class members should feel free to ask each person questions to get a more complete impression. After the introductions, each person should write down some first impressions of the other class members (if you each display a large name card, this is much easier). Those who want to may share their first impressions with the class. Then reactions to those impressions also may be shared and discussed.

2. Interpersonal Perceptions

Separate into groups of five, and fill out the Preliminary Scale of Interpersonal Perceptions on each of the other four group members. Pass the completed scales to each person in the group. Examine the feedback you get, and discuss these with the others in the group. You may want to share with one another the behaviors that led to these perceptions.

PRELIMINARY SCALE OF INTERPERSONAL PERCEPTIONS
_____

Group Member's Name _____

On the scale below each question, circle the number that best describes the way you see this person's participation in group discussion. Try to distinguish between those areas where the person rates high and those where he/she rates less well.

1. How well does this person understand himself/herself in relation to this group? (Circle one numeral)

5	4	3	2	1
He/she has a very good understanding				He/she has very little understanding

2. How effective do you think this person is in contributing ideas, insights, and suggestions that help the group solve problems and achieve its goals? (Circle one numeral)

5	4	3	2	1
He/she is exceptionally effective				He/she is very ineffective

3. How effective do you think this person is in performing functions that build the group and keep it working well? (Circle one numeral)

5	4	3	2	1
He/she is exceptionally effective				He/she is very ineffective

4. In your opinion, how able is this person to express himself/herself freely and comfortably in the group? (Circle one numeral)

5	4	3	2	1
He/she is exceptionally free and comfortable				He/she is very restricted and tense

5. To what extent do you feel that this person really understands your ideas and feelings? (Circle one numeral)

5	4	3	2	1
He/she has a very good understanding				He/she has very little understanding

3. Group Consensus Activity

Form into groups of five, and then read and discuss the following article on cloning. As an agenda, try to answer the questions that follow the article.

*SCIENTISTS REPORT CLONING OF MOUSE—FIRST FOR MAMMALS**
By WALTER SULLIVAN, The New York Times
   NEW YORK—Scientists in Switzerland have reported the first authenticated cloning of a mammal. Using cells from mouse embryos, they say they have produced three mice that are genetically identical to the original embryos.
   Cloning is the production of a plant or animal identical with one from which a cell or cell nucleus has been taken and activated to become a complete organism. In plants, the procedure, using a cutting, is relatively routine. Cloning has been performed to a limited extent in frogs and other amphibians, but the possibility of cloning mammals had not previously been demonstrated.
   The mice were cloned by taking nuclei from embryonic rather than adult cells, the scientists reported. Whether it will be possible to produce clones from adult mice or other adult mammals, including man, remains uncertain.
   Some researchers hope to mass-produce prize livestock in this manner. Others believe such experiments can provide an understanding of the development of individuals from embryos to adults, including the origin of birth defects.
   In the mouse experiments, each clone was produced by taking a nucleus obtained from a mouse embryo at an early stage of development and inserting it into a fertilized egg from another mouse. The original nuclear material in that egg was then extracted, leaving only the inserted nucleus.
   The egg, after being cultured about four days, was placed in the womb of a mouse that then gave birth to an offspring with all the genetic features of the embryo from which the nucleus had been taken. The offspring bore no relationship to the mouse whose egg had been used or to the mother that bore it.

Two of the three mouse clones later produced seemingly normal offspring. The third died after seven weeks, but an autopsy revealed no abnormalities related to the cloning.

Earlier reports that mammals, and even a human being, had been cloned have never been authenticated or taken seriously by biologists.

The achievement shows that cloning, because it has been successfully performed in amphibians, is also possible with embryonic mammals, presumably including humans. It also suggests that the ability of amphibians to regenerate body parts may not be entirely beyond reach in mammals. Regeneration would be possible if genetic information within the nuclei of cells of an adult could be reactivated to perform roles, such as producing a new limb or new individual, other than those assigned to that specialized cell.

The transplants of the nuclei were performed at the University of Geneva by Dr. Karl Illmensee and Dr. Peter C. Hoppe, who is from the Jackson Laboratory in Bar Harbor, Maine. Their work has been reported at several scientific meetings and will be described later this month in the journal Cell, published by the Massachusetts Institute of Technology in Cambridge, Mass.

As in earlier nuclear transplants, the nucleus was extracted by a glass tube, or pipette, honed to hairlike sharpness. Under observation with a microscope, the pipette, controlled by a mechanical micromanipulator, was inserted into a cell taken from a mouse embryo at an early stage of development (the spherical, or blastocyst, stage, reached a few days after fertilization).

The pipette was then inserted into an egg from another mouse so recently fertilized that the sperm nucleus had not yet joined with the egg nucleus. The pipette was then used to extract the two original nuclei.

Altogether, 542 transplants were performed. Of these, 363, including the three that produced live mice, were of nuclei derived from the inner cell mass of an embryo at the blastocyst stage. It is the inner cell mass that evolves into the fetus.

The remaining nuclei were from cells forming the outer part of the blastocyst sphere, or the trophectoderm. These cells normally evolve into such structures as the uterus and umbilical cord. Their nuclei were apparently incapable of being sufficiently activated within the egg to produce an individual.

Of the 363 transplants of nuclei from the inner cell mass, 142 survived the micromanipulation and were cultured in glass vessels. Of these, 96 subdivided at least once, and within four days 48 had developed into many-celled blastocysts.

Of these embryos, 16 that appeared normal were transferred into the wombs of five white mice prepared for pregnancy by hormone treatment. The embryos had developed from eggs taken from black mice, but the nuclei inserted into them were from mice colored either grey or agouti (the color of wild mice).

Specially prepared mice also received 44 embryos taken from white mice and not subject to nuclear transplants. The added embryos enabled the prepared mice to produce litters of normal size. They all become pregnant and gave birth to a total of 35 mice. All but the three mice recognized as clones were white. None had the black fur of the strain that provided the egg cells.

The three clones had the color of the strains from which the transplanted nuclei were derived. Two, a male and female, were gray. The third was an agouti female. Tiny samples of tissue were taken from the ear, tail and skin of these mice to be cultured for genetic screening. Enzymes from the mice were also analyzed as genetic markers.

> In all respects the mice resembled the embryos from which the nuclei had been taken, rather than the egg donor or the mouse prepared for pregnancy.

What are the implications of this case for the cloning of humans? Would clones be human? Would they have souls? What rights should they have? Is it desirable to clone humans? What should be U.S. policy toward the cloning of humans?

4. Ice-Breaking Exercises

Fill out the two forms that follow; then get into groups of five or so, and share answers. Later, you can discuss what you as a group experience from these exercises.

1. The person in the group I would like to get to know better is

   _____

2. The person in the group who seems to be most like myself is

   _____

3. The person in the group whom I would like to know, that I care and am concerned about, is

   _____

4. The person who has been the most helpful is

   _____

5. A person I would like to hitchhike around the country with is

   _____

6. A person I would trust to fold my parachute before jumping from an airplane is

   _____

7. A person I would like to have a deep discussion with is

   _____

8. A person I would like most to keep in touch with is

   _____

9. A person I would trust with my secrets is

   _____

10. A person whom I feel I know least well is

   _____

What other things would you like to say to someone in this group? Take a risk (be constructive).

_____

_____

What person in this group:

_____ 1. Has the darkest eyes?

_____ 2. Has the longest name?

_____ 3. Could hide in the smallest place?

_____ 4. Has the biggest hands?

_____ 5. Has the oldest brother or sister?

_____ 6. Can give the biggest smile?

_____ 7. Can make the scariest face?

_____ 8. Has the most brothers and sisters?

_____ 9. Has the fewest brothers and sisters?

_____ 10. Has the lightest hair?

_____ 11. Has the most freckles?

_____ 12. Can make the highest mark on the wall without jumping?

_____ 13. Is wearing the most colors?

_____ 14. Has the longest hair?

_____ 15. Has the shortest name?

_____ 16. Has lived in the most places?

_____ 17. Has had the most pets?

_____ 18. Can hum the lowest note?

_____ 19. Has the smallest waist?

_____ 20. Can stand on one foot for the longest time without holding on to something?

5. Group Decision Making

Separate into groups of five or so. Choose one of the cases described below, and decide as a group what you would do in the situation. Then discuss your group processes.

WHAT WOULD YOU DO?*

Every day, doctors, nurses, patients and patients' families face life-and-death decisions. There is rarely an obvious "right" choice; each of them is, in some way, bad. Here are some real cases that present painful alternatives. The choices made by those responsible—and the results of their actions—appear below.

1. Doctors at a university hospital examined a 10-year-old boy whose bone cancer of the upper arm had recurred in spite of radiation treatments. The physicians advised amputation of the limb and warned that without the operation, the child would almost certainly die. But the boy, an enthusiastic Little Leaguer, begged his parents and the doctors to let him keep his arm so that he could continue to play baseball. *Advise amputation, boy is to young to make decision.*

2. A 7-year-old girl was suffering from a progressive neurological disease that had made her totally dependent on a respirator. She could talk and think normally, but the rest of her body functions were deteriorating rapidly and she was obviously in pain. Attempts to "wean" her from the respirator were unsuccessful, and doctors eventually realized it was unlikely she would ever recover. The parents, who were deeply religious, agonized over a decision about whether to turn off the machine. *Choose life still had mind & ability to communicate*

3. A young woman, who was dying of multiple sclerosis, finally lapsed into an irreversible coma. She remained totally unresponsive for about a week, and her doctors agreed there was nothing more they could do to help her. One evening the patient, still comatose, began to gasp for breath. Her parents, who were sitting by the bedside, summoned the nurse and asked her to call a doctor.

4. A 6-year-old boy had severe renal failure in both kidneys; his best chance of survival would be a transplant from a sibling. Each of his two older sisters, 8 and 12, was willing to donate a kidney in an effort to save the boy. The risk to either girl—from the operation or from living with one kidney—was quite small. But common medical practice dictated that young donors should not be used, except in the case of a twin. *Transplant minimal risk envolved siblings willing – problem sibling to young to make decision*

5. At the student-health service of a major university, a young man told his psychotherapist that we wanted to kill a young woman who lived nearby but who was then on a trip abroad. The therapist conferred with two colleagues, and, in a limited breach of professional confidentiality, informed the campus police; they picked up the student and detained him for questioning. Concluding that the youth was harmless, the police decided to release him after extracting a promise

---

**Copyright © 1981, by Newsweek, Inc. All Rights Reserved. Reprinted by Permission.*

that he would not bother the woman he had spoken of murdering. The health service thought it unnecessary to take any further action. *Police should have warned the women of threat,*

1. The family decided against surgery. Now, nearly a year later, the boy is receiving radiation and chemotherapy—and playing baseball. Physicians say it is too soon to estimate his chances of recovery.

2. The physician asked the parents if they wanted to discover whether God wished the child to breathe on her own. The distraught couple agreed and, as they sat vigil, the respirator was removed; the child died about four hours later.

3. The nurse requested that the parents leave the room. Instead of summoning the doctor immediately, she waited until the patient had stopped breathing. Then she went, with a physician, to tell the parents that their daughter had died. "It was the hardest thing I ever did in my life," the nurse admits.

4. The doctors refused the sisters as donors, on the ground that they were too young to make a major medical decision that could affect their whole lives. The brother has survived for four years on dialysis.

5. Two months later, shortly after the woman's return, the student went to her home and killed her. Her parents sued the university—and won. The state supreme court ruled that the health service and the university had a "duty" to warn the girl of the threat on her life.

READINGS: OVERVIEW

The systems model presented in Figure 1.1 represented an attempt to show the interrelated nature of twenty-four variables relevant to the study of small group interaction (six variables in each of the four columns in the model). Dorwin Cartwright's article shows how three variables fit together as he discusses the tremendous influence groups can have in changing people. The eight principles in the article are as relevant today as when he presented them over forty years ago. This fact helps to emphasize both the predictability of and the importance of knowing group dynamics principles. It is also interesting to note that these principles fit quite comfortably within the systems approach to studying small group interaction, which is the conceptual model around which this book is structured.

The second article, by Bradford and Cohen, shows the complexity and power of management's effective use of small groups.

Achieving Change in People: Some Applications of Group Dynamics Theory

Dorwin Cartwright

What principles of achieving change in people can we see emerging? To begin with the most general proposition, we may state that the behavior, attitudes, beliefs, and values of the individual are all firmly grounded in the groups to which he belongs. How aggressive or cooperative a person is, how much self-respect and self-confidence he has, how energetic and productive his work is, what he aspires to, what he believes to be true and good, whom he loves or hates, and what beliefs and prejudices he holds—all these characteristics are highly determined by the individual's group memberships. In a real sense, they are properties of groups and of the relationships between people. Whether they change or resist change will, therefore, be greatly influenced by the nature of these groups. Attempts to change them must be concerned with the dynamics of groups.

In examining more specifically how groups enter into the process of change, we find it useful to view groups in at least three different ways. In the first view, the group is seen as a source of influence over its members. Efforts to change behavior can be supported or blocked by pressures on members stemming from the group. To make constructive use of these pressures the group must be used as a *medium of change.* In the second view, the group itself becomes the *target of change.* To change the behavior of individuals it may be necessary to change the standards of the group, its style of leadership, its emotional atmosphere, or its stratification into cliques and hierarchies. Even though the goal may be to change the behavior of *individuals,* the target of change becomes the group. In the third view, it is recognized that many changes of behavior can be brought about only by the organized efforts of groups as *agents of change.* A committee to combat intolerance, a labor union, an employers association, a citizens group to increase the pay of teachers—any action group will be more or less effective depending upon the way it is organized, the satisfaction it provides to its members, the degree to which its goals are clear, and a host of other properties of the group.

An adequate social technology of change, then, requires at the very least a

Dorwin Cartwright, "Achieving Change in People: Some Applications of Group Dynamics Theory" from Human Relations, *Vol. 4, 1951. Reprinted by permission of Plenum Publishing Corporation.*

scientific understanding of groups viewed in each of these ways. We shall consider here only the first two aspects of the problem: the group as a medium of change and as a target of change.

The Group as a Medium of Change

Principle No. 1   If the group is to be used effectively as a medium of change, those people who are to be changed and those who are to exert influence for change must have a strong sense of belonging to the same group.

Kurt Lewin described this principle well. "The normal gap between teacher and student, doctor and patient, social worker and public, can . . . be a real obstacle to acceptance of the advocated conduct." In other words, in spite of whatever status differences there might be between them, the teacher and the student have to feel as members of one group in matters involving their sense of values. The chances for reeducation seem to be increased whenever a strong we-feeling is created (5). Recent experiments by Preston and Heintz have demonstrated greater changes of opinions among members of discussion groups operating with participatory leadership than among those with supervisory leadership (12). The implications of this principle for classroom teaching are far-reaching. The same may be said of supervision in the factory, army, or hospital.

Principle No. 2   The more attractive the group is to its members the greater is the influence that the group can exert on its members.

This principle has been extensively documented by Festinger and his co-workers (4). They have been able to show in a variety of settings that in more cohesive groups there is a greater readiness of members to attempt to influence others, a greater readiness to be influenced by others, and stronger pressures toward conformity when conformity is a relevant matter for the group. Important for the practitioner wanting to make use of this principle is, of course, the question of how to increase the attractiveness of groups. This is a question with many answers. Suffice it to say that a group is more attractive the more it satisfies the needs of its members. We have been able to demonstrate experimentally an increase in group cohesiveness by increasing the liking of members for each other as persons, by increasing the perceived importance of the group goal, and by increasing the prestige of the group among other groups. Experienced group workers could add many other ways to this list.

Principle No. 3   In attempts to change attitudes, values, or behavior, the more relevant they are to the basis of attraction to the group, the greater will be the influence that the group can exert upon them.

I believe this principle gives a clue to some otherwise puzzling phenomena. How does it happen that a group, like a labor union, seems to be able to exert such strong discipline over its members in some matters (let us say in dealings with management), while it seems unable to exert nearly the same influence in other matters (let us say in political action)? If we examine why it is that members are attracted to the group, I believe we will find that a particular reason for belonging seems more related to some of the group's activities than to others. If a man joins a union mainly to keep his job and to improve his working conditions, he may be largely uninfluenced by the union's attempt to modify his attitudes toward national and international affairs. Groups differ tremendously in the range of matters that are relevant to them and hence over which they have influence. Much of the inefficiency of adult education could be reduced if more attention were paid to the need that influence attempts be appropriate to the groups in which they are made.

Principle No. 4   The greater the prestige of a group member in the eyes of the other members, the greater the influence he can exert.

Polansky, Lippitt, and Redl (11) have demonstrated this principle with great care and methodological ingenuity in a series of studies in children's summer camps. From a practical point of view it must be emphasized that the things giving prestige to a member may not be those characteristics most prized by the official management of the group. The most prestige-carrying member of a Sunday school class may not possess the characteristics most similar to the minister of the church. The teacher's pet may be a poor source of influence within a class. This principle is the basis for the common observation that the official leader and the actual leader of a group are often not the same individual.

Principle No. 5   Efforts to change individuals or subparts of a group which, if successful, would have the result of making them deviate from the norms of the group will encounter strong resistance.

During the past years a great deal of evidence has been accumulated showing the tremendous pressures which groups can exert upon members to conform to the group's norms. The price of deviation in most groups is rejection or even expulsion. If the member really wants to belong and be accepted, he cannot withstand this type of pressure. It is for this reason that efforts to change people by taking them from the group and giving them special training so often have disappointing results. This principle also accounts for the finding that people thus trained sometimes display increased tension, aggressiveness toward the group, or a tendency to form cults or cliques with others who have shared their training.

These five principles concerning the group as a medium of change would appear to have readiest application to groups created for the purpose of producing changes in people. They provide certain specifications for building effective training or therapy groups. They also point, however, to a difficulty in producing change in people in that they show how resistant an individual is to changing in any way contrary to group pressures and expectations. In order to achieve many kinds of changes in people, therefore, it is necessary to deal with the group as a target of change.

The Group as a Target of Change

Principle No. 6   Strong pressure for changes in the group can be established by creating a shared perception by members of the need for change, thus making the source of pressure for change lie within the group.

Marrow and French (9) reports a dramatic case-study which illustrates this principle quite well. A manufacturing concern had a policy against hiring women over 30 because it was believed that they were slower, more difficult to train, and more likely to be absent. The staff psychologist was able to present to management evidence that this belief was clearly unwarranted at least within their own company. The psychologist's facts, however, were rejected and ignored as a basis for action because they violated accepted beliefs. It was claimed that they went against the direct experience of the foremen. Then the psychologist hit upon a plan for achieving change which differed drastically from the usual one of argument, persuasion, and pressure. He proposed that management conduct its own analysis of the situation. With this help management collected all the facts which they believed were relevant to the problem. When the results were in they were now their own facts rather than those of some "outside" expert. Policy was immediately changed without further resistance. The important point here is that facts are not enough. The facts must be the accepted property of the group if they are to become an effective basis for change. There seems to be all the difference in the world in changes actually carried out between those cases in which a consulting firm is hired to do a study and present a report and those in which technical experts are asked to collaborate with the group in doing its own study.

Principle No. 7   Information relating to the need for change, plans for change, and consequences of change must be shared by all relevant people in the group.

Another way of stating this principle is to say that change of a group ordinarily requires the opening of communication channels. Newcomb (10) has shown how one of the first consequences of mistrust and hostility is the avoidance of communicating openly and freely about the things producing the tension. If you look closely at a pathological group (that is, one that has trouble making decisions or effecting coordinated efforts of its members), you will certainly find strong restraints in that group against communicating vital information among its members. Until these restraints are removed there can be little hope for any real and lasting changes in the group's functioning. In passing it should be pointed out that the removal of barriers to communication will ordinarily be accompanied by a sudden increase in the communication of hostility. The group may appear to be falling apart, and it will certainly be a painful experience to many of the members. This pain and the fear that things are getting out of hand often stop the process of change once begun.

Principle No. 8   Changes in one part of a group produce strain in other related parts which can be reduced only by eliminating the change or by bringing about readjustments in the related parts.

It is a common practice to undertake improvements in group functioning by providing training programs for certain classes of people in the organization. A training program for foremen, for nurses, for teachers, or for group workers is established. If the content of the training is relevant for organizational change, it must of necessity deal with the relationships these people have with other subgroups. If nurses in a hospital change their behavior significantly, it will affect their relations both with the patients and with the doctors. It is unrealistic to assume that both these groups will remain indifferent to any significant changes in this respect. In hierarchical structures this process is most clear. Lippitt has proposed on the basis of research and experience that in such organizations attempts at change should always involve three levels, one being the major target of change and the other two being the one above and the one below.

These eight principles represent a few of the basic propositions emerging from research in group dynamics. Since research is constantly going on and since it is the very nature of research to revise and reformulate our conceptions, we may be sure that these principles will have to be modified and improved as time goes by. In the meantime they may serve as guides in our endeavors to develop a scientifically based technology of social management.

In social technology, just as in physical technology, invention plays a crucial role. In both fields progress consists of the creation of new mechanisms for the accomplishment of certain goals. In both fields inventions arise in response to practical needs and are to be evaluated by how effectively they satisfy these needs. The relation of invention to scientific development is indirect but important. Inventions cannot proceed too far ahead of basic scientific development, nor should they be allowed to fall too far behind. They will be more effective the more they make good use of known principles of science, and they often make new developments in science possible. On the other hand, they are in no sense logical derivations from scientific principles.

I have taken this brief excursion into the theory of invention in order to make a final point. To many people "group dynamics" is known only for the social inventions which have developed in recent years in work with groups. Group dynamics is often thought of as certain techniques to be used with groups. Role playing, buzz groups, process observers, post-meeting reaction sheets, and feedback of group observations are devices popularly associated with the phrase "group dynamics." I trust that I have been able to show that group dynamics is more than a collection of gadgets. It certainly aspires to be a science as well as a technology.

This is not to underplay the importance of these inventions nor of the function of inventing. As inventions they are all mechanisms designed to help accomplish important goals. How effective they are will depend upon how skillfully they are used and how appropriate they are to the purposes to which they are put. Careful evaluative research must be the ultimate judge of their usefulness in comparison with alternative inventions. I believe that the principles enumerated in this paper indicate some of the specifications that social inventions in this field must meet.

References

1. Cartwright, D. Some principles of mass persuasion: Selected findings of research on the sale of United States war bonds. *Human Relations,* 1949, 2(3), 253–67.
2. Cartwright, D. *The research center for group dynamics: A report of five years' activity and a view of future needs.* Ann Arbor: Institute for Social Research, 1950.
3. Coch, L. and French, J. T. P., Jr. Overcoming resistance to change. *Human Relations,* 1948, *1*(4), 512–32.
4. Festinger, L., *et al. Theory and experiment in social communication:* Collected papers. Ann Arbor: Institute for Social Research, 1950.
5. Lewin, K. *Resolving social conflicts,* p. 67. New York: Harper & Bros., 1951.
6. Lewin, K. *Field theory in social science,* pp. 229–36. New York: Harper & Bros., 1951.
7. Lewin, K., Lippitt, R., and White, R. K. Patterns of aggressive behavior in experimentally created "social climates." *Journal of Social Psychology,* 1939, *10,* 271–99.
8. Lippitt, R. *Training in Community Relations.* New York: Harper & Bros., 1949.
9. Marrow, A. J. and French, J. T. P., Jr. Changing a stereotype in industry. *Journal of Social Issues,* 1945, *1*(3), 33–37.
10. Newcomb, T. M. Autistic hostility and social reality. *Human Relations,* 1947, *1*(1), 69–86.
11. Polansky, N., Lippitt, R., and Redl, F. An investigation of behavioral contagion in groups. *Human Relations,* 1950, *3*(4), 319–48.
12. Preston, M. G. and Heintz, R. K. Effects of participatory vs. supervisory leadership on group judgment. *Journal of Abnormal and Social Psychology,* 1949, *44,* 345–55.

Managing for Excellence

David L. Bradford and Allan R. Cohen

I. Dealing with Subordinates: Only One-Third of the Manager's Job

In writing a book about how to create excellence, we have told only part of the story. In order to do justice to the complexity of how to deal with subordinates, we have had to limit our discussion of dealing with peers and superiors to how the manager can gain the autonomy to use a Developer approach. But this emphasis is not meant to downplay the importance of these other key managerial issues. Departments and leaders do not exist in splendid isolation; it is the rare manager whose success isn't highly dependent on successful interactions with colleagues and superiors. In most cases it is impossible to create excellence without considerable skills in managing laterally and upwards, as well as down. These other players can have a major impact in terms of their willingness to share information, deliver resources, provide support, and cooperate in implementing decisions.

Furthermore, these three aspects of managing interact with each other so that success in one area influences outcomes in the others. Having clout with your boss gains respect from subordinates and peers; being influential with colleagues lets you deliver what your boss wants and your subordinates need; and high performing subordinates increase your power sideways and upwards because you can deliver on your obligations and promises.

Although a full exploration of how to be more effective with these other two aspects of the manager's job is the subject for another book, it is worth noting that:

> Many of the skills needed to get the most from subordinates are useful in dealing with boss and peers. For example, the ability to build common vision and compatible goals is important laterally and upwards. Skills in negotiation, confrontation, and joint problem-solving also apply to all three directions. You as a manager not only lead and have to develop your own team but are a member of your boss's team; group development skills are crucial in the latter situation as well.

From: David L. Bradford and Allan R. Cohen, Managing for Excellence. *New York: Wiley, 1984, pp. 280–289. Copyright © 1984, John Wiley & Sons, Inc. Reprinted by permission of John Wiley & Sons, Inc.*

The Developer model, once it is reasonably in place, frees you from many of the burdens of managing downward. If subordinates are genuinely sharing responsibility so that you do not have to carry all the weight on your shoulders, considerable time and energy are released for the work needed outside your unit. What we have seen with managers who operate under heroic assumptions is the extent to which their time and energy are consumed in putting out the constant internal brush fires that prevent them from adequately dealing with these external functions.

These points speak to a concern frequently raised by many of the managers who are considering the Developer approach. When we have taught the model, the response is often one of worry: "If I share my managerial responsibility with subordinates, won't that take away my job? Won't subordinates see me as superfluous?" With unemployment among middle managers an increasing phenomenon, many fear that the best way to justify their existence is to manage (downwards) in a more visible fashion.

However, the opposite is true. Creating a team that is committed to departmental success frees the manager to spend more time on those functions which often only the leader can do. This includes not only interfacing with other units in the organization but dealing with the powers-that-be. In an increasingly turbulent world, the leader has to manage the core processes of innovation and change. As Kanter (1983) has demonstrated in *The Change Masters,* leaders have to sense opportunities from above and outside, formulate new possibilities, build coalitions with peers to support cross-departmental change, and sell higher-ups on the ways these innovations will help achieve corporate goals. These are the ways in which effective middle and upper-middle managers get things done—and make themselves more valuable in the process.

All of that not only takes time but is difficult to deliver without a strong department and willing subordinates. The Developer model is useful insofar as it can ultimately free you to spend most of the time where your skills are ultimately needed and where the largest payoffs are.

II. Manager-as-Developer: Making the Most of Your Imperfect World

We began this guide to achieving excellence by declaring that something is wrong with leadership in American organizations. In that initial chapter we reported some of the experiences of managers who did operate at an excellent level. In our consulting and training work, we frequently have posed the question, "What does it take to get excellence." We have raised this question in several ways and, to come full cycle from that first chapter, we want to describe a conversation we had with a group of savvy middle managers from some of America's leading companies.

We raised the following hypothetical issue: "How would you respond if the president of your organization came to you and said, 'I want you to take over Department X and make it perform at an excellent level. What would it take for you to do that?' '' The managers in this session quickly agreed that they could deliver on the president's request if the following three conditions were met:

First, "Let me pick my own staff so that I can have highly competent people who will work well together."
Second, "Give me an exciting assignment that is important to this organization."
Third, "Give me a boss who doesn't interfere or tell me exactly what to do."

We then asked this group of managers how frequently those conditions are given to them; they laughed. If you can by skill, luck, or magic acquire these loaded-for-success conditions, life would be considerably easier than it is now. But one way to think about the message of this book is that it tells you how to build these conditions when they are not so fortuitously given to you. Few managers can completely pick their own staff—what we have shown is how you can develop high performers and a mature team with the individuals you presently have. Few leaders in any organization are anointed by the president with just the perfect, crucial mission—what we have illustrated is how you can take the department's function and reconceptualize it into a challenging and exciting goal. Finally, few of us are blessed with the perfect superior—but we have given some hints about ways you can negotiate with your boss so that you can have the necessary autonomy and support.

III. Some Concluding Paradoxes

Rather than being dependent on those fortuitous but rare events when the perfect conditions are laid in your lap, this book is about how you can take control of what happens to you. By now, you should have a clear idea of how to go about countering the tendencies of organizational units to perform at levels far below what is possible. With determination, careful planning, and a willingness to risk doing things differently, you can produce excellence in the department you manage. You can make it a place where all the members are committed to the unit's goals, feel personal responsibility for its success, take initiative rather than wait passively for directions, and share a dedication to quality.

The experiences of managers who have begun using the Developer model show that it can work in a variety of conditions. Extra effort is needed when subordinates, superiors, or peers are resistant or unprepared, but these obstacles can be overcome. The key is to set up a process where you and your subordinates, working jointly, can discover the approach that best fits your specific situation. The act of sharing the responsibility for finding your ways to the shared-responsibility team is itself more important than following the model to a T.

Keep that paradoxical admonition in mind as you turn to our final words of wisdom, which we have formulated as a series of six paradoxes for postheroic managing.

PARADOX 1.

The Manager-as-Developer has to be both less active and more active than the heroic manager.

On the one hand, the postheroic manager has to back away from feeling solely responsible for solving all problems and managing the department. That obligation can be paralyzing at first, especially if you are used to achieving daily satisfactions from carrying the world on your shoulders. Although it is by no means appropriate to withdraw and go passive, you may not be able to see what else to do when you are trying to let go of heroic riding to the rescue. You might perceive heroism's apparent opposite as standing by while the damsel is run over by the onrushing locomotive.

Nevertheless, this dichotomy is false. We are not advocating management-by-absence; excellence can't be achieved by leader abdication. The Manager-as-Developer has to be quite active, but in a very different way from conventional heroics. While the traditional leader focused activity almost exclusively on solving task issues, Developers have to be active in managing procedural issues. Except when they have clearly greater expertise than their subordinates on that topic, Developers concentrate on managing the process so that full use is made of subordinate ability. The Developer's hard work and initiative are directed at seeing that the real issues are raised, arguments are joined, and commitments are made. Great activity is required of the Developer—to develop individuals and groups so that they can perform well in solving the problems and in sharing in the management of the unit.

Once a department is reasonably developed, there are fewer managerial demands on the Developers, but that hardly means that they have created their own unemployment. "Development" is not an end state in which the manager withers away. Improved performance just surfaces a new set of problems—redefined tasks, increased responsibilities, more complex issues. There will always be new people coming into the department who have to be integrated or changes in external conditions that require adjustments. And, as pointed out earlier, any time saved by the manager's not having to deal with internal issues can well be spent with the other crucial aspects of the leader's job: dealing sideways with other departments, upward with the boss, or outside the organization. The problem of having nothing to do or being reduced to watching the action from outside while longing to get into the game is not a problem in this postheroic world.

PARADOX 2.

The Manager-as-Developer must give greater autonomy to subordinates while establishing more controls.

To allow subordinates to share responsibility requires that the leader be willing to give up some of the conventional controls. The Developer must loosen the reins on problem solving, task assignment, and meeting agendas. Yet this loss of manager-based control is balanced by the increased controls that evolve when all subordinates are personally committed to departmental success. Collective acceptance of the same central overarching goal is a form of control. If members feel responsible for managing the unit, they will be more willing to pressure (exert control over) peers who are not coming through. If they accept the team as theirs, they will believe it is right for them to influence each other. All of this activity produces far more control than could be exerted by even the most watchful manager. Of course, these controls affect you as well as your subordinates; you become accountable to subordinates for commitments made, and they are more likely to push you to perform.

PARADOX 3.

Managers-as-Developers increase their own power by giving subordinates greater power.

Power and influence are not a fixed sum. In most organizations, there is too little power to produce excellence. Leaders who sense they are in low-power situations are hesitant about giving their subordinates increased influence in the decision-making process—in determining how the department is to be run and in deciding how best to carry out their assignments. Yet giving power begets power; subordinates who feel empowered and committed to the departmental goal are not only more motivated but are also more willing to be influenced by their peers and by you. People with low power most resist the power of others. The best way for you to increase your influence with subordinates is to increase their power with each other, with you, and with others outside the unit. This procedure is better defined as power-enhancement, rather than power-sharing.

PARADOX 4.

The Manager-as-Developer builds a team as a way to support member individuality.

Groups can be dangerous forces toward conformity in thought and behavior. Too many people experience their organizations as constraining. But groups can also support individuality. As a team develops, it moves from a collection of individuals who are suspicious of each other (and therefore want to limit differences among themselves) into a cohesive but consensual group where individual differences are valued and supported. A genuinely collaborative team can allow more diversity and autonomy than one that clings together for mutually distrustful motives.

In this vein, the Manager-as-Developer needs to hold meetings so that the team can develop to a point where fewer meetings are needed! So many presentday organizations support far more meetings than are necessary. The majority of unnecessary meetings are held because people don't trust each other or the manager is afraid that people will all march to their separate drummers. When the team has developed so that trust has developed and everybody is committed to the same goals, members know what to do and can usually act on their own in ways that are close to what the group and manager would have directed.

PARADOX 5.

The Manager-as-Developer model requires an optimistic faith in subordinate possibilities but tough implementation to work.

The Manager-as-Developer model is optimistic in several ways. First, the model is based on the premise that virtually everyone wants to do well—that no reason exists for basic incompatibility between what the organization needs (in its search for excellence) and what individuals want to produce (in terms of performing competently). Second, the model optimistically posits that most people basically do not seek to empire-build, play politics, and do each other in unless the organizational situation makes it difficult to accomplish anything otherwise. Nasty behavior arises mostly when members feel blocked from legitimate methods for getting their work done, not as a result of an innate component of personal nastiness. Finally, the model's optimism is revealed in its tenet that most people can change—their behaviors, not personalities. Under the proper conditions, which include a manager who functions as a Developer, a relatively high percentage of subordinates can learn and grow.

Many managers resist this optimism. There is a kind of comfort taken in cynicism—in hanging onto the beliefs that people are not to be trusted, are out for their own self-interest, and can't change. The developmental approach cannot be utilized without giving up this cynicism.

At the same time, the Manager-as-Developer model is basically a tough approach. It is tough in setting high standards (and holding people to them). It is tough in requiring that the manager hold subordinates' feet to the fire when they may want to avoid the difficult issues. It is tough in pushing for conflicts to be identified and worked through rather than smoothed over. It is tough in requiring that people be confronted (rather than shunted aside, or ignored) when they don't come through. And it is tough in demanding that the manager be willing to be open to confrontation as well.

Many managers avoid this toughness. Some are so concerned about being liked that they do not even raise the important issues. But even many of the managers who think themselves hard-boiled are not very tough in important dimensions. There is a difference between hardness and toughness. The manager can be hard by not listening to subordinate complaints, exploiting others for the sake of short-term productivity, or by showing a hard exterior to prevent subordinates from broaching difficult issues. Such hardness is not toughness. Being tough is fully listening to subordinates, acknowledging validity in their complaints, and still being able to take the difficult actions when appropriate. Toughness is not dropping bombs on distant, impersonal targets; insisting on performance despite closeness and caring is far tougher.

PARADOX 6.

Although the Developer model requires new behavior, the best way to improve your performance as a manager is to focus on the needs of others, rather than on yourself.

It is easy to become frozen by self-help books. Although we have tried to avoid detailed, step-by-step advice, we have drawn your attention to a lot of things at once, many of them involving changes in your attitudes, skills, and even behavior. This multi-faceted process can be like trying to learn how to play tennis by memorizing each motion in microscopic, sequential detail. By the time you remember how to hold the racket, where to plant your feet, how to line up parallel to the net, what to look at, and the angle of your arm, the ball is long since dead. At some point in your playing progress, you might benefit from minute examination of some aspect of your game, but only after you have the basic idea and rhythm of tennis to depend on. To build the idea and rhythm, you need to use the Zen tennis approach: Focus on the ball going back over the net and where you want it to land. Your swing and positioning will follow naturally.

Managing by a new style requires something similar to this attitude. You need to maintain your focus outward, on your subordinates and their needs, the nature of the tasks you all face, and the kind of results you desire. Too close attention to how you're doing—where your feet are planted (or how precisely you are executing the model)—only causes ungainly awkwardness.

Learning anything new requires a period of awkwardness, so don't let the prospect be discouraging. More important, even while checking once in a while to see how you are doing, don't become so self-conscious that you come to the fate of the centipede who was asked how he coordinated 100 legs: You can't move at all.

Remember, a long journey starts with small steps, even while your eye is on the guiding star. You have to do both at once. Happy trip.

Relevant Background Factors

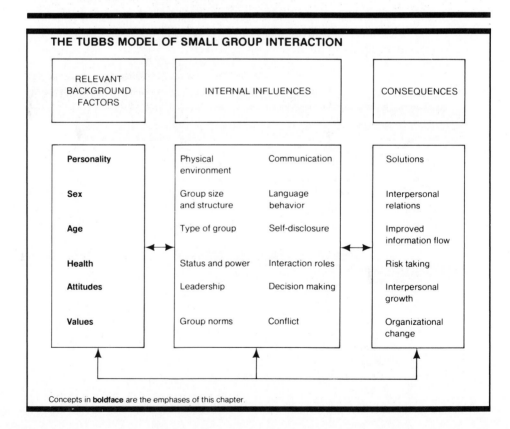

THE TUBBS MODEL OF SMALL GROUP INTERACTION

RELEVANT BACKGROUND FACTORS	INTERNAL INFLUENCES		CONSEQUENCES
Personality	Physical environment	Communication	Solutions
Sex	Group size and structure	Language behavior	Interpersonal relations
Age	Type of group	Self-disclosure	Improved information flow
Health	Status and power	Interaction roles	Risk taking
Attitudes	Leadership	Decision making	Interpersonal growth
Values	Group norms	Conflict	Organizational change

Concepts in **boldface** are the emphases of this chapter.

The purpose of Chapter Two is to study closely the relevant background factors that partially compose the Tubbs Model of Small Group Interaction. The six relevant background factors are personality, sex, age, health, attitudes, and values. These six factors relate directly to "why we do what we do" when placed in situations involving a small group. The chapter also discusses Maslow's hierarchy of needs. These needs tend to help explain further the six relevant background factors.

GLOSSARY

Inclusion: Inclusion is our need for belonging, feeling a part of, and being together with others.

Control: Control is our need to influence, lead, and develop power over others or to be influenced, led, or have others exert power over us.

Affection: Affection refers to the friendship and closeness between people.

Attitudes: An attitude is a mental state that exerts influence over an individual's behaviors. Attitudes have three components: (1) a cognitive component, which refers to a concept, (2) an affective component, which is emotion, and (3) a behavioral component, which is the readiness to act.

Consistency Theories: Consistency theories all are based on the assumption that human beings have a strong psychological need for consistency. This is often referred to as a need to maintain cognitive balance.

Values: Values are fewer in number than attitudes and serve as important predictors of behavior. They appear to be more stable and long lasting than attitudes.

CASE STUDY: Simpson vs. Engineering

When our supervisor, Bud Thomas, retired after thirty-seven years of service, the men in the department threw one of the biggest retirement parties that Engineering had ever seen. Bud was well liked by everyone, and we were sorry to see him go. As far as the engineers he supervised were concerned, he was the ideal boss. Bud was the type of supervisor who provided support when an employee needed it while managing to supervise not so closely that his employees felt that they had someone constantly looking over their shoulders. He was the type of supervisor who always made sure that we received credit for jobs well done.

After Bud's retirement, everyone was speculating as to who would be promoted to his vacancy. The majority of the engineers felt that one of our department's older men who had been on the job for years would be promoted. We were wrong.

Upper management decided to promote one of the younger engineers, who had seven years of seniority in another engineering section. His name was John Simpson. John was twenty-nine years old and a competent engineer. He came to our division as a low-level college graduate in-training employee in 1981. By 1986 he had worked his way up to engineer, and now, with Bud's retirement, to a supervisory position over our section.

All went well the first few months. The older employees with more seniority were a bit resentful at first, but after a couple of weeks the initial "grumbling" faded away, and the department resumed its business-as-usual atmosphere.

After John had been our supervisor for about three weeks, he called a meeting of the eleven people he supervised to announce some changes. First of all, John announced that he thought we should have a group meeting every day at 7 A.M. He thought that this would enable him to get a better picture of "what is going on" on a daily basis. John also stated that he felt that because he was working 6:30 A.M. to 3:30 P.M. each day, all of us should be on the same schedule. When some of the employees complained that this violated the current flextime policy on working hours and also conflicted with what was being allowed in other engineering groups in our division, John asserted that flextime was his prerogative and that he could set working hours, as he is our supervisor.

Some of the engineers were so mad that they took their case for flextime to the head engineer. He told them that flextime could be waived at the discretion of the supervisor. So we had to start at 6:30 each morning.

Therefore, at the first 7 A.M. meeting, John did all the talking, with the engineers talking only when spoken to. The engineers managed to limit the amount of information about the jobs they were working on. So John never had a clear picture of "what is going on."

The only change John achieved by the elimination of flextime and the mandatory attendance at morning meetings was the alienation of himself from other engineers. This became more evident as each day passed.

When John asked for volunteers to attend a conference and give a brief presentation about a topic in engineering, everyone turned him down. The same was true on the issue of overtime; John always had a hard time convincing anyone to stay over a couple of hours.

John furthered his alienation from the department when he announced that the company car we used to go from building to building (our plant complex is 2 miles long) and run errands with would be eliminated. He said that this was an upper-management decision over which we had no control.

Our productivity sagged so much after this that we started missing deadlines. For the first time, our group started to have morale problems.

At this point, John decided that the best way to solve our problems would be to have a Quality of Work Life meeting at which we could air our problems. When the meeting was held,

John asked what our main problem was, and we replied that he was our problem. Three days later, John transferred to another division.

---

1. What issues or problems can you identify in this case? *Need for Control* *Initially resentment, background factors such as: Age, Personality, Attitude. John was to authoritative, not flexible, didn't take into consideration*
2. How would have you have handled this situation if you had been John Simpson? *the needs of his subordinates. He didn't listen to his employees. no communication. made changes without regard as to how these changes would effect the staff. He alienated himself, productivity & morale declined.*

I would have observed & evaluated the current system to see if it was working before making any changes. If I felt changes were absolutely necessary, I would have presented the problem to the employees and asked them to brain storm to see if they could come up with any workable solutions, remained sensitive to employee needs & flexible.

This case clearly illustrates the very complex systems nature of group dynamics. The attitudes of John Simpson were at the heart of the problem. Yet the attitudes, age, work values, and seniority of the work group interacted with John's attitudes, age, values, and behaviors. If John had not been so young, their attitudes might have been more receptive. If he had been female, it would have added still another dimension that might have influenced their attitudes. The short-term result was a decrease in productivity. The longer-term result was that John was relieved of his supervisory position. Although the case doesn't follow up the incident, probably the group's attitudes will be strengthened and its cohesiveness increased; the new supervisor will likely face an even more close-knit group.

In this chapter we will examine six factors that we refer to as relevant background factors. They are personality, sex, age, health, attitudes, and values. Several of these are illustrated in the case of Simpson versus Engineering. One of the basic premises of systems theory is that all these factors are interrelated, so that a change in one part of the system creates changes in other parts of the system.

EXPLAINING WHY WE DO WHAT WE DO

Perhaps you may have wondered why John or the rest of the group acted the way they did. Or more generally, why do any people behave the way they do? This question has intrigued people for centuries. Behaving in specific ways is usually seen as an attempt by the individual to meet certain needs. For example, have you ever been in a group situation and wondered why you were there? Suppose you look out a classroom window and see a beautiful sky; it is a great day for being outside. You begin to experience competing needs—the need to go outside and have fun and the need to accomplish whatever the group's purpose is (such as studying for an upcoming exam). Whichever need is more intense will most probably determine the behavior you pursue.

Probably one of the best-known models for explaining people's needs is Maslow's (1970) hierarchy of needs (see Figure 2.1).

Physiological needs must be met in order to survive. Some groups were formed in the days of the cave dwellers to fight off saber-toothed tigers, as well as other unfriendly cave people, and to help gather food.

Security needs often motivate the formation of groups by individuals who lack

---

FIGURE 2.1   MASLOW'S NEED HIERARCHY

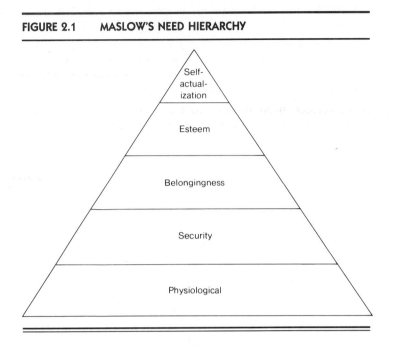

---

sufficient power on their own. This is demonstrated by the union movement, which resulted from the fact that there were far more workers than jobs. With ten people waiting to fill each job, workers were somewhat hesitant to make demands of bosses. Unions helped workers gain power and, eventually, job security.

Belongingness needs are easy for most people to identify with. Think about what you felt like during your first week as a college freshman. One student member of a freshman discussion group wrote about this belongingness need not being fulfilled: "During our discussion, I felt like I wasn't even supposed to be in my group. The others seemed like they were all very familiar with each other and discussed almost entirely among themselves. They took over the discussion basically by looking only at each other and asking a lot of questions of each other (and cracking a lot of really funny jokes). I tried to contribute but felt ignored. It was very uncomfortable and I became quiet after a few more attempts to contribute. I'm glad I didn't receive a grade on that discussion because I was annoyed at how little I participated." Eventually, the feelings of aloneness begin to subside as people develop their own circles of friends (social groups).

Esteem needs may also be met by groups. Often people are attracted to certain fraternities or sororities because of the prestige of membership, which adds to their feeling of self-esteem. All people need to feel that they are important, and being a part of a good group or organization is one very good way to accomplish that goal.

Self-actualization needs are the highest-level needs Maslow identified. A person may be attracted to a group because of the need for self-development. Encounter groups are one particular type of group devoted to the growth and development of members. Educational groups or work groups also may help individuals achieve a higher lever of human potential.

Maslow argued that the needs lowest on the hierarchy must be satisfied before the higher-level needs are activated. For example, we worry less about self-actualization in a job when we are unemployed and the bills haven't been paid.

Probably one of the reasons Maslow's theory has been so popular is because it seems intuitively valid. It is important to have an understanding of what motivates people (including ourselves). When we are in a group and one person talks a lot, it may be that he or she is trying to meet a belongingness need. If they brag, they are probably trying to satisfy an esteem need. If they consistently offer creative ideas that seem quite unusual, they may be trying to meet a self-actualization need.

PERSONALITY

Because each of us is a member of numerous groups throughout our lives, have you ever wondered what motivates us to join groups in the first place? Although there are many personality theories, one seems particularly relevant to small group behavior. Schutz (1958, 1967, 1971) hypothesized that most people share three needs that groups help fulfill: needs for inclusion, control, and affection. You will find Schutz's theory explained in detail at the end of this chapter. It is called the FIRO—B theory. FIRO—B stands for Fundamental Interpersonal Relations Orientation—Behavior. It means that everyone relates or orients themselves to others in ways that can be identified, measured, and predicted. If you are trying to lead a work group, it is very useful to be able to understand what motivates you and your group members.

Schutz's work began at the Naval Research Laboratory in Washington, D.C., nearly forty years ago. The FIRO—B test has been used to select submarine crews as well as astronaut teams whose members would have personality styles that would help them work more efficiently together under high-stress conditions. The major premise of Schutz's theory is that people need people and that we join groups to help fill this need. Each person, from childhood on, develops a fundamental interpersonal relations orientation with differing levels of needed inclusion, control, and affection.

All of us have felt the need for inclusion. If you have ever been in a physical education class in which teams were chosen, you know this feeling. Do you remember waiting to be chosen and fearing not being chosen? Some people have also experienced the need for control. If you are trying to lead a group, and several conversations are going on simultaneously, it brings out the need to control the discussion. Finally, if a group pays a lot of attention to certain members, it can make us feel the need to have some attention and affection directed our way, too. These are important needs in all people, but obviously they vary in intensity from person to person.

Inclusion

Inclusion refers to our need for belonging, feeling a part of, and being together with others. Have you ever been in a group in which you felt ignored? Perhaps you have felt this way in this very class, especially on the first or second day. This is because you were not being responded to as much as your need for inclusion required. Other people may not necessarily disagree with what you are saying; they just may not be responding. Such behavior violates our need to be included in the group. On a more basic level, it also makes us doubt our self-worth. If this exclusion happens over and over, most of us will begin to doubt our intrinsic worth as people.

On the job, if people go to lunch and don't invite us, our need for inclusion may not be met. On the other hand, if we prefer to do things on our own and people are constantly around us, this violates our *low* need for inclusion. Most of us want to be included in some groups and prefer to avoid others. If we are ignored by the attractive groups and sought after by the unattractive groups, this also violates our need for inclusion.

Even the rich and famous need to feel included. Blair (1988, p. 334) wrote about the tragic life of NBC News anchorwoman Jessica Savitch. She writes:

> Recently, however, Savitch had asked Linda Ellerbee to dinner at Hurley's. "Jessica wanted to be one of the guys, to be associated with those of us who did what we were paid to do," Ellerbee said. "She wanted to talk journalism war stories, but hers all had to do with hairdressers and missed planes and missed opportunities." As Ellerbee sat there listening to Savitch, who was talking so loudly that other diners' heads were turning, she felt any remaining envy dissolve into pity for the blond anchorwoman. "NBC was a good place for women to work," Ellerbee said. "We stuck together. But Jessica never got into any of that. She was terrified of being found out, so she never got close to anybody at work. She never trusted any of us."

The late Sammy Davis, Jr., wrote a gripping example of how he felt the opposite of inclusion (exclusion) when he first went into his group in the U.S. Army in 1942. He wrote,

> It was impossible to believe they were talking about me.
> "Yeah, but I still ain't sleepin' next to no nigger." . . . The corporal beckoned from the doorway. "Okay, c'mon in," he snapped, "on the double." We picked up our gear and followed him through the door. I felt like a disease he was bringing in. . . . I looked around the barracks. The bed nearest ours was empty. All the cots were about two feet apart from each other except ours, which were separated from the rest by about six feet—like we were on an island. . . . A sergeant came in and from the center of the barracks announced, "I'm Sergeant Williams. I'm in charge of this company. . . . There is only one way we do things here and that's the Army way! There will be exactly three feet of space, to the inch, between every bed in this barracks. You have sixty seconds to replace the beds as you found them. *Move!*" (Davis and Boyar 1989, pp. 6–7)

The inclusion issue raises its head over and over throughout our lives. Each time we take a new job, join a new work group, or meet a new group socially, we feel it. Problems occur when we are not sensitive to another person who is new in the group. They are experiencing the feeling, but we may not be tuned into their needs. Often, when a person comes in late for a meeting, the others do not make any attempt to orient that person or bring him or her up to date. All of us have a need for inclusion that must be met before we are able to function fully in a group. Keep in mind that this need recurs, much as our need to eat.

Control

Control refers to our need to influence, lead, and develop power over others or to be influenced, led, or have others exert power over us. If you have ever been in a group with no appointed leader, you know how uncomfortable it is to break the ice and get the discussion started. Those who attempt to get the group organized are trying to exert control over the others. At first, this may be welcomed, but often people begin to resent the control takers and will eventually ask them to stop being so pushy, with comments such as, "Who died and left you boss?" The issue of who is in control remains alive throughout the life of any group. Especially as membership changes, the pecking order is reshuffled and has to be reestablished. Here is an account of an M.B.A. class exercise in which resentment of a control taker is very obvious:

> The group consisted of seven people. The purpose of the class exercise was to form a manufacturing company and produce products. One individual chose himself as General Manager and also appointed an Assistant General Manager. The remaining members formed the assembly line workers. . . . The General Manager was a very forceful, energetic individual. He chose his own Assistant and appointed himself almost before we had formed the group. He is a very impatient individual. His entire manner left everyone in doubt as to the final outcome of the exercise. . . . The practice run was a complete disaster. We didn't know what the product was, let alone how to build it. Step by step instructions were available for everyone to read, but we weren't given time to read them. The General Manager didn't pay attention to his duties. He was more interested in production line speed than he was in purchasing materials or financial matters. He couldn't get quality products because of the haphazard organization of the work force. We had to start over again and again. The third time through, we got fairly decent quality. By that time it was too late. Dissension in the ranks of the group was rampant. . . . We were not motivated to do a good job, the only challenge was to beat the opposition (i.e., management).

Control, power, and leadership are closely related subjects. Why do you suppose so much has been written about them? Who is in control seems to be one of life's basic issues. Some studies have shown that whenever two people meet for the first time, a dominant-submissive relationship is established within the first sixty seconds. The perceptions of who is dominant between two people have been found to correlate over 90 percent with carefully constructed personality tests measuring the same phenomenon. Some books on power and control go to extreme lengths to help people gain control over others. Korda (1975) suggests that in order to gain and hold control over others, you should position your desk with your back to a window so that the other person has to look into the sunlight, thus putting him or her at a disadvantage.

The control issue is relevant to every organization on a daily basis, from the formal organization and the so-called span of control, to who talks the most in meetings. Supervisors typically talk more than subordinates. They also usually control the topic of conversation. Control is often demonstrated in rather subtle ways, too. I once saw an office worker throw a report on a secretary's desk. He said, "Sandy, I need to have this typed for the 3:00 meeting today." You could tell by her expression that she did not like the way he talked to her. Later that day, he came to pick up the finished report. She said, "Gee, Dave, I'm really sorry. I just didn't have time to get it done. Mr. Jenkins [the top boss] had me on another project all day." She was giving Dave a lesson in organizational control. Any experienced supervisor knows how much control his or her subordinates have if they choose to use it.

Affection

Affection refers to the friendship and closeness among people. Often our best friends are co-workers. Why is it that when we have time off from the job, we will organize bowling leagues, golf outings, and baseball leagues with co-workers? Some of these activities, such as the company picnic or Christmas party, may be more or less required. But for the most part, we socialize off the job as well as on because we want to; picture the many winning-team locker-room scenes with the champagne pouring over people's heads and players hugging each other as extreme examples of this affection.

Schutz (1967) compares inclusion, control, and affection in the following way: "A difference in inclusion behavior, control behavior, and affection behavior is illustrated by the different feelings a man has in being turned down by a fraternity, failed in a course by a professor, and rejected by his girl. . . . Inclusion is concerned with the problem if in or out, control is concerned with top or bottom, and affection with close or far." In each of these areas we have both the need to receive these behaviors from others and the need to express such needs towards others. Wanted inclusion would be hoping to be asked to go to lunch or coffee or to have a beer with the group; expressed inclusion would be inviting someone else to go. A compatible need level would exist when a person's wanted and expressed needs are at about the same level of intensity. Compatibility among individuals seems to occur when their needs are similar on the inclusion and affection dimensions and complementary or different on the control dimension. A group may suffer from too many power struggles if members are all high in need to control. Compatibility on these three dimensions tends to reduce conflict and increase group cohesiveness and satisfaction.

A carefully controlled laboratory study found that Schutz's predictions were substantiated. Liddel and Slocum (1976) constructed groups that were neutral, compatible, or incompatible on the basis of FIRO—B scores. When the groups were allowed to work on a problem-solving task, the compatible groups completed their tasks significantly faster than the neutral groups, which were significantly more efficient than the incompatible groups.

FIRO—B also has been found to be useful in organizational development. Varney and Hunady (1978) conducted a study in a 50-year-old heavy metal production plant with 900 employees and 95 managers. They used the FIRO—B test as a tool to give feedback to the work groups regarding their own individual needs and to give them insight into each other. The plant manager originally described the organization's needs in the following summary:

> There is a considerable amount of disagreement and disharmony among members of the management staff, resulting in a failure on the part of individuals as well as the team as a whole to accomplish set tasks. The performance indictors for the plant are in almost all cases below the normal, and we ranked among a total of six plants in our division as the lowest performer. The basic problem seems to be that people cannot work together

when it comes to sorting out problems, and they spend a lot of time blaming each other for the failures that occur. (p. 445)

As a result of the study, the researchers reported numerous changes in the behavior of the employees involved in the study. They concluded, "FIRO—B is a powerful stimulus to change. In the research reported here, we have demonstrated the value of the use of a "high energizer" such as the FIRO—B in team-building interventions" (p. 445).

Although personality is one of the most important background factors in small group communication, other factors are also involved. *Organismic* factors or variables are those that are part of the organism. These include a number of characteristics, but three seem to be especially pertinent to small group interaction: sex, age, and health.

SEX

Perhaps the most obvious thing about groups that include both sexes is that they are most interesting! Schutz (1971, p. 226) writes, "Usually, if there's a girl in the group who attracts me I find more interest in the group as a whole, and must watch myself because I tend to find everything she says and does somehow much more fascinating than I do anyone else's contribution." Women emphatically point out that the increased arousal brought about by a member of the opposite sex is every bit as much a part of the feminine response pattern as it is the masculine.

Sex does seem to play an increasing role in work groups. Blotnick (1986) surveyed 1800 professional women between the ages of 18 and 45. They had a median age of 32 and an average income of $26,000. He found that an astonishing 56 percent reported having had an affair with a co-worker, customer, or client. This compared to only 7 to 9 percent in the 1970s and even lower percentages in the 1950s and 1960s. These statistics lead to the conclusion that sex is a volatile and extremely relevant background factor to consider in work group settings.

More recently, Maineiro (1990, p. 5) wrote of recent surveys involving sex and the work group:

> Over eighty-six percent of the employees whom they interviewed had been aware of, or had been involved in, an office romance. A survey of 444 readers showed . . . over fifty percent of those surveyed had been sexually propositioned by someone at work; a quarter had sex in their place of work and another eighteen percent had sex with a co-worker during work hours!

These statistics are even more shocking given that Thomas (1986, p. 26) reports that 53 percent of all the full-time workers in America are women and that of all the women in the country between ages twenty-five and thirty-five, fully 66 percent are working full time.

Differences in behavior between the sexes have for years been known to be a function of cultural influences and childhood learning experiences. Margaret Mead (1968) found as early as 1935 that certain behaviors the Western world had assumed were innately masculine or feminine were, instead, culturally determined. In her studies of New Guinea tribes, she found certain societies in which women dominated. She writes (p. 259): "Among the Tchambuli the woman is the dominant, impersonal, managing partner, the man the less responsible and the emotionally dependent person." Mead describes the husband, on the other hand, as being catty toward other men but charming toward women. He danced in the tribal ceremonies, spent hours on his personal makeup, and gossiped about the other *men* in the village. Obviously, such behaviors cannot be an inherent function of one's sex.

Berg and Bass (1961) report that men tend to be more task oriented in groups, whereas women are more concerned with interpersonal harmony. Kibler, Barker, and Cegala (1970) found no differences between sexes in ability to comprehend and retain information from orally communicated messages. Furthermore, in a more recent study, Rosenfeld and Christie (1974) found no significant differences in persuasibility between men and women. They cite four other studies between 1968 and 1973 that also failed to find sex differences in persuasibility, whereas older studies, from 1935 to 1968, more often than not found women more persuasible. Rosenfeld and Christie (1974, p. 253) concluded, "If earlier studies were correct concerning persuasibility . . . women are gradually growing away from the 'traditional' dependence upon others and acquiring more confidence in their own judgments. It is futile to attempt to conclude that one sex is more persuasible than another based upon the present study and other available research." Recent literature (Dunegan & Duchon, 1989) suggests that a relationship between risk taking and task complexity exists in regard to the sexes. When tasks are simple, requiring a more "legitimate role performance," women are less likely to emit risk-taking behaviors. However, as tasks become more complex and the need for "legitimate role performance" becomes more blurred, women and men will take risks on an equal basis.

It would seem that the same futility presently exists in attempting to predict *group* communication behaviors on the basis of sex alone. However, it is important to emphasize that certain stereotypes concerning male and female roles are probably outdated and that new research is needed to establish if any sex differences do exist regarding small group behaviors. For example, review the stereotypes listed below.

How to Tell a Businessman from a Businesswoman

A businessman is aggressive; a businesswoman is pushy.

A businessman is good on details; she's picky.

He loses his temper because he's so involved in his job; she's bitchy.

When he's depressed (or hung over), everyone tiptoes past his office.

She's moody, so it must be her time of the month.

He follows through; she doesn't know when to quit.

He's confident; she's conceited.

He stands firm; she's impossible to deal with.

He's firm; she's hard.

His judgments are her prejudices.

He is a man of the world; she's been around.

He drinks because of excessive job pressure; she's a lush.

He isn't afraid to say what he thinks; she's mouthy.

He exercises authority; she's power mad.

He's close-mouthed; she's secretive.

He's a stern taskmaster; she's hard to work for.

It seems reasonable to predict that groups comprised of both sexes will be different from those whose members are all of the same sex. We might expect that sexually heterogeneous groups would have more socially oriented behaviors and fewer task-oriented behaviors, because members would be more interested in promoting social relationships than in homogeneous groups. A clever study by Rosenfeld and Fowler (1976) found that sex and personality combined to influence an individual's leadership style. The most interesting finding of this study seems to be that men and women who act similarly are perceived differently. According to Rosenfeld and Fowler (1976, p. 324), "Whereas democratic males were characterized as forceful, analytical, and as valuing the love of people . . . democratic females were characterized as open-minded and nurturing. The democratic male may appear to group members as analytical and thereby aloof, while the democratic female may appear to be warm and affectionate." This study illustrates what is meant by the systems aspects of small group interaction. Personality, sex, style of leadership behavior, and the resulting perception of the person behaving are all interrelated.

Morrison, White, and Van Velsor (1990, p. 290) conducted extensive interviews with seventy-six successful women in Fortune 100 companies. On the basis of this research, they identified six factors associated with women's career success. They are:

1. Help. Mentors from above offered advice and inspiration.

2. Achievement. A track record of proven successes.

3. Desire. This is demonstrated through hard work, long hours, and personal sacrifice.

4. Management. The ability to get people to perform while maintaining their respect and trust.

5. Risk taking. Career moves requiring relocation and travel were examples.

6. Tough, decisive, and demanding. Being aggressive, making hard decisions, and being willing to fight for what they believed was right.

It would seem from this list that there is nothing that would differentiate these characteristics from those of successful male executives. However, Loden (1990) found that women approach teamwork and participatory management differently from men. She found that "they are less likely to 'pull rank' and more likely to stress cooperation than competition" (p. 298). As women's roles in our society change, more modern research can help to clarify and probably disprove some long-held beliefs.

For a comprehensive discussion of gender and communication, see Eakins and Eakins (1978).

AGE

Obviously, communication patterns differ from childhood through adolescence to adulthood and old age. Older group members in college-age groups (for example, married students, veterans, and so forth) tend to be more influential, on the basis of their relatively greater number of years of experience. Although this may not always hold true, it tends to be the case. There is some evidence (Bass, Doll, and Clair 1953) that older college women are held in higher esteem than younger college women. It generally takes time to develop leadership qualifications. In fact, one study (Quinn 1973) indicated that one reason younger people in general have lower job satisfaction is that they tend to have lower-level jobs, which are inherently less satisfying. On the other hand, as they gain in age and experience, they move into more challenging job capacities and gain in satisfaction.

Zenger and Lawrence (1989) found that age similarity of group members had a positive effect on the communication of information within project groups. This stems from earlier notions that people tend to communicate with those who are similar to themselves. Similar age ranges lead to similar life experiences and interests. Communication channels produced by nonwork-related conversations will influence the ease of work-related communications.

Finally, Shaw (1981, pp. 181–182), summarizing the literature on age and group behavior, stated:

> [T]here is good evidence that chronological age of the group member is related to several aspects of group interaction. With increasing age, the individual has an increasing . . . selectivity of contacts and greater complexity of . . . interaction. . . . Age is related to behavior in groups, it provides the time required for the individual to learn appropriate social responses . . . in most cases it is not the mere fact that the individual has aged that is important, but rather that he has had greater experience in social situations.

It is also interesting to speculate that groups with age heterogeneity would perform differently than those with age homogeneity. A number of studies indicate that some member heterogeneity relates positively to such group outcomes as cohesion (Hare 1962). It is apparent that age, and the experiences that go along with age, will affect group interaction and subsequent group outcomes. For the time being, however, the exact nature of these relationships is not clear.

Although health may not be a highly significant factor in the study of small groups, it does play a part. Deficiencies in both physical and mental health would seem to impede group performance. A member who fails to attend meetings or who is unable to carry his or her portion of the group workload will sooner or later reduce total group output. Also, physical health frequently affects stamina. Strength and stamina may not be important in relatively short discussions (lasting up to an hour); however, discussions and conferences frequently last for days. Labor-management negotiations may go twenty hours a day for a week or even longer. In one case, a local labor agreement was settled after a prolonged strike; the week after the agreement was reached, the local union president died of a heart attack. So physical health and stamina can play an important part in small group interaction.

Those who are spaced out on drugs or who are hung over from the night before will also harm group performance. In one case a college professor was consistently abusive and aggressive in department meetings. He later admitted that he had been so high on drugs he didn't even remember being at the meetings. Yet his behavior caused severe setbacks in his department, because he argued vociferously against all attempts to cover the items in the group's agenda; he also seriously hurt the feelings of other group members through his verbal assaults. Physical and mental health factors are out of the control of other group members, yet they have an effect on the group's end results.

Bo Schembechler, the legendary former football coach of the University of Michigan (and current president of the Detroit Tigers) writes the following account of how health affects his life:

Sure enough, five weeks later, I was in the hospital for another catheterization when I started to have that second heart attack, and a day that was supposed to be back-to-work turned into the day they cut my chest open and did my second open-heart surgery. That one, I thought, would be the clincher. *God, just let me live.* My heart was becoming like an old car; parts were hard to find. I really figured my life would change after that, and I'd be lucky to be walking, let alone coaching, again. . . .

So what have I learned from my troubled heart? Well I figure it's God's way of keeping me in check. Just like my bowl record. Without that, I'd have nothing but success in football; my ego would go through the roof. Same thing with my heart. Without that, I might lose all sight of what life is really about. I might just coach myself into oblivion, let little things depress me, never have a good laugh or shoot the breeze with players. But because of all the times I've been in that damn hospital wondering if I'd ever get out, I've really come to enjoy life, as crazy as it is.

My heart has given me a certain perspective. I never get depressed. Little things don't upset me anymore. I'm a different guy than most people figure from watching the games or reading newspapers. All my screaming and carrying on is strictly in football—and most of that is for effect. Privately, I'm a fairly sensitive person, and I enjoy life, and I have a decent sense of humor. I like to laugh, I like people, and I'm pretty easy to please when it comes to doing things or going places. Why worry?

As long as I hear that ticky, ticky, ticky, I'm a happy guy. (Schembechler and Albom 1989, pp. 225–226)

As each of us develops through childhood and adolescence, a myriad of experiences shape our view of the world. Because we each have different experiences, we would expect our outlooks to differ also. These experiences are called developmental factors, and we will look at three that are related to small group interaction: attitudes, values, and anxieties.

ATTITUDES

Almost fifty years ago, Allport (1935) defined an *attitude* as "a mental and a neural state of readiness, organized through experience, exerting a directive or dynamic influence upon the individual's response to all objects and situations with which it is related." According to Triandis (1971), attitudes have three components: (1) a cognitive component, which refers to an idea or a concept, such as "Chevrolets," (2) an affective component, or the emotion toward the idea (Chevrolets are good), and (3) a behavioral component, which is the readiness to act (that is, to drive or buy a Chevrolet).

McGrath and Altman (1966) indicate that group members may hold several types of attitudes that are relevant to their participation in small groups. For example, they have attitudes toward the task itself, toward the situation within which the group is operating, toward people inside and outside of the group, and toward other issues that may be related to the one under discussion. All these attitudes will ultimately affect their behavior in the group, which in turn will affect the group's results. How many times have you been a member of a project team or group in which either you or others in the group have found that you just couldn't seem to get too enthusiastic about accomplishing the task? Or perhaps you would ordinarily be interested in the task, but it comes at a time when you are preoccupied with other things, such as romantic difficulties or financial worries. These illustrations help to indicate the important role that attitudes may play in determining one's actions in the group.

Another variable in the background factors of small group communication is race. Perhaps it is difficult for you to recognize the relevance of discussing race differences in small group communication. Remember that each group member brings his or her own individual history to the group. Race and religious persuasion have proven to be associated with attitudes.

A recent study (Greenhaus, Parasuraman, and Wormley, 1990) discussed the elements of "access discrimination" and "treatment discrimination" in organizations. The same principles apply to group communication. Access discrimination prevents members of a subgroup of the population (not necessarily a minority group) from entering a particular group. Treatment discrimination occurs when subgroup members receive fewer opportunities and fewer rewards within a particular group. For instance, remember the "grandfather clause" that was instituted for voting rights in the early part of the century. Blacks were given the right to vote (were allowed equal access) if their grandfather had voted (not allowed equal treatment).

When we speak about organizations as groups, access discrimination has been successfully reduced within the last few years. But in many organizations, treatment discrimination is holding fast. Greenhaus and others (1990) found that although minority groups, particularly blacks, have come to occupy considerably more managerial positions in organizations in the last few years, they still receive fewer opportunities to excel in the organization. Compared to white managers, black managers felt less accepted in their organizations, perceived themselves as having less discretion on their jobs, received lower ratings from their supervisors in job performance and promotability, were more likely to have reached career plateaus, and experienced lower levels of career satisfaction.

A group environment that is conducive to equal opportunities should produce minimal race differences and will result in a more successful group effort.

Some of the most intuitive yet provocative theories concerning attitudes are the so-called cognitive consistency theories. These closely related theories are all based on the assumption that human beings have a strong psychological need for consistency. Heider (1958), the first of the consistency theorists, refers to this as a need to maintain *balance*. He reasons that if we hold an attitude X and another person holds the same value, then we are likely to feel positively toward that person. For example, if Lance likes motorcycles and Brad also likes motorcycles, Lance is likely to have positive feelings toward Brad. This can be illustrated in Figure 2.2. If, on the other hand, Brad does not like motorcycles, Lance would feel some imbalance and would be motivated to resolve it in one of several ways. First, he could try to change Brad's evaluation of motorcycles. Second, he could change his feeling toward Brad. Finally, he could change his own evaluation of motorcycles. The specific alternative Lance chooses would depend on the relative strength of his attitudes toward Brad and toward motorcycles.

Heider predicts that balanced triads are rewarding, or pleasant to experience, whereas imbalanced triads result in pressure to restore balance. An easy rule of thumb for differentiating between balanced and imbalanced triads is that if the algebraic product of the three elements in the triad is positive, the triad is balanced. If the algebraic product is negative, the triad is imbalanced. Which of the triads in Figure 2.3 is imbalanced, thus creating pressure to restore balance? How could balance be restored?

A related consistency theory is called *cognitive dissonance theory* (Festinger 1957). In this theory, *consonance* is the same as Heider's concept of balance, and *dissonance* is equivalent to imbalance in that it serves to motivate a change back to consonance. One of the interesting finds of research in this area is that a severe initiation for attaining group membership creates a high level of dissonance, which is

FIGURE 2.2

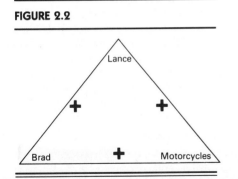

FIGURE 2.3

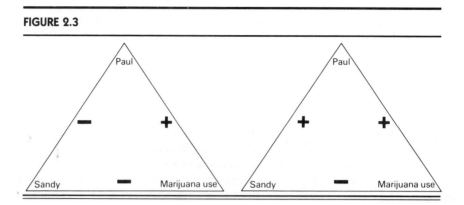

usually resolved by the person valuing membership in the group more than if the initiation was less severe (Aronson and Mills 1959).

Fraternities and sororities have used pledging as a device to increase the severity of initiation into membership. The result is usually that one who endures these experiences reduces the dissonance caused by them and begins to believe they are necessary and even desirable for the new pledge class to endure. The traditional pride in being a United States Marine has also resulted largely from the severity of initiation experienced in Marine Corps boot camp.

Group interaction may also create dissonance. If you are confronted in a discussion with an opinion contrary to your own, some degree of dissonance will result. The dissonance will increase if you value the other person and if the issue over which you disagree is one of high relevance. According to Festinger and Aronson (1968) you may reduce the dissonance in these five ways (starting with the most likely and going to the least likely approach): (1) Devalue the importance of the issue; (2) derogate the disagreeing person; (3) attempt to change his or her attitude; (4) seek additional social support for your view; and (5) change your attitude. Aronson (1973) posits that although people like to think of themselves as rational animals, they are more likely than not "rationalizing animals." It is important to point out that we all use these methods of dissonance reduction, and we need to have them. Although rationalizing may sound like something we should avoid, it can be a helpful tool if we are consciously aware of using it.

Organ and Bateman (1986, p. 218) remind us of the difficulty of attempting to change a person's attitude when they write:

> We would expect people to be jealous of their freedom with respect to attitudes that are central to their self-concepts. Attempts to change such attitudes represent, in essence, attempts to change their identities. Consider the workers who like to use certain materials and procedures because they are so closely linked to their self-images as meticulous artisans. A supervisor trying to alter their sentiments toward those methods is, perhaps unwittingly, striking at the core of their vocational self-images. It would not be surprising if they defended their freedom to hold such attitudes by valuing their procedures and materials all the more, in response to influence attempts.

On the other hand, actual research evidence has shown that successful attitude change can be accomplished. For example, Miller and Monge (1985, p. 382) studied the impact of communication regarding organizational change on employee attitudes and anxiety level. From their research, they conclude:

> The results of this study have several implications for organizational managers interested in improving employees' attitudes toward work or the organization or helping them adjust to organizational change . . . managers should also be aware of employee interaction and consider information a means of reducing anxiety and stress, improving worker satisfaction, or influencing other job attitudes.
>
> Second, this research indicates that any information is better than no information, so managers facing change should try to provide employees with as much information as possible. Third . . . managers should attempt to isolate needs relevant to the change and see that the needs are being met in the new situation and help employees to know that their needs are being considered.

VALUES

Although an overwhelming amount of research has been conducted on attitudes and attitude change, Rokeach (1968, 1971, 1973) has argued that people's *values* are also important as a predictor of behavior. His rationale is that we have thousands of different attitudes, but we have only several dozen values. Values, then, are seen as more fundamental than attitudes and are more stable and long-lasting. For an exercise concerning your own values and how they relate to the values of others, see the exercises at the end of this chapter.

People are both products and producers of their environment. As outlined in a social cognition theory by Wood and Bandura (1989), *reciprocal determinism* represents the "bidirectional influence" of our behavior. We respond, with our own personal values and experiences, to others, with their own personal values and experiences. Others respond to our responding to them, and our behavior determines and is determined by our environment. The process is both reciprocal and perpetual.

Value differences may significantly influence the course of any given group discussion. Suppose you are in a group attempting to determine a policy regarding pregnancy leaves of absence for employees of a company. Suppose also that your committee consists of six women, three who have been to college and three who have not. On the basis of the study data in Figure 2.4, how likely to you think it would be that the committee might achieve consensus on this issue?

This research indicates that educational differences would generate severe value differences between the two subgroups on the committee. If one group, the noncollege women, basically valued motherhood and devalued careers for women, it would probably be difficult for them to agree with the others on a leave-of-absence policy decision. Similar difficulties arise in discussions dealing with sexual behaviors, obscenity, abortion, religion, and politics, for example. Any discussion on a topic on which people have strong value differences is likely to be complicated by such differences.

With the graduating class of 1986, there were two nationally publicized examples of values influencing graduation committees' decisions. At Rice University in Houston, Texas, two graduates who were vegetarians asked administrators to allow them to have diplomas printed on paper rather than on sheepskin. One of the graduates said, "I don't participate in eating meat. If I draw the line there, why not draw it one step further?" (AP, May 10, 1986). At Tufts University in Boston, the medical school students no longer wanted to take the 2000-year-old Hippocratic oath because they no longer believed in the values it upheld. Instead, they vowed to "stress prevention over cure, tend to their patients' psychological needs, seek help from others, and, above all, 'not play God' " (AP, May 18, 1986).

At every university, committees decide such policies. It is conceivable that the values of the administrators on those committees played a part in determining the decisions described above. In fact, Naisbitt (1982) argues that these are simply examples of one "megatrend," which he calls "From either/or to Multiple Option." As other examples, he cites the number of television channels that used to be available (3 networks) compared to cable television's 40. If you have a satellite dish, you may be able to get over 100. An organizational example would be the so-called cafeteria of compensation and benefits approach, in which employees can select from a wide variety of company benefits to suit their own particular needs (e.g.,

FIGURE 2.4
Bar graph from the *Flint Journal,*
November 13, 1974

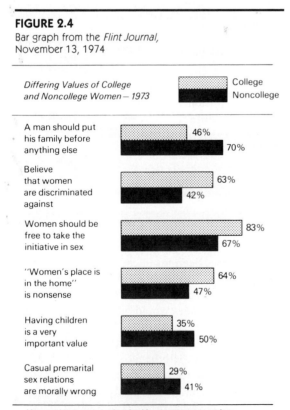

*Differing Values of College
and Noncollege Women — 1973*   College
                                        Noncollege

A man should put his family before anything else — 46% / 70%

Believe that women are discriminated against — 63% / 42%

Women should be free to take the initiative in sex — 83% / 67%

"Women's place is in the home" is nonsense — 64% / 47%

Having children is a very important value — 35% / 50%

Casual premarital sex relations are morally wrong — 29% / 41%

Women's movement has had its warmest reception on America's campuses. The recent Yankelovich "Study of American Youth" reports that the values of Women's Lib have created a wide schism between women in college and women who do not have a college education.

tuition refund, versus optional life insurance, versus tax sheltered employee investment programs, versus increased retirement contributions). These are all current examples of changing values influencing our behaviors.

Earlier we discussed the influence of age on values and behaviors. Payne, Summers, and Stewart (1973) studied subjects from three generations (college students, their parents, and their grandparents). They were asked to respond on a seven-point scale (1) "not at all bad" to (7) "extremely bad" to each of eighty-five items. Sample items were:

- Becoming involved in unusual sex practices with persons of the opposite sex
- Being unpatriotic
- Cheating on your income tax
- Cheating on an exam and getting caught
- Going to a party in casual clothes and finding that everyone is dressed up
- Having to go on welfare to feed or clothe your children adequately

The researchers found that college students were significantly less severe in their judgments than were their parents, who were in turn less severe than the grandparents.

Although differences exist among generations, it is also likely that major differences exist among individuals in the same age group. A question arises as to the degree of value differences that can be tolerated in a group before these differences become a major obstacle to group functioning. Fortunately, some related research sheds light on this question. Rogers and Shoemaker (1971) discussed this issue with regard to homophily and heterophily of relationships. *Homophily* is defined as "the degree to which pairs of individuals who interact are similar in certain attributes (beliefs, values, education, social status)" (McCroskey 1971, p. 174). Rogers and Bhowmik (1971, p. 213) state that "heterophilic interaction is likely to cause message distortion, delayed transmission, restriction of communication channels, and may cause cognitive dissonance, as the receiver is exposed to messages that may be inconsistent with his existing beliefs and attitudes, an uncomfortable psychological state." In other words, two students would probably communicate more easily than a student and a professor. Although considerable research has been conducted on the effect of homophily-heterophily on the diffusion of innovations, more research is needed to determine the effects these factors have on group functioning and group outcomes.

The culture that someone was raised in may also lead to differences in values among group members. One author (Weisinger 1989, p. 242) discussed the hazard of criticizing group members for behavior that is culturally motivated. He told this story:

An AT&T manager had a talented engineer whose ideas never got recognized. The problem was that the young man in question was rather reserved and rarely spoke up at meetings. The times that he did, he was so timid that the other engineers, a rather aggressive bunch, either did not pay attention to what he said or challenged him into silence. Wanting the young man to receive his due, the manager took him aside and explained that if he were ever going to make his knowledge known he had best speak up in a forceful manner. The engineer replied that in his culture, it was seen as inappropriate to express one's opinions so directly. The manager was stymied.

With the increase in international trade, it is more than likely that most of you will at sometime be involved in a group project with someone raised in a culture different from your own. It is also important for you to remember that there are many different cultures right here in the United States. You don't have to go across the ocean to find someone with cultural values different from your own. As Weisinger (1989) points out, it is important not to force a person to act in a way that contradicts his/her cultural norms. If such a situation arises, make sure that everyone in the group knows one another's cultural rules. Being aware of such differences will help group members learn the best way to respond to one another.

THE SYSTEMS PERSPECTIVE

As we pointed out in Chapter 1, small group interactions are the result of influences that can be labeled inputs, throughputs, and outputs. These factors are in a constant state of simultaneous and reciprocal influence. This chapter has focused on some of the inputs—namely, the relevant background factors of the group members. Through the discussion of personality, we tried to illustrate the role personality plays in shaping individual behavior. For example, those high on inclusion will probably be more inclined to join groups in the first place (if we assume that membership is voluntary). Those high on affection are very likely to smile more, express more feelings both verbally and nonverbally than low affiliators, give more direct eye contact to more members of the group, and agree more than low affiliators. We would expect that high affection members would have higher satisfaction resulting from harmonious group experiences, and greater dissatisfaction with groups that experience a high degree of conflict and disagreement. The person low on need for inclusion would tend to avoid meetings and group memberships whenever possible and would avoid talking in the groups he or she was forced to be in. Group interaction would generally be viewed by the introvert as threatening and therefore less satisfying than engaging in the same activity alone. However, if the group were conducted by a supportive and nonthreatening leader, the introvert's satisfaction level would increase dramatically (Giffin and Bradley 1969).

High control members tend to enjoy working on task-oriented projects, because they are more task oriented than most others and find that the group tends to slow down their progress. The exception, of course, would be a group composed of a lot of high controllers. In this case, high cohesion or high conflict might result, depending on the way the members decided to reward their efforts. Thus group norms, leadership style, and communication patterns all tend to influence the satisfaction level of group members. In the example at the beginning of this chapter, the group including John Simpson provided an illustration of a controller that resulted in a low level of satisfaction. John was seen by the rest of the group as too domineering. He got into one argument after another with other members. In this case, his high degree of dominance and dogmatism seemed to overshadow most of his expertise.

The three organismic factors discussed in this chapter were sex, age, and health. A group with both sexes tends to have more socially oriented communication patterns and fewer task-oriented comments resulting.

This chapter also dealt with age as an organismic variable. Age seems to be somewhat similar to attitudes and values in that the more similar group members are (in age, attitudes, and values), the easier it is for them to communicate in a way that leads to higher satisfaction. It stands to reason that it is more comfortable to be in groups with people like ourselves (in terms of age, attitudes, and values) than it is to be in groups in which we feel we "don't fit in" as well. However, some of the most interesting experiences occur when we meet someone of a drastically different age group who shares our attitudes and values. Conversely, even people of one's own age may differ so much an attitude or personality that hard feelings result.

In the readings at the end of this chapter, William Schutz shows the importance of the need for inclusion, control, and affection in relation to several aspects of group behavior. The second selection, by Widgery and Tubbs, applies attitude change theory to supervision.

EXERCISES

1. Employee Selection Problem

You are a member of a personnel selection committee. You need to hire two people as first-line supervisors in an industrial foundry. The supervisors would be in charge of thirty-person (mostly male) work groups who do machining processes (grinding, drilling, polishing) on metal castings made from molten metal in a different part of the foundry. Examine all five information sheets, which describe the candidates who have passed the physical examination and are available for immediate employment.

1

NAME: Sally A. Peterson   AGE: 23

MARITAL STATUS: Married   NUMBER OF CHILDREN: 0

NUMBER OF DEPENDENTS OTHER THAN SELF (explain relation): 1—husband

EDUCATION:

	Years	Degree or Diploma	Major (where applicable)
Elementary	8	Yes	
High School	4	Yes	College prep.
College	4	Yes (B.A.)	Sociology

CURRENT EDUCATIONAL OR VOCATIONAL SITUATION: Has been management trainee for four months with XYZ Aircraft Company. Began with XYZ immediately after serving two years with Peace Corps.

VOCATIONAL SKILLS OR EXPERIENCE: None other than a few elementary skills learned while in Peace Corps.

POLICE RECORD: None

ADDITIONAL COMMENTS: Currently active in volunteer community social work. Has taken over Junior Achievement group in underprivileged neighborhood.

2

NAME: Thomas Browne   AGE: 26

MARITAL STATUS: Married   NUMBER OF CHILDREN: 0

NUMBER OF DEPENDENTS OTHER THAN SELF (explain relation): 1—wife

EDUCATION:

	Years	Degree or Diploma	Major (where applicable)
Elementary	8	Yes	
High School	4	Yes	College prep.
College	4	Yes (B.A.)	Economics
	$\frac{1}{2}$	(toward M.A.)	Economics

CURRENT EDUCATIONAL OR VOCATIONAL SITUATION: Is completing first year in graduate school working toward M.A. in economics, which should be completed in one more semester. Is classified in top third of his graduate school class. Is currently a research assistant to leading economist in graduate school of business.

VOCATIONAL SKILLS OR EXPERIENCE: None

POLICE RECORD: Arrested with a number of other students involved in campus disturbance—released without charges being made.

ADDITIONAL COMMENTS: None

3

NAME: William Cross   AGE: 20

MARITAL STATUS: Married   NUMBER OF CHILDREN: 0
                                     (expecting first child in 6 months)

NUMBER OF DEPENDENTS OTHER THAN SELF (explain relation): 1—wife

EDUCATION:

	Years	Degree or Diploma	Major (where applicable)
Elementary	8	Yes	
High School	4	Yes	Vocational
College			

CURRENT EDUCATIONAL OR VOCATIONAL SITUATION: Plumber's apprentice completing second year of apprenticeship. Employed by large building contractor.

VOCATIONAL SKILLS OR EXPERIENCE: Plumbing, some automotive repair skills, welding. General construction work.

POLICE RECORD: Two arrests, no convictions.
First arrest while in high school—no details because of juvenile status. Second arrest for disorderly conduct—charges dismissed.

ADDITIONAL COMMENTS: None

4

NAME: Jane Williams   AGE: 24

MARITAL STATUS: Single   NUMBER OF CHILDREN: 0

NUMBER OF DEPENDENTS OTHER THAN SELF (explain relation): 0

EDUCATION:

	Years	Degree or Diploma	Major (where applicable)
Elementary	8	Yes	
High School	4	Yes	College prep.
College	4	Yes (B.A.)	Sociology
	$1\frac{1}{2}$	Yes (M.B.A.)	Production Management

CURRENT EDUCATIONAL OR VOCATIONAL SITUATION: Completing second year of graduate school. Has B.A. in sociology, working toward Ph.D., which should be completed in 3 to 4 semesters. Ranks in middle third of graduate class. Working one-half time as a teaching assistant. Doing volunteer work, and beginning research on urban sociology project.

VOCATIONAL SKILLS OR EXPERIENCE: None

POLICE RECORD: None

ADDITIONAL COMMENTS: None

5

NAME: Robert Smith   AGE: 21

MARITAL STATUS: Single   NUMBER OF CHILDREN: 0

NUMBER OF DEPENDENTS OTHER THAN SELF (explain relation): 0

EDUCATION:

	Years	Degree or Diploma	Major (where applicable)
Elementary	8	Yes	
High School	4	Yes	College prep.
College	3½	B.S. expected at end of semester	Business Administration

CURRENT EDUCATIONAL OR VOCATIONAL SITUATION: College senior expecting degree at end of current (spring) semester. "A–" student.

VOCATIONAL SKILLS OR EXPERIENCE: Typing. Has also worked part time in selling, construction work, and on farms.

POLICE RECORD: None

ADDITIONAL COMMENTS: Father unemployed for medical reasons. Mother works to support family. It is known that he has worked his way through college and has incurred a small debt in the form of a student loan.

Group Task After reviewing all five information sheets, meet as a group for thirty minutes to decide which two candidates should get the jobs. Each of you in the group will be assigned to argue in favor of one of the five candidates. After each of you presents the best "case" for your candidate, you must work together collectively to determine in the best interest of everyone concerned who should be hired. Your company is an equal opportunity/affirmative action employer.

2. Self-Esteem Exercise

Rate yourself on the following list of terms. First put an *I* in the appropriate blank indicating how you would like to be *ideally*. After completing all the items, begin the list again. This time put an *R* in the appropriate blank indicating how you think you *really* are. After you have rated your ideal self and your real self, compare the two. You may want to talk to others to see how their ratings compare.

1. Attractive   ___:___:___:___:___:___   Unattractive

2. Intelligent   ___:___:___:___:___:___   Unintelligent

3. Weak   ___:___:___:___:___:___   Strong

4. Passive   ___:___:___:___:___:___   Active

5. Fair   ___:___:___:___:___:___   Unfair

6. Kind   ___:___:___:___:___:___   Unkind

7. Quiet   ___:___:___:___:___:___   Loud

8. Introverted ___:___:___:___:___:___   Extroverted

9. Nervous   ___:___:___:___:___:___   Relaxed

10. Liberal   ___:___:___:___:___:___   Conservative

11. Happy   ___:___:___:___:___:___   Sad

12. Boastful   ___:___:___:___:___:___   Humble

13. Controlled ___:___:___:___:___:___   Uncontrolled

14. Vulnerable ___:___:___:___:___:___   Invulnerable

15. Excited   ___:___:___:___:___:___   Calm

16. Sexy   ___:___:___:___:___:___   Unsexy

17. Trusting   ___:___:___:___:___:___   Untrusting

18. Powerful   ___:___:___:___:___:___   Weak

19. Conforming ___:___:___:___:___:___   Independent

20. Sensitive ___:___:___:___:___:___   Insensitive

3. Personal Styles Exercise

Read the descriptions of the tough battler, friendly helper, and objective thinker that follow. Then anonymously rate volunteer class members on these three dimensions by placing an X inside a triangle as illustrated.

After this has been done, distribute the ratings to the people who have been rated. Class members may ask questions to get more feedback on what behaviors create these impressions on fellow students.

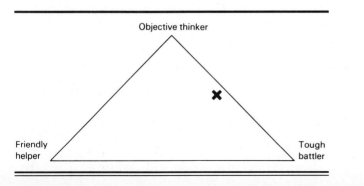

PERSONAL STYLES IN GROUPS AND ORGANIZATIONS*

Listed below are three characteristic types that may be found in any group or organization.

	Tough Battler	Friendly Helper	Objective Thinker
Emotions	Accepts aggression, rejects affection	Accepts affection, rejects aggression	Rejects both affection and interpersonal aggression
Goal	Dominance	Acceptance	Correctness
Influences others by	Direction, intimidation, control of rewards	Offering understanding, praise, favors, friendship	Factual data, logical arguments
Value in organization	Initiates, demands, disciplines	Supports, harmonizes, relieves tension	Defines, clarifies, gets information, criticizes, tests
Overuses	Fighting	Kindness	Analysis
Becomes	Pugnacious	Sloppy, sentimental	Pedantic
Fears	Being "soft" or dependent	Desertion, conflict	Emotions, irrational acts
Needs	Warmth, consideration, objectivity, humility	Strength, integrity, firmness, self-assertion	Awareness of feeling, ability to love and to fight

Above are shown characteristic emotions, goals, standards of evaluation, and techniques of influence of each type, and his/her service to the organization.

Each can be overdone and distorted. The *Tough Battler* would be a better manager, a better parent, a better neighbor, and a more satisfied person if he/she could learn some sensitivity, accept his/her inevitable dependence on others, and come to enjoy consideration for them. The Tough Battler would be more successful if he/she recognized that some facts will not yield to pugnacity.

The *Friendly Helper* would be a better manager, parent, citizen, and person if he/she could stand up for his/her own interests and for what is right, even against the pleas of others. This type needs firmness and strength and courage not to evade or smooth over conflicts. He/she must face facts.

The *Objective Thinker* would be a better human being and a better business leader if he/she could become more aware of his/her own feelings and the feelings of others. The Objective Thinker needs to learn that there are times when it is all right to fight and times when it is desirable to love.

*This material is adapted from the *Reading Book* of the NTL Institute for Applied Behavioral Science, associated with the National Education Association. The papers were originally prepared for theory sessions at the Institute's laboratories.

4. Gender Conditioning and the Stress It Produces

In groups of five or so, discuss your feelings about the following statements on the topics of sex roles and gender conditioning. The outline that follows this list may help you get started.

1. I am moving away from the idea that there is one role for men and one role for women, but I feel guilty when the man or woman in my life does something I have traditionally felt responsible for.

2. I know that society's views of a man's showing emotion or its traditional rules of what he may eat or wear are no measure of the man; but by openly breaking these rules, he is just asking for people to question his sexuality, and it's not worth the hassle.

3. Women's liberation, carried to the extreme, is responsible for the high rate of male impotency and homosexuality we find today.

4. Right or wrong, a man's sexuality is measured by his status and ability to make money. By many people's standards, all a women needs to be successful is to find a man who will take care of her.

5. The thing a man should be most proud of is his success in his work. Mainly, he works to provide the "good life" for his wife and family. Not having a job is the worst thing that can happen to him.

6. I think I (my husband) work(s) too hard; but not maintaining our present lifestyle would cause more problems and be even harder to deal with than my (his) overwork.

For Men:

1. Since adulthood I have found it difficult to become close friends with another male. It really doesn't matter, though, because once I become involved with a woman, I find I really don't need any other close friends.

2. I understand that the woman in my life has a need to be liberated; but I am still doing everything that I always did, and constantly she wants more from me. Her liberation is costing me mine.

For Women:

1. The man in my life finds activities he can do without me that bring him satisfaction, partly because we agree that everyone is responsible for his own happiness. I don't enjoy going out without him. Social events seem to be designed for couples, and I feel out of place when I am alone or with women.

2. For the first time the man in my life feels that it is important for me to know who I am and what I want out of life. I am so accustomed to "not wanting anything" that I can't answer those two questions. I jump from one idea to another, and it is driving us both crazy.

I. Gender conditioning distorts one's "world consciousness"

   A. His vision of the world situation

   B. Her vision of the world situation

II. Gender conditioning distorts one's body consciousness

   A. View of pain: Male denies pain—e.g., drops dead at fifty-four. Female affirms pain—e.g., lives in Palm Springs till age ninety.

   B. View of dependency: Male denies dependency—e.g., won't go to doctor. Female affirms dependency—e.g., likes doctors.

   C. View of passivity: Male feels need to be aggressive. Female feels need to be dependent/passive.

   D. View of diet: Male equates food with masculinity—the more food, the more masculine. Female is obsessed with diet.

   E. View of touching: Male gets touched only as prelude to sex. Female desires to be touched often.

   F. View of emotions: Male denies emotions. Female affirms emotions.

Summary: The process (gender conditioning) undermines the content (feelings) of a relationship.

III. What holds traditional relationships together?

   A. Role: Male knows what society expects of his role, and so does female.

   B. Ritual: Life is programmed by events.

   C. Religion: Sanctifies traditional relationship.

IV. Actor/reactor: The roles created by society over the centuries

   A. Actor = Male = Mr. Macho—is aggressive, emotionless, does not have needs, is a sexual performer and initiator and feels like a machine

   B. Reactor = Female = Earthmother—is passive, indirect aggressor, gives up autonomy, is sexually submissive, is emotional, sees self as a child who is controlled and used

   C. Result can be withdrawing, passive men and raging women who destroy one another

5. A Fable

Read the following fable, and rank the characters on the basis of how much you like each person. Your number-one rank will be the person you like best; number five, the person you like the least. This information will be shared.

Once upon a time, four people lived on a river. On one side of the river lived Ann and Jack. On the other side of the river, Ralph and Mike lived. None of the people could cross the river, because they had no boats and there were no bridges or safe places to swim across. The river was infested with crocodiles and piranhas. It was possible to talk across the river, and over a period of time, Ann and Ralph fell in love and spent a great deal of time looking at and talking to one another. They became engaged but had no way of getting together.

Ann and Jack were friends, and Jack was Ann's confidant. On the other side of the river, Mike and Ralph were also friends.

One day a sailor, Sinbad, came down the river on his boat. He was hailed by Ann, who asked him to take her across the river so that she could be with Ralph, her betrothed. Sinbad agreed to do this on one condition—that she let him sleep with her.

Ann was placed in a deep conflict by this offer, and she sought help from Jack, her friend and confidant. Jack spent several hours talking with Ann. He was most sympathetic to her plight but essentially communicated that he had confidence that Ann could make up her own mind about this decision.

Ann decided to take up Sinbad's offer. She spent the night with Sinbad on his boat, and the next day Sinbad deposited her on the opposite shore. Ralph was awaiting her landing, and they embraced at once.

After a while, Ralph asked her how she had managed to convince Sinbad to take her across, and Ann told him the whole story.

Upon hearing the story, Ralph pushed Ann away and said he would have nothing more to do with her.

Just at this time, Mike came by. He had overheard what had happened, and as soon as he saw Ralph pushing Ann away, he moved in and beat up Ralph thoroughly.

6. The New Hire Case

Andrea Turner was a new faculty member at a small private college (150 faculty members). This was her first teaching job after receiving her Ph.D. from one of the most prestigious graduate schools in the country. She worked in the psychology department, which employed twenty-five faculty and three secretaries. Andrea commuted from a city 50 miles away. Therefore, she came to work only on the three days she taught classes and on other days did her other work at hime.

When she was at work, she always kept her office door closed. Most others in the department left theirs open. Occasionally faculty members would go to the student center for coffee breaks in groups of three or four. Andrea was invited but almost never went. After a while, the others stopped asking her to

Rank Order
1. _____
2. _____
3. _____
4. _____
5. _____

join them. She was busy writing her first book for a prestigious publishing house.

Andrea was an effective teacher and participated on several faculty commitees. She was a prolific writer and scholar. Over the course of three years, Andrea performed well above average for a new faculty member.

When it came time for her review for promotion, a great division was apparent among the other faculty members in their attitudes toward Andrea. A few felt that her work was very strong and that she deserved to be promoted. About two-thirds of the professors on the committee felt that she was too much of a loner and did not contribute to the overall needs of the department, only to her own personal success. After much heated discussion, the decision was made not to promote her.

Within three months, Andrea resigned and took a new teaching job at an excellent university. She left without the usual farewell party for departing colleagues. She apparently cleared out her office one night after everyone had left work. Nobody remembered saying good-bye to her.

Postscript: Several other women faculty members had been promoted in this department, and there was a favorable attitude toward affirmative action among the group. So it can be assumed that sex discrimination was not a factor in this case.

Discussion Questions

1. How would you analyze this case in light of Schutz's theory?

2. How would you analyze it from Andrea's viewpoint?

3. From the department's viewpoint?

4. Would you have done anything about this situation if you had been Andrea's department head?

5. Would you have done anything if you had been one of her colleagues in the department?

6. How typical do you think this case is?

7. What implications does this case (and Schutz's theory) have for you?

READINGS: OVERVIEW

William Schutz has been studying the influence of personality needs on interpersonal and small group interaction for over forty years. During this time he has identified the three basic needs described in this chapter of *inclusion*, *control*, and *affection*. In this article he elaborates on the manner in which these needs consistently influence our interaction patterns with others.

The second article examines some practical applications of attitude change theory for the supervisor.

The Interpersonal

William Schutz

Our self-concept is largely derived from our relations with other people. In our dealings we exchange various commodities with these people and must make adjustments. In order to understand this interpersonal level I will use a framework first introduced in my book *FIRO*.

Each person has three basic interpersonal needs that are manifested in behavior and feelings toward other people. But this activity is rooted in a person's feeling about himself, his self-concept. The three basic need areas are posited to be *inclusion, control,* and *affection.*

Inclusion refers to feelings about being important or significant, of having some worth so that people will care. The aspect of the self-concept related to *control* is the feeling of competence, including intelligence, appearance, practicality, and general ability to cope with the world. The area of *affection* revolves around feelings of being lovable, of feeling that if one's personal core is revealed in its entirety it will be seen as a lovely thing.

Inclusion behavior refers to associations between people, being excluded or included, belonging, togetherness. The need to be included manifests itself as wanting to be attended to, and to attract attention and interaction. The college militant is often objecting mostly to the lack of attention paid him, the automated student. Even if he is given negative attention he is partially satisfied.

Being a distinct person—that is, having a particular identity—is an essential aspect of inclusion. An integral part of being recognized and paid attention to is that the individual be distinguishable from other people. The height of being identifiable is to be understood, since it implies that someone is interested enough to discover a person's unique characteristics.

An issue that arises frequently at the outset of group relations is that of commitment, the decision to become involved in a given relationship. Usually, in the initial testing of a relationship, individuals try to present themselves to one another partly to find out what facet of themselves others will be interested in. Frequently a member is silent at first because he is not sure that people are interested in him.

Inclusion is unlike affection in that it does not involve strong emotional attachments to individual persons. It is unlike control in that the preoccupation is with prominence, not dominance. Since inclusion involves the process of formation, it usually occurs first in the life of a group. People must decide whether they do or don't want to form a group.

A person who has too little inclusion, the undersocial, tends to be introverted and withdrawn. He consciously wants to maintain this distance between himself and others, and insists that he doesn't want to get enmeshed with people and lose his privacy. Unconsciously, however, he definitely wants others to pay attention to him. His biggest fears are that people will ignore him and would just as soon leave him behind. His unconscious attitude may be summarized by, "No one is interested in me, so I'm not going to risk being ignored. I'll stay away from people and get along by myself." He has a strong drive toward self-sufficiency as a technique for existence without others. Behind his withdrawal is the private feeling that others don't understand him. His deepest anxiety, that referring to the self-concept, is that he is worthless. He thinks that if no one ever considered him important enough to receive attention, he must be of no value whatsoever.

The oversocial person tends toward extroversion. He seeks people incessantly and wants them to seek him out. He is also afraid that they will ignore him. His unconscious feelings are the same as those of the withdrawn person, but his overt behavior is the opposite. His unconscious attitude is summarized by, "Although no one is interested in me, I'll make people pay attention to me in any way I can." His inclination is always to seek companionship, for he is the type who can't stand to be alone. All of his activities will be designed to be done in a group.

The interpersonal behavior of the oversocial type of person is designed to focus attention on himself, to make people notice him, to be prominent. The direct method is to be an intensive, exhibitive participator. By simply forcing himself on the group, he forces the group to focus attention on him. A more subtle technique is to try to acquire power (control) or to be well-liked (affection), but it is still for the primary purpose of gaining attention.

To the individual for whom inclusion was resolved in childhood, interaction with people presents no problem. He is comfortable with or without people. He can be a high or low participant in a group without anxiety. He is capable of strong commitment to and involvement with certain groups, but can also withhold commitment if he feels it is appropriate. Unconsciously, he feels that he is a worthwhile, significant person.

On the physical level, inclusion has to do with penetration of the boundaries between the self and the rest of the world, and therefore deals primarily with the periphery of the body, the skin and sense organs, the eyes, ears, nose, and mouth. Attitudes toward these organs may be related to attitudes toward being included with people. If contact with people is a fearsome thing, then the eyes keep people from intruding by not seeing others clearly, and then in order to see them clearly, it is permitted to put up a barrier—a barrier called glasses. When eyes are in the active process of seeing, and don't really want to see, they become dull and seem to retire toward the back of the head. Ears which don't want inclusion hear people who are close as if they were far away. Closeness is not accepted and people are kept at a distance. The mouth and lips become tight and impenetrable. The skin shies away from being touched; it is easily tickled, gets rashes and hives easily so that people will not come near. The muscles of the skin may also become tightened so that feeling is minimized, resulting in a leathery touch feeling.

All of these devices need not be used by one individual. There are probably special circumstances that bring about the preeminence of one over the other. The rock opera *Tommy* describes a boy who sees his mother in bed with another man and becomes blind, who hears them talking and becomes deaf, and who is told never to tell anyone what he saw and heard and becomes mute. In a dramatic form this is probably a good example for the reason for specifying which sense organ is the preferred one for avoiding inclusion.

On a recent trip that involved discussing work with a large number of people, my voice started getting hoarse, which I took to mean that I didn't want to talk any more. But then I noticed my hearing becoming erratic. Of course it was psychological; I simply didn't want to listen to all these people anymore. I began to understand how desirable and possible it would be to become deaf, at least in that situation.

If being included is important, the body may reflect it by having these peripheral organs perform in the opposite way. The eyes become vigilant, looking for people in order to see them clearly. They try to see people who are far away as actually being closer. Possible outcomes of this are especially good vision and perhaps vertical lines between the eyebrows reflecting the effort put into seeing clearly. You can try this right now by looking at some object, preferably a person, in two ways. First look at him dully, as if your eyes were open but actually way back in your head and seeing as little as possible while appearing to give attention. Then look at the same object and feel your eyes leap out and grab him, taking in every aspect of him. The difference in the two feelings is usually very marked and gives some sense of how voluntary such a common phenomenon as looking can be.

The person with a high need for inclusion will have acute senses of smell and hearing, bringing far things near. The skin is receptive to touch and probably is open and soft. This is the pure inclusion pattern. Very quickly complications arise. The person open to inclusion can be sensitive to rejection and develop a barrier. Or he may allow touch and then be afraid.

An interesting body difference occurred in a class in Rolfing. One man, who was learning to be a Rolfer, reacted to the assaults of the teacher Ida Rolf—who uses assault as a teaching method—by immediately responding with a defense, a self-justification, a counterattack, a lengthy explanation. I on the other hand responded to her attacks with utter coolness and calm, allowing her to continue unabated, sometimes agreeing with her point, possibly joking away some of her steam, while underneath, quietly knowing that I was right.

When it came to Rolfing each of us, a startling difference appeared in the way we responded at the periphery of our bodies, the skin. When my friend was physically penetrated he would scream and holler, ask for time out, complain, cry, and reassess the competence of the Rolf practitioner. I would feel most of those things, too, but be very stoic and allow the practitioner to penetrate quite far. But then he would be disconcerted by two things. When he took his hand out my skin would spring back to where it was like rubber, apparently unaffected by his push. Also, if he pushed deeply enough into the flesh, he met a barrier that felt like steel. In other words, he and I represented in our bodies almost the identical reactions we made psychologically, his immediate response, my apparent acceptance but deeper resistance.

Another possibility in exploring the physical correlates of inclusion comes from a comment about sexual intercourse, and brings up physical function to add to the structural physical considerations I have been talking about. In the sexual act, various phrases can be distinguished that parallel inclusion, control, and affection. Inclusion problems refer to the initial phases of the act, the feelings about penetration. A male with problems of inclusion will probably have erection problems. His conflict over whether or not to penetrate would be reflected in the nervous enervation of the penis and its willingness or not to be ready to enter. A similar situation arises for a woman where inclusion problems are reflected in the readiness of her vagina to receive the penis, whether she's loose enough and moist enough. Also, the pelvic muscles for both that should be relaxed for maximum pleasure may be tightened if conflict still exists.

Breathing is also primarily an inclusion phenomenon. It's the way of entering or leaving any situuation. If no commitment is desired the breath is cut off along with a tightening of the muscles. This cuts down virtually all vital functions. A full commitment of a person's time and energy involves full breathing, a charged-up body. The Indians and yogis have recognized the importance of breathing control, pranayama, for centuries. It is the key to someone's involvement. Routinely, when I'm giving a lecture or demonstration to a large group, I will begin by doing some activity that requires them to breathe deeply, either screaming, pounding, deep breathing, or anything that gets them pumped up. I find it makes a big difference in the audience's attention and presence.

The same holds for an encounter group. Whenever a member shows a lack of involvement, getting him into some activity requiring deep breathing almost inevitably brings him in. Breathing patterns become ingrained early in life, and a person is usually not aware of his lack of full breathing. Improving the breathing pattern is probably one of the fastest ways to change the feeling of the entire organism. In bioenergetic therapy, the "air or breath is equivalent to the spirit, the pneuma of ancient religions, a symbol of the divine power residing in God, the father figure. Breathing is an aggressive act in that inspiration is an active process. The body sucks in the air. The way one breathes manifests one's feeling about his right to get what he wants from life."

In terms of the body systems, not only are the sense organs and respiration related to inclusion, but so are the digestive and excretory systems, which focus on exchange with the environment and which deal with whether an object will be in or out of the body. These systems express the body's desire to incorporate or reject outside objects. A person with a desire to exclude will reject food and/ or excrete readily and, in the extreme, develop vomiting and diarrhea. One who is anxious to include will go in the other direction, namely, overeating and constipation. A well-resolved relation in the inclusion area should result in good digestion and elimination.

If we consider the interaction between a person and his body, the inclusion problem is one of energy. A body excludes itself in the world by being energyless. The difference between living and not living is the difference between having the flows of energy, nerve impulses, blood circulation, breathing, and so on, and not having them. When a body includes itself, it is filled with energy and feeling.

Hence the problem of inclusion is in or out; the interaction centers on encounter, and the physical aspect is that of energy.

Control behavior refers to the decision-making process between people and areas of power, influence, and authority. The need for control varies along a continuum from the desire for authority over others (and therefore over one's future) to the need to be controlled and have responsibility lifted from oneself.

An argument provides the setting for distinguishing the inclusion-seeker from the control-seeker. The one seeking inclusion or prominence wants very much to be one of the participants in the argument, while the control-seeker wants to be the winner, or, if not the winner, on the same side as the winner. If forced to choose, the prominence-seeker would prefer to be the losing participant, while the dominance-seeker would prefer to be a winning nonparticipant.

Control is also manifested in behavior directed toward people who try to control. Expressions of independence and rebellion exemplify lack of willingness to be controlled, while compliance, submission, and taking orders indicate various degrees of accepting control. There is no necessary relation between an individual's behavior toward controlling others and his behavior toward being controlled. The sergeant may domineer his men, for example, and also accept orders from his lieutenant with pleasure and gratefulness, while the neighborhood bully may dominate his peers and also rebel against his parents.

Control behavior differs from inclusion behavior in that it does not require prominence. The power behind the throne is an excellent example of a role that would fill a high-control need and a low need for inclusion. The joker exemplifies a high-inclusion and low need for control. Control behavior differs from affection behavior in that it has to do with power relations rather than emotional closeness. The frequent difficulties between those who want to get down to business and those who want to get to know one another better illustrate a situation in which control behavior is more important for some and affection behavior for others.

Concern about one's competence, especially in the area of masculinity, leads to overmasculine responses. This is often seen in politics, where concern about one's assertiveness often leads to absurd overreaction to physical threats, especially when a government official has police or soldiers at his disposal.

Control problems usually follow those of inclusion in the development of a group or of an interpersonal relationship. Once the group has formed, it begins to differentiate; different people take or seek different roles, and often power struggles, competition, and influence become central issues. In terms of interaction, these issues are matters of confrontation, to use a term now in vogue.

The extreme person who is too low on control, called an abdicrat, is one who tends toward submission and abdication of power and responsibility in his interpersonal behavior. He gravitates toward a subordinate position where he will not have to take responsibility for making decisions, where someone else takes charge. He consciously wants people to relieve him of his obligations. He does not control others even when he should; for example, he would not take charge even during a fire in a children's schoolhouse in which he was the only adult. He never makes a decision if he can refer it to someone else.

For the individual who has successfully resolved his relations in the control area in childhood, power and control present no problem. He feels comfortable giving or not giving orders, taking or not taking orders, whatever is appropriate to the situation. Unlike the abdicrat and autocrat, he is not preoccupied with fears of his own helplessness, stupidity, and incompetence. He feels that other people respect his competence and will be realistic with respect to trusting him with decision-making.

Speculation on the physical concomitants of control behavior begins with control of the muscles through tightening and through intellectual or nervous system activity. The central nervous system, along with the endocrine system, is generally credited with controlling the anatomy.

Ida Rolf has a fascinating concept of the relation of the core of the body, by which she means the head and spinal column, to the envelope, which includes the two girdles, the pelvic and shoulder girdles with attached appendages, legs and arms. Her idea is that the core represents *being* and the envelope *doing*. Some people develop one and not the other, both, or neither.

For a male, a great deal of control is usually expressed in the formation of the upper arms, shoulders, and neck. Attaining masculinity is frequently related to having hulking, heavily developed shoulders and neck and back muscles. Wrestlers and football linemen typify this formation in the extreme, as the large muscle that goes from the middle of the back up into the neck, the trapezius, is so overdeveloped that it appears that they have no necks.

The feeling of being out of control, and thereby vulnerable, was brought home to me personally when a Rolfer working on my neck freed the trapezius muscle that I had held chronically tight so that my head and neck began to rise up out of my shoulders. As I stood there with my head elevated to a place where it felt both unfamiliar and wonderfully free, I felt frightened. The image that came to mind was of the boy in the circus who sticks his head through the bullseye of a target for people to throw balls at. I felt very exposed, very much in plain sight for everyone to see, with no place to hide. You may capture some of that feeling by standing up straight, putting your chin in and letting your head rise up as if it had a string through the crown, and let your shoulders relax down. When you get as high as you can, look around. When this happened to me I had a clear feeling of why my head had sunk into my shoulders. It was safer, more protected, and less vulnerable.

In general, the pattern of muscle tensions represents the defense pattern of a person. It is the way in which he controls himself so that he can cope with the world. A pattern of no chronic muscle tensions—as opposed to muscle tone— would then represent a nondefensive state, perhaps something like the ego- lessness of the Eastern mystics.

Intellectual control involves voluntary shaping of the body propensities. Control is exercised over the body's desires by moral codes and in line with parental upbringing so that thought is used to govern action.

In the interaction between a person and his body, the control problem is one of centering. A body undercontrolled is disorganized; a body overcontrolled is rigid. A well-controlled body functions with integration among its parts so that they flow easily and appropriately. Inappropriate movement and coordination result when the body is uncertain of what it is doing. Centering means placing everything in its appropriate place so that one is "hooked-up." Being off center makes all movement slightly disconnected.

In the sexual act, control has to do with the occasion and timing of the orgasms and the direction of movement. Withholding an orgasm is an act of personal control that often has a hostile motive, "you can't satisfy me." Sexual control problems would include difficulty of orgasm, premature ejaculation, and the lack of ability to let go.

Thus the problem of control is top or bottom; the primary interaction is confrontation, and the physical aspect is that of centering.

Affection behavior refers to close personal emotional feelings between two people, especially love and hate in their various degrees. Affection is a dyadic relation, that is, it can occur only between pairs of people at any one time, whereas both inclusion and control relations may occur either in dyads or between one person and a group of persons.

Since affection is based on building emotional ties, it is usually the last phase to emerge in the development of a human relation. In the inclusion phase, people must *encounter* each other and decide to continue their relation; control issues require them to *confront* one another and work out how they will be related. To continue the relation, affection ties must form and people must embrace each other to form a lasting bond, and also to say goodbye.

The person with too little affection, the underpersonal type, tends to avoid close ties with others. He maintains his one-to-one relations on a superficial, distant level and is most comfortable when others do the same with him. He consciously wishes to maintain this emotional distance, and frequently expresses a desire not to get emotionally involved, while unconsciously he seeks a satisfactory affectional relation. His fear is that no one loves him, and in a group situation he is afraid he won't be liked. He has great difficulty in genuinely liking people, and distrusts their feelings toward him.

His attitude could be summarized by, "I find the affection area very painful since I have been rejected, therefore I shall avoid close personal relations in the future." The direct technique of the underpersonal is to avoid emotional closeness or involvement, even to the point of being antagonistic. The subtle technique is to be superficially friendly to everyone. This behavior acts as a safeguard against having to get close to, or become personal with, any one person.

In his self-concept, the underpersonal believes that if people knew him well, they would discover traits that make him unlovable. As opposed to the inclusion anxiety that the self is worthless and empty, and the control anxiety that the self is stupid and irresponsible, the affection anxiety is that the self is nasty and unlovable.

The overpersonal type attempts to become extremely close to others. He definitely wants others to treat him in a very close way. The unconscious feeling on which he operates is, "My first experiences with affection were painful, but perhaps if I try again they will turn out to be better." Being liked is extremely important to him in his attempt to relieve his anxiety about being always rejected and unloved. The direct technique for being liked is an overt attempt to gain approval, be extremely personal, ingratiating, intimate, and confiding. The subtle technique is more manipulative and possessive, to devour friends and subtly punish any attempts by them to establish other friendships.

The basic feelings for the overpersonal are the same as those for the underpersonal. Both responses are extreme, both are motivated by a strong need for affection, both are accompanied by a strong anxiety about ever being loved and basically about being unlovable, and both have considerable hostility behind them stemming from the anticipation of rejection.

For the individual who successfully resolved his affectional relations in childhood, close emotional interaction with another person presents no problem. He is comfortable in such a personal relation as well as in a situation requiring emotional distance. It is important for him to be liked, but if not he can accept the fact that the dislike is the result of the relation between himself and one other person; in other words, the dislike does not mean that his is a totally unlovable person. And he is capable of giving genuine affection.

The primary interaction of the affection area is that of embrace, either literal or symbolic. The expression of appropriate deeper feelings is the major issue, particularly in group situations, where a paradox arises. At the beginning of the group there are many expressions as to how difficult it is to express hostility to people. It often later develops that there is only one thing more difficult—expressing warm, positive feelings.

A difference between inclusion, control, and affection behavior is illustrated by the different feelings a man has in being turned down by a fraternity, failed in a course by a professor, and rejected by his girl. The fraternity excludes him, telling him that as a group they don't have sufficient interest in him. The professor fails him and says, in effect, that he finds him incompetent in his field. His girl rejects him, implying that she doesn't find him lovable.

The affectional aspect of the sexual act is the feeling that follows its completion. This can be anything from a flood of warm, affectionate, loving feelings to a revulsion and thoughts of "what am I doing here?" It depends partly on how well the heart and genitals are connected. The circulatory (heart) and reproductive (genital) systems are most directly related to the area of affection.

In the interaction between a person and his body, the affectional problem is one of *acceptance*. The body may be charged up with energy and coordinated through centering, but the problem of body acceptance remains. An accepted body can allow feeling to flow through it without avoiding any part. Sensation is not blocked. An unaccepted body works against itself, trying to become sickly or dissociated. Thus, the ideal body feels energetic, centered, and acceptable.

With respect to an interpersonal relation, inclusion is concerned primarily with the formation of a relation, whereas control and affection are concerned with relations already formed. Within existent relations, control is the area concerned with who gives orders and makes decisions, whereas affection is concerned with how emotionally close or distant the relation becomes.

In summary, the problem of affection is close or far; the interaction is embrace, and the physical aspect is acceptance.

Gaining Commitment: Applying Persuasion Theory to the Workplace

Robin N. Widgery and Stewart L. Tubbs

Persuasion Theory

Do managers and business leaders understand the fundamentals of human behavior well enough to be effective in gaining the commitment of others? Do they know how to communicate with peers and subordinates in ways that foster support for their ideas and instructions? Such commitment marks the difference between work done enthusiastically and work done apathetically, or not at all. One can hardly pick up a book that is written by a successful manager (Iacocca 1984, McCormack 1984, Keller 1989) or in some cases even an academician (Bradford and Cohen 1984, Kilman 1989) without encountering criticism of management education as being severely out of touch with the real world of managing, especially with regard to interpersonal influence.

It should be of major concern to management educators that there is such an abundance of criticism from such highly respected sources. The implied message weaving its way through these criticisms is compelling: To be an effective manager and leader, one must be able to influence positively the attitudes of others—to motivate them toward productive behaviors. A great deal is known about why and how people commit themselves to various activities. Attitude change theory is a rich body of knowledge. If translated to the work environment, it can show managers how to stimulate, inspire, and motivate their peers and employees.

Attitude change theory is but one example of a theoretical body of knowledge that has great promise for application in the real world. For several decades, numerous scholars have found this area of study to be a relevant part of the organizational communication and organizational behavior literature (Rogers and Shoemaker 1971; Goldhaber 1990; Farace, Monge, and Russell 1977; Goldhaber et al. 1979; Sussman and Krivonos 1979; Hunt 1980; Fisher 1981; Hawkins and Preston 1981; Seiler, Bauduin, and Scheulke 1982; Timm and Peterson 1982; Pace 1983; Brown and Weiner 1984; Argyris 1985; Harris 1985; Bryman 1986; Schuster 1986; Humphrey 1987; Jablin et al. 1987; Kilmann 1989; and Gardner 1990).

Perhaps the most popular explanations of attitude change are to be found among the consistency theories. Although different researchers have proposed many variants of these theories (Newcomb 1953; Festinger 1957; Osgood,

Suci, and Tannenbaum 1957; and Heider 1958), the first to record a theory of cognitive consistency was Heider (1946). He developed the now famous Balance Theory. The basic premise of the theory is that people prefer to have psychological or cognitive comfort and avoid situations and information that involve a logical or psychological inconsistency or imbalance. These terms describe a state of psychological stress occurring when beliefs, feelings, values, perceptions, or behaviors seem to conflict. For example, an employee (E) who feels negatively toward the performance of a task (T) but who receives a directive from a respected superior (S) would suffer some psychological pressure to change his attitudes about the task and/or the supervisor. The important elements demonstrating this relationship are presented in Diagram A.

DIAGRAM A

An Unbalanced System

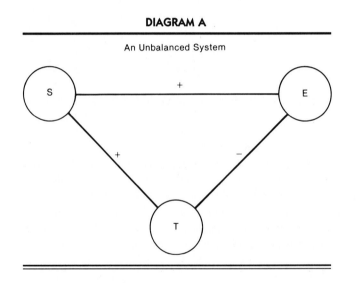

These basic principle of Heider's theory is that if the algebraic product of the signs in the triad (E/S/T) is positive, the attitude system of the E (employee) is balanced. If it is negative, the system is unbalanced. A positive sign can be considered as a positive relationship, or logical association, between the elements within the triad. The positive sign may represent respect, liking, trust, or other positive feelings or relationships by the employee (E). A negative sign can be considered to be a negative relationship, or a disassociation. The negative sign may represent disrespect, dislike, distrust, or other negative feelings or relationships by the employee (E).

The practical implication of this is that when the attitude system is unbalanced, the employee (E) is motivated to change his attitude(s) or perceptions to restore balance. But if the system is balanced, no psychological pressure exists to motivate a change in attitude. In Diagram B below are the eight permutations called cognitive triads. These represent all possible balanced and unbalanced relationships between the E, S, and T.

DIAGRAM B

Imbalanced Conditions (attitude change pressure)

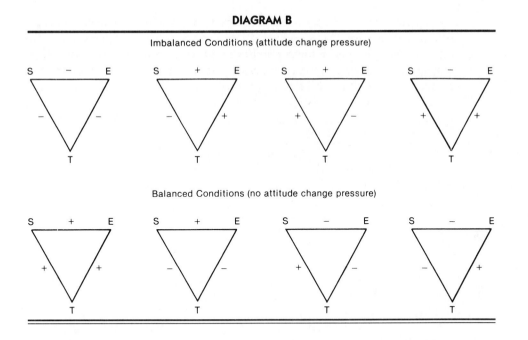

Balanced Conditions (no attitude change pressure)

If there is an unbalanced condition, there is psychological pressure for the person to restore balance. Summarizing considerable research on this issue, Festinger and Aronson (1968) indicate that there are three predictable ways that balance may be restored. First, the employee's (E's) attitude toward the supervisor (S) may change. In fact, this is the most likely part of the system to change. If a supervisor (S) orders us to do something we don't want to do, we may discredit that person rather than change our attitude toward the task (T). The new balanced triad is diagrammed below.

DIAGRAM C

Employee's Attitude Changes Toward the Supervisor

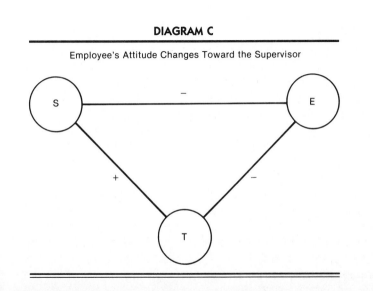

A second possibility is for the employee's perception of the supervisor's attitude toward the task to change ($S + T$ to $S - T$). In this instance, the employee can rationalize the supervisor's attitude toward the task instead of actually changing his own attitude toward the task. This change can also result in a balanced triad like the one below in Diagram D.

DIAGRAM D

Employee's Perception of Supervisor's Attitude Toward the Task Changes

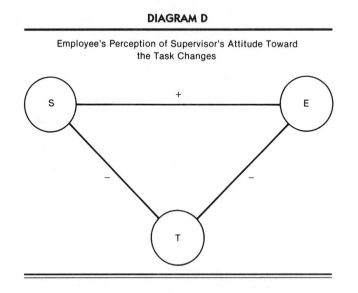

A third way for the E (employee) to restore balance is to change his attitude toward the T (task) itself. This is the outcome preferred by the supervisor. However, as we have seen, it is the least likely to occur, given the other two alternatives. This possibility is diagrammed below.

DIAGRAM E

Employee's Attitude Toward the Task Changes

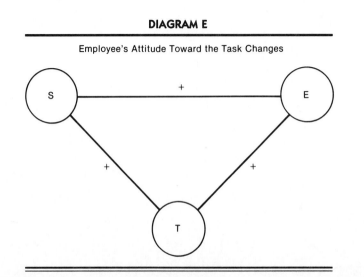

Implications for Supervisors

Supervisors and theorists alike are interested in how attitude change can be made to occur through appropriate management behaviors. In this section we will explore a method for influencing constructive attitude change within the employee. First, if we know that in an unbalanced condition one likely relationship to change is the supervisor/employee (S/E) link, then the first priority is to bolster that link. If the supervisor wants to increase her credibility with the employee, she must generally demonstrate that she holds certain key values that employees associate with effective management behavior.

For example, Hellriegel, Slocum, and Woodman (1983) argue that the overwhelming bulk of leadership research would support the conclusion that most employees value competence, consistency, fairness, concern, clarity of directions, honesty, and sensitivity to feelings of the employee. If the supervisor emphasizes these aspects of her behavior toward her subordinates consistently, she may then draw on her image, much like a bank account, when her influence is needed to gain commitment for unattractive tasks. If her image is strong and positive, it becomes more difficult for the employee (E) to change this part of the triad (E + S to E − S) in order to restore balance in the system. This is illustrated in Diagram F by adding a secondary triad to the primary triad in Heider's model. If the E's attitude toward the S changes from (+) to (−),

DIAGRAM F

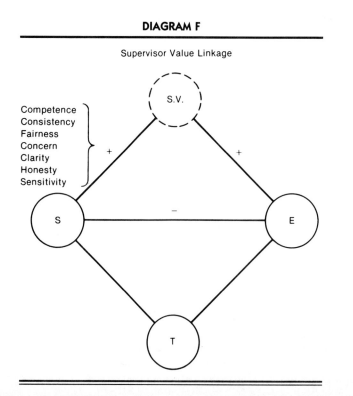

Supervisor Value Linkage

it will create a new imbalance in the supervisor values linkage. This places pressure on the E to maintain a positive attitude toward the S.

As stated above, a second possible change used to restore balance to the attitude system is for the employee to change (reshape) his perception of the supervisor's attitude toward the task (S + T to S − T). This may occur through rationalization, which allows the employee's system to restore balance without the employee having to actually change his attitude toward the task itself. The supervisor can try to keep such rationalization from occurring by demonstrating sincerity, commitment, enthusiasm, excitement, and unambiguous support for the task (O'Donnel and Kable 1982, Smith 1982). When the supervisor demonstrates these behaviors as related to the specific task, it will be harder for the employee to rationalize that the supervisor doesn't really believe in what she is saying about the task. In other words, if the S/T relationship is seen by the E to be negative, he would be replacing one imbalance with a new imbalance in the commitment values linkage. This would place psychological pressure on the E to continue to perceive the S/T relationship as positive. (See Diagram G.)

DIAGRAM G

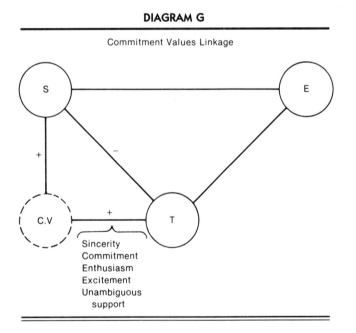

Commitment Values Linkage

The third alternative for restoring balance to the attitude system is for the employee to actually change his attitude toward the task (E − T to E + T). In order for this to happen, he has to see which of his own needs will be met by doing the task (T) with a high degree of commitment.

All of us want to have our actions result in positive outcomes. Extending Maslow and Herzberg's theories, Dubrin (1982) lists twenty two specific outcomes that most employees would consider as meeting their needs. They are:

Feedback on desired behavior

Praise encouragement, and related rewards

Approval

Recognition

Comradeship

Job Security

Money

Favorable performance appraisal

Privy to confidential information

Challenging work assignments

Freedom to choose one's own work activity

Opportunity to see oneself become more important, mose useful

Seeing results of one's work

Chance to use one's mind

Power to influence co-workers and management

Promotion

Improved working conditions

Capable and congenial co-workers

Business luncheaon

Time off from work

Attendance at trade show or convention

Status symbols

The manager is more likely to be successful in creating productive attitude change if she can show the positive relationships between one or more employee needs to the task. Once the E perceives a positive relationship between need gratification and the unattractive task (T), the pressure is on the E/T linkage to change to positive. To resist change leaves the E with an unbalanced needs values linkage. (See Diagram H on page 92.) If we put together the basic (E/S/T) triad and the three secondary triads, we can see how the entire system looks. (See Diagram I on page 92.)

DIAGRAM H

Needs Values Linkage

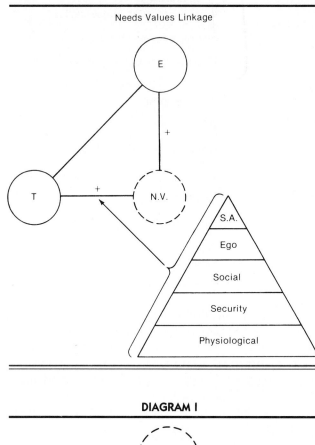

DIAGRAM I

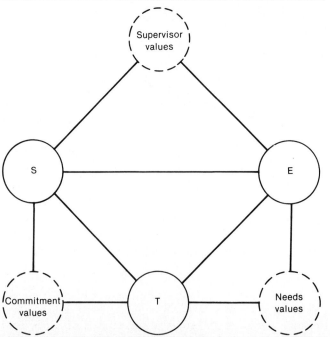

Finally, if we put in the appropriate signs, we can see how the system looks with all parts balanced. The balanced source values linkage supports the positive E/S linkage. The balanced commitment values linkage supports the positive S/T linkage. And, a balanced need values linkage places psychological pressure on the E/T linkage to change from negative to positive. (See Diagram J.)

DIAGRAM J

A Balanced System

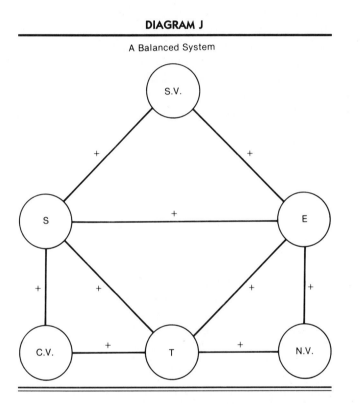

As you can see from this example, balance theory offers a useful model for creating commitment by using the employee's own need for psychological consistency as a directive force for attitude change. In order to assure the desired change, however, other more readily changeable alternatives must be reinforced so that the employee changes the desired attitude toward the task. From this model come three important guidelines for managers who would create commitment for unattractive tasks:

1. Communicate with peers and subordinates from a position of credibility. Without perceived integrity, competence, and sensitivity to the feelings of fellow workers, it is difficult to inspire or gain the commitment of others.

2. Show your own commitment and enthusiasm toward the tasks of the workplace, even those that are unattractive. It's not easy to rationalize that "even the supervisor isn't excited with the task," if the supervisor demonstrates unambiguous commitment to the importance of the task.

3. Make the employee aware that even the unattractive task is important in satisfying his various needs. When the task is seen to be the avenue through which needs may be attained, the employee will be more likely to invest those energies in the task that leads to higher levels of productivity and mutual reward for him and the organization.

The authors' four decades of experience, both as university professors and as management consultants to *Fortune 500* companies, has demonstrated to us that the approach discussed can result in improved employee motivation and commitment. We have learned the value of going beyond the discussion of theoretical models to make behavioral science practical to those who must apply it to the challenges of the work environment. Managers and business leaders always prefer the practical to the theoretical. Commenting on the role of theory, Kurt Lewin said, "Nothing is more practical than a good theory."

References

Argyris, Chris, 1985. *Strategy, change and defensive routines.* Marshfield, Mass.: Pittman.

Bormann, Ernest G., William S. Howell, Ralph Nichols, and George L. Shapiro, 1969. *Interpersonal communication in the modern organization.* Englewood Cliffs, N.J.: Prentice-Hall.

Bradford, David L., and Allan R. Cohen, 1984. *Managing for excellence: the guide to developing high performance in contemporary organizations.* New York: John Wiley.

Brown, Arnold, and Edith Weiner, 1984. *Supermanaging: how to harness change for personal and organizational success.* New York: McGraw-Hill.

Bryman, Alan, 1986. *Leadership and organizations.* London: Routledge & Kegan Paul.

Dubrin, Andrew J., 1982. *Contemporary applied management.* Plano, Tex.: Business Publication, Inc.

Farace, R. Vince, Peter R. Monge, and H. M. Russell, 1977. *Communicating and organizing.* Reading, Mass.: Addison-Wesley.

Festinger, Leon, 1957. *A theory of cognitive dissonance.* Evanston, Ill.: Row, Peterson.

Festinger, Leon, and Elliot Aronson, 1968. Arousal and reduction of dissonance in social contexts. In Dorwin Cartwright and Alvin Zander (eds.). *Group dynamics: research and theory* (3rd ed.). New York: Harper & Row, pp. 125–136.

Fisher, Dalmar, 1981. *Communication in organizations.* St. Paul: West.

Gardner, John, 1990. *Leadership.* New York: Free Press.

Geneen, Harold, 1984. *Managing.* New York: Doubleday.

Goldhaber, Gerald M., 1990. *Organizational communication* (5th ed.). Dubuque, Iowa: Wm. C. Brown.

Goldhaber, Gerald M., Harry S. Dennis, Gary M. Richetto, and Osmo Wiio, 1979. *Information strategies: new pathways to corporate power.* Englewood Cliffs, N.J.: Prentice-Hall.

Harris, Phillip R., 1985. *Management in transition.* San Francisco: Jossey-Bass.

Hawkins, Brian L., and Paul Preston, 1981. *Managerial communication.* Santa Monica: Goodyear.

Heider, Fritz. "Attitudes and Cognitive Organization," *Journal of Psychology,* 1946, 21, 107–112.

Heider, Fritz, 1958. *The psychology of interpersonal relations.* New York: John Wiley.

Hellriegel, Don, John W. Slocum, and Richard W. Woodman, 1983. *Organizational behavior* (3rd ed.). St. Paul: West, Ch. 13.

Humphrey, Watts, 1987. *Managing for innovation.* Englewood Cliffs, N.J.: Prentice-Hall.

Hunt, Gary T., 1980. *Communication skills in the organization.* Englewood Cliffs, N.J.: Prentice-Hall.

Huseman, Richard C., Cal M. Logue, and Dwight L. Freshley, 1969. *Readings in interpersonal and organizational communication.* Boston: Holbrook Press.

Iacocca, Lee, 1984. *Iacocca.* New York: Bantam Books.

Jablin, Frederick, et al., 1987. *Handbook of organizational communication.* Newbury Park, Calif.: Sage.

Keller, Maryann, 1989. *Rude awakening.* New York: William Morrow.

Kilman, Ralph H., 1989. *Managing beyond the quick fix.* San Francisco: Jossey-Bass.

McCormack, Mark, 1984. *What they don't teach you at the harvard business school.* New York: Bantam Books.

Newcomb, Theodore, 1953. An approach to the study of communicative acts. *Psychological Review* **60**: 393–404.

O'Donnel, Victoria, and June Kable, 1982. *Persuasion: an interactive-dependency approach.* New York: Random House, Ch. 6.

Osgood, Charles, George J. Suci, and Percy H. Tannenbaum, 1957. *The measurement of meaning.* Urbana: University of Illinois Press.

Pace, R. Wayne, 1983. *Organizational communication: foundations for human resource development.* Englewood Cliffs, N.J.: Prentice-Hall.

Rogers, Everett M., and F. Floyd Shoemaker, 1971. *Communication of innovations.* New York: Free Press.

Ruch, Richard, and Ronald Goodman, 1983. *Image at the top.* New York: Free Press.

Schuster, Frederick E., 1986. *The Schuster report: the proven connection between people and profits.* New York: John Wiley.

Seiler, William J., E. Scott Bauduin, and L. David Scheulke, 1982. *Communication in business and professional organizations.* Reading, Mass.: Addison-Wesley.

Smith, Mary John, 1982. *Persuasion and human action: a review and critique of social influence theories.* Belmont, Calif.: Wadsworth, Ch. 9.

Sussman, Lyle, and Paul D. Krivonos, 1979. *Communications for supervisors and managers.* Sherman Oaks, Calif.: Alfred.

Timm, Paul R., and Brent D. Peterson, 1982. *People at work.* St. Paul: West.

Zelko, Harold, and Frank E. X. Dance, 1965. *Business and professional speech communication.* New York: Holt, Rinehart, and Winston.

Group Circumstances and Structure

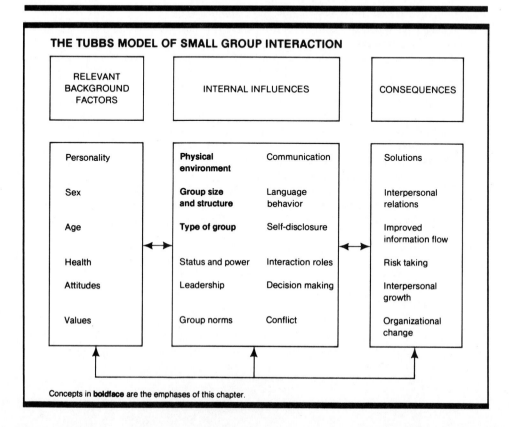

THE TUBBS MODEL OF SMALL GROUP INTERACTION

RELEVANT BACKGROUND FACTORS	INTERNAL INFLUENCES		CONSEQUENCES
Personality	**Physical environment**	Communication	Solutions
Sex	**Group size and structure**	Language behavior	Interpersonal relations
Age	**Type of group**	Self-disclosure	Improved information flow
Health	Status and power	Interaction roles	Risk taking
Attitudes	Leadership	Decision making	Interpersonal growth
Values	Group norms	Conflict	Organizational change

Concepts in **boldface** are the emphases of this chapter.

In Chapter 1, the internal influences of the Tubbs Model of Small Group Interaction were introduced briefly. Chapter 3 includes a more in-depth treatment of physical environment, group structure, and group type. Physical environment is the setting in which small group interaction takes place. Two topics that fit under physical environment are territoriality and seating patterns. Group size and structure are often connected to the notion that people in a group are related in a number of ways. One relationship is characterized by communication networks. The third internal influence is the type of group. It is obvious that groups will interact differently depending on what types of groups they are. Some examples included in Chapter 3 are primary groups, casual and social groups, work groups, and educational groups.

GLOSSARY

Territoriality: The word "territoriality" was coined by Edward Hall and defined as "the tendency for humans and other animals to lay claim to and defend a particular area or territory."

Seating Patterns: Seating patterns often affect the type and volume of interaction of a group.

Communication Networks: Communication networks are the five different networks that demonstrate the different forms of communicating to one another.

Primary Groups: Primary groups are groups that usually include one's family and closest friends.

Casual and Social Groups: Casual and social groups include neighborhood groups, fraternities, and even classmates. The impact on behavior of these relationships is often quite profound.

Educational Groups: Educational groups are groups that interact for the sole purpose of study or instruction.

Work Groups: Work groups are the formation of people on the job.

Problem-Solving Groups: Problem-solving groups are groups that form in order to solve one or more problems.

CASE STUDY: The Emergency Room

John Jones arrived at the emergency room (ER) via stretcher and paramedics at 10:00 P.M. While in transport, the paramedics radioed the ER that a 60-year-old white male had called 911 because of chest pain. The patient was very short of breath; chest pain was radiating to his neck and left arm; he was perspiring; and he was experiencing palpitations. Mr. Jones was becoming more anxious and indicated that the pain and pressure were worse and that he could hardly catch his breath. Suddenly, he was no longer breathing, and his heart stopped.

The cardiac resuscitation team went into action. Members included a physician, two nurses, a pharmacist, a radiologic technologist, a respiratory therapist, a medical technologist, and an orderly. Dr. Wells immediately placed a tube into Mr. Jones's trachea to enable the respiratory therapist to provide artificial respiration. Nurse Hanna listened to the chest and reported that the lungs were not being ventilated equally. She said, "I think the tube will have to be moved." "Bullshit," snapped Dr. Wells.

Then the respiratory therapist reported that the blood gas analysis supported Nurse Hanna's evaluation of the lungs. Dr. Wells replied, "Well then bag the hell out of him" (i.e., ventilate him vigorously). He then told an orderly to begin performing external chest compression.

Once the ABC's of cardiopulmonary resuscitation (CPR) had been established (airway, breathing, and circulation), Dr. Wells proceeded with further evaluation and pharmacologic treatment of the patient. These measures were necessary to reestablish and maintain the heartbeat. Dr. Wells asked the pharmacist for an antiarrythmic drug. The pharmacist disagreed and recommended a different choice. "Goddam it, just prepare what I tell you" Dr. Wells exploded.

Once the drugs had begun to take effect, further evaluation of the patient was necessary. Dr. Wells monitored the heart's response to therapy with the electrocardiogram and requested the medical technologist to draw blood samples to assess the patient's electrolyte balance. Additionally, the respiratory therapist drew a blood sample to evaluate the effectiveness of artificial respiration and the patient's acid-base status. Last, Dr. Wells asked the radiologic technologist to obtain a chest X ray to ascertain proper placement of the breathing tube and to further assess the heart and lungs. The technologist reported that the X ray showed that the tube was in the right lung and the left lung was collapsed. Dr. Wells said, "I guess I'll have to move the damn tube."

The electrocardiogram began to show irregular heartbeats, which soon went into fibrillation. Dr. Wells called for the shock paddles, which restored the heartbeat. After the breathing tube was moved, subsequent laboratory tests and the chest X ray were reported to be within normal limits. Mr. Jones's heart was stabilized, no longer requiring external chest compression. But the electrocardiogram showed evidence of recent damage to the heart muscle. Mr. Jones was transferred to the Coronary Care Unit (CCU) for further monitoring, evaluation, and therapy.

Prior to transfer, Nurse Knight had telephoned a report (background information about Mr. Jones's admission and treatment in the ER) to the nurse in charge of the CCU. Dr. Wells also had telephoned Mr. Jones's family physician to notify him about Mr. Jones's condition and hospital admission.

Mr. Jones's doctor consulted with Dr. Hayes, a cardiologist who recommended cardiac catheterization to evaluate the degree of heart damage suffered as a result of the heart attack. In the specialized cardiac catheterization laboratory, Dr. Hayes surgically inserted and manipulated specialized tubes to facilitate injection of dye into the heart's arteries. The procedure was accomplished with the assistance of nurses who monitored Mr. Jones's vital signs and radiologic technologists who operated specialized radiographic equipment. The end result was a moving fluoroscopic picture of the heart demonstrating cardiac blood distribution through the coronary arteries and effectiveness of the heart's pumping action.

The cardiac catheterization showed almost complete obstruction of three coronary arteries. Mr. Jones was then referred to Dr. Barnes for surgical evaluation for possible coronary artery bypass surgery.

1. What examples of teamwork are illustrated in this case?

2. How would you improve this team's functioning?

By James S. Sheahan, staff perfusionist for Cardiovascular Perfusionists, Inc., in Ft. Myers, Florida, and Cynthia L. Sheahan, R.N., staff nurse for the Eye Center of Florida in Ft. Myers.

The case study beautifully illustrates a work group. In this chapter we will be looking at several very different types of groups, ranging from the family, or primary group, to street gangs, encounter groups, and problem-solving groups. Although each type of group differs from the others, some common conceptual links connect all types of groups. The first factor that is relevant to all groups is the so-called ecology of the group.

The dispute over the size and shape of the negotiating table at the Paris peace talks in 1968 represents one of the most significant examples in our nation's history of ecology in group discussion. The disagreement lasted eight months and was typical of the many political implications of each issue under negotiation. McCroskey, Larson, and Knapp (1971, p. 97) explain the reasons for the dispute:

> The United States (US) and South Viet Nam (SVN) wanted a seating arrangement in which only two sides were identified. They did not want to recognize the National Liberation Front (NLF) as an "equal" party in the negotiations. North Viet Nam (NVN) and the NLF wanted "equal" status given to all parties—represented by a four-sided table. The final arrangement was such that both parties could claim victory. The round table minus the dividing lines allowed North Viet Nam and the NLF to claim all four delegations were equal. The existence of the two secretarial tables (interpreted as dividers), the lack of identifying symbols on the table, and an AA, BB speaking rotation permitted the United States and South Viet Nam to claim victory for the two-sided approach. Considering the lives lost during the eight months needed to arrive at the seating arrangement, we can certainly conclude that territorial space has extremely high priority in some interpersonal settings.

In this chapter we will look more closely at small group ecology as well as other internal influences in small group interaction.

Chapter 1 defined *internal influences* on a group as factors that are influenced by the individual characteristics of group members and that in turn influence a group's functioning and its ultimate end results. Internal influences are somewhat under the control of group members (that is, members are able to change them). In this chapter we will examine three major types of internal influence: (1) physical environment, (2) group structure, and (3) type of group.

PHYSICAL ENVIRONMENT

For many years writers have hypothesized that a room's environment influences the interaction within it. Supposedly, "warm" colors—hues of orange, red, and brown—facilitate interaction, whereas "cool" hues of blue and green tend to encourage reserved, formal conversation. A series of studies conducted to test these assumptions (Maslow and Mintz 1956, Wong and Brown 1923, Bilodeau and Schlosberg 1959) found that people consistently associated an ugly room with monotony, fatigue, irritability, headache, discontent, and hostility. A beautiful room evoked such reactions as pleasure, enjoyment, importance, comfort, and a desire to remain in the room. The ugly room was stark, gray, and disheveled, whereas the beautiful room had carpeting, drapes, and warm beige walls. These studies also showed that mental functioning was better in beautiful rooms. Both memory and ability to solve problems were found to be better in the beautiful room. Along this same line, Barnlund (1968, p. 514) writes: "A colleague after attending a meeting in a conference room created by [Frank Lloyd] Wright was similarly impressed, confessing that he believed interpersonal antagonism could not be provoked in such a setting." Although it is doubtful that we could ever design a room that would eliminate all antagonism, it seems plausible that rooms can be designed that at least do not act as a source of irritation. It is also interesting to speculate that inadequate ventilation, heating, lighting, and roominess might serve to detract from the overall effectiveness of groups. Zalesny and Farace (1987) found that work settings have symbolic value that influences employees' perceptions of their environment and their work. An environment that is conducive to more communication, such as the less traditional "open office," is often more conducive to success on group tasks.

Territoriality

Edward Hall (1959) coined the term "territoriality" to describe the tendency for humans and other animals to lay claim to and defend a particular area or territory. We are all familiar with this behavior among dogs, birds, and gorillas, but we may be less aware of our own attempts to defend our territories. It has been estimated that college students begin to identify a particular seat in the class as "their chair" by as early as the second class period. Although we probably would not ask a person to give up the chair, we would feel some annoyance at having to move to another one. This is reminiscent of the home court advantage in basketball: Teams traditionally play better on the home court than they do at "away" games.

In addition to identifying certain places as our territory, we also move about in a portable space bubble of about 18 inches in each direction that we let only certain people violate. This is referred to as our *personal space*. Sommer (1959, p. 248) distinguishes personal space from territory in the following way:

> The most important difference is that personal space is carried around while territory is relatively stationary. The animal or man will usually mark the boundaries of his territory so that they are visible to others, but the boundaries of his personal space are invisible. Personal space has the body at its center, while territory does not.

Kinzel (1969) conducted a study of inmates at the United States Medical Center for Federal Prisoners. He found that men who had committed violent crimes had a personal space, or "body buffer zone," twice as large as that of prisoners classified as nonviolent. The violent group stated that they felt threatened when a person came close to them, as if the person were an intruder who was "looming up" or "rushing in" at them.

Hall (1959) describes the humorous situation in which people with different-sized space bubbles try to communicate. Arabs or South Americans will try to step closer, reducing the distance between them and their listeners. North American or German listeners will then step backward to reestablish what they feel is a comfortable distance for conversation. And so it continues as one individual ends up backing the other all the way around the room. Rosenfeld (1965) found that personality factors influenced the size of one's personal space. Those high in need for affiliation (see Chapter 2) sat an average of 57 inches away from a target person, whereas those low in affiliation averaged 94 inches in distance.

personal space: culture influence personality factors

Hall (1959) refers to the study of personal space and distance as *proxemics*. He has identified four zones that seem to influence interaction in North American culture. He points out, however, that these distances do not apply to other cultures that have different zones. The four types of distances are intimate, personal, social, and public.

Intimate distance extends from touching to about 18 inches. This distance encourages soft whispers about very confidential matters. It also allows us to use more of our senses in communicating (for example, touching, smelling, and even tasting). *Personal distance* ranges from 18 inches to about 4 feet. Conversation is usually soft, and topics are usually personal. *Social distance* refers to the distance between 4 and 12 feet. At this distance voices are usually raised, and the topics are nonpersonal public information for anyone to hear. *Public distance* refers to 12 feet and beyond. This requires a loud voice and impersonal topics. As we shall see later in this chapter, different groups may at one time or another involve the use of all of these four distances. Encounter groups frequently include physical touching, whereas large committees may be seated around tables more than 25 feet in diameter. Figure 3.1 gives more examples of various distances and kinds of communication.

Seating Patterns

Have you ever noticed the difference in interaction between a group sitting on the grass or the floor and one whose members are seated indoors around a rectangular table? One difference is that sitting on the floor or grass allows greater informality and tends to facilitate interaction. However, research has shown that even the seating patterns around rectangular tables have a major impact on interaction. Strodbeck and Hook (1961) found that those seated at the head of the table were chosen significantly more often as the leader. Hare and Bales (1963) found that those seated in positions marked A, C, and E in Figure 3.2 were frequent talkers and frequently scored high on dominance in personality tests.

Sommer (1969) also studied several possible seating patterns (see Figure 3.3). The corner-to-corner or face-to-face arrangements were most often preferred for casual conversation, whereas cooperating pairs (studying together) preferred the

FIGURE 3.1

Adapted from Hall 1959, p. 163–164. Chart from *The Silent Language* by Edward T. Hall. Copyright © 1959 by Edward T. Hall. Reprinted with permission of Doubleday & Company, Inc.

Distance	Content	Vocal Shifts
3–6 inches	Top secret	Soft whisper
8–12 inches	Very confidential topics	Audible whisper
12–20 inches	Confidential topics	Soft voice
20–36 inches	Personal topics	Soft voice
4½–5 feet	Nonpersonal topics	Full voice
5½–8 feet	Public information	Loud voice
8–20 feet	Public information to a group	Very loud voice
20–100 feet	Hailing and departing comments	Very loud voice

FIGURE 3.2   SEATING PATTERN

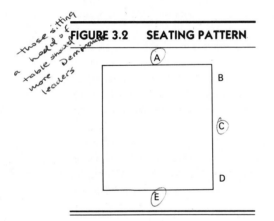

those sitting at the head of a table should be more Democratic leaders

side-by-side arrangement. Competing pairs chose the face-to-face or the distant-opposite arrangements about equally often. Russo (1967) found that people seated in the more distant positions (when all positions around the rectangular table were occupied) were perceived to be less friendly, less well acquainted, and less talkative than those seated closer to the person filling out the questionnaire.

Hearn (1957) verified a phenomenon known as the "Steinzor effect" (Steinzor 1950), in which members of groups with minimal leadership directed many more comments to those facing opposite them than to those sitting on either side. However, with a dominant, assertive leader, the behaviors were reversed, and significantly more conversation was directed to those sitting next to them.

Sommer (1965) also studied the seating preferences at round tables (Figure 3.4). He found that conversing or cooperating pairs preferred to sit side by side, whereas

FIGURE 3.3   SEATING PATTERNS AT
RECTANGULAR TABLES:
(A) CORNER-TO-CORNER,   – casual
(B) FACE-TO-FACE,   – casual – competing pairs
(C) DISTANT-OPPOSITE,
(D) CORNER-TO-END,
(E) SIDE-BY-SIDE, AND
(F) END-TO-END   more often chosen as leaders

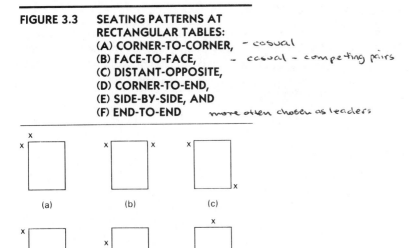

competing pairs preferred to sit at distant-opposite points. These findings have been corroborated by Batchelor and Goethals (1972), who found much the same result with groups who had no tables at all but simply were allowed to move their chairs to positions they preferred.

All this research taken collectively indicates that groups with differing personalities and tasks will exhibit predictable seating patterns. Also, dominant seating positions at the ends of rectangular tables will tend to give some members a leadership advantage and will result in some frustration and disenchantment for those in the "blind spots" on the sides of the tables.

FIGURE 3.4   SEATING PREFERENCES AT
ROUND TABLES: (A) SIDE-
BY-SIDE,
(B) DISTANT-OPPOSITE, AND
(C) SIDE-TO-END

GROUP SIZE AND STRUCTURE

The concept of group structure refers to the idea that groups are made up of people who are related to one another in a number of ways. Although group structure may include a number of interrelated topics, we will be concerned with only two: (1) communication networks and (2) group size.

Communication Networks

The research on communication networks commonly employs five different networks, which are illustrated in Figure 3.5. Leavitt (1951) found that the central person in a network such as the wheel usually becomes the leader and enjoys the position more than those on the periphery, whose communication is much more restricted. That is, the central person can communicate to any of them, but they must direct *all* of their comments through the center. Both the chain and the Y networks have characteristics similar to the wheel. On the other hand, the circle and the all-channel patterns are much less centralized and are sometimes leaderless.

A person who dominates the discussion will sometimes create a network similar to the wheel. Although this may be more centralized and efficient, it results in dependence on the leader and lower group satisfaction for everyone but the leader. The chain or the Y network allow members to communicate with one or two other persons but not with all others in the group. This produces subgroups, decreased satisfaction, and a relatively poor amount of idea sharing.

The all-channel network may be relatively slow, but it is superior in terms of idea sharing and member satisfaction. Feedback is more immediate, and, as a result, accuracy of communication is better. Shaw (1964) summarized the findings of eighteen group network studies by concluding that *centralized networks,* such as the chain and the wheel, are better for solving simple problems such as identifying colors or picturelike symbols. However, when the problem is complex (as most real-life problems are), the *decentralized networks,* such as the circle and the all-channel, are faster and more accurate and result in higher member satisfaction. It seems clear that the all-channel network is the most desirable for most problem-solving situations a group would be likely to encounter. An example of a centralized network would be a boss who requires all information to pass through him or her.

Group Size

Perhaps one of the questions most frequently asked by students of small group interaction is this: What is the best size of group to work with? On one hand, it seems that a relatively small group would be more efficient; on the other hand, larger groups would have more resources. A great deal of research has been conducted on this question, and some fairly clear results emerge.

less than 5 not enough resources

Groups of only two people may find themselves deadlocked in statements on many questions. They also suffer the disadvantage of having too few members to contribute ideas. Groups of three are still too small and tend to result in two-against-one coalitions that leave one person out. Groups of four begin to be effective, but because of their even number of members may end up with tie votes on decisions.

FIGURE 3.5   COMMUNICATION NETWORKS: (A) WHEEL, (B) CHAIN, (C) Y, (D) CIRCLE, AND (E) ALL-CHANNEL
By permission of News America Syndicate.

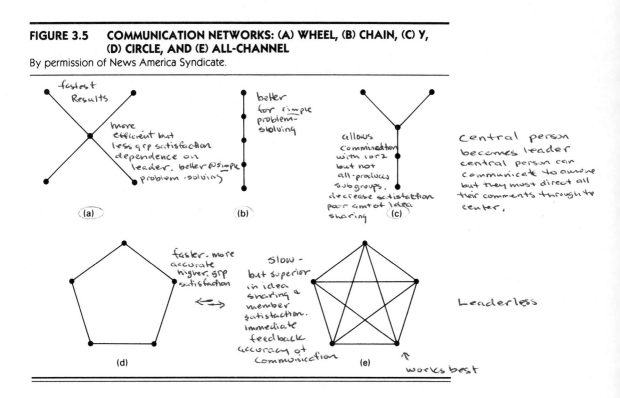

(a) fastest Results / more efficient but less grp satisfaction dependence on leader, better @simple problem-solving

(b) better for simple problem-solving

(c) allows communication with 1 or 2 but not all-produces subgroups. decrease satisfaction poor amt of idea sharing / central person becomes leader central person can communicate to anyone but they must direct all their comments through the center.

(d) faster. more accurate higher grp satisfaction ⟷ slow - but superior in idea sharing a member satisfaction. immediate feedback accuracy of communication

(e) Leaderless / works best

Bales (1954) found that the optimum group size appeared to be five. This size seems to be small enough for meaningful interaction yet large enough to generate an adequate number of ideas.

As groups grow larger than five, members complain that the group is too large and that they are not able to participate as often as they would like. Also, as size gets larger, there is an increasing tendency for subgroups to form, which may carry on side conversations that annoy the rest of the group and detract from group progress. Groups of ten or more tend to spend an inordinate amount of time simply organizing themselves, so that more attention is diverted away from the task and toward simply maintaining the group's functioning.

more than 5 too large - unable to participate

The influence of the number of members within a group is mixed with other variables such as the function of the group and its membership composition. Luft (1984) concludes that "Cohesion tends to be weaker and morale tends to be lower in larger groups than in comparable smaller ones. How often groups meet varies inversely with size and duration and directly with closeness of feelings" (p. 23).

As the group's size increases arithmetically (linearly), the potential number of interactions increases geometrically (exponentially). Bostrom (1970, p. 257) shows how rapidly these interaction patterns multiply. In a dyad (two people) only two relationships are possible, A to B and B to A, but in a triad (three people) there are nine possibilities:

A to B	B to C	A to B and C
A to C	C to B	B to A and C
B to A	C to A	C to A and B

The calculations from group sizes two to eight are (Bostrom 1970, p. 258):

Number in Group	Interactions Possible
2	2
3	9
4	28
5	75
6	186
7	441
8	1056

Bostrom (p. 263) concludes from his study: "The data here seem to indicate that the individual who sends more than he receives is not only more often chosen as a good discussant but is also more satisfied with the discussion than the member who receives more than he sends . . . satisfaction apparently comes from talking, not listening."

Markham, Dansereau, and Alutto (1982) have suggested that there can be a positive relationship between size and absenteeism when within-group overtime is applied. This could be explained by a number of possibilities. Perhaps greater strain is placed on the supervisor of that unit as the quality of supervision declines. Or members' perceptions of the new situation might help them rationalize a few extra days' absence when more labor is available to the work group.

"Social loafing" refers to the decreased effort of each individual member as the number of people in a group increases (Latané, Williams, and Harkins 1979). Recent studies (Harkins 1987, Harkins and Syzmanski 1989) suggest that social loafing occurs because participants perceive that their individual efforts cannot be evaluated. This concept can be useful in that it alerts managers to a probable negative influence on group productivity and provides a rationale for analyzing the effect of group size on group productivity and the design of organizational units. The studies made to date provide no clear conclusions. However, these guidelines are suggested (Albanese and Van Fleet 1985, p. 253):

1. To the extent that group members act rationally in their decision to contribute to a group's public good, a free-riding tendency will operate in groups.

2. As group size increases, the average contribution of group members to the group's public good may decrease, even though the total public good provided by the group may increase.

3. The basic strategy for countering the free-riding tendency is to build various private goods that are contingent on the provision of the group's public good into the group member's incentive system.

Actually, management is most concerned with point 3. Through effective use of power, design of organizations (size of organizational units included), as well as control of rewards and punishment, management influences the incentive system of group members. As a result of these findings, it would seem desirable to keep the group size to about five *whenever possible,* unless some other objective, such as increased widespread participation, seems to be worth increasing group size. Even when increasing participation (for example, including all members of a fraternity or sorority) is the goal, subcommittees of about five would allow the widespread participation *as well as* the efficiency and satisfaction of working in a small group. This optimal size, however, depends on the type of group. Five is the recommended size for a problem-solving group. Obviously, a work group, family group, or even some problem-solving groups may require a different number of members, depending on the particular situation.

TYPE OF GROUP

One of the confounding problems in the study of small groups is the variety in types of groups that have been studied. It is obvious that certain critical differences will emerge when the term "group" is applied to studies of primitive tribes, street gangs, factory work groups, and artificially formed laboratory groups. Although there may be some important similarities among these groups, we would also expect to find some real confusion resulting from attempts to compare different groups across the board. In addition, it seems likely that differing group types will have an effect on subsequent interaction and group outcomes or end results. For example, social groups will interact differently from work groups, and the outcomes of their separate group interactions will be different. In this section we will look at six commonly recognized types of groups.

Primary Groups

Primary groups usually include one's family and closest friends. Certainly the vast majority of attitudes and values people hold are a result of the influences of their primary groups. Primary groups influence self-concept as well as personality from childhood to adulthood. The members of our primary groups are sometimes referred to as our "significant others," because they are probably the most important people in our lives. Although we may sometimes develop deep friendships from other associations on the job, in school, and so forth, family members usually remain our most significant others throughout our lives.

Obviously, the nuclear family has undergone drastic changes in modern times. For example, the divorce rate has doubled (now at 50 percent) since 1965. Sixty percent of second marriages also fail. One-third of all the children born in the 1980s will live in a stepfamily, and one-fourth of all the children in America are being raised by a single parent. Over one-fifth of the children born today are born to unwed mothers.

"An astonishing two-thirds of all mothers are in the labor force, roughly double the rate in 1955, and more than half of all mothers of infants are in the work force" (Footlick 1990, p. 16).

These statistics are even more alarming when combined with some other research findings. Roark (1989) cites research from the *Journal of Pediatrics* stating that "latchkey" children are twice as likely to use cigarettes, alcohol, and marijuana as youngsters who are cared for by adults after school (p. A9).

Perhaps even more basic than that, Pennsylvania State University psychologist Jay Belskey states that

> mounting research indicates that babies less than 1 year old who receive nonmaternal care for more than 20 hours a week are at greater risk of developing insecure relationships with their mothers; they're also at increased risk of emotional and behavioral problems in later childhood. (Wingert and Kantrowitz 1990, p. 89)

And yet in spite of all its shortcomings, the family is still one of the most important sources of gratification in our lives. Locke (1989) reports that 81 percent of those surveyed listed the family as one of their top two sources of pleasure, with friends the next most mentioned source.

The annual national survey of incoming college freshmen revealed that 67 percent rated getting married and raising a family as one of the highest of their life goals. Only "becoming an authority in his or her field" (72 percent) and "being very well off financially" (73 percent) rated higher (*The Chronicle of Higher Education,* September 6, 1989, p. 17).

Family communication often occurs around the dinner table. Shapiro (1990) reports that

> According to a study by *Better Homes and Gardens* magazine and the Food Marketing Institute, . . . seven out of 10 families eat dinner together three or more times a week, and more than half of the families surveyed eat together every night. . . . Nearly half the respondents admit to keeping the TV on; even so, most families describe their 32 minutes at the table (35 on weekends) as calm and enjoyable. (p. 78)

Casual and Social Groups

Casual and social groups include neighborhood groups, fraternities, bowling partners, golf partners, and, in some cases, fellow members of street gangs. Although these relationships may be relatively short-lived, their impact on behavior can be quite profound.

More recently, Mydans (1990) reported on California gangs in the following way:

> Separating their gang identities from their home lives, the South Bay Family members give themselves nicknames they carry in elaborate tatoos around the backs of their necks. . . . They are "wanna bes," with nothing happening around them to show them it's real dangerous, until they run afoul of real gang members, and then they end up dead.
>
>   Bare chests, tattoos, Budweiser beer, . . . seemed to be the fashion. . . . There were knives and a deer rifle in evidence, and some said they had pistols. . . . "Right or wrong, your bros are your bros." (p. B4)

Haroldson (1989) reported that a major study of 3382 10–14-year-olds showed that they suffered a great deal from stress. One of the recommendations from the researcher was that schools "should consider having more interaction among students to talk about their fears, stress, and concerns. One form of this interaction might be placing . . . students in 'cooperative group learning situations.' . . . Parents, teachers and students . . . need to be more supportive. . . . Listen to them, help them in developing problem-solving and decision-making skills and serving as a general support system" (p. B4). This example illustrates the importance of the social group.

These studies of street gangs and friendship groups show the profound influences that social groups have on each of us. It may very well be that we profoundly influence the social groups as well. It is worth keeping in mind that we are all creatures of experience and that these experiences help shape us for a lifetime.

Educational Groups

Educational groups also may be called learning groups or enlightenment groups. They get together for the primary purpose of study or instruction. These may include, for example, management training seminars, orientation meetings, or quarterback clubs. These groups may discuss recent books, movies, childrearing, meditation, martial arts, or many other topics centering around personal development. Brilhart (1984) refers to an enlightenment discussion as one in which members may attempt to solve problems without having authority to implement their decisions. Small group interaction classes frequently conduct problem-solving discussions concerning national or international issues. Unfortunately, although these groups may develop worthwhile answers to important real-world problems, they are not usually in a position to implement their decisions. The experience of attempting to improve problem-solving skills, however, is a worthwhile result even if the group's decision does not always affect reality. It is interesting to note that even when we *do* have the authority to implement, the results are sometimes not as dramatic or satisfying as we might like. For example, one group determined an excellent solution to a campus parking problem. The solution was accepted by the university administration. However, because of a major construction program, the parking lot was torn up and replaced by a new classroom building before the new plan could be implemented.

At Harvard Business School, each class includes eighty-five people. Kelly and Kelly (1986, pp. 14–15) describe the extremely competitive class atmosphere in the Harvard Business School classroom.

> In an eighty-minute class, one student is asked to "open" the discussion by presenting the case, analyzing the situation, and recommending an approach to solving the business problem or carrying the company forward toward its stated goals. These openings generally take between ten and twenty minutes.
>
> Then, all hell breaks loose, with eighty-four other students scrambling to argue how they would deal with the situation differently and why their approach would be better. Some teachers gently guide the discussion, others prod, while still others are highly aggressive and intimidating in their questioning. . . . In some sections, students have been known to gang up on less-qualified students, forcing them out of school early—

usually between 5 and 10 percent of each section drops out or is forced out in the first year. In other sections, people have worked hard to make sure everyone stays in by making sure that no one student performs badly in more than one or two courses.

The classes are also broken up into smaller study groups of ten people each. This discussion group then becomes the class's working unit and is small enough for members to relate effectively to. Students learn from each other in discussion groups. Over the course of the term, the discussion groups often become social groups and, for some, surrogate families as well. Thomas (1989) argues persuasively on behalf of the use of small groups as a teaching methodology for virtually any subject matter.

In 1985, *The Organizational Behavior Teaching Review Journal* devoted an entire issue to the use of groups in teaching. The editor (1985) explained it this way:

> This special issue is devoted to promoting an increased understanding of why groups should be used in teaching and how they can be used effectively. These issues are becoming increasingly important to everyone in higher education, in part because there is a growing recognition that learning groups provide a potential solution of some of our most difficult pedagogical problems. (p. 1; see also Tubbs 1985)

Work Groups

Some of the most influential small group research ever to be conducted has occurred in work groups. The now-classic studies conducted by Harvard Business School in the Western Electric Hawthorne plant in Chicago are a case in point. This company was a subsidiary of AT&T and manufactured telephone equipment for the Bell System. The studies lasted from 1927 to 1932 and are described in detail by Mayo (1933) and Roethlisberger and Dickson (1939).

The studies were originally designed to determine the influence of illumination on industrial productivity. It was hypothesized that improved lighting would improve productivity. The first study showed that productivity increased whether lighting levels were increased or *decreased* to a level darker than moonlight (three footcandles). This, of course, puzzled the researchers.

A second study was conducted to determine the effect of periodic rest breaks on productivity. Once again it was found that productivity kept incresing whether a rest break was added or taken out of the work schedule. The researchers hypothesized that the productivity increases resulted from the workers' changed social situation, increased satisfaction, and new patterns of social interaction brought about by the creating of an experimental condition and paying of special attention to the workers. This productivity increase resulting from special attention has since been labeled the *Hawthorne effect*.

In order to more carefully determine the influence of these social factors on productivity, a second set of studies was designed and labeled the Bank Wiring Observation Room experiment. Workers were observed as they wired, soldered, and inspected switchboards or "banks" of switches. Workers were on an economic incentive system that allowed them to earn more pay if they produced more. The experiment showed that workers were producing far below what they were capable of producing, because of the group's social norm enforced by the co-workers. The researchers referred to this as artificial restriction of output.

The group norm or unwritten rule was to set a relatively low level of work, which was called a fair day's work for a fair day's pay. Anyone who produced much more was branded a "rate buster" or a "speed king." Those who underproduced were called "chiselers," and those who might tell anything to a supervisor that would get them in trouble were called "squealers." In each case, the person who violated the group's norm was punched hard in the arm or shoulder, a punishment affectionately referred to as "binging." These social practices did, indeed, influence the workers' output more than the opportunity to earn more money for more work. The major findings of the Hawthorne studies were summarized by Miner (1988, p. 263).

1. The level of productivity is set by social norms, not by physiological capacities.

2. Noneconomic rewards and sanctions significantly affect the behavior of the workers and largely limit the effect of economic incentive plans.

3. Often workers do not act or react as individuals but as members of groups.

See the reading by Hatvany and Pucik at the end of this chapter for an example of the effective use of work groups.

It was also found that the informally chosen group leader was the best liked and that he or she most represented the values of the group. This leader was often more influential than the appointed leader (the supervisor). On the basis of these studies, management theorists began to stress (1) the importance of communication within the work group, (2) the importance of participation in the decision-making process, and (3) the potential values of democratic leadership. The emphasis on these three factors was later to be referred to as the *human relations* approach to management.

Andrew S. Grove is president of Intel Corporation, a computer chip and microprocessor company in Silicon Valley. In his best-selling book, *High Output Management* (1983, p. 71), Grove discusses the importance of groups to his company:

> a big part of a middle manager's work is to supply information and know-how, and to impart a sense of the preferred method of handling things to the groups under his control and influence. A manager also makes and helps make decisions. Both kinds of managerial tasks can occur during face-to-face encounters, and therefore only during meetings. Thus I will assert again that a meeting is nothing less than the MEDIUM through which managerial work is performed. That means we should not be fighting their very existence, but rather using the time spent in them as efficiently as possible.

Problem-Solving Groups

Although we have looked at other types of groups, by far the greatest emphasis in group discussion textbooks has been on improving problem-solving and decision-making abilities (Barnlund and Haiman 1959, Collins and Guetzkow 1964,

Harnack and Fest 1964, Gulley 1968, Sattler and Miller 1968, Bormann 1969, Patton and Giffin 1973, Applbaum et al. 1974, Gouran 1974, Goldberg and Larson 1975, and Brilhart and Galanes 1989).

The terms "task-oriented," "problem-solving," and "decision-making" groups have been used interchangeably to stress the emphasis on the cognitive end products of group discussion. Although interpersonal relations are often discussed, they are considered not as important and merely a means to an end (that is, to solve a problem).

Among the many kinds of decision-making groups in organizations, quality circles have become a highly successful mechanism for increasing employee involvement and solving company problems. Mohr and Mohr (1983) illustrate the value of problem-solving groups in the following instances:

■ A study done at B. F. Goodrich of vendors' invoices showed that the top 11 percent accounted for 68 percent of the dollars recovered.

■ At Westinghouse, a purchasing department quality circle discovered that 78 percent of their vendor overshipment problems was caused by 12.5 percent of the causes identified by the circle members.

■ In a machine and sheet metal shop at Sunnyvale, California, 77 percent of the rejected parts resulted from 15 percent of the causes.

Pareto Principle
80-20 rule
80% of problems
are caused by 20%
of the issues.

As these examples suggest, most organizations find that a few key issues typically cause most of the problems demanding attention. This idea originated with the nineteenth-century Italian economist Vilfredo Pareto, whose studies showed that a small percentage of the population held a high percentage of the wealth, whereas the great majority lived in poverty. Many authors since Pareto have confirmed his principle that some issues (a vital few) result in the largest percentage of problems, whereas most issues (the trivial many) result in relatively few problems. Another name for the Pareto principle is the 80–20 rule: 80 percent of the problems are caused by 20 percent of the issues (Mohr and Mohr 1983, pp. 131–132).

Kanter (1983) states that groups are the cornerstone of participative decision making in American organizations. She writes:

> It is hard to mention "teams" or "participation" anymore without someone's labeling them "Japanese-style management." In the first place this is faintly ridiculous. . . . Innovating companies emphasize teamwork, but they also reward individuals, and they give internal entrepreneurs free rein to pioneer—as long as they can also work with the team. So "American-style" participation does not and should not mean the dominance of committees over individuals, the submergence of the individual in the group or the swallowing of the person by the team, but rather the mechanism for giving more people at more levels a piece of the entrepreneurial action. (p. 364)

Types of Discussion Questions

Problem-solving groups must spend a great deal of time and energy in careful deliberation. Generally, the group will be attempting to provide some answer or answers to the discussion question. Sample discussion questions include these:

1. How can we keep from eliminating the earth's ozone shield?

2. What can be done about the problem of cheating in our school?

3. How do we determine local obscenity and pornography standards?

4. What are the long-term effects of marijuana use?

5. How do we achieve equal opportunity for women and minorities?

6. How can we reduce energy consumption?

7. Should abortion or contraception be made mandatory for families that already have two children?

8. What is an acceptable level of unemployment?

9. Should marijuana be legalized?

10. Should handguns be outlawed?

11. Has the decline of civilization begun in this country?

12. How can we curb drug abuse in industry?

An effective problem-solving discussion begins with an effectively structured discussion question. First, a topic should be limited to one issue. Notice that question 7 includes both abortion and contraception. These two issues may require different answers, so only one should be included in the discussion question. An improved version of number 7 would be, "How can we help curb population growth?"

QUESTIONS OF FACT   Questions of fact deal with truth and falsity. Is it or is it not so? "What are the long-term effects of marijuana use?" is a question of fact. "Can the disease AIDS (Acquired Immune Deficiency Syndrome) be transmitted by casual contact in a school classroom?" is another.

Discussions involving questions of fact require evidence and documentation to establish whether or not the phenomenon exists. For example, "Does the Bermuda Triangle really pose a major threat to ships and planes traveling in the area?" or "Does intelligent life exist in outer space?" Frequently, such questions remain somewhat unresolvable, but they are interesting to discuss anyway.

QUESTIONS OF DEFINITION   Questions of definition are fairly narrow but are often quite difficult to answer. The problem of defining obscenity and pornography has been with us for decades. The emotionalism experienced in numerous states over textbook wording is but one of many examples of disagreement over what is obscene. Several years ago the Supreme Court ruled that no one definition could be made for all communities, so each local community had to define obscenity and pornography for itself.

In the medical arena, lawsuits are arising over differences in the medical definition of death. If accident victims become organ transplant donors, what signs do doctors use to determine if the donor is dead? Cessation of the heartbeat is certainly not a reliable sign, because numerous people walking around today have had their hearts stop temporarily. What about cessation of brain activity? The point is that the definition is important and is not as easily determined as it might first appear.

QUESTIONS OF VALUE   Questions of value invoke an evaluation of the issues once the facts and the definitions have been determined. Whereas facts can be verified by others, values are personal and often differ drastically from one individual to another. Perhaps we can agree on a definition of affirmative action as *unequal* opportunity for women and minorities to undo the wrongs that have existed for decades. Yet can we agree that *unequal* opportunity of any kind is desirable? Some judges have ruled that this is still another form of discrimination (against white males) and is inconsistent with the ideals of the Equal Employment Opportunity Commission. Yet others feel strongly that reverse discrimination is required to tip the scales of justice to where they should have been a long time ago.

Differences in values are at the base of the controversies over abortion and contraception, as well. Those who believe in the right of the unborn child see abortion and even contraception as unthinkable. Those on the other side feel that the individual women should have the right to decide whether she wants a child and that these decisions should not be dictated by others. Here is another case in which the ''right'' answer will definitely vary depending on one's own personal and very individual value system.

QUESTIONS OF POLICY   Questions of policy involve establishing the facts, determining definitions, discussing values, and determining the ways and means of solving a problem. "What can be done to solve the problems of drug abuse?" "What should our state's policy be toward abortions?" "Should the United States provide more public service jobs for the unemployed?" "How can the misuse of handguns be reduced?" All these are examples of policy questions. Discussions regarding questions of policy are often the most complicated, because they encompass some of the other three types of discussion questions (fact, definition, and value). Let us look at one topic (equal rights for women) as it might be discussed in each of the four ways.

1. *Fact:* "Do women have equal rights in this country?"

2. *Definition:* "What do we mean by the term *equal rights for women?*"

3. *Value:* "Is it desirable to change women's role in our society?"

4. *Policy:* "How can we achieve equal rights for women in this country?"

As you can see, the policy question assumes, to some extent, that (1) equal rights do not presently exist, (2) agreement on a definition of equal rights can be reached, (3) equal rights for women are desirable, and (4) something ought to be done to bring about equal rights for women. It is important to remember that policy discussions may bog down on these earlier questions if all group members do not agree on these assumptions.

In addition to trying to find a solution to the problem, policy questions frequently must deal with the question of how to implement the solution. Should equal rights be dictated by law? Should they evolve through generations of attitude change produced by the mass media and word of mouth? Should they be implemented at the local level, like obscenity laws, or at the national level, like crimes against the government? All these questions deal with the specifics of how the solution actually gets enacted.

Figure 3.6 summarizes the elements involved in various types of discussion questions.

Discussion Group Formats

Discussion questions may be approached in a variety of different small group formats. The selection of an appropriate format largely depends upon group members' own needs and circumstances. Although there are any number of possible formats, these five are representative of most problem-solving discussions:

Dialogue: The dialogue is simply a discussion or conversation between two people. It may be conducted privately or in front of an audience.

Panel: The panel discussion usually involves a small number of people (up to five or six) conducting an informal discussion on a topic they have all thought about and possibly researched beforehand. One person is appointed moderator to help move the group along its planned agenda. Conversation is mostly spontaneous, and participants may interrupt one another.

Symposium: The symposium includes several participants, each of whom gives a short formal presentation on a prepared topic usually built around a central theme. Participants do not interrupt each other during the formal presentations, but a less formal discussion usually follows.

FIGURE 3.6   ELEMENTS INVOLVED IN DISCUSSION QUESTIONS

Elements Included	Type of discussion			
	Fact	Definition	Value	Policy
Facts	X	X	X	X
Definitions		X	X	X
Values			X	X
Policies				X
Implementation				X

Forum: A forum is a question-and-answer period designed to allow audience members to interact with the discussion group. A forum period often follows a panel discussion or a symposium. It is customary for the chairperson to introduce the panel or symposium members and to serve as a moderator for the forum period.

Colloquy: A colloquy may take a number of forms, but each involves the questioning of experts by the other experts on the panel, laypersons on a second panel, or laypersons in the audience. This format is very similar to the panel discussion except that experts are involved and a second panel of laypersons may also be involved.

Discussion Group Techniques

In addition to the major formats discussed above, there are a number of subformats or techniques that may be employed in discussion groups. These techniques are often used for short periods of time as *part* of a discussion group format.

Phillips 66: Phillips 66 is a specific technique developed by J. D. Phillips (1948). It simply allows all the members of an audience to form groups of about six people to discuss a specific topic for about six minutes and then report the group's conclusion through a spokesperson. Realistically, this technique is more useful if longer time limits are allowed (up to an hour or so). The general term for this, when time and group size are not limited to six, is a *buzz group* or *buzz session.* The technique offers the advantage of allowing a lot of people to participate in a fairly efficient manner. The results from all groups are compiled and used to solve the problem faced by the entire assembly.

Case Discussion: A case discussion is an educational discussion centered on a real or hypothetical event. The case problem is presented to the group, and members attempt to solve it as best they can. A case problem is included at the beginning of each chapter in this book to illustrate the way in which small group theory and research apply to real-life problems.

Role Playing: Role playing simply allows participants to adopt a new "role" or set of behaviors other than their own. For example, quiet individuals may be assigned the role of leader, or argumentative members may be assigned the role of harmonizer or compromiser. Meek members may be asked to play the role of the "devil's advocate." In each case the individual gets an opportunity to practice a role in an attempt to build his or her group skills. This helps develop role flexibility so that participants can adopt new and different role behaviors as the need arises. Role playing also may be used to demonstrate to the rest of the group what a given role may do to a group discussion. The chronic nonconformist role can be secretly given to one member to demonstrate how the others will react. The typical reaction is that that person gets a lot of attention from the rest of the group for a while but will be ignored after a time if he or she continues to deviate (see Chapter 4 for more on deviation).

Another version of role playing is the role reversal. In this case, participants try to take the part of another person (usually one with whom they have a conflict). Biracial groups, labor-management groups, and others frequently use this technique to develop empathy for the other person's point of view. It often results in funny situations, which also help relieve some of the tension. Try some of the role-playing exercises in this book to help get a feel for what role playing is like—for example, Exercise 1 at the end of Chapter 2.

Fishbowl: The fishbowl technique has one small group attempt to solve a problem for a specified period of time (often thirty minutes), while a second group, seated around the outside of the first group, observes the process. After the discussion, the observer group gives feedback to the first group as to what behaviors they were able to identify as helpful or harmful to the group's progress. Then the two groups reverse positions and roles: The observers become the observed, and vice versa. This technique may be aided by the use of videotape equipment.

Conference: A conference is a series of meetings on topics of common interest between and among people who represent different groups. For example, representatives from different colleges and universities may gather at a conference to discuss problems of finance, curriculum, community service, and others. Conferences often involve hundreds of people and may last several days. For the past several years, different countries have hosted world food conferences in an attempt to plan for the feeding of the world's population. Conferences may also be quite small and last a short period of time. The critical element is that different groups are represented. An example of the latter type of conference is the plant manager's weekly conference in a manufacturing plant where representatives from production, engineering, maintenance, inspection, personnel, and other departments get together to organize their efforts and to solve common problems.

NGT: The Nominal Group Technique (NGT) was developed by Delbecq, Van de Ven, and Gustafson (1975) as a technique to reduce the effects of group conformity pressure. The NGT method has six phases. First is a silent, independent generation of ideas written down on paper. Second is a round-robin listing of ideas on a large sheet of newsprint or blackboard so everyone can see. The third step is a clarification of points without any critique. Fourth, everyone individually ranks the ideas. Fifth is a clarification of the vote. Sixth is a final ranking of the ideas. Jarobe (1988) has found that this method results in better decisions than less-structured group discussions. Clearly, this method incorporates the advantages of a group in that several people's ideas are used. At the same time, it minimizes the disadvantage that often occurs when group members' ideas are subject to self-censorship based on one's fear of being rejected by other group members.

THE SYSTEMS PERSPECTIVE

In this chapter we have looked at some of the elements that constitute the internal influences section of our model. In systems theory these elements would be called part of the *throughput* of small groups. Early in the chapter we examined territoriality, physical environment, and seating behavior in groups. As suggested by the Vietnam negotiations, different cultures have drastically differing perceptions of how to position furniture or whether to have furniture at all. This illustrates the way in which relevant background factors influence such internal influences as territoriality, physical environment, and seating behavior. For example, in Western culture we typically place furniture along the walls with open space in the middle of the room. The Japanese tend to cluster furniture in the center of the room, leaving the space along the walls open. Also, imagine conducting a group discussion while seated barefoot on the floor around very low tables. This should help you picture the importance of background factors in relation to seating behaviors.

Probably the most important internal influence in the model is the type of group. Obviously, the procedures, norms, expectations, and outcomes of a work group will be radically different from those of a social group. For example, a norm of openness in both self-disclosure and candid feedback to others exists in many social groups. However, you might find that to tell your boss or friend exactly what you do *not* like about them is certainly inappropriate. The type of group has an enormous impact on the way in which that group functions.

In this chapter we also looked at the literature on communication networks. We saw that the all-channel network was best for group member satisfaction, whereas the wheel produced the fastest results. As our systems perspective leads us to believe, determining the "best" network depends, among other things, on the demands of the situation.

When we discussed the issue of group size, we began to see the connection between the type of group and the appropriate group size. All other things being equal, five seems to be the optimum size for a problem-solving group. However, the optimum size for a group discussion in a classroom may be radically different from that of a work group on an assembly line or in a large office. Even the idea of the "right" size of family group depends on each of our relevant background factors. Typically, people have quite strong feelings about what is the "right" sized family. These feelings usually result from a lifetime of attitude formation influenced by parents, friends, and, perhaps, religious affiliation.

Group size is also related to the idea of communication networks. As the size increases, the all-channel network begins to bog down in the confusion, and a more controlled network tends to be more appropriate. Group size is also related to the consequences of group interaction. Larger groups tend to produce lower levels of satisfaction and interpersonal relations among participants. Bostrom's research, cited in this chapter, is very revealing. It showed that most people like to talk far more than they like to listen in groups.

In the preceding section of this chapter we looked at different group formats and techniques (for example, panel, symposium, role playing, fishbowl, conference). Obviously, there is a connection between type of group and appropriate format. Can you imagine the U.S. president's cabinet engaging in role-playing and fishbowl simulations? Certainly, educational groups use these formats and techniques with a great deal of success, but work groups would be more likely to use panels, symposiums, and conferences.

The type of group format is also related to the desired group outcome. If personal growth is the goal, then role playing or fishbowls are helpful. On the other hand, if the group goal is to solve a task-oriented problem, such as how to cut energy consumption by 10 percent, the panel discussion is probably more appropriate. As usual, it all depends.

1. Discussion of Case Studies

Divide into five-person groups. Each group can discuss *one* of the cases below.* Each of these cases describes real-life psychological studies involving naive human subjects. Ask yourself, "How do I feel about the use of this procedure in social research?" Then, within each group, try to agree on one of the six reactions listed below.

(a) I am totally unopposed to its use.

(b) I am basically unopposed to its use.

(c) I am slightly more unopposed to its use.

(d) I am slightly more opposed than unopposed to its use.

(e) I am basically opposed to its use.

(f) I am opposed to its use under any circumstances.

After you have arrived at group agreement on one of the six reactions above, each group should share its reaction and the reasoning behind it. Discuss the different reactions among the groups.

Case 1—Homosexual Attitudes

Men are recruited to participate in an experiment on sexual attitudes, although they are not told that it is actually a study of attitudes toward homosexuality. Participants are led to believe that a "psycho-galvanometer" used in the experiment is capable of detecting sexual arousal. They are also told that if the galvanometer registers when an individual looks at slides of nude males, the individual is probably a latent homosexual. The galvanometer is rigged so that all participants are led to believe they are latent homosexuals. Following the

*These cases were used in a study on ethics in social research practices conducted by Edwin A. Rugg (personal correspondence, May 20, 1975).

experiment, the researcher informs the participants that the galvanometer was rigged and gives detailed information about the study and its true purpose.

Case 2—Obedience

Individuals are recruited to participate in an experiment on memory and learning, although the actual purpose of the experiment is to study obedience. Participants are given the role of "teacher" and told to administer increasingly strong electric shocks to the "learner" whenever the learner makes an error in the memory task. The learner is actually an assistant to the researcher and receives no actual shocks. He only pretends to experience pain as the shock level becomes more and more severe. The psychological dilemma for the participant involves deciding whether to obey the experimenter, who insists that the participant continue to shock the learner, or to side with the learner, who begs the participant to stop administering shocks. When the participant refuses to continue or when the highest shock level is reached, the experiment is over. At that point, the participant is told that the shocks and cries of pain were faked. The true purpose and details of the study are explained.

Case 3—Reactions to Fear and Anxiety

Students, participating in a series of experiments for course credit, are told when they arrive at one of the research laboratories that they will receive an electric shock as part of the experiment. The researcher is interested in the reactions of groups under conditions of fear and anxiety. In order to facilitate anxiety arousal, the researcher describes in detail the pain and uncomfortable side effects that usually accompany the electric shock. Actually, no shocks are ever administered. Following the experiment, the researcher informs the participants that they will not be shocked after all. He then explains the actual experiment that took place and why they were purposefully misled.

Case 4—Self-concept and Achievement

Students at a teacher's college complete a series of placement tests but are not told that the tests are actually part of a psychological experiment. The experiment involves giving half of the students false test results that indicate that they are unfit for a teaching career. The researcher is interested in studying the effects of lowered self-concept on subsequent achievement. Two weeks later the study is completed, and the researcher tells the students that the test results were falsified and explains the details of the research project.

Case 5—Reward and Performance

Individuals are promised $2 if they participate in an experiment that involves performing a simple but boring task. Some of the participants are later led to believe that they may receive up to $20 for their participation, even though the researcher has no intention of paying participants more than $2 for their time. The researcher is interested in the effects of different anticipated rewards on attitudes toward the task and the quality of task performance. At the end of the experiment, the researcher explains why he/she cannot pay participants more than the $2 initially agreed upon and discusses the purpose and nature of the research.

READINGS: OVERVIEW

In the first article, Tubbs discusses educational groups and the parallels between the changing nature of leadership in business and the changing nature of leadership in the classroom.

In the second article, Hatvany and Pucik describe the important role groups play in the Japanese method for achieving high productivity in their society. To what extent do you think these group methods could be used in the Western world?

Teacher as Leader/Developer

Stewart L. Tubbs

Those who would find fault with American education today are legion. On the other hand, there appear to be two promising and parallel developments, one in business leadership, the other in classroom leadership. Between the two, there is an approach that points toward a brighter future.

The new paradigm is based on the premise that the "heroic" form of leadership is obsolete, and that "developmental" leadership is the more appropriate model for the future.

Business Leadership

Leadership in business has evolved from the traditional model of Manager-as-Hero to the contemporary model of Manager-as-Developer. In this model, leaders dedicate their efforts to increasing the skill levels and utilizing the expertise of their subordinates. One of the exciting examples of this concept in action is the new Saturn Corporation.

Saturn Corporation, a wholly owned subsidiary of General Motors, has a radical new organizational structure which uses teams as the basic supervisory unit. GM has invested over $5 billion in this bold new venture.

In fact, the name "Saturn" was chosen to reflect the concentric rings of decision-making groups that run the organization. Tichy and Devanna (1986) describe the various levels of group activity represented by the "rings of Saturn" compared to the traditional role of an individual manager of that level (p. 231).

The traditional GM plant has six levels of management: plant manager, production manager, central superintendent, down to production supervisor or foreman.

In contrast, the Saturn organization has teams at each level doing the work normally accomplished by individual managers. The teams represent different functional specialties such as engineering, manufacturing, marketing, and so on.

General Motors is not the only company to use new manufacturing procedures. Smith (1985) cites the "Team Taurus" concept at Ford Motor Company in which teams were responsible for bringing out the Ford Taurus and the Mercury Sable, two extremely successful new car lines. He writes:

Stewart L. Tubbs, "Teacher as Leader/Developer," From The Journal of Professional Studies, *Fall 1989, 4–16. Reprinted by permission.*

Some 15,000 workers enrolled in employee-involvement programs are involved in Taurus/Sable. If ten years ago they heard of our repair-rate targets, they would have laughed. Back then, 10 to 15 of every 100 cars built were diverted after assembly for repair. We've cut that back to five, two, and one. (p. 33)

The GM and Ford examples are but two of many that illustrate the important way in which groups are becoming an inherent part of a very different way of managing modern organizations. Bradford and Cohen (1984) have argued persuasively in their best-selling book, *Managing for Excellence*, that the Manager-as-Hero style which worked well in the past has given way to the Manager-as-Developer, the style for today and the future. In their book, they identify four myths of the heroic management style:

1. The good manager knows at all times what is going on in the department.

2. The good manager should have more technical expertise than any subordinate.

3. The good manager should be able to solve any problem that comes up (or at least solve it before a subordinate can).

4. The good manager should be the primary (if not the only) person responsible for how the department is working. (pp. 10–11)

These myths emerge out of a common assumption. The "good manager" is assumed to be—and to function as—the "superior." But our experience tells us that these assumptions can block solutions to problems. Today, solutions are coming from our supposed "inferiors." Here are three examples.

Two summers ago, my 15-year-old son had a student internship at a high tech company. From him I learned about fax machines. Last year we installed one in the office and have come to know and love it.

A graduate student recently sent an electronic mail message to all the faculty on our local area network describing how to configure our disk for an expanded network. Here faculty are learning from a graduate student.

I recently talked to a man with a Harvard MBA who is the CEO of a $10 billion company. When I asked him a question, he responded "I don't really know. You'll have to talk to my training director about that."

Are these examples atypical? I don't think so. The knowledge explosion is such that none of us can keep up with it. The most basic lesson taught to those who are moving into general management is that they must rely on the expertise within their organizations.

George Elges was once General Manager of Cadillac. He tells the story of turn signal indicator lights shorting out. He and his top engineers and managers tried repeatedly to solve the problem, to no avail. Finally, he went down on the assembly line and asked the hourly workers. Within minutes they told him that the sharp metal on the inside of the fenders was cutting through the insulation on the wires. They suggested placing a rubber washer inside the hole in the fender where the wire went through.

Bradford and Cohen (1984) state:

> The solution that worked yesterday is only slightly appropriate today and will be
> irrelevant tomorrow. Task complexity virtually assures that no one person can
> have all the necessary knowledge which forces a heightened degree of in-
> terdependence among subordinates (and a much greater demand for coordina-
> tion) if work is to be successfully accomplished, especially at an excellent level . . .
> Heroism may be motivating for the superior, but it has the opposite effect on
> subordinates. . . . Today there are far more subordinates who want to be chal-
> lenged by work; they place "challenging jobs" and "a chance to grow and
> develop" ahead of such rewards as pay, status, and job security. (pp. 12, 15)

Classroom Leadership

The most abrupt shock I encountered on my first full-time teaching job was the
contrast between the one-on-one competition of the classroom and the need
for effective teamwork with my teaching colleagues. Employers regularly criticize business students (usually MBA holders) for being too self-absorbed in
their careers, and not sufficiently team-oriented. It is not surprising that we
don't have much in the way of team-oriented skills. Few of our classes teach
this type of skill.

As a result of this lack of skill-oriented teaching, the American Assembly of
Collegiate Schools of Business (AACSB) has been pursuing what it calls the
"Outcome Measures Project."

This project is designed to measure student gains as a result of having been
through a business education.

Outcomes are of two types:

- Cognitive outcomes include knowledge of such disciplines as Accounting, Economics, Finance, Management, Marketing, Quantitative Analysis, etc.

- Non-cognitive (I don't like the term) outcomes include such skills as
  leadership, oral communication/presentation skills, written communication, planning and organizing, information gathering and problem analysis, decision-making, delegation and control, self-objectivity, and disposi-
  tion to lead.

The Outcomes Measures project represents a significant step toward
legitimizing skill development as part of university teaching. Students can learn
these skills if they do them constantly in the classroom.

Such a development has been occurring in college classrooms. The traditional model of instruction has had the instructor as expert, but this is evolving
into the model of instructor as developer.

Arrington (1989) and Kraft (1985) have described this approach as Group-
Inquiry. Students are divided into groups of five to actively analyze and report
on structured topics.

Tubbs (1985) has also reported on a Consulting Teams methodology in which student teams serve as consultants to business organizations off campus, and report their results in class.

Dr. Ziad Kronfel, associate professor of psychiatry at The University of Michigan Medical School, is my next door neighbor. Recently he mentioned that the professors in his school were trying to reduce the problem of excessive absences from their lectures.

I asked him if they had diagnosed the problem. He said that the medical students told them that the lectures were a waste of time. They preferred to meet on their own in groups of three or four to discuss the material. I asked him if this type of group discussion might be held in class. He said that they were experimenting with a technique that had been successful in one course entitled "Introduction to Clinical Practice."

Under the careful guidance and coaching of the instructor, the students are divided into teams of three. One student role-plays the physician. One plays the patient, and one videotapes and critiques the physician's techniques. He said both the faculty and students were very satisfied with this teaching method.

The philosophical underpinnings of these approaches are based on the principle that active learning is more effective than passive learning (Tubbs, 1973, 1987, 1988). This philosophy leads us to six paradoxes which parallel those of Bradford and Cohen (1984).

Paradox 1

The Teacher-as-Developer has to be both less active and more active than the heroic teacher.

In 1965, I was student teaching Biology in Lakewood (Ohio) High School. After observing me teaching dissection in a laboratory one day, my supervising teacher, Mr. Coleman, told me, "You're working too hard. Let them do more for themselves. They will learn it better." This advice has served me well throughout my career.

It takes great skill to use student participation effectively. The greatest tendency of managers when attempting participative management is to go from autocratic to laissez-faire leadership. Similarly, when instructors attempt to change from lectures to group discussions, they tend to withdraw too much and the student discussions may go nowhere.

What we need to develop is the ability to develop constant student interaction, but with very active structuring, questioning, and coaching from the instructor. So we are less actively lecturing, but more active in prodding, provoking, structuring, and guiding student discovery.

Paradox 2

The Teacher-as-Developer must give greater autonomy to students while establishing more control.

One of my most successful teaching experiences has been with classes of student "Consulting Teams" (Tubbs, 1985). The approach is to divide students into teams of five.

Each team is assigned to work for a United Way agency as volunteer consultants. They negotiate and write a contract that identifies mutually agreed-upon objectives for the students and client organizations to meet.

Since the students are off campus, they have greater autonomy than they would normally have meeting in the classroom under my caring but watchful eye.

However, at the same time, I had to develop more guidelines (or controls) so students would know what was expected of them, and what behaviors were inappropriate for the assignment.

For example, some members of the team would chronically complain that not all group members would live up to the contract. Thus, I had to establish a peer rating as part of the evaluation process leading to their project grade.

This illustrates the new challenges presented by Paradox 2.

Paradox 3

Teachers-as-Developers increase their own power by giving students greater power.

There is a big difference between position power and personal power. Position power is the authority of our position. For example, the university gives us the authority to make assignments, assign grades, etc.

However, personal power is the credibility which we earn based on our knowledge, experience, and interpersonal skills. As we allow greater participation and ownership of group outcomes, we also increase our personal power by building stronger support and loyalty.

It doesn't take much teaching experience to realize that our formal authority or power over students is very limited. However, the enthusiasm and excitement that results from getting students turned on to the subject matter is substantial.

A student once told me, "You get excited over ideas." I had never thought about it that way, but she was right. That kind of power to excite people through ideas rarely occurs through position power.

Paradox 4

The Teacher-as-Developer builds a team as a way to support member individuality.

Think about being new in a group. How free do you feel to express your opinions, especially whey they deviate from those expressed in the group? Now think about a group in which you feel very secure. How free do you feel to express a deviant opinion now?

Janis, in his well known book, *Groupthink* (1982), advises that groups can institute processes that actually increase individual thinking in cohesive groups where "groupthink" would otherwise tend to occur. Obviously, a high level of skill in running groups is required. (For more on this see Tubbs, 1988.)

The implication for teachers is that we need to allow students the freedom to disagree with one another and with us. At the same time, we need to teach them the difference between idea opponents and personal opponents. The trick is to keep from turning an idea opponent into a personal opponent. The skill required is persuasion.

Paradox 5

The Teacher-as-Developer model requires an optimistic faith in student possibilities but demands tough implementation to work.

In this context, Bradford and Cohen (1984) state:

The Manager-as-Developer model is optimistic in several ways. First, the model is based on the premise that virtually everyone wants to do well—that no reason exists for basic incompatibility between what the organization needs (in its search for excellence) and what individuals want to produce (in terms of performing competently). . . . At the same time, the Manager-as-Developer model is basically a tough approach. It is tough in setting high standards (and holding people to them). It is tough in requiring that the manager hold subordinates' feet to the fire when they may want to avoid the difficult issues. (p. 287)

In business, no person better illustrates this principle than Lee Iacocca. He has been the savior of Chrysler Corporation. Yet most people don't know that he has fired more than 25 Chrysler vice presidents in the process of turning that company around.

The popular 1989 movie, "Lean on Me," is the true story about Joe Clark, a controversial high school principal in Paterson, New Jersey. He took over a school infested with dope dealers and maladroits. Through tough new policies and practices, he was able to spur students to much higher levels of academic achievement. He exemplifies all of us who believe our students have the potential to reach new heights, but we may have to get tough in the process.

Paradox 6

Although the Developer model requires new behavior, the best way to improve your performance as a teacher is to focus on the needs of students, rather than on yourself.

The most contemporary paradigm for leadership is the situational model. Hersey and Blanchard (1988) argue persuasively that leadership is most effective when adapted to the specific needs of the situation, most particularly, the individual follower.

It is axiomatic that to be an effective teacher, one must diagnose the needs of students, and then help to meet those needs. The common complaint about teachers is that they really know the subject matter, but can't get it across. Clearly, to "snow" students with our knowledge and vocabulary does little to advance learning.

Resistance to Change

It has been said that the only person who likes change is a baby with a wet diaper. Obviously, those of us who have been successful with a didactic teaching style will find many reasons not to change.

Similarly, Fred Herr, former vice president of Product Assurance for Ford, said in a speech once that one of Ford's top managers found the new employee-oriented management methods so distasteful that he resigned and retired. The manager reportedly said, "For years you have encouraged me to be an attack dog. Now you want me to be a pussycat. I can't do it."

The catalyst for change in industry is the ravaging of our industries by foreign competition. The catalyst for change in education is the avalanche of criticism from tuition-paying customers who are becoming increasingly less satisfied with the education they are getting for their precious dollars.

The ironic thing is that changes can be difficult for students too. I remember teaching a class at the University of Kansas more than 20 years ago in which a student got angry with me for not "teaching." He asked, "What are you getting paid for if we have to teach ourselves?"

I'm sure that whatever I said to convince him was not very effective. Today I might quote Carl Rogers (1969), who wrote:

> I have come to feel that the only learning which significantly influences behavior is self-discovered, self-appropriated learning. Such learning, . . . assimilated in experience, cannot be directly communicated to another. (pg. 153)

On the other hand, after hundreds of classes and thousands of students (and three awards for outstanding teaching), I am more convinced than ever that the secret to success is through the methods advanced in this paper. Teams of workers and teams of students can support each other to discover for themselves what they need to learn, how they need to grow, and how problems might be solved. This kind of togetherness describes the future. And it works—in corporations, and in classrooms.

EXHIBIT 1

	Teacher-as-Hero Model	Teacher-as-Developer Model
Assumption	Lessons are best revealed to students through lectures	Lessons are best acquired by students through experience-based activities.
Method	Primarily one-way communication	Primarily group-centered, two-way communication.
Emphasis	Increasing information, passivity	Development of skills, activity, creativity
Locus of Responsibility	Instructor	Instructor/Students
Incentives	Grades	Grades, ego involvement, skill development
Culture	Formal, parent-child, competitive	Informal, adult-adult, cooperative
Cognitive Approach	Analysis	Synthesis
Student-Teacher Relations	Distant, sometimes adversarial	Closer, more collaborative
Power	Centralized	More distributed
Organizational Criteria	Efficiency	Effectiveness

References

Bradford, D. L. & Cohen, A. R. (1984). *Managing for excellence: The guide to developing high performance in contemporary organizations.* New York: John Wiley.

Faculty Center for Instructional Effectiveness (Producer), & Arrington, P. G. (Director). (1989). *Group-inquiry: A method for learning* [Videotape]. Ypsilanti, MI: Eastern Michigan University.

Hersey, P., & Blanchard, K. (1988). *Management of Organizational Behavior* (5th ed.). Englewood Cliffs, N.J.: Prentice-Hall.

Janis, I. (1982). *Groupthink* (2nd ed.). Boston: Houghton-Mifflin.

Kraft, R. G. (1985). Group-inquiry turns passive students active. *College Teaching, 33* (4), 149–154.

Rogers, C. (1969). *Freedom to learn.* Columbus: Charles E. Merrill.

Schein, E. H. (1978). *Career dynamics.* Reading, MA: Addison-Wesley.

Smith, D. C. (February, 1985). Team Taurus: Ford's $3 billion mid-market plunge. *Ward's Auto World,* 26–33.

Tichy, N. M., & Devanna, M. A. (1986). *The transformational leader.* New York: Wiley.

Tubbs, S. L. (1973). Reactions to sensitivity training from the standpoint of a participant and trainer. *Michigan Speech Association Journal, 8*(1), 32–35.

Tubbs, S. L. (1984–85). Consulting teams: A methodology for teaching integrated management skills. *The Organizational Behavior Teaching Review, 9*(4), 52–57.

Tubbs, S. L., & Moss, S. (1987). *Human Communication* (5th ed.). New York: Random House.

Tubbs, S. L. (1988). *A systems approach to small group interaction* (3rd ed.). New York: Random House.

Japanese Management Practices and Productivity

Nina Hatvany and Vladimir Pucik

The [United States] is the most technically advanced country and the most affluent one. But capital investment alone will not make the difference. In any country the quality of products and the productivity of workers depend on management. When Detroit changes its management system we'll see more powerful American competitors.

> —Hideo Suguira, Executive Vice-President, Honda Motor Co.

Productivity—or output per worker—is a key measure of economic health. When it increases, the economy grows in real terms and so do standards of living. When it declines, real economic growth slows or stagnates. Productivity is the result of many factors, including investment in capital goods, technological innovation, and workers' motivation.

After a number of years of sluggish productivity growth, the United States now trails most other major industrial nations in the rise in output per worker, although it still enjoys the best overall rate. This state of affairs is increasingly bemoaned by many critics in both academic and business circles. Some reasons suggested to "explain" the U.S. decline in productivity rankings include excessive government regulation, tax policies discouraging investment, increases in energy costs, uncooperative unions, and various other factors in the business environment.

Some observers, however—among them Harvard professors Robert Hayes and William J. Abernathy—put the blame squarely on American managers. They argue that U.S. firms prefer to service existing markets rather than create new ones, imitate rather than innovate, acquire existing companies rather than develop a superior product or process technology and, perhaps most important, focus on short-run returns on investment rather than long-term growth and research and development strategy. Too many managers are setting and meeting short-term, market-driven objectives instead of adopting the appropriate time-horizon needed to plan and execute the successful product innovations needed to sustain worldwide competitiveness.

The performance of the American manufacturing sector is often contrasted with progress achieved by other industrialized countries—particularly Japan. Japan's productivity growth in manufacturing has been nearly three times the U.S. rate over the past two decades—the average annual growth rate between 1960 and 1978 was 7.8 percent. In the last five years alone, the productivity

Reprinted by permission of the publisher, from Organizational Dynamics, *Spring 1981.* © 1981 *by American Management Association, New York. All rights reserved.*

index has increased by more than 40 percent and most economists forecast similar rates for the 1980s. Such impressive results deserve careful examination.

Students of the Japanese economy generally point out that Japanese investment outlays as a proportion of gross national product are nearly twice as large as those in the United States, and this factor is backed by a high personal savings ratio and the availability of relatively cheap investment funds. Also, a massive infusion of imported technology contributed significantly to the growth of productivity in Japan. Among noneconomic factors, the Japanese political environment seems to support business needs, especially those of advanced industries. In addition, the "unique" psychological and cultural characteristics of the Japanese people is frequently cited as the key reason for Japan's success.

It is indeed a well-known fact that absenteeism in most Japanese companies is low; turnover rates are about half the U.S. figures, and employee commitment to the company is generally high. But although cultural factors are important in any context, we doubt that any peculiarities of Japanese people (if they exist) have much impact on their commitment or productivity. In fact, several recent research studies indicate that Japanese and American workers show little or no difference in the personality attributes related to performance. Rather, we join Robert Hayes and William Abernathy in believing that, in this context, productivity stems from the superior management systems of many Japanese firms. But the focus of our analysis is not on such areas as corporate marketing and production strategies. Instead, we will examine management practices in Japan as they affect one key company asset: human resources.

Our analysis is guided by our experience with subsidiaries of Japanese firms in the United States. Typically, these companies are staffed by a small group of Japanese managers with varying levels of autonomy relative to the company's parent. The rest of the employees are American. Although they operate in an alien culture, many of these subsidiaries are surprisingly successful. While it is often very difficult to measure the performance of newly established operations, it is no secret that production lines in several Japanese subsidiaries operate at the same productivity rate as those in Japan (for example, the Sony plant in San Diego).

This example—as well as others—serves to demonstrate that what works in Japan can often work in the United States. The techniques used by the management of Japanese subsidiaries to motivate their American workers seem to play an important part in the effort to increase productivity. Therefore, a careful examination of management practices in Japan is useful not only for a specialist interested in cross-cultural organization development, but also for the management practitioner who is losing to foreign competition even on his or her home ground. What is it that the Japanese do better?

Our discussion attempts to answer this question by presenting a model of the Japanese management system that rests on a few elements that can be examined in different cultural settings. The model will be used to highlight the relationship between the management strategies and techniques observed in Japan and positive work outcomes, such as commitment and productivity. Our review is not intended to be exhaustive, but rather to suggest the feasibility of integrating findings from Japan with more general concepts and theories. We will therefore focus on relationships that may be verified by observations of behavior in non-Japanese, especially U.S., settings.

We propose that positive work outcomes emanate from a complex set of behavioral patterns that are not limited to any specific culture. The emphasis is on management practices as a system and on the integration of various strategies and techniques to achieve desired results. We hope thus to provide an alternative to statements—often cited but never empirically supported— that the high commitment and productivity of Japanese employees is primarily traceable to their cultural characteristics.

A Management System Focused on Human Resources

Most managers will probably agree that management's key concern is the optimal utilization of a firm's various assets. These assets may vary—financial, technological, human, and so on. Tradeoffs are necessary because utilization of any one asset may result in underutilization of another. We propose that in most Japanese companies, *human assets are considered to be the firm's most important and profitable assets in the long run.* Although the phrase itself sounds familiar, even hollow, to many American managers and OD consultants, it is important to recognize that this management orientation is backed up by a well-integrated system of strategies and techniques that translate this abstract concept into reality.

First, long-term and secure employment is provided, which attracts employees of the desired quality and induces them to remain with the firm. Second, a company philosophy is articulated that shows concern for employee needs and stresses cooperation and teamwork in a unique environment. Third, close attention is given both to hiring people who will fit well with the particular company's values and to integrating employees into the company at all stages of their working life. These general strategies are expressed in specific management techniques. Emphasis is placed on continuous development of employee skills; formal promotion is of secondary importance, at least during the early career stages. Employees are evaluated on a multitude of criteria—often including group performance results—rather than on individual bottom-line contribution. The work is structured in such a way that it may be carried out by groups operating with a great deal of autonomy. Open communication is encouraged, supported, and rewarded. Information about pending decisions is circulated to all concerned before the decisions are actually made. Active observable concern for each and every employee is expressed by supervisory personnel (Figure 1). Each of these management practices, either alone or in combination with the others, is known to have a positive influence on commitment to the organization and its effectiveness.

We will discuss these practices as we have observed them in large and medium-size firms in Japan and in several of their subsidiaries in the United

States. Although similar practices are often also in evidence in small Japanese companies, the long-term employment policies in these firms are more vulnerable to drops in economic activity and the system's impact is necessarily limited.

Strategies

Once management adopts the view that utilizing human assets is what matters most in the organization's success, several strategies have to be pursued to secure these assets in the desired quality and quantity. These strategies involve the following:

Provide Secure Employment   Although Japanese companies typically provide stable and long-term employment, many smaller firms find it difficult to do so in times of recession. The policy calls for hiring relatively unskilled employees (often directly from high schools or universities), training them on the job, promoting from within, and recognizing seniority.

The implicit guarantee of the employee's job, under all but the most severe economic circumstances, is a marked departure from conventional managerial thinking about the need to retain flexibility in workforce size in order to respond efficiently to cyclical variations in demand. However, this employment system, at least as practiced in large corporations in Japan, is far from being inflexible. Several techniques can be applied to ride out recession with a minimum burden of labor cost while keeping a maximum number of regular workers on the jobs—a freeze on new hiring, solicitation of voluntary retirement sweetened by extra benefits, use of core employees to replace temporaries and subcontractors doing nonessential work, and so forth. Thus a labor force cut of approximately 10–15 percent in a short time period is not an unusual phenomenon. In addition, across-the-board salary and bonus cuts for all employees, including management, would follow if necessary.

Japanese managers believe that job security has a positive impact on morale and productivity, limits turnover and training costs, and increases the organization's cohesiveness. For that reason, they are willing to accept its temporary negative effect in a period of reduced demand. Long-term employment security is also characteristic of all the U.S. subsidiaries that we have visited. Layoffs and terminations occur extremely rarely. For example, the Kikkoman Company instituted across-the-board wage cuts in an attempt to preserve employment during the last recession. Murata instituted a four-day workweek, and at Matsushita's Quasar plant, a number of employees were shifted from their regular work to functions such as repairs, maintenance, and service. It should be noted that there are several well-known U.S. corporations—for example, IBM and Hewlett-Packard—that follow similar practices when the alternative would be layoff.

In Japanese companies, even poor performers are either retrained or transferred, instead of simply being dismissed. The plant manager in an electronics

---

FIGURE 1   JAPANESE MANAGEMENT PARADIGM

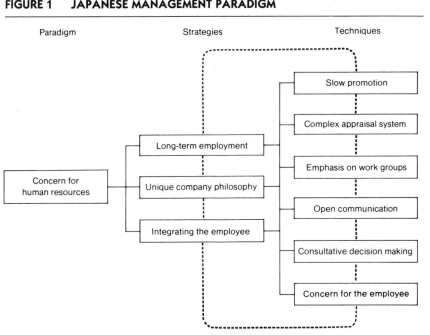

---

component factory explained how the company copes with personal failures: "We give a chance to improve even if there has been a big mistake. For example, the quality control manager didn't fit, so we transferred him to sales engineering and now he is doing fine."

Research on behavior in organizations suggests that the assumptions of Japanese managers and some of their U.S. colleagues about the positive impact of job security are, at least to some degree, justified. It has been shown that long tenure is positively associated with commitment to the organization, which in turn reduces turnover. High commitment in conjunction with a binding choice (employees of large firms in Japan have difficulty finding jobs of the same quality elsewhere, given the relatively stable labor market) also leads to high satisfaction, but whether this contributes to high productivity still remains to be proved. It is, however, necessary to view the policy of secure employment as a key condition for the implementation of other management strategies and techniques that have a more immediate impact on the organization's effectiveness.

Articulate a Unique Company Philosophy   A philosophy that is both articulated and carried through presents a clear picture of the organization's objectives, norms, and values—and thus helps transform commitment into productive effort. Familiarity with organizational goals gives direction to employees' actions, sets constraints on their behavior, and enhances their motivation. The understanding of shared meanings and beliefs expressed in the company philosophy binds the individual to the organization and, at the same time, stimulates the emergence of goals shared with others, as well as the stories, myths, and symbols that form the fabric of a company philosophy. William Ouchi and Raymond Price suggest that an organizational philosophy is an elegant informational device that provides a form of control at once pervasive and effective; at the same time it provides guidance for managers by presenting a basic theory of how the firm should be managed.

An explicit management philosophy of how work should be done can be found in many successful corporations in both Japan and the United States; examples in the United States include IBM, Texas Instruments, and U.S. Homes. Nevertheless, it is fair to say that the typical Japanese firm's management philosophy has a distinct flavor. It usually puts a heavy emphasis on cooperation and teamwork within a corporate "family" that is unique and distinct from that of any other firm. In return for an employee's effort, the family's commitment to the employee is translated into company determination to avoid layoffs and to provide a whole range of supplementary welfare benefits for the employee and his or her family. Naturally, without reasonable employment security, the fostering of team spirit and cooperation would be impossible. The ideal is thus to reconcile two objectives: pursuit of profits and perpetuation of the company as a group.

In a number of cases, a particular management philosophy that originated within the parent company in Japan is also being actively disseminated in its U.S. subsidiaries. Typically, claims of uniqueness range from the extent of the company's concern for employees' worklives to the quality of service to the customer. We quote from the in-house literature issued by one of the fastest growing Japanese-owned electronics component makers in California:

Management Philosophy
Our goal is to strive toward both the material and the spiritual fulfillment of all employees in the Company, and through this successful fulfillment, serve mankind in its progress and prosperity.

Management Policy
[. . .] Our purpose is to fully satisfy the needs of our customers and in return gain a just profit for ourselves. We are a family united in common bonds and singular goals. One of these bonds is the respect and support we feel for our fellow family co-workers.

Integrate Employees into the Company   The benefits of an articulated company philosophy are lost, however, if it's not visibly supported by management's behavior. A primary function of the company's socialization effort, therefore, is to ensure that employees have understood the philosophy and seen it in action. Close attention is given to hiring people who are willing to endorse the values of the particular company and to the employees' integration into the organization at all stages of their working life. The development of cohesiveness within the firm, based on the acceptance of goals and values, is a major focus of personnel policies in many Japanese firms.

Because employees are expected to remain in the company for a major part of their careers, careful selection is necessary to ensure that they fit well into the company climate. In many U.S.-based Japanese firms also, new hires at all levels are carefully screened with this aspect in mind. As in Japan, basic criteria for hiring are moderate views and a harmonious personality, and for that reason a large proportion of new hires come from employee referrals. In general, "virgin" workforces are preferred, since they can readily be assimilated into each company's unique environment as a community.

The intensive socialization process starts with the hiring decision and the initial training program and continues in various forms thereafter. Over time, the employee internalizes the various values and objectives of the firm, becomes increasingly committed to them, and learns the formal and informal rules and procedures, particularly through job rotation. That process usually includes two related types of job transfers. First, employees are transferred to new positions to learn additional skills in on-the-job training programs. These job changes are planned well in advance for all regular employees, including blue-collar workers. Second, transfers are part of a long-range experience-building program through which the organization develops its future managers; such programs involve movement across departmental boundaries at any stage of an employee's career.

While employees rotate semilaterally from job to job, they become increasingly socialized into the organization, immersed in the company philosophy and culture, and bound to a set of shared goals. Even in the absence of specific internal regulations that might be too constraining in a rapidly changing environment, a well-socialized manager who has held positions in various functions and locations within the firm has a feel for the organization's needs.

Techniques

The basic management orientation and strategies that we have just discussed are closely interrelated with specific management techniques used in Japanese firms and in their subsidiaries in the United States. The whole system is composed of a set of interdependent employment practices in which the presence of one technique complements as well as influences the effectiveness of others. This interdependence, rather than a simple cause-effect relationship, is the key factor that helps maintain the organization's stability and effectiveness. Additional environmental variables may determine which of the strategies or techniques will require most attention from top management, but in their impact on the organization no single technique listed below is of prime importance.

Slow Promotion, Job Rotation, and Internal Training   All Japanese subsidiaries that we have visited have seniority-based promotion systems. At one of them, a medium-size motorcycle plant, a seniority-based promotion system has been reinstituted after an experiment with a merit-based system proved highly unpopular with employees. Training is conducted, as expected, mostly on the job, and as one textile company executive noted, career paths are flexible: "You can get involved in what you want to do." Hiring from outside into upper-level positions is rare. According to another Japanese plant manager: "We want someone who understands the management system of the company. We want to keep the employees with us; we want to keep them happy."

Although promotion is slow, early informal identification of the elite is not unusual and carefully planned lateral job transfers add substantial flexibility to job assignments. Not all jobs are equally central to the workflow in an organization, so employees—even those with the same status and salary—can be rewarded or punished by providing or withholding positions in which they could acquire the skills needed for future promotions.

Job-rotation in U.S.-based Japanese firms seems less planned or structured than in Japan and more an ad-hoc reaction to organizational needs—but in general, the emphasis on slow promotion and job rotation creates an environment in which an employee becomes a generalist rather than a specialist in a particular functional area. For the most part, however, these general skills are unique to the organization. Several of the Japanese manufacturers that invested in the United States were forced to simplify their product technology because they were not able to recruit qualified operators versatile enough to meet their needs, and there was not enough time to train them internally.

In Japan, well-planned job rotation is the key to the success of an in-company training program that generally encompasses all the firm's employees. For some categories of highly skilled blue-collar workers training plans for a period of up to ten years are not unusual. Off-the-job training is often included, again for managers and nonmanagers alike. However, whether such an extensive training system will be transferred to U.S. subsidiaries remains to be seen.

In addition to its impact on promotion and training, job rotation also promotes the development of informal communication networks that help in coordinating work activities across functional areas and in resolving problems speedily. This aspect of job rotation is especially important for managerial personnel. Finally, timely job rotation relieves an employee who has become unresponsive to, or bored with, the demands of his or her job.

Some observers argue that deferred promotion may frustrate highly promising, ambitious employees. However, the personnel director of a major trading company has commented: "The secret of Japanese management, if there is any, is to make everybody feel as long as possible that he is slated for the top position in the firm—thereby increasing his motivation during the most productive period of his employment." The public identification of "losers," who of course far outnumber "winners" in any hierarchical organization, is postponed in the belief that the increased output of the losers, who are striving hard to do well and still hoping to beat the odds, more than compensates for any lags in the motivation of the impatient winners. By contrast, top management in many American organizations is preoccupied with identifying rising stars as soon as possible and is less concerned about the impact on the losers' morale.

Complex Appraisal System   In addition to emphasizing the long-term perspective, Japanese companies often establish a complex appraisal system that includes not only individual performance measures tied to the bottom line, but also measures of various desirable personality traits and behaviors—such as creativity, emotional maturity, and cooperation with others as well as team performance results. In most such companies, potential, personality, and behavior, rather than current output, are the key criteria, yet the difference is often merely symbolic. Output measures may easily be "translated" into such attributes as leadership skills, technical competence, relations with others, and judgment. This approach avoids making the employee feel that the bottom line, which may be beyond his or her control, in part or in whole, is the key dimension of evaluation. Occasional mistakes, particularly those made by lower-level employees, are considered part of the learning process.

At the same time, evaluations do clearly discriminate among employees because each employee is compared with other members of an appropriate group (in age and status) and ranked accordingly. The ranking within the cohort is generally not disclosed to the employees, but of course it can be partially inferred from small salary differentials and a comparison of job assignments. At least in theory, the slow promotion system should allow for careful judgments to be made even on such subjective criteria as the personality traits of honesty and seriousness. However, the authors' observations suggest that ranking within the cohort is usually established rather early in one's career and is generally not very flexible thereafter.

Employees are not formally separated according to their ability until later in their tenure; ambitious workers who seek immediate recognition must engage in activities that will get them noticed. Bottom-line performance is not an adequate criterion because, as noted, it is not the only focus of managerial evaluation. This situation encourages easily observable behavior, such as voluntary overtime, that appears to demonstrate willingness to exert substantial effort on the organization's behalf. The evaluation process becomes to a large degree self-selective.

Several other facets of this kind of appraisal system deserve our attention. Because evaluations are based on managerial observations during frequent, regular interactions with subordinates, the cost of such an evaluation system is relatively low. When behavior rather than bottom-line performance is the focus of evaluation, means as well as ends may be assessed. This very likely leads to a better match between the direction of employee efforts and company objectives, and it encourages a long-term perspective. Finally, since group performance is also a focus of evaluation, peer pressure on an employee to contribute his or her share to the group's performance becomes an important mechanism of performance control. Long tenure, friendship ties, and informal communication networks enable both superiors and peers to get a very clear sense of the employee's performance and potential relative to others.

Among the management techniques characteristic of large Japanese enterprises, the introduction of a complex appraisal system is probably the least visible in their U.S. subsidiaries. Most of their U.S.-based affiliates are relatively young; thus long-term evaluation of employees, the key point in personnel appraisal as practiced in Japan, is not yet practicable. Furthermore, the different expectations of American workers and managers about what constitutes a fair and equitable appraisal system might hinder acceptance of the parent company's evaluation system.

Emphasis on Work Groups   Acknowledging the enormous impact of groups on their members—both directly, through the enforcement of norms, and indirectly, by affecting the beliefs and values of members—Japanese organizations devote far greater attention to structural factors that enhance group motivation and cooperation than to the motivation of individual employees. Tasks are assigned to groups, not to individual employees, and group cohesion is stimulated by delegating responsibility to the group not only for getting the tasks performed but also for designing the way in which they get performed. The group-based performance evaluation has already been discussed.

Similarly, in the U.S.-based Japanese firms that we have visited, the group rather than an individual forms the basic work unit for all practical purposes. Quality of work and speed of job execution are key concerns in group production meetings that are held at least monthly, and even daily in some companies. The design function, however, is not yet very well developed; many workers are still relative newcomers unfamiliar with all aspects of the advanced technology. Intergroup rivalry is also encouraged. In one capacitor company, a group on a shift that performs well consistently is rewarded regularly. Sometimes news of a highly productive group from another shift or even from the Japanese parent is passed around the shop floor to stimulate the competition.

In Japan, group autonomy is encouraged by avoiding any reliance on experts to solve operational problems. One widely used group-based technique for dealing with such problems is quality control (QC) circles. A QC circle's major task is to pinpoint and solve a particular workshop's problem. Outside experts are called in only to educate group members in the analytical tools for problem solving or to provide a specialized technical service. Otherwise, the team working on the problem operates autonomously, with additional emphasis on self-improvement activities that will help achieve group goals. Fostering motivation through direct employee participation in the work process design is a major consideration in the introduction of QC circles and similar activities to the factory floor.

Nevertheless, work-group autonomy in most work settings is bound by clearly defined limits, with the company carefully coordinating team activities by controlling the training and evaluation of members, the size of the team, and the scope and amount of production. Yet within these limits, teamwork is not only part of a company's articulated philosophy, it actually forms the basic fabric of the work process. Job rotation is encouraged both to develop each employee's skills and to fit the work group's needs.

From another perspective, the group can also assist in developing job-relevant knowledge by direct instruction and by serving as a model of appropriate behavior. The results of empirical studies suggest that structuring tasks around work groups not only may improve performance, but also may contribute to increased esteem and a sense of identity among group members. Furthermore, this process of translating organizational membership into membership in a small group seems, in general, to result in higher job satisfaction, lower absenteeism, lower turnover rates, and fewer labor disputes.

Open and Extensive Communication   Even in the Japanese-owned U.S. companies, plant managers typically spend at least two hours a day on the shop floor and are readily available for the rest of the day. Often, foremen are deliberately deprived of offices so they can be with their subordinates on the floor throughout the whole day, instructing and helping whenever necessary. The same policy applies to personnel specialists. The American personnel manager of a Japanese motorcycle plant, for example, spends between two and four hours a day on the shop floor discussing issues that concern employees. The large number of employees he is able to greet by their first name testifies to the amount of time he spends on the floor. "We have an open-door policy—but it's their door, not management's" was his explanation of the company's emphasis on the quality of face-to-face vertical communication.

Open communication is also inherent in the Japanese work setting. Open work spaces are crowded with individuals at different hierarchical levels. Even high-ranking office managers seldom have separate private offices. Partitions, cubicles, and small side rooms are used to set off special areas for conferences with visitors or small discussions among the staff. In one Japanese-owned TV plant on the West Coast, the top manager's office is next to the receptionist—open and visible to everybody who walks into the building, whether employee, supplier, or customer.

Open communication is not limited to vertical exchanges. Both the emphasis on team spirit in work groups and the network of friendships that employees develop during their long tenure in the organization encourage the extensive face-to-face communication so often reported in studies involving Japanese companies. Moreover, job rotation is instrumental in building informal lateral networks across departmental boundaries. Without these networks, the transfer of much job-related information would be impossible. These informal networks are not included in written work manuals, thus they are invisible to a newcomer; but their use as a legitimate tool to get things done is implicitly authorized by the formal control system. Communication skills and related behavior are often the focus of yearly evaluations. Frequently, foreign observers put too much emphasis on vertical ties and other hierarchical aspects of Japanese organizations. In fact, the ability to manage lateral communication is perhaps even more important to effective performance, particularly at the middle-management level.

Consultative Decision Making   Few Japanese management practices are so misunderstood by outsiders as is the decision-making process. The image is quite entrenched in Western literature on Japanese organizations: Scores of managers huddle together in endless discussion until consensus on every detail is reached, after which a symbolic document, "ringi," is passed around so they can affix their seals of approval on it. This image negates the considerable degree of decentralization for most types of decisions that is characteristic in most subsidiaries we have visited. In fact, when time is short, decisions are routinely made by the manager in charge.

Under the usual procedure for top-management decision making, a proposal is initiated by a middle manager (but often under the directive of top management). This middle manager engages in informal discussion and consultation with peers and supervisors. When all are familiar with the proposal, a formal request for a decision is made and, because of earlier discussions, is almost inevitably ratified—often in a ceremonial group meeting or through the "ringi" procedure. This implies not unanimous approval, but the unanimous consent to its implementation.

This kind of decision making is not participative in the Western sense of the word, which encompasses negotiation and bargaining between a manager and subordinates. In the Japanese context, negotiations are primarily lateral between the departments concerned with the decision. Within the work group, the emphasis is on including all group members in the process of decision making, not on achieving consensus on the alternatives. Opposing parties are willing to go along, with the consolation that their viewpoint may carry the day the next time around.

However, the manager will usually not implement his or her decision "until others who will be affected have had sufficient time to offer their views, feel that they have been fairly heard, and are willing to support the decision even though they may not feel that it is the best one," according to Thomas P. Rohlen. Those outside the core of the decision-making group merely express their acknowledgement of the proposed course of action. They do not participate; they do not feel ownership of the decision. On the other hand, the early communication of the proposed changes helps reduce uncertainty in the organization. In addition, prior information on upcoming decisions gives employees an opportunity to rationalize and accept the outcomes.

Japanese managers we have interviewed often expressed the opinion that it is their American partners who insist on examining every aspect and contingency of proposed alternatives, while they themselves prefer a relatively general agreement on the direction to follow, leaving the details to be solved on the run. Accordingly, the refinement of a proposal occurs during its early implementation stage.

Although the level of face-to-face communication in Japanese organizations is relatively high, it should not be confused with participation in decision making. Most communication concerns routine tasks; thus it is not surprising that research on Japanese companies indicates no relationship between the extent of face-to-face communication and employees' perceptions of how much they participate in decision making.

Moreover, consultation with lower-ranking employees does not automatically imply that the decision process is "bottom up," as suggested by Peter Drucker and others. Especially in the case of long-term planning and strategy, the initiative comes mostly from the top. Furthermore, consultative decision making does not diminish top management's responsibility for a decision's consequences. Although the ambiguities of status and centrality may make it difficult for outsiders to pinpoint responsibility, it is actually quite clear within the organization. Heads still roll to pay for mistakes, albeit in a somewhat more subtle manner than is customary in Western organizations: Departure to the second- or third-ranking subsidiary is the most common punishment.

Concern for the Employee   It is established practice for managers to spend a lot of time talking to employees about everyday matters. Thus they develop a feeling for employees' personal needs and problems, as well as for their performance. Obviously, gaining this intimate knowledge of each employee is easier when an employee has long tenure, but managers do consciously attempt to get to know their employees, and they place a premium on providing time to talk. The quality of relationships developed with subordinates is also an important factor on which a manager is evaluated.

Various company-sponsored cultural, athletic, and other recreational activities further deepen involvement in employees' lives. This heavy schedule of company social affairs is ostensibly voluntary, but virtually all employees participate. Typically, an annual calendar of office events might include two overnight trips, monthly Saturday afternoon recreation, and an average of six office parties—all at company expense. A great deal of drinking goes on at these events and much good fellowship is expressed among the employees.

Finally, in Japan the company allocates substantial financial resources to pay for benefits for all employees, such as a family allowance and various commuting and housing allowances. In addition, many firms provide a whole range of welfare services ranging from subsidized company housing for families and dormitories for unmarried employees, through company nurseries and company scholarships for employees' children, to mortgage loans, credit facilities, savings plans, and insurance. Thus employees often perceive a close relationship between their own welfare and the company's financial welfare. Accordingly, behavior for the company's benefit that may appear self-sacrificing is not at all so; rather, it is in the employee's own interest.

Managers in the U.S.-based companies generally also voiced a desire to make life in the company a pleasant experience for their subordinates. As in Japan, managers at all levels show concern for employees by sponsoring various recreational activities or even taking them out to dinner to talk problems over. Again, continuous open communication gets special emphasis. However, company benefits are not as extensive as in Japan because of a feeling that

American employees prefer rewards in the form of salary rather than the "golden handcuff" of benefits. Furthermore, the comprehensive government welfare system in the United States apparently renders such extensive company benefits superfluous.

In summary, what we observed in many Japanese companies is an integrated system of management strategies and techniques that reinforce one another because of systemic management orientation to the quality of human resources. In addition to this system's behavioral consequences, which we have already discussed, a number of other positive outcomes have also been reported in research studies on Japanese organizations.

For example, when the company offers desirable employment conditions designed to provide job security and reduce voluntary turnover, the company benefits not only from the increased loyalty of the workforce, but also from a reduction in hiring, training, and other costs associated with turnover and replacement. Because employees enjoy job security, they do not fear technical innovation and may, in fact, welcome it—especially if it relieves them of tedious or exhausting manual tasks. In such an atmosphere, concern for long-term growth, rather than a focus on immediate profits, is also expected to flourish.

An articulated philosophy that expresses the company's family atmosphere as well as its uniqueness enables the employee to justify loyalty to the company and stimulates healthy competition with other companies. The management goals symbolized in company philosophy can give clear guidance to the employee who's trying to make the best decision in a situation that is uncertain.

Careful attention to selection and the employee's fit into the company results in a homogeneous workforce, easily able to develop the friendship ties that form the basis of information networks. The lack of conflict among functional divisions and the ability to communicate informally across divisions allow for rapid interdivisional coordination and the rapid implementation of various company goals and policies.

The other techniques we've outlined reinforce these positive outcomes. Slow promotion reinforces a long-range perspective. High earnings in this quarter need not earn an employee an immediate promotion. Less reliance on the bottom line means that an employee's capabilities and behaviors over the long term become more important in their evaluations. Groups are another vehicle by which the company's goals, norms, and values are communicated to each employee. Open communication is the most visible vehicle for demonstrating concern for employees and willingness to benefit from their experience, regardless of rank. Open communication is thus a key technique that supports consultative decision making and affects the quality of any implementation process. Finally, caring about employees' social needs encourages identification with the firm and limits the impact of personal troubles on performance.

What we have described is a system based on the understanding that in return for the employee's contribution to company growth and well-being, the profitable firm will provide a stable and secure work environment and protect the individual employee's welfare even during a period of economic slowdown.

The Transferability of Japanese Management Practices

As in Japan, a key managerial concern in all U.S.-based Japanese companies we have investigated was the quality of human resources. As one executive put it, "We adapt the organization to the people because you can't adapt people to the organization." A number of specific instances of how Japanese management techniques are being applied in the United States were previously cited. Most personnel policies we've observed were similar to those in Japan, although evaluation systems and job-rotation planning are still somewhat different, probably because of the youth of the subsidiary companies. Less institutionalized concern for employee welfare was also pointed out.

The experience of many Japanese firms that have established U.S. subsidiaries suggests that the U.S. workers are receptive to many management practices introduced by Japanese managers. During our interviews, many Japanese executives pointed out that the productivity level in their U.S. plants is on a level similar to that in Japan—and occasionally even higher. Other research data indicate that American workers in Japanese-owned plants are even more satisfied with their work conditions than are their Japanese or Japanese-American colleagues.

The relative success of U.S.-based Japanese companies in transferring their employment and management practices to cover the great majority of their U.S. workers is not surprising when we consider that a number of large U.S. corporations have created management systems that use some typical Japanese techniques. Several of these firms have an outstanding record of innovation and rapid growth. A few examples are Procter & Gamble, Hewlett-Packard, and Cummins Engine.

William Ouchi and his colleagues call these firms Theory Z organizations. Seven key characteristics of Theory Z organizations are the following:

1. Long-term employment.

2. Slow evaluation and promotion.

3. Moderately specialized careers.

4. Consensual decision making.

5. Individual responsibility.

6. Implicit, informal control (but with explicit measures).

7. Wholistic concern for the employee.

The Theory Z organization shares several features with the Japanese organization, but there are differences: In the former, responsibility is definitely individual, measures of performance are explicit, and careers are actually moderately specialized. However, Ouchi tells us little about communication patterns in these organizations, the role of the work group, and some other features important in Japanese settings.

Here's an example of a standard practice in the Theory Z organization that Ouchi studied in depth:

> [The Theory Z organization] calculated the profitability of each of its divisions, but it did not operate a strict profit center or other marketlike mechanism. Rather, decisions were frequently made by division managers who were guided by broader corporate concerns, even though their own divisional earnings may have suffered as a result.

A survey by Ouchi and Jerry Johnson showed that within the electronics industry perceived corporate prestige, managerial ability, and reported corporate earnings were all strongly positively correlated with the "Z-ness" of the organization.

It is also significant that examples of successful implementation of the Japanese system can be found even in Britain, a country notorious for labor-management conflict. In our interpretation, good labor-management relations—even the emergence of a so-called company union—is an effect, rather than a cause, of the mutually beneficial, reciprocal relationship enjoyed by the employees and the firm. Thus we see the coexistence of our management paradigm with productivity in companies in Japan, in Japanese companies in the United States and Europe, and in a number of indigenous U.S. companies. Although correlation does not imply cause, such a causal connection would be well supported by psychological theories. Douglas McGregor summarizes a great deal of research in saying: "Effective performance results when conditions are created such that the members of the organization can achieve their own goals best by directing their efforts toward the success of the enterprise."

Conclusion

Many cultural differences exist, of course, between people in Japan and those in Western countries. However, this should not distract our attention from the fact that human beings in all countries also have a great deal in common. In the workplace, all people value decent treatment, security, and an opportunity for emotional fulfillment. It is to the credit of Japanese managers that they have developed organizational systems that, even though far from perfect, do respond to these needs to a great extent. Also to their credit is the fact that high motivation and productivity result at the same time.

These strategies and techniques we have reviewed constitute a remarkably well-integrated system. The management practices are highly congruent with the way in which tasks are structured, with individual members' goals, and with the organization's climate. Such a fit is expected to result in a high degree of organizational effectiveness or productivity. We believe that the management paradigm of concern for human resources blends the hopes of humanistic thinkers with the pragmatism of those who need to show a return on investment. The evidence strongly suggests that this paradigm is both desirable and feasible in Western countries and that the key elements of Japanese management practices are not unique to Japan and can be successfully transplanted to other cultures. The linkage between human needs and productivity is nothing new in Western management theory. It required the Japanese, however, to translate the idea into a successful reality.

Acknowledgments

The authors would like to thank Mitsuyo Hanada, Blair McDonald, William Newman, William Ouchi, Thomas Roehl, Michael Tushman, and others for their helpful comments on earlier drafts of this paper. We are grateful to Citibank, New York, and the Japan Foundation, Tokyo, for their financial support of the work in the preparation of this paper.

Selected Bibliography

Robert Hayes and William Abernathy brought the lack of U.S. innovation to public attention in their article, "Managing Our Way to Economic Decline" (*Harvard Business Review,* July–August 1980).

Thomas P. Rohlen's book, *For Harmony and Strength: Japanese White-Collar Organization in Anthropological Perspective* (University of California Press, 1974), is a captivating description of the Japanese management system as seen in a regional bank. Peter Drucker has written several articles on the system, including "What We Can Learn from Japanese Management" (*Harvard Business Review,* March–April 1971). His thoughts are extended to the United States by the empirical work of Richard Pascale, "Employment Practices and Employee Attitudes: A Study of Japanese and American Managed Firms in the U.S." (*Human Relations,* July 1978).

For further information on the Theory Z organization see "Type Z Organization: Stability in the Midst of Mobility" by William Ouchi and Alfred Jaeger (*Academy of Management Review,* April 1978), "Types of Organizational Control and Their Relationship to Emotional Well-Being" by William Ouchi and Jerry Johnson (*Administrative Science Quarterly,* Spring 1978), and "Hierarchies, Clans, and Theory Z: A New Perspective on Organization Development" by William Ouchi and Raymond Price (*Organizational Dynamics,* Autumn 1978).

Douglas McGregor explains the importance of a fit between employee and organizational goals in *The Human Side of Enterprise* (McGraw-Hill, 1960).

Leadership and Social Influence Processes

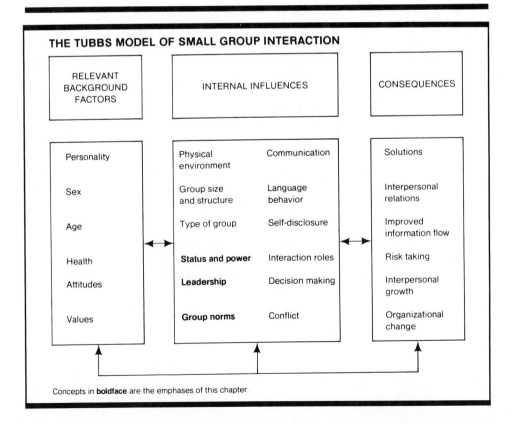

THE TUBBS MODEL OF SMALL GROUP INTERACTION

RELEVANT BACKGROUND FACTORS	INTERNAL INFLUENCES		CONSEQUENCES
Personality	Physical environment	Communication	Solutions
Sex	Group size and structure	Language behavior	Interpersonal relations
Age	Type of group	Self-disclosure	Improved information flow
Health	**Status and power**	Interaction roles	Risk taking
Attitudes	**Leadership**	Decision making	Interpersonal growth
Values	**Group norms**	Conflict	Organizational change

Concepts in **boldface** are the emphases of this chapter.

Chapter 4 covers quite extensively three more of the internal influences in the Tubbs Model of Small Group Interaction. These influences are status and power, leadership, and group norms. There are two types of status, ascribed and attained. There are five types of power (i.e., reward, legitimate, referent, expert, and coercive). The chapter also contains information on leadership and the several different perspectives on how a leader is developed. Three perspectives are the trait theory, the circumstances theory, and the function theory. Situational leadership is also discussed. Followership styles are discussed briefly, because every successful leader has followers. The last subject in Chapter 4 is conformity and the processes of social influence.

GLOSSARY

Ascribed Status: Ascribed status is the prestige that goes to a person by virtue of his or her birth.

Attained Status: Attained status is the prestige that goes to a person on the merits of his or her own individual accomplishments.

Reward Power: Reward power is the power an individual has to give or withhold rewards.

Legitimate Power: Legitimate power is the influence we allow others, such as our bosses, to have over us on the basis of their positions.

Referent Power: Referent power is based on identification with the source of power, that is, having admiration for someone.

Expert Power: Expert power is our acceptance of influence from those whose expertise we respect.

Coercive Power: Coercive power is the power an individual has to give or withhold punishment.

Followership Styles: Followership styles are behavioral tendencies people have toward authority figures (e.g., obedient versus rebellious).

Groupthink: Groupthink refers to the tendency for group members to share common assumptions; it frequently leads to mistakes.

CASE STUDY: Department 8101

Background Information

Department 8101, where I was employed, was considered one of the top areas to work in Plant Eight. Its personnel consisted of twelve light classification people, all with relatively high seniority, and seven general classification people, all with relatively low seniority. Also, the department had two job setters with fifteen or more years of seniority. This department was a cohesive and sound working unit. It had the distinction of being the top-producing department in the division—a proven money-maker with good to excellent personnel.

The Key Players

Hank—Supervisor of 8101 until July 1. Hank is sixty-two years old and had been a member of management for over twenty-five years. Hank had been supervisor of 8101 for the past six years. Hank's management philosophy can best be described as laissez-faire. "As long as the job gets done" were Hank's favorite words. Hank was well liked by all his subordinates and was a close drinking buddy of both the job setters.

Terry—Junior Job Setter. Terry had fifteen years' seniority, the last five in Department 8101. Terry can best be described as a little scrapper who didn't take guff from anyone. Terry is one hell of a worker who knew his job inside and out and would perform it well if left alone. Terry distrusted almost every manager but Hank. His first words after hearing of Hank's impending retirement were, "We're going to have to break the S.O.B. (the new manager) in quick so he doesn't get any weird ideas."

Denny—Senior Job Setter. Denny had seventeen years' seniority, the last eight in Department 8101. Denny had been and continues to be a powerful force in the local labor union. Former plant committeeman, Denny is respected by peers and managers alike. Quiet but extremely perceptive and smart, Denny is without question the informal leader of this department. Hank had given Denny unlimited discretion in making decisions concerning the line. As stated, he is respected by everyone in the department, but in particular, by Terry and Helen.

Helen—Relief Woman. Thirty years' seniority, the last fifteen in Department 8101. Extremely nice woman as long as you agreed with her; if you didn't—watch out! Helen worked hand in hand with Denny in the day-to-day operations of Department 8101. Helen had only one bias— she disliked female managers. Told me once that the company started going downhill when it began hiring female supervisors.

Me—job title, General. Two years' seniority. Still wet behind the ears and overwhelmed by everything that takes place in a factory. I was twenty years old and back for my second summer in Department 8101 after an educational leave. I watched people and did my job. Best learning experience I ever had.

Group Expectations

Thirty-minute lunch rather than twenty-four-minute lunch.
Two thirty-minute breaks rather than two twenty-three-minute breaks.
Fifteen-minute wash-up period at the end of the shift rather than five minutes.

Minimal supervision.
Allowing worker discretion on the job.
No busy work should be handed out.
No hassle for missing an occasional day now and then.

Group Standards

While on the job, every worker would perform to the utmost of his or her capabilities.

Horseplay and slacking off were dealt with by the group, as were abusers of the tardiness and absenteeism policies.

Training of new members was carried out by the group. Time and care were taken when breaking in these new workers. They were not left alone until they performed the job right.

High attention was given to quality.

Finally, this was a tight-knit group that liked being known as the top-producing department. Therefore, if a person failed to work within these standards, they were ignored and maybe even asked to leave.

As one can see by looking at Department 8101, training, discipline, and even determining how the work was to be performed were carried out by the group. The only thing the supervisor really had to do was to make sure the department had the materials to perform the work. The rest, the group would take care of.

What was needed, after Hank, was a manager who could work within the system. What we got was Rita.

The Case

On Friday, Hank retired.

On Monday, Rita arrived and was introduced to each one of us by the first-shift supervisor. As I shook her hand, I looked into her eyes to try to get a reading on her—to see if she really was the person we had all heard about through the grapevine the last two weeks.

Through Denny and his connections, we learned that Rita was a former Marine sergeant, forty-eight years old, who had just recently retired from the military. She had hired into the company as a supervisor and had spent the last six months as a fill-in supervisor. The word was she followed the book to the letter. If this were true, based on my experiences in Department 8101, I knew our department would be in for a long, hot summer.

The first-shift supervisor stayed over four hours every night, and the third-shift supervisor came in four hours early every night for the first week. Rita observed and listened to them but made no effort at all to talk to the workers. She was, from the start, aloof.

On Monday morning of week two, Rita called for a meeting to take place during our first break. During this meeting, Rita said she had observed a few things in our department that she didn't quite like. Terry immediately shot me an "I told you so" glance. Rita continued and discussed the things she didn't like and felt had to be changed. "Due to the fact we are losing one-half hour a night in production time, this department will return to a twenty-four-minute lunch break, a twenty-three-minute break period, and a five-minute wash-up period at the end of the shift."

Rita went on to say that the lackadaisical view given to tardiness and absenteeism would not continue. She stated that if you were tardy you would not be given your regular job. If you came in and if you were absent without an excuse, you could expect to be written up (with a reprimand).

Further, Rita said she would like to generate more flexibility into the department and would like to begin job rotation on an experimental basis beginning the following week. She concluded the meeting by saying she looked forward to working with us and that she hoped the department could be even more productive than in the past. I couldn't wait for our twenty-four-minute lunch period at the corner bar to see the reaction.

Terry: Who the hell made her a supervisor? She's nuts! We've got to get rid of her—she's a power-crazy dyke. (These were some of the nicer things Terry was saying about our new supervisor.)

Helen: That's the way all women supervisors are—bossy! They have to go around proving who's boss. She has no business being a supervisor any more than I do.

Denny (Interjecting a calmer voice): She's new and inexperienced. Let's give her a little time and see if she settles down and wises up.

After a little more bickering, the group agreed with Denny. Rita would be given a chance to wise up before any "radical" measures were taken.

However, as the days and weeks passed, Rita was not wising up. She began applying the pressure harder and harder to do things her way. People were getting written up right and left for tardiness, absenteeism, coming back late from lunches and breaks, etc. Jim, a popular person in the work group, got a one-day suspension when he and Rita got into a heated argument over packing labels. Helen was put on notice for failure to clean up her work area. Terry was written up for drinking, tardiness, almost anything Rita could nail him with.

In addition to this, Rita started taking on more and more changeovers for our shift and wouldn't tell Denny and Terry about it until the last minute. For unlike Hank, Rita wouldn't let Terry and Denny see the intershift report to find out the day's activities. They were told what to do just like everybody else. Rita was in command, and she wanted everybody to know it, especially Denny.

All of this activity took place during the course of July. By August, I knew that a major explosion along the lines of Hiroshima would take place within our department soon.

Around the middle of August it happened. Terry got drunk during lunch and came back to work in a surly mood. Rita walked over to him and Denny and said that we were going to be changing over at eight o'clock. Terry looked her straight in the eye and said, "I'm not doing a damn thing." Rita then gave Terry a direct order. Terry promptly told Rita what to do with her direct order, and Rita suspended him on the spot. By this time the argument had heated up enough that everybody was watching the action. Denny stepped in to try to cool the argument down, but Rita told him to "Stay out of this, Denny. This is between me and Terry." I could see the anger in Denny. Terry grabbed his coat and made his way over to a neutral area to await a union committeeman. Rita then looked at Denny and simply said someone would be over to help him change over.

That night in the bar the war council took place. Terry just sat there muttering how he wished Rita was a guy so he could punch her. Denny led the discussion, and a consensus formed quickly that Rita had to go—and fast. But how? Ideas were kicked back and forth, and finally Denny decided that as a whole the group had to screw up all over the place. Mistake on top of mistake. It was to be a group sabotage of the entire department. Denny then asked the group if they were united in this plan of action. One by one, each member of the group nodded "yes," until it got to me.

I worked eight hours a day with these people, and I had grown to like many of them. I knew that if I didn't agree to this, I would no longer be a member of the group. I was stuck, and I knew it. I shook my head "yes," knowing that I would assist only in a limited way. The actions were to begin immediately.

By the end of August, Rita was a basket case; she looked much older than her forty-eight years. Rita had lost control, and she knew it, as did everyone else. Every day our department went down for one reason or another, and our production numbers reflected this as they kept getting worse and worse. Quietly, unceremoniously, Rita was removed as supervisor of 8101 just before Labor Day. A victory party took place at the bar the night we learned Rita would no longer be our supervisor. We had won. Rita not only ended up leaving our department, she ended up leaving the company.

1. What mistakes do you think Rita made as a leader in this case?

2. What, specifically, would you have done differently if you had been Rita?

In this case study we see a problem that is not unique to a manufacturing department. The problem has to do with being able to develop effective leadership behaviors. Each of us from time to time will be called upon to act in the role of a group leader. For some, the role may seem comfortable; others will have to work hard to grow into it. In any case, leadership is a topic that seems to capture the interest of most students of small group interaction.

An indication of the times is revealed in the story that if a Martian spaceman were to land on Earth and demand, "Take me to your leader," we would not know where to take him. No subject in the small group literature has received more attention than leadership. As members of an achievement-oriented society, Americans are almost obsessed with the topic of leadership. We build and destroy heroes like so many clay pigeons. In a recent article, Zaleznik (1990) responded to what he felt was a desperate need in education to recognize qualities of good leadership rather than train students to be managers. Professional managers, Zaleznik argues, carry a bag of tools that can coordinate and control. However, a good leader, with good ideas and exciting directions, can generate enthusiasm, support, and cohesion in a group or organization. Compare this orientation to that of the Japanese, whose ancient proverbs include the saying, "A nail that protrudes is hammered down," and among whom the idea of standing out above one's peers is considered in poor taste. This chapter will examine the process of personal influence and its various ramifications. We begin with a discussion of power and status, then move to the ever-popular topic of leadership, and conclude with an analysis of the uses and abuses of social influence.

STATUS AND POWER

Most farmers who have raised poultry are familiar with the chickens' pecking at one another in an attempt to determine which animal dominates. The eventual result is that one chicken rises to the dominant position, a second chicken dominates all others but the top chicken, the third chicken dominates all but the top two, and so on down the line. This order of dominance is generally referred to as the *pecking order,* and when a new chicken is introduced to the barnyard, it must fight all the others to establish its position in the pecking order.

Pecking orders are also found in human interaction. Most often they are informal and adhered to almost unconsciously. They may also be formalized, as in an organization chart. An example of such a pecking order in the United States government is referred to as the "order of precedence"; it formally designates who precedes whom in the pecking order (or in order of importance as they might be officially introduced to a visiting dignitary or head of state). James Symington (1971, pp. 94–95) remarked that, as Chief of Protocol, "It was always a humbling reminder to read over this list" (since he was at the bottom).

Table of Precedence

The President of the United States

The Vice-President of the United States

The Speaker of the House of Representatives

The Chief Justice of the United States

Former Presidents of the United States

The Secretary of State

The Secretary-General of the United Nations

Ambassadors of Foreign Powers—individually ranked by order of date of presentation of credentials

Widows of former Presidents of the United States

United States Representative to the United Nations

Ministers of Foreign Powers (Chiefs of Diplomatic Missions)

Associate Justices of the Supreme Court of the United States and Retired Associate Justices

The Cabinet

    The Secretary of the Treasury

    The Secretary of Defense

    The Attorney General

    The Postmaster General

The Secretary of the Interior

The Secretary of Agriculture

The Secretary of Commerce

The Secretary of Labor

The Secretary of Health, Education and Welfare

The Secretary of Housing and Urban Development

The Secretary of Transportation

The Senate

Governors of States (unless the function in question occurs in a Governor's own State, in which he ranks after the Vice-President)

Former Vice-Presidents of the United States

The House of Representatives

Charges d'affaires of Foreign Powers

The Under Secretaries of the Executive Departments and the Deputy Secretaries

Administrator, Agency for International Development

Director, United States Arms Control and Disarmament Agency

Secretaries of the Army, the Navy, and the Air Force

Director, Office of Management and Budget

Chairman, Council of Economic Advisers

Chairman, Board of Governors, Federal Reserve

Chairman, Joint Chiefs of Staff

Chiefs of Staff of the Army, the Navy, and the Air Force (ranked according to date of appointment)

Commandant of the Marine Corps

(5-Star) Generals of the Army and Fleet Admirals

The Secretary-General, Organization of American States

Representatives of the Organization of American States

Director, Central Intelligence Agency

Administrator, General Services Administration

Director, United States Information Agency

Administrator, National Aeronautics and Space Administration

Administrator, Federal Aviation Administration

Chairman, Civil Service Commission

Chairman, the Atomic Energy Commission

Director, Defense Research and Engineering

Director, Office of Emergency Planning

Director, the Peace Corps

Director, Office of Economic Opportunity

Special Assistants to the President

Deputy Under Secretaries

Assistant Secretaries of the Executive Departments

United States Chief of Protocol

Types of Status

Status is defined as one's position or rank relative to the others in a group. High status tends to result in greater personal power or ability to influence others. Increased power, in turn, tends to elevate an individual's status level. Power and status tend to go hand in hand, reciprocally influencing one another.

Think of the many ongoing groups you have joined. They often have an established pecking order into which you must insert yourself. How does this pecking order come about in the first place? *Ascribed status* refers to the prestige that goes to a person by virtue of some characteristic such as his or her family wealth, good looks, or age. One man who attended an Ivy League school remarked that it was a bit awesome to be in classes with the children of *the* Rockefellers, *the* Firestones, *the* Kennedys. Those born into such families are likely to have high status even though as individuals they have done nothing to earn it.

But what about the many occasions in which a new group forms and there is no established pecking order? How does one get established? What are the effects once it has been set up? Those who rise to positions of status on the basis of the merits of their own individual accomplishments acquire what is called *attained status*. The United States is known as one country in which the Horatio Alger story can still occur—where the person from humble origins can still rise from one socioeconomic class to a higher one more easily than in many other countries.

What kinds of behaviors enable a person to acquire a position of attained status? Goldhamer and Shils (1939) hypothesized that power and status is a function of the ratio of the number of successful power acts to the number of attempts to influence:

$$\frac{Number\ of\ successful\ power\ acts}{Number\ of\ attempts\ made} = power\ and\ status$$

One student stated: "The impact of this ratio dawned on me during our fraternity's officer elections. One brother tried many times, all unsuccessful, for a variety of positions. He is a good worker, so that was not his problem. His problem was that within the fraternity he did not have any status. The number of attempts made was many, but the number of successful acts was zero. His status fell further with each new failure."

The effects of social status are not limited to an individual's reactions to other people. An individual's status can influence his or her own behavior, as well. This is particularly true in group interaction. In a 1989 study, Jemmott and Gonzalez randomly assigned high-status ("boss") and low-status ("helper") labels to grade school children. These children were randomly assigned to small groups, where only one child in the group was assigned a status level different from the other children. For instance, there would be four bosses with one helper or four helpers with one boss.

As was expected, children who were assigned a high-status label performed significantly higher on tasks than children assigned a low-status label. Moreover, Jemmott and Gonzalez found some interesting interactions among the variously labeled children. The performance of children with low status was even lower if they were alone in their group. The performance of children with high-status labels was either unaffected or further enhanced by the absence of other common-status children.

Jemmott and Gonzalez (1989) attribute their findings to the effects of *tokenism,* which is when one member of a group is of very different status from other members of the group. Group members will tend to minimize the differences among themselves and emphasize the differences from the token member.

Jemmott and Gonzalez (1989) discuss tokenism in light of what has been described as "chronic status," a status that people have at all times. Gender, race, and religious affiliation are all examples of chronic status. One interesting case of tokenism and chronic status occurred when a young man was hired into the corporate office of a company run primarily by women. He became the "token male" and was ostracized by his fellow employees. As in the Jemmott and Gonzalez study, he was not as successful—most likely because he was assigned a label of low status and he was alone in his group.

Obviously, the success rate and relative status of any individual will vary from group to group. Most of us find that we have a relatively higher status level in high school than we achieve when we attend college. This is usually because colleges and universities draw from a much larger population than most high schools, and the competition gets tougher as the size of the population increases.

Types of Power

Although each of us has encountered situations in which people have power over one another, we may not have been very systematic in identifying the types of sources of that power. French and Raven (1959) identified five different types of power that can be brought to bear in groups. They classify them as (1) reward power, (2) coercive power, (3) legitimate power, (4) referent power, and (5) expert power.

Reward power refers to the ability an individual has to give or withhold rewards. A company executive obviously has this type of power, which can take the form of financial rewards through raises and promotions as well as of social rewards such as recognition and compliments or praise. *Coercive power* is the opposite of reward power in that it utilizes punishment rather than reward. A supervisor can reprimand, discipline, and even fire an employee who does not live up to certain behavioral standards. An IBM employee was once sent home when he showed up for work without a tie. Most companies reserve the right to set what they believe to be appropriate standards for employees' dress. Coercive power is sometimes used to enforce these standards.

Legitimate power is defined as the influence we allow others to have over us on the basis of the value we place on certain of their characteristics. For example, we feel that it is legitimate for a judge to determine a sentence in a court case or for a supervisor to determine work schedules or assignments. A person who is elected to office is felt to have a legitimate right to exercise the power of that office. Of course, this right may be abused, and the official may be removed from office.

Referent power is extremely potent, because it is based on the person's identification with the source of power. If you had a teacher you really admired, you would do many things (such as studying hard or putting off social activities) to accomplish things that would bring approval or praise from that teacher. Ringwald et al. (1971, p. 47) studied different types of college students and found that one type (which they called cluster four students) was especially prone to identify with the professor and to be the "model student" in the eyes of the professor. These students were described as "self-confident, interested, involved; tend to identify with [the] teacher and see him as a colleague. Older than average [mostly upperclassmen]." Although Ringwald et al. studied only undergraduates, this description would also apply to a large segment of graduate students.

Expert power refers to our acceptance of influence from those whose expertise we respect. We accept the advice of lawyers in legal matters, of physicians in medical matters, or of others whom we perceive as having credibility on a given topic. In a group discussion concerning the dangers of heroin addiction, the speakers who had the most expert power of persuasion were the former addicts who told tragic stories of how heroin had destroyed parts of their lives.

Yates (1985, p. 123) makes an interesting point about power when he writes:

> Thus, a fundamental shortcoming of organizational behaviorists . . . is that they tend to ignore or underemphasize the importance of power relationships and differing authority roles in the group process. If a decision making group is, in reality, a small representative body comprising a variety of broader interests and institutional claims and statuses, it will function as a group, as a microcosm of larger forces and conflicts, in the organization. To that extent, to treat individual relations in the group as the essential stuff of decision making risks missing the forest for the trees.

In other words, we need to be aware not only of the power relationships that exist within a group context but also of those that grow out of the group and that act as an entity in the larger organizational context.

Kotter (1986, p. 129) offers some practical advice on how to build a power base for those starting out in their careers. He writes:

> [You could ask yourself,] over the past twelve months, how much have I really learned about the products or services, the markets, the technologies, and the people with whom I deal?

In the past year, how many people have I gotten to know at work? How many people have I strengthened or improved my relationship with? Have I alienated anyone? Is my reputation as good or better than it was a year ago? If not, why not?

As we think in terms of status and power, we might want to keep in mind that the different types of power usually overlap. A person may be in a position to use reward power as well as coercive power but may prefer to rely on referent power, legitimate power, or expert power. In any event, there are different types of power that can be used (and abused).

If we assume that different group members have different levels of status and power, what effect does this fact have on the interaction in the group? Cartwright and Zander (1968, p. 415) state that if you were to observe a company board meeting, you would be able to differentiate between a lower-status person (the junior executive) and the vice-president by the following differences in their behavior:

> The man whom you believe to be the junior executive addresses the majority of his remarks to the man you believe to be the vice-president. Moreover, he chooses his words with care in order that he not seem to imply any criticism of the other man or appear inadequate. He listens carefully to what the vice-president has to say and is usually ready to see the reasonableness of the arguments made by him. He is friendly toward the boss, ready to tell a joke or talk about his family, and to copy some of the older man's mannerisms.
>
> In contrast, the vice-president talks pretty much to the entire group. He freely offers information, advice, and even criticism to others. He seldom makes critical remarks about himself. Nor is he nearly so ready as the younger man to listen to statements made by the rest of the group. He is more likely to defend his own position than to see the value in the points made by the staff. And on the whole he is less inclined to idle talk than is the junior executive.
>
> You may come away from the meeting feeling that the two men acted the way they did because they had quite different personalities, and you would undoubtedly be correct—in part. If, however, you were to see the junior executive in a meeting with *his* staff in which he is now the boss, you would probably be surprised to see how differently he behaves. Now it is likely that you would find the young man acting toward others in a way very similar to that shown by the vice-president in the earlier meeting.

The scene described above is one example of the *results* of differences in status or power. We also know that information directed toward high-status persons tends to be "whitewashed" in that it is more often positive than negative.

Another application of power in groups is the use of the group itself by a higher authority to develop support for decisions. Pfeffer (1981, pp. 175–176) writes:

> Given that committees are established to legitimate decisions and provide outlets for the expression of various interest, the important aspect of committees in organizational politics is not their function as much as their very existence. It is the process of cooptation, the process of interest representation, and the process of meeting and conferring which is critical in providing acceptance and legitimacy of decisions. These processual aspects may be as important as the substance of the decisions actually reached.

Thus the very process of involving groups in making decisions may increase the boss's power to have those decisions implemented.

It also has been found that comments in small groups tend to be directed more often (by direction of eye contact) to higher-status group members than to those of lower status. If you quickly want to determine the high-status members of any group, just notice to whom people direct their comments. Thibaut and Kelley (1986) found this phenomenon in an experimental study and hypothesized that this type of upward communication acts as a substitute for a member's own upward mobility in the group's pecking order. Thus, if we can't be football stars or sorority presidents, we can at least try to become friends with them.

Finally, high status results in a group's being willing to tolerate deviation on the part of a group member. Highly successful people are notoriously idiosyncratic. It has been suggested that a person who is idiosyncratic but not successful is simply considered weird. Albert Einstein and Thomas Edison both were considered eccentric, yet their eccentricities were tolerated because of the magnitude of their contributions. Most groups will tolerate deviations from those who are highly valued in the group. One rule of thumb is that new members are not allowed to deviate nearly as much as those who are old-timers. This is true among college faculty members, in companies, in government agencies, and even in prisons. We discuss deviation and conformity pressure further later in this chapter.

LEADERSHIP

Definitions of leadership are numerous, but we like that of Tannenbaum, Wechsler, and Massarik (1961), who define leadership as:

> Interpersonal influence, exercised in [a certain] situation and directed, through a communication process, toward the attainment of a specified goal or goals. Leadership always involves attempts on the part of a leader (influencer) to affect (influence) the behavior of a follower (influencee) or followers in [a certain] situation.

Gardiner (1990, p. 10), in his excellent book on leadership, adds the following insight to the definition: "when I use the word *leader,* I am in fact referring to the leadership team. No individual has all the skills—and certainly not the time—to carry out all the complex tasks of contemporary leadership." With these two definitions in mind, let us examine what people have historically thought about leadership.

Historic Trends

During the eighteenth and nineteenth centuries, philosophers argued the relative merits of two viewpoints regarding leadership. These were the trait, or "great man," theory and the circumstances theory. Although we have come a long way in our study of leadership, it is still interesting to go back and examine the evolution of the different approaches.

Trait Theory   Leaders are born, not made

Trait theory grew out of the idea that leaders are born, not made. Examples from history could include Alexander the Great, Corazone Aquino, John F. Kennedy, and George Bush. The assumption was that certain physical traits or personality traits enable a person to be a leader.

The physical traits associated with leadership were height, weight, and physical attractiveness and body shape. In our culture, taller people are sometimes associated with higher status, and vice versa. In one study (Wilson 1968) a speaker named Mr. England was introduced to each of five different college classes by a different title:

- Class 1—a student from Cambridge

- Class 2—a demonstrator in psychology from Cambridge

- Class 3—a lecturer in psychology from Cambridge

- Class 4—Dr. England, senior lecturer from Cambridge

- Class 5—Professor England from Cambridge

When students were asked to estimate the speaker's height, the average estimate increased from Class 1 to Class 5. In other words, the more prestigious England's title, the taller the students thought he was. A study at the University of Pennsylvania showed that height in inches correlated more closely with a graduate's starting salary after graduation than any other index (such as grade-point average, number of extracurricular activities, parents' education level). Although correlation does not prove causality, it is still interesting to see the anecdotal evidence supporting the belief that height is viewed positively. As one student aptly put it, "I would define a leader as someone I can look up to, both figuratively and literally."

A more recent study (Bradley-Steck 1987) surveyed 1200 M.B.A. graduates of the University of Pittsburgh. The researchers found a combination of height and weight predicted starting salary. For example,

> The average salary of those surveyed was $43,000, but a typical six foot professional earned $4,200 more than his 5 foot 5 counterpart. If the taller man was trim and the shorter man fat, the difference translated to about $8,200. . . . Height and weight weren't as important factors among women. It was hypothesized that middle of the road (height and weight) for women was preferred. Men's heights seemed to be an advantage up to about 6-4. However, at 6-6 or 6-7 the height seemed to be a disadvantage. (p. A1)

What relationship might there be between weight and leadership? The heavier the better? No, actually the predicted relationship is curvilinear (see Figure 4.1). Thus, people who are too thin or too heavy would be considered either too weak and fragile or too self-indulgent and undisciplined to be good leaders. In one unpublished study conducted in a large company, employees were divided into groups, one whose members weighed within 10 percent of their "desirable" weight (based on a doctor's chart of height and weight) and one whose members deviated more than 10 percent above or below their charted body weight. The percentage of promotions was

**FIGURE 4.1   HYPOTHETICAL RELATIONSHIP BETWEEN
WEIGHT AND LEADERSHIP**

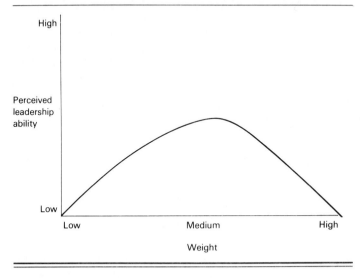

tabulated for the two groups, and it was found that the medium-weight group had more promotions.

In a study conducted by a Madison Avenue employment agency with branches in forty-three American cities, it was found that overweight persons may be losing as much as $1,000 a year for every pound of fat. According to the agency's president, Robert Hall (1974), the survey showed that among executives in the $25,000–50,000 salary group, only 9 percent were more than 10 pounds overweight. In the $10,000–20,000 group, only 39 percent were more than 10 pounds overweight (according to the standards established by life insurance companies). Hall said that the overweight "are unfairly stereotyped as slow, sloppy, inefficient, and overindulgent. When important, high-paying jobs are at stake and candidates are under close scrutiny, the overweight are less likely to be hired or promoted into them." Hall also stated that companies frequently specify their preference for slim candidates, but only once in twenty-five years did a company request a plump executive; the company was a manufacturer of oversized clothing.

Closely related to body weight is body type. Sheldon (1940, 1942, 1954) identified three different body types, or *somatotypes.* The very thin person is called an *ectomorph,* the very heavy and soft person an *endomorph,* and the medium weight, muscular type is the *mesomorph.* Intuitively, we might expect leaders to come from the mesomorphic body type. Although there are no studies to support or refute this prediction, it is a provocative theory that might someday be tested. For example, those who are successful in political campaigns and in movie careers seem to be more often than not mesomorphic. We also know from several research studies that more attractive people are perceived as having higher credibility (for example, higher expertise and better character) on the basis of their looks alone (Mills and Aronson 1965; Widgery and Webster 1969; Widgery 1974).

In addition to physical traits, certain personality traits were thought to be associated with leadership. A list of some of these traits includes self-confidence, dominance, enthusiasm, assertiveness, responsibility, creativity, originality, dependability, critical thinking ability, intelligence, and ability to communicate effectively. Although all these traits have some commonsense appeal, Bird (1940) and Stogdill (1948) surveyed over 200 leadership studies and found that out of all the identified traits, only 5 percent were common to four or more of the studies surveyed. In a recent update, however, Stogdill (1974, p. 93) has had somewhat greater success in securing a level of agreement among leadership trait studies. His results appear in Figure 4.2.

FIGURE 4.2 FACTORS APPEARING IN THREE OR MORE STUDIES

Reprinted with permission of The Free Press, a Division of Macmillan, Inc. from *Stogdill's Handbook of Leadership,* rev. ed., by Bernard M. Bass. Copyright © 1974, 1981 by The Free Press.

Factor No.	Factor Name	Frequency
1	Social and interpersonal skills	16
2	Technical skills	18
3	Administrative skills	12
4	Leadership effectiveness and achievement	15
5	Social nearness, friendliness	18
6	Intellectual skills	11
7	Maintaining cohesive work group	9
8	Maintaining coordination and teamwork	7
9	Task motivation and application	17
10	General impression (halo)	12
11	Group task supportiveness	17
12	Maintaining standards of performance	5
13	Willingness to assume responsibility	10
14	Emotional balance and control	15
15	Informal group control	4
16	Nurturant behavior	4
17	Ethical conduct, personal integrity	10
18	Communication, verbality	6
19	Ascendance, dominance, decisiveness	11
20	Physical energy	6
21	Experience and activity	4
22	Mature, cultured	3
23	Courage, daring	4
24	Aloof, distant	3
25	Creative, independent	5
26	Conforming	5

In summarizing his latest thoughts on the trait theory, Stogdill (1974, p. 413) states:

> Although leaders differ from followers with respect to various aspects of personality, ability, and social skills, tests of such traits have been of limited value for selection of leaders. Traits do not act singly but in combination. . . . The leader who acquires leadership status in one group tends to emerge as leader when placed in other groups. Thus, perhaps the best prediction of future leadership is prior success in this role.

On the other side of the coin, Geier (1967) was able to identify five negative traits that consistently prevented group members from emerging as leaders. Such members were (1) uninformed about the problem being discussed, (2) nonparticipative, (3) extremely rigid in holding to pet ideas, (4) authoritarian in bossing others around, and (5) offensive and abusive in language style. Although the trait theory has not held as many answers as early philosophers and theorists had hoped, it has provided us with some helpful information and insight.

Bennis and Nanus (1985, pp. 223–224) interviewed ninety contemporary American leaders, from Ray Kroc, founder of McDonalds, to John H. Johnson, publisher of *Ebony,* to John Robinson, coach of the Los Angeles Rams. They concluded:

> Myth 3. Leaders are Charismatic. Some are, most aren't. Among the ninety there were a few—but damned few—who probably correspond to our fantasies of some "divine inspiration," that "grace under stress" we associated with J.F.K. or the beguiling capacity to spellbind for which we remember Churchill. Our leaders were all "too human"; they were short and tall, articulate and inarticulate, dressed for success and dressed for failure, and there was virtually nothing in terms of physical appearance, personality, or style that set them apart from their followers. Our guess is that it operates in the other direction; that is, charisma is the result of effective leadership, not the other way around, and that those who are good at it are granted a certain amount of respect and even awe by their followers, which increases the bond of attraction between them.

They summarize their research this way: "Managers do things right, leaders do the right thing."

Circumstances Theory —Leader in one area but not necessarily in another Circumstance makes the Leader

Ira Hayes was an American Indian who became famous for having been one of the United States Marines who lifted the American flag after the battle of Iwo Jima in the South Pacific during World War II. Ira Hayes just happened to be standing nearby when the photographer solicited a group to pose for the picture that later became world-famous. Ira instantly became a national hero and was sent on cross-country United States Savings Bond drives to raise money for the American war effort. Ira's pride made him feel so guilty for being a "counterfeit hero" that he began to drink. He eventually died an alcoholic.

Ira Hayes is the classic example of a person being at the right place at the right (or wrong) time. This is sometimes called the *circumstances theory of leadership.* Another facet of this theory is that a person may be an effective leader in one circumstance but perform poorly in a different circumstance. Therefore, some theorists would argue that the circumstances make the leader. A good example of this is the student/faculty softball, football, or basketball teams that are found on some campuses. Although the professors are usually the leaders in the classroom (because of a relatively higher level of expertise in the subject), the students are usually the leaders on the athletic field, where they often know more about the game and are almost always in better physical shape than the professors.

Like trait theory, circumstances theory seems to have some validity. However, there are many exceptions to the rule. Charles Percy was president of Bell and Howell Corporation at age 30 and has also functioned effectively as a United States senator. Robert McNamara functioned well as president of Ford Motor Company, United States Secretary of Defense, and head of the World Bank organization. George Schultz and John Glenn are two more individuals who have succeeded in numerous capacities in and out of government. Circumstances theory, although somewhat valid, leaves something to be desired in explaining the complex phenomenon of leadership.

Function Theory   *Leaders are made, not born*

A theory that deviates rather dramatically from the first two is function theory. Underlying this theory is the notion that leaders are made, not born. That is, leadership consists of certain behaviors or *functions* that groups must have performed. These functions are identifiable behaviors that can be learned by anybody. We can all improve our potential as leaders by learning to perform these key functions more effectively. Although trait and circumstance theories assume there is little we can do to become leaders if we aren't a certain height or if we never seem to be in the right place at the right time, function theory offers hope for those of us who may not have been born Kennedys or Rockefellers or who are not asked to be in famous photographs.

The two important functions that have been consistently identified are referred to by a variety of terms, but are basically the same concepts. They are (1) task orientation and (2) people orientation. The terms used to describe these concepts are summarized in Figure 4.3.

Wood, Phillips, and Pedersen (1986, p. 80) summarize the literature on this point by writing:

> Designated leaders perform a variety of important functions. They provide liaison with groups or other individuals in the surrounding environment, they furnish a central point of responsibility, which is especially significant in organizational settings that demand clear lines of accountability; they represent a central point when there are problems, changes in plans, complications, and so on. Without one person who assumes responsibility for these functions, a group may factionalize, become chaotic, or operate inadequately.

Penley and Hawkins (1985, p. 82) measured interpersonal communication between supervisors and subordinates. They conclude:

> The results emphasize the need to focus attention on leaders' communication, including their relational messages.

FIGURE 4.3   SUMMARY OF COMPARABLE TERMS FOR LEADERSHIP FUNCTIONS

	Task Orientation	People Orientation
Bales 1950	Task	Social-emotional
Halpin and Winer 1957	Initiating structure	Consideration
Cartwright and Zander 1968	Goal achievement	Group achievement

Much of the research concerning communication and leadership has focused primarily upon the communication behavior of the effective supervisor (Jablin, 1979) rather than upon communication as the observable behavior of leadership. Earlier, Redding (1972) summarized this research. He stated that effective supervisors (1) were more communication-oriented than the ineffective leader and enjoyed speaking up, (2) tended to be receptive and responsive to subordinate inquiries, (3) tended to ask or persuade rather than to tell and (4) gave advance notice of changes and explained the why of things—that is, were more open.

This study contributes one description of supervisor-subordinate communications that is characteristic of attributed leadership qualities. Subordinates perceive that supervisors who show consideration communicate more task and career messages and are more responsive in their communication.

A negative example is provided by Bennis and Nanus (1985), who write about Jimmy Carter's leadership style. They quote one of his loyal cabinet officers, who said: "Working for him was like looking at the wrong side of a tapestry—blurry and indistinct" (pp. 36–37).

With function theory, the emphasis has shifted away from the leader as a person and toward the specific behavioral acts that facilitate group success. Leadership may be "possessed" by any group member who performs these leadership functions. The task-oriented behaviors are those directed toward the group's accomplishing its goal. The people-oriented behaviors are directed toward the maintenance of the interpersonal relationships in the group. It is assumed that people-oriented activities ought to have an indirect effect on helping accomplish the group's task. An analogy would be that of a machine. The machine operates to accomplish a task (producing parts). However, if the machine is not cleaned and lubricated, it will break down sooner or later, thus halting its productivity. Similarly, although task-oriented groups may require a leader who can help them accomplish their goal, they may cease functioning if they become too bogged down in personality conflicts or counterproductive interpersonal friction. Both task-oriented and people-oriented behaviors are required to enable a group to progress. Bales, in Figure 4.4, offers a summary of the twelve types of specific behavioral acts (six task-oriented, six people-oriented) and the average percentage of the interaction in any given group discussion that would probably fall into each category. Ross summarizes the work of Bales and

FIGURE 4.4

Adapted from *Personality and Interpersonal Behavior* by Robert F. Bales. Copyright © 1970 by Holt, Rinehart & Winston, Inc. Reprinted by permission of Holt, Rinehart & Winston, Inc.

	Category	Percentage	Estimated Norms
People-oriented (positive)	1. Seems friendly	3.5	2.6– 4.8
	2. Dramatizes	7.0	5.7– 7.4
	3. Agrees	18.5	8.0–13.6
Task-oriented	4. Gives suggestions	3.8	3.0– 7.0
	5. Gives opinions	24.5	15.0–22.7
	6. Gives information	8.3	20.7–31.2
	7. Asks for information	10.3	4.0– 7.2
	8. Asks for opinions	12.5	2.0– 3.9
	9. Asks for suggestions	2.3	0.6– 1.4
People-oriented (negative)	10. Disagrees	1.0	3.1– 5.3
	11. Shows tension	7.8	3.4– 6.0
	12. Seems unfriendly	0.5	2.4– 4.4
		Total: 100.0	

others in an extended model of the twelve Bales Interaction Process Analysis (IPA) categories (Figure 4.5).

The function theory of leadership seems to hold the most promise for teaching most of us how to improve our own leadership abilities. For example, many students hesitate to participate in discussions for fear of "saying something stupid." Yet several research studies indicate that simply participating at all is one primary requirement of becoming more of a leader (Morris and Hackman 1969; Hayes and Meltzer 1972; Regula and Julian 1973). Other studies show that individuals who are able to perform both task- and people-oriented functions in groups are likely to get better results from their groups than those who are less effective in performing these two functions.

Effective leadership on the job emphasizes a high concern for people and a high concern for task in the workplace. Under such conditions the workplace becomes a "worthplace" (Karlins and Hargis 1988, p. 665). In a worthplace, production and quality of the product are high, and employee satisfaction is high. "Unfortunately a significant number of American managers persist in over-emphasizing 'task' concerns, while ignoring or downplaying the importance of 'people' concerns in the workplace" (Karlins and Hargis 1988, p. 665). In a report of a recent survey of large organizations (Karlins and Hargis 1988), managers' perceptions of their own leadership styles were found to be very different from their employees' perceptions. This investigation of fifty-two large organizations found that most managers (88%) perceived themselves as striking a balance between task and people concerns, with a high concern for both (9.9 on the Blake Mouton Grid). However, most subordinates (85%) reported that they worked for managers who emphasized a high concern for tasks and a low concern for people.

These skewed perceptions of leadership likely have a detrimental effect on management. When a leader of a group perceives himself or herself as being effective

FIGURE 4.5 INTERACTION PROCESS ANALYSIS, CATEGORIES OF COMMUNICATIVE ACTS

Based on Robert F. Bales, *Interaction Process Analysis*, Reading, Mass: Addison-Wesley, 1950, p. 9; A. Paul Hare, *Handbook of Small Group Research*, New York: Free Press of Glencoe, 1962, p.66; and Clovis R. Shepherd, *Small Groups: Some Sociological Perspectives*, San Francisco: Chandler, 1964, p. 30.

	Major Categories	Subcategories	Illustrative Statements or Behavior
Social emotional area	Positive reactions	1. Shows solidarity	Jokes, gives help, rewards others, is friendly
		2. Shows tension release	Laughs, shows satisfaction, is relieved
		3. Shows agreement	Passively accepts, understands, concurs, complies
Task area	Attempted answers	4. Gives suggestion	Directs, suggests, implies autonomy for others
		5. Gives opinion	Evaluates, analyzes, expresses feeling or wish
		6. Gives information	Orients, repeats, clarifies, confirms
	Questions	7. Asks for information	Requests orientation, repetition, confirmation
		8. Asks for opinion	Requests evaluation, analysis, expression of feeling
		9. Asks for suggestion	Requests direction, possible ways of action
Social emotional area	Negative reactions	10. Shows disagreement	Passively rejects, resorts to formality, withholds help
		11. Shows tension	Asks for help, withdraws, daydreams
		12. Shows antagonism	Deflates other's status, defends or asserts self, hostile

Key: a. Problems of communication b. Problems of evaluation c. Problems of control
     d. Problems of decision e. Problems of tension reduction f. Problems of reintegration

in meeting the needs of the group and the group members do not perceive the same, the system breaks down. In order to transform a workplace into a "worthplace," managers must learn to have more accurate perceptions of their leadership styles.

The final important implication to grow out of the function theory of leadership is that these functions need not be performed by the one person designated as group leader. In fact, the implication is the reverse. To the extent that all group members learn to perform these two functions, overall group leadership will be improved. This is often referred to as *shared* or *democratic* leadership, which we will examine in the next section.

Leadership Styles

A great deal of attention has been paid to the different types of available leadership styles since the early studies conducted by Kurt Lewin and his associates (Lewin, Lippitt, and White 1939; White and Lippitt 1968). The early studies identified three different styles: autocratic, democratic, and laissez-faire.

The issue in these three leadership styles is the degree and location of control. The authoritarian, or autocratic, leader has a high need to maintain control of the group himself or herself. Some might even say that the autocratic leader has an obsession for control. When this obsession reaches the extreme, it is manifested in the following types of behaviors (Sattler and Miller 1968, pp. 250–251):

1. The authoritarian leader usually plans to get to the conference room when everyone else is assembled. He fears getting to the meeting early, for he has no interest in carrying on nontask-related conversation. This does not mean that the leader is a latecomer—he isn't; if the meeting is scheduled to start at 3:10 p.m., you will be sure that the leader will be present and the meeting will start on the proper split second.

2. Often the leader will present an extended introduction to start a meeting, in part because he wishes others to know how well informed he is.

3. Sometimes the authoritarian will outline precise procedures on how the discussion is to be conducted. Thus, he might tell the group that Mr. A will comment on Item 1, B and C on Item 2, and D on Item 3. Such advice on procedure is not given in order to be helpful to others; largely, it seems, the authoritarian uses rules of order to make his own task easier.

4. Authoritarians, more than other leaders, specialize in questions directed to specific persons such as, "Jones, what are your facts . . . ?" . . . "Now I want to hear from Smith. . . ." Such leaders do not frequently use open or "overhead" questions that any person in the group may answer.

5. Authoritarians appear to be unable to withstand pauses in discussion—if such leaders cannot get rapid verbalization from others, they will themselves supply verbal noises.

6. The leader almost invariably maintains strict control over the order and sequence of topics; he appears to love placing group members in a "straitjacket" of restrictions.

7. The authoritarian leader interrupts others often, for at least three reasons: to correct errors whether major or insignificant, to keep persons talking about what he desires, and in general to show who is in command.

8. Clever authoritarians at times encourage group members to discuss irrelevant matters at considerable length. This is true, of course, only when to discuss the irrelevant is in keeping with the leader's designs.

9. When the leader clarifies contributions he is sometimes guilty of changing the intent of statements to make them more acceptable to himself. (Here, of course, we have both procedural and content control.)

The laissez-faire style of leadership goes to the opposite extreme. Not only is there no concern for control, but there is no direction, concern for task accomplishment, or concern for interpersonal relationships. The laissez-faire style is not really a style of leadership at all; it is nonleadership.

The democratic leadership style represents an attempt to find a reasonable compromise between the other two extremes. The leader does attempt to provide direction and to perform both task and social leadership functions, but at the same time he or she tries to avoid dominating the group with one person's views. Some would argue that no matter how hard an individual tries, some domination cannot be avoided.

Which leadership style is best? In order to answer this question, we must determine the criteria for judging effectiveness. Some criteria would include (1) the quality of the group output, (2) the time taken to accomplish the task, (3) the satisfaction of the group members, (4) the absenteeism of group members, and (5) the independence developed in group members. White and Lippitt (1968) reported (1) that the quality of group output in their study was better under democratic leadership, (2) that democratic leadership took more time than autocratic, (3) that member satisfaction was higher under democratic leadership (in fact, hostility was thirty times as great in the autocratic groups, and nineteen out of twenty preferred the democratic group to the autocratic), (4) that the democratic group had the lowest absenteeism, and (5) that the democratic group fostered more independence, whereas the autocratic style bred dependence and submissiveness among group members.

The democratic style got better results in each case except in time taken to accomplish the task. However, subsequent studies (Likert 1967) have shown that the autocratic leader gets fast results in the short run, but that these results may be of poor quality or may be resisted by others. The net effect is that the solution may not be enacted, and the problem will have to be dealt with again on future occasions. Because this amounts to less efficiency, the democratic style may even prove to be less time-consuming in the long run (see Chapter 7 for more on this). In addition, the hostility bred by autocratic leadership produces counterproductive results. For example, in industrial groups, absenteeism, grievances, work stoppages, and sabotage are all ways in which employees attempt to "get back" at what they consider to be harsh leadership. "Goldbricking" in the military is another typical example. An autocratic leadership style fosters group norms that say, "Do as little as possible to get by, and look busy when the boss is around. However, when the cat's away . . ."

Barrett and Carey (1989, p. 3) note, "History records that Abraham Lincoln sought input from his cabinet officers regarding the appointment of Ulysses S. Grant as Commander of the Grand Army of the Republic. When each cabinet member spoke against the appointment, Lincoln responded that the vote was seven nays and one aye—and that the ayes had it. Communication is important to the democratic leader because he or she relies so heavily on the input and support of group members. In an organization the leader has the ultimate responsibility of communicating the vision, or "strategy," of the company to those who run it. Barrett and Carey (1989) outlined a method for communicating business strategy for leaders that is primarily democratic in nature. After all, a strategy, no matter how eloquent, is successful only to the extent that it is effectively communicated to the whole group. The three-point strategy of communication includes: (1) communicating the strategy inside and outside of the business (to employees and consumers), (2) communicating in person (not by videotape or vicariously through other subordinates), and (3) telling the whole story (including all information that will be relevant to the success of the business). "The [leader of group] should enjoy telling and selling the strategy to the troops" (p. 3). It is this vision that leads the group, and the democratic leader cannot succeed without its understanding and support.

Group-centered leadership, or nondirective leadership, is a method that has grown out of the desire to develop more effective forms of democratic leadership. Haiman (1951, p. 40) wrote: "Probably the most important single concept that has emerged in the last twenty years from the ever growing wealth of psycho-therapeutic experience is the realization that the most effective way to direct the behavior of human beings is simply to help them direct themselves." Forty years later we can see that, if anything, Haiman's conclusion is even more relevant than it was when written.

Gordon (1955) outlined the philosophy of group-centered leadership in further detail. He criticized the long-held assumption that leadership involves functions that should be carried out by one person. We have already encountered this fallacy in the section on the functional theory. In addition, we have seen that the autocratic leadership style breeds dependence and submissiveness. The group-centered approach would be to allow each member to grow and develop whatever leadership skills he or she possesses. (See Figure 4.6.)

The group-centered, or nondirective, approach lends itself more to the social group or the unstructured encounter group than the work group or the task-oriented discussion group. However, certain aspects of the group-centered approach may be applied to any group situation.

The group-centered leadership philosophy is well summarized in the famous words of Lao-tzu:

FIGURE 4.6 TWO CONTRASTING APPROACHES TO LEADERSHIP IN SMALL GROUPS

Based on Thomas Gordon, *Group-Centered Leadership* (Boston: Houghton Mifflin, 1955), pp. 197–200.

Group-Centered	Leader-Guided
Principal Behaviors	
1. Allows group to diagnose its needs. Tries to facilitate communication in group during this process.	1. Finds out as much as possible about group's needs, in order to provide group with situation where it can get what it needs.
2. Allows group to plan its own experiences. Tries to facilitate communication during this process.	2. Plans specific learning situations and/or group experiences from which group may draw insights.
3. Avoids making decisions for group, except those which facilitate bringing members together initially.	3. Makes decisions for group when group seems too immature to make correct decisions.
4. Preparation involves doing things that will improve his own contributions to group.	4. Preparation involves doing things that will improve his own contribution and things that he feels group needs.
5. Tries to lose his special status position so that he can participate in decision making without having his contributions given special consideration by group.	5. Uses influence of his special status position in group to bring about decisions or to guide group in certain directions.
6. Leaves responsibility with each member for participating. Tries to facilitate group's developing a permissive and accepting atmosphere by being as permissive and accepting as he can.	6. Facilitates participation by subtle or direct methods of involving each member in group activities.
7. Sets limits in terms of his own ability to be accepting of group action.	7. Sets limits more in terms of what will be best for group.
8. Wants to contribute resources just like any other member of group. Tries to avoid being used by group as *only* or *chief* resource person.	8. Wants group members to use him as the special resource person, and generally lets himself be used by group in this way.
9. Tries to understand members' expressed wishes for him to behave in some particular role, but does not always feel compelled to do so.	9. Usually accedes to members' wishes that he play some particular role or else tries to convince them that another role is best.
10. Tries not to influence others to play some particular role.	10. Often influences or directly manipulates members to play some particular role.
11. Tries not to think beyond the level of expressed understanding of group members, feeling that only meaningful insights will be those arrived at by members themselves.	11. Often interprets group's behavior in order to give members understandings they might not acquire themselves.
12. Tries not to be perceived as "the leader," believing that, as long as he is so perceived, group members will not be completely free to be themselves and often will react to his contributions either submissively and uncritically or with hostility and resistance.	12. Tries to be perceived as "the leader," believing that he will thus be better able to control the situation to meet group's needs.
13. Takes no special responsibility for seeing that group evaluates its achievement or its progress.	13. Takes special responsibility to ensure that evaluative function is carried out in group.
14. Tries to lose his "official role" in order to be free to resist group's needs for dependence and to reduce his own anxiety about the outcome of group action.	14. Tries to reinforce his "official role" in order to have more influence on the group action.
15. Takes no special responsibility to reduce anxiety, to resolve tension, etc. Feels such elements are inevitable consequence of group interaction.	15. Takes special responsibility to reduce anxiety and to resolve tension. Feels such elements hinder group purposes and should be avoided.

Group Leadership Philosophy Summarized

A leader is best
When people barely know that he exists,
Not so good when people obey and acclaim him,
Worse when they despise him.
"Fail to honor people,
They fail to honor you";
But of a good leader who talks little,
When his work is done, his aim fulfilled,
They will say, "We did it ourselves."

In a two-year national study of college presidents, Fisher and Tack (1990) found that effective college presidents were very different from representative college presidents in many ways. In a recent article, Fisher and Tack outlined "Attributes of Effective College Presidents, and the special qualities of Effective College Presidents in Social Relationships." In their 1990 study, Fisher and Tack found that the most common attributes of effective college presidents include:

- Self-confidence and a positive outlook; tending to view problems as unrealized opportunities

- Tendency to work countless hours to achieve goals

- High level of confidence in those with whom they worked

- Willingness to take calculated risks, more so than other chief executives

- Strategic, thinking carefully about what they say and do

In particular, Fisher and Tack felt that the qualities of these college presidents reinforced the link between self-control and effectiveness in leadership.

In social relationships, effective college presidents relate to and think about others in a manner dramatically different from their representative counterparts. For instance, effective college presidents:

- Believe more strongly in gaining respect than in fostering popularity

- Are more inclined to encourage staff and faculty to take risks and to be creative

- Surround themselves with exceedingly able people who are futurists

- Actively solicit input from constituents and encourage faculty and staff to share ideas (no matter how diverse)

- Display a willingness to move against the mainstream

As an example of these qualities among effective college presidents, Fisher and Tack cite the willingness of these people to support merit pay. That is, effective college presidents recognize the importance of letting productive people know their efforts are appreciated. In general, these effective leaders appear more confident, are more willing to take risks, and show genuine support and appreciation for the role of others in decision making. These constitute signs of excellence in leadership, as opposed to just good management.

FOLLOWERSHIP

Although leadership is written about more than most topics relating to small group interaction, followership is much less frequently discussed. Because leadership is defined as successful attempts to influence, followers are required to make leaders. In fact, leadership and followership go hand in hand. Earlier we saw that one style of leadership (democratic) in many cases seems to be best. What style of followership is best? Let us first look at three alternative followership styles.

Followership Styles

Milgram (1974) summarizes almost fifteen years of research on this topic in his book *Obedience to Authority*. In Milgram's experiments, subjects were told to administer electric shocks to other subjects as part of an experiment in learning associations between word pairs. The victim was strapped in a chair and was unable to escape the shocks. The control panel on the shock generator indicted voltage up to 450 volts, which level was labeled, "Danger: Severe Shock." As the voltage was increased, the victim screamed, "Get me out of here; I can't stand the pain; please, I have a heart condition." These protests were continued for any and all shocks administered above 150 volts. (No actual shocks were given, but the subjects really thought they were shocking the victims.)

A group of psychiatrists was asked to predict how much shock the subject would administer to the victim. They predicted that almost every subject would refuse to obey the experimenter, that those who administered any shocks at all would stop at 150 volts, and that only about one in a thousand would go all the way to 450 volts (the end of the control panel). Out of Milgram's original forty subjects, however, twenty-six (65 percent) obeyed the experimenter's orders and administered the shocks right up to the 450-volt limit. However, Milgram found that as situations were changed (for example, if the victim was brought into the same room with the subject), the subject was less willing to shock the victim. The behavior found in Milgram's experiments illustrates what might be termed a *dependent* style of followership.

Large organizations such as the military, organized religions, and government and industrial organizations frequently produce a higher level of dependence in people. James McCord, one of the convicted Watergate burglars, was described by Woodward and Bernstein (1974, p. 22) as "deeply religious, . . . ex- FBI agent, . . . military reservist, . . . [and] as the consummate 'government man'—reluctant to act on his own initiative, respectful of the chain of command, unquestioning in following orders." Lt. Col. Oliver North is another person who seems to fit the description. As we saw earlier, autocratic leadership produces a higher level of dependent followership. Most of us are caught up to some degree in the obedience syndrome, but with much less harmful or dramatic results.

A second type of follower is the *counterdependent* person. Counterdependence is a type of behavior that is rebellious and antiauthoritarian. Although the dependent personality is thought to result from overly punitive parents, the counterdependent personality is thought to result from overly permissive parents. People who are used to doing things more or less their own way resent a leader or any authority figure who intervenes. This type of person would be dissatisfied with almost any style of leadership. It may not be too much of an exaggeration to say that this group consists of misfits who are pretty much chronic problems. In the industrial work force they create major problems for leaders wherever they go. Steinmetz (1969, pp. 10–11) quoted Edward Cole, former president of General Motors, as stating:

> A research study found that a relatively few employees—28%—filed 100% of the grievances and accounted for 37% of the occupational hospital visits; 38% of the insurance claims, 40% of the sick leaves, 52% of the garnishments, and 38% of the absenteeism experienced at a certain factory. Thus not only are there a comparatively small proportion of people who are absentee-oriented, but these same people tend also to be the ones who create a significant number of all the other problems generated within the organization.

This type of follower would be hard for any leader to lead. We saw earlier that a democratic leadership style tends to produce higher levels of member satisfaction. However, Runyon (1973) found in an industrial chemical plant that some hourly employees (primarily young workers) did not have high job satisfaction regardless of type of supervisory style. Even a participative (democratic) style did not produce a high level of satisfaction. Perhaps it is fair to say that some people are simply difficult to lead, and that in dealing with them, one leadership style would be about as good (or bad) as any other. The problem then would be to try to bring the followers to a point where they could accept legitimate leadership from others.

(3) The third followership style is the *independent*. The independent is one who can either take over and lead when the situation demands or follow the lead of others when that role is more appropriate. Benjamin Franklin once said, "He that cannot obey cannot command." This implies the role flexibility required of both an effective leader and an effective follower.

Interestingly enough, in a totally different context, Milgram (1974) found that when he asked subjects to shock the victims in his studies, psychiatrists (professional group) predicted that they would disobey rather quickly, whereas other middle-class adults (nonprofessional group) predicted that they would obey somewhat longer and give more intense shocks. It appears that, to some extent, education and perhaps the subsequent self-confidence tends to correlate with independence of followership and decision making.

To illustrate the contingency aspects of leadership, one student wrote:

Example As a second grade instructional aide, I led dependent followers. For these students, who were highly motivated, "gifted" children, I found that a group-centered approach was best, because it forced the students to make decisions which affected them. This improved their academics and matured their thinking processes. As a resident adviser, I led counterdependent followers. The beginning of the year was handled democratically but after about six weeks the autocratic method proved more effective. Those students who became dissatisfied changed their followership style, so that they would be treated more democratically; those students who did not change at least accomplished the basic tasks—to establish a community conducive to study and to obey the rules of the school and the laws of Michigan and the U.S., which they were not doing under a democratic style of leadership. Finally, as the vice-president of a fraternity, I found a democratic style to be most effective. This provides for personal development and satisfaction, while still accomplishing the tasks which are outlined. However, becoming too group-centered can be a detriment because of the physical size of the membership, and the nature of the tasks which are accomplished.

This is an excellent example of the systems aspect of small group interaction. In each of the situations described above, several factors were acting in combination to influence and determine the most effective leadership style. "If you believe in people's abilities, they will come to believe in them" (Conger 1989).

An independent follower requires an empowering leader. Research suggests that the practice of *empowering* employees leads to independent followership styles. Empowerment—instilling a sense of power in subordinates—seeks to strengthen an individual's beliefs in his or her sense of effectiveness. Empowering leaders will provide a positive emotional atmosphere for their employees, reward and encourage their employees in personal ways, express confidence in their employees, and foster responsibility and initiative among their employees (Conger 1989).

In this section we have looked at three styles of followership. We have labeled them the dependent, the counterdependent, and the independent types. On the basis of this discussion, which followership style seems to describe your predominant style? How does your style change in response to different leaders and different situations? Note the trends shown in Figure 4.7.

CONTINGENCY THEORY

Building on the previous theories, two approaches have been offered that are highly consistent with the systems approach taken in this book. Fiedler (1967) has developed a *situational,* or *contingency,* theory of leadership. Hersey and Blanchard (1982) have developed a somewhat different theory. Although these models are both

---

FIGURE 4.7   LEADERSHIP AND FOLLOWERSHIP STYLES

Leadership Styles	Followership Styles
Autocratic	Dependent
Democratic	Independent
Laissez-faire	Counterdependent (rebellious)

referred to as situational theories, the term "contingency theories" also seems appropriate, because the leader's effectiveness is contingent, or dependent, upon the combination of his or her behaviors and the situation.

Fiedler and Chemers (1974) argue that a combination of three separate factors determine a leader's effectiveness: (1) leader-member relations, (2) task structure, and (3) position power. For example, leader-member relations are roughly equivalent to what we have come to know as a person's interpersonal skills or people orientation. If a leader is people oriented, the leader-member relations are likely to be good. If, on the other hand, his or her orientation is that people are a necessary evil in getting something done, then the leader-member relations are likely to be poor.

Task structure is the second variable in Fiedler's theory. If a group's task is highly structured and the leader has a manual of procedures to be followed, it would be harder for group members to challenge the leader's approach. On the other hand, if the task is highly ambiguous, such as trying to determine policy by predicting future events, then the group members might have quite a bit of legitimate input that could be as good or better than the leader's idea alone.

The third variable is position power. This can be either strong or weak. If the leader heading a work group has the power to hire and fire, to promote or not, and to determine raises or punishment, then the leader has strong position power. If, on the other hand, the group is comprised of volunteers working for a church committee or a student organization, the leader has weak position power to get people to do the task. In the model shown in Figure 4.8, we see the results of Fiedler's research. This model clearly shows that these three variables have a strong influence on the leader's effectiveness; in other words, leadership effectiveness is congruent upon these three

FIGURE 4.8   FIEDLER'S CONTINGENCY LEADERSHIP MODEL
From Fiedler and Chemers, *Leadership and Effective Management* (Glenview, Ill.: Scott, Foresman, 1974), p. 80. Copyright 1974 Scott, Foresman & Co. Reprinted by permission of the author.

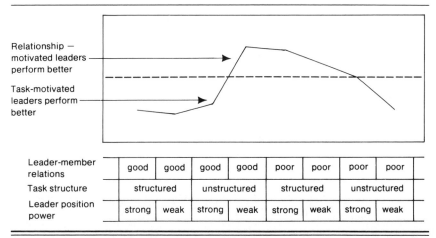

Leader-member relations	good	good	good	good	poor	poor	poor	poor	
Task structure	structured		unstructured		structured		unstructured		
Leader position power	strong	weak	strong	weak	strong	weak	strong	weak	

variables. If we take the example described above in which a leader is working with a group of volunteers for a student organization and the task is fairly unstructured (without clear guidelines on how to proceed), then the person who is not people oriented will be very ineffective. In fact, the group members will simply not come back to the next meeting. This theory is fascinating in its implications for leadership, because the same leader acting in the same way would likely be very successful in leading a military group where the operations manual supported "going by the book" and where followers who didn't obey would end up in the guardhouse.

Over two decades ago Barnlund (1962, p. 52) wrote: "Leadership [effectiveness] is dependent upon situational variables, at least two of which seem to be changes in group task and membership." More recently, Hersey and Blanchard's 1982 model very clearly pointed out the role of these variables on leadership effectiveness.

Building on the ideas we presented earlier in the functions theory section, these authors also stress the two leadership functions of (1) task-oriented behavior, and (2) people-oriented, or relationship, behavior. To these they add a third important variable, (3) the maturity of the followers. Maturity level could be defined in various ways, but Hersey and Blanchard define it in terms of three components. The first is the ability of the group members. If their ability is quite low, the leader has to be more directive than if the group members have high ability. Second, if the followers have high levels of motivation to achieve, they need less direction than followers who are not "self-starters." In fact, one professor gave a motivation test to a group so low in motivation that they would not even fill out the test! They simply didn't care about it.

The third component of follower maturity is the level of education or experience with that particular task. If a follower is totally inexperienced with fixing a malfunctioning car engine, a high level of ability and motivation may not be enough.

For more on determining the maturity level of the followers, see the article by Hersey and Blanchard at the end of this chapter.

As we see in Figure 4.9, when the maturity of followers is lowest (M1), the leadership style most likely to be effective is S1, or *telling*. With an M2 level, the S2 style, *selling*, is best. *Participating* goes best with a higher level of follower maturity, and *delegating* is the recommended supervisory style for the highest level of follower maturity.

Although it is important to develop some flexibility in our approaches to leadership in different situations, it is also important to realize that we all have limitations. As one colleague remarked, "We can't be a chameleon changing drastically for each situation." Hersey and Blanchard recognize that each of us tends to prefer one or two of these leadership patterns (that is, telling, selling, participating, and delegating). In most situations we gravitate toward whichever of these patterns has worked well for us in the past. The difficulty comes when the leadership that is *required* is different from the one we feel comfortable choosing. For example, George Steinbrenner, the former owner of the New York Yankees, used a *telling* leadership pattern. However, because he had severely unhappy players and

**FIGURE 4.9   HERSEY AND BLANCHARD'S (1982)
CONTINGENCY MODEL OF
LEADERSHIP**

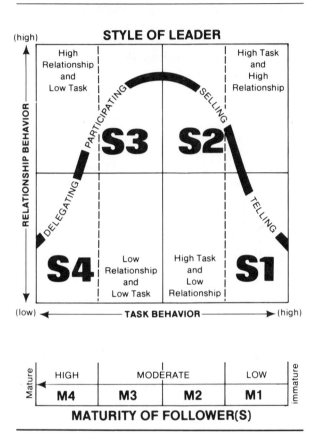

managers, maybe a different pattern (for example, delegating to his manager) would have been more appropriate. Yet it is probably quite hard for Mr. Steinbrenner to move to this other style because of his strong personality. Another factor to keep in mind is that if he had not been the owner of the team and a millionaire, his behavior pattern probably would have been even less tolerated by others in the organization.

In spite of their limitations, contingency models seem to offer the most promising theories to help guide us in determining the most effective leadership behaviors. They also fit well into the systems approach taken in this book.

GROUP NORMS: SOCIAL INFLUENCE AND CONFORMITY

This entire chapter deals with the process of social influence. In earlier sections we have seen that some people tend more to be the influencers and others the influencees. In this section we will explore some of the results of social influence—namely, conformity pressure.

Like individuals, groups form habits. When people have been together for a time, they develop standardized ways of managing tasks, procedures, and the environment. Wood, Phillips, and Pedersen (1986) define *norms* as "standardized patterns of belief, attitude, communication and behavior within groups. They grow out of member interaction. Then, in systematic fashion, they influence future interaction" (p. 40). Note this contemporary example:

> It had to start somewhere. Every third teenager on the street is wearing them—perfectly good blue jeans ripped to shreds.
>
> The most important determinant of a trend, however, is neither merchandisers nor the media. It's the vast, ineffable plasma of intra-teen peer pressure. At some point between the time the media first transmits the image and the time the merchandisers begin to sell it, peer pressure is critical. Ashley Camron, Teen magazine editor Roxanne Camron's 13-year-old daughter, is an eighth grader at Colina Intermediate School in Thousand Oaks, Calif. Ashley picked up on ripped jeans about three years ago, cutting holes in some denim shorts after seeing the look on models and actors. But she didn't have the nerve to wear them to school until her friends started wearing them, too: "If you see it on your friends, then you can wear it in public." Now, she says, everyone's wearing them. (Barol 1990, pp. 40-41)

Every one of us undoubtedly has felt the pressure to conform at one time or another. We notice pressure from the childhood challenges where we are "chicken" if we don't go along with the group, to the high school or college scene where we are labeled "brown-noses" if we appear to be spending more time in the teacher's office than our classmates think is normal.

Although norms can be described in terms of their functional value to the group, this does not imply that members of the group deliberately develop norms with the conscious intention of achieving positive group benefits. According to Thibaut and Kelley (1986, p. 141):

> The development process underlying the emergence of norms are likely to yield rules that have positive functional values for the relationship. As norms are decided upon, imported from other relationships, and tried out, only the more useful ones are likely to be retained. This is not to say that the norms found in any group will be the best solutions to various problems of control, coordination, and synchronization.

Actually, the term "norms" refers to the written or unwritten laws or codes that identify acceptable behavior. Obviously, norms will vary drastically from one group to another. Ouchi (1981, p. 28) writes:

> The influence of cultural assumptions is clearly reflected in the contrast between Japanese and American styles of decision making. Typically, the Japanese devote extensive time to defining and analyzing problems, but move with great speed in making final decisions. Americans follow an opposite path in which minimum time is devoted to analysis, while making the final decision consumes substantial time. No wonder international negotiations are often so frustrating for all parties.

The Japanese norms for group productivity have been widely admired and written about in our country. Perhaps the most fascinating spin-off is where Japanese companies have started firms in the United States and have brought their norms here. Hatvany and Pucik (1981, p. 14), in their comprehensive analysis of successful Japanese management policies, write:

> Acknowledging the enormous impact of groups on their members—both directly, through the enforcement of norms, and indirectly, by affecting the beliefs and values of members—Japanese organizations devote far greater attention to structural factors that enhance group motivation and cooperation than to the motivation of individual employees. Tasks are assigned to groups, not to individual employees, and group cohesion is stimulated by delegating responsibility to the group not only for getting the tasks performed, but also for designing the way in which they get performed.

A recent study reported by Mydans (1990) found that poor academic achievement by black students was, in part, because of group norms. He states that, "Many black students may perform poorly in high school because of a shared sense that academic success is a sellout to the white world. . . . The study argues that this grows out of the low expectations that white Americans have of blacks, low expectations that have taken root among blacks themselves." The research was conducted in a predominantly black high school in Washington, D.C. Because it was important to the students to maintain a black identity, some black students shunned schoolwork. "They chose to avoid adopting attitudes and putting in enough time and effort in their schoolwork because their peers (and they themselves) would interpret their behavior as 'white'." Other behaviors considered to be acting "white" were, "speaking standard English, . . . going to the opera or ballet, studying in the library, going to the Smithsonian Institution, doing volunteer work, camping or hiking, and being on time" (p. B6). Clearly, group norms serve as a powerful force to inhibit these students' future success.

By now you may have asked yourself, "Why do we even need to have norms?" Actually, norms often serve to reduce ambiguity and to help us feel more at ease. We often feel uncomfortable when we don't know what behaviors are acceptable in a given situation—for example, when moving from elementary school to junior high or middle school, going from junior high to high school, or graduating from high school and going to college. Remember the uneasiness you felt during your first day in each of these new situations. Only after we have learned some of the common practices or norms can we begin to relax and "be ourselves." One student who went to Harvard a few years ago learned that the norm was to buy expensive sweaters and then take scissors to fray the elbows so that the sweaters didn't look like new. A reverse attitude is prevalent today toward designer jeans. Nobody would be caught dead in what looked like old baggy jeans.

The norms in our society regarding clothing are quite strong. It is interesting to note that even going without clothes involves certain norms. On a nude beach, wearing clothes or even a bathing suit is frowned upon. Jones (1981) writes that at Black's Beach in San Diego, forty to fifty thousand nude bathers gather on a given day. He describes the norms there as follows:

Nude beaches usually are pretty remote. Gawkers aren't interested in walking very far. . . .

If someone is obnoxious, if some guy keeps his clothes on and stares at the women, it's a matter of peer pressure telling him, hey buddy, what's your problem? Why don't you move on now? This isn't a peep show.

Thirty years ago, a psychologist named Leon Festinger hypothesized a theory of social comparison (1954). This theory pointed out the need each of us has to check out our own ideas with those of others. The more ambiguous the situation, the greater is this need. In addition, when we find ourselves at odds with others, we feel pressure to reduce the discrepancies one way or another. The more we are attracted to the group, the more pressure we will feel to change toward the group norms.

On the hunch that this theory might have some relevance in predicting attitude influence on pot smoking, one student (Unger 1974) conducted a modest study in which he asked, "What has been the most significant source of influence on your views toward pot smoking?" The largest source of influence (43 percent) was from peers; the second largest (37 percent) was from authoritative written documents; the next (8 percent) was from lectures; and 12 percent said from other sources. These data would seem to confirm Festinger's thesis that we are inclined to look to others to help us determine the guidelines for our own opinions and behaviors. It is also significant to note that, as we saw from the study at Bennington College discussed in Chapter 3, the value changes we undergo in college are likely to last for a lifetime (Newcomb 1943).

Conformity: Research and Applications

One of the earliest conformity studies was conducted by Muzafer Sherif (1936) in the late 1930s. He showed subjects a pinpoint of light projected onto a wall in a completely darkened room. The light appeared to move even when the subjects knew that it was stationary. This optical illusion is called the *autokinetic effect*. Subjects were tested alone and in groups. Subjects were told to report when the light appeared to move and to judge about how far it moved. When tested individually, subjects estimated the light's range of movement at 3.6 inches. After they had discussed their experiences in groups of two and three, the average range of estimated movement had reduced to 0.4 inches. Clearly, the group discussion provided an influence on each person's judgment of the amount of the light's movement. This resulted in the reduced range of estimates of the light's movement. This clearly fits Kiesler and Kiesler's (1969, p. 2) definition of conformity as "a change in behavior or belief . . . as a result of real or imagined group pressure."

Solomon Asch (1952) conducted a classic series of conformity studies during the early 1950s. View the two cards with vertical lines drawn on them shown in Figure 4.10. Which line on card B is the same length as that on card A? If you had been in Asch's study, you and the other seven subjects would have announced your decisions in order as you were seated in the room. You are the seventh to answer out of eight. For the first two rounds there is unanimous agreement. However, on the third trial, everyone in the group agrees that line 1 is equal in length to line X. You think it is line 2, instead. What do you do? This goes on through eighteen experimental trials. In twelve of the trials you are the only one disagreeing with the

FIGURE 4.10

others. Actually, the others in the group were Asch's paid stooges, or confederates. The experiment was designed to create pressure on you to conform or yield to the others.

Asch (1955) found that, out of 123 naive subjects, 37 percent conformed to the majority opinion, whereas control subjects, judging independent of group pressure, made virtually no errors.

Another technique for constructing a conformity-inducing situation was developed by Crutchfield (Kretch, Crutchfield, and Ballachey 1962, pp. 504–511). With this method five naive subjects at a time were seated at booths that were partitioned from each other. The front of each booth had panels of signal lights and switches. The lights supposedly indicated the responses the others made to the stimuli presented to them (these also indicated that the subject's judgment would be different from the four others). Actually, none of the panels was connected to any other panel. Rather, the investigator rigged the signal lights so that the subject would always be a minority of one. In several studies a total of more than 600 people participated as naive subjects. Some of the results are summarized below.

1. Group pressure does, indeed, produce conformity.

2. Yielding can be induced even on attitudes having personal relevance.

3. Yielding is greater on difficult decisions than on easy ones.

4. There are large differences in amounts of yielding for different individuals.

5. When subjects are tested again without the group pressure, a major part of the original yielding disappears.

Some situational factors that were found to be pertinent to the conformity process include group size, perceived competence of group members, group unanimity, extremity of group opinion, and group cohesiveness. The size of the group affects conformity in that group pressure increases to a maximum with four people composing the opposing majority. Numbers larger than four, even up to fifteen, produce only slightly more yielding. Higher perceived group competence produced more conformity pressure. For example, Crutchfield (1959) found that some high-level mathematicians conformed to group pressure (from other mathematics experts) on the answers to simple arithmetic problems, giving answers that were wrong and that would very likely not have been given under normal circumstances. Group unanimity appears to have a highly significant effect on conformity. Asch (1956) found that when at least one other member of the group reinforced the one-member minority, the resistance to group pressure was significantly increased. With regard to extremity of majority opinion, Tuddenham (1961) found that when the majority opinion lies well outside the range of acceptable judgments, yielding occurs among fewer individuals and to a lesser degree. Group cohesiveness caused an increase in conformity, and the second-higher status group member conformed the most of anyone in the group (Harvey and Consalvi 1960).

Individual personal factors also have been studied in relation to conformity (see also Chapter 2). Some of the results of the conformity research include the following (Tuddenham 1961):

1. Conformists are less intelligent.

2. Conformists are lower in ego strength and in their ability to work in stress situations.

3. Conformists tend toward feelings of personal inferiority and inadequacy.

4. Conformists show an intense preoccupation with other people, as opposed to more self-contained, autonomous attitudes of the independent person.

5. Conformists express attitudes and values of a more conventional (conservative) nature than nonyielders.

The pressure to conform is eloquently described by Walker and Heynes (1967, p. 98) in the following way:

> If one wishes to produce Conformity for good or evil, the formula is clear. Manage to arouse a need or needs that are important to the individual or the group. Offer a goal which is appropriate to the need or needs. Make sure that Conformity is instrumental to the achievement of the goal and that the goal is as large and as certain as possible. Apply the goal or reward at every opportunity. Try to prevent the object of your efforts from obtaining an uncontrolled education. Choose a setting that is ambiguous. Do everything possible to see that the individual has little or no confidence in his own position. Do everything possible to make the norm which you set appear highly valued and attractive. Set it at a level not too far initially from the starting point of the individual or group and move it gradually toward the behavior you wish to produce. Be absolutely certain you know what you want and that you are willing to pay an enormous price in human quality, for whether the individual or the group is aware of it or not, the result will be *Conformity*. (See also Paulus 1989.)

Have you ever noticed what happens to the person who does try to deviate from the group? By definition this person is a *nonconformist*. He or she gets many times more comments directed toward him or her as these variables increase (that is, group cohesion and relevance of topic, as well as the acting in a noticeably different way).

Think of Suicidal Tendencies and Violent Femmes and others of the "punk rock" genre as examples.

In a quantitative study of the group's reaction to a deviant, Schachter (1951) predicted that the deviant would be talked to the most (frequency of communication) and that the reaction to the deviant would depend upon (1) relevance of the discussion topic, (2) degree of group cohesiveness, and (3) degree to which the person deviated. These predictions are summarized in the chart in Figure 4.11, which is included because the actual data supported virtually all the predictions.

In other words, we are more likely to get hot under the collar when a person deviates from a neighborhood group discussing cross-district busing of our children (high cohesion, high relevance) than if a person deviates from a group of strangers deciding on what color to paint the walls in the school gymnasium (low cohesion, low relevance). Notice that the deviant gets many times more comments directed toward him as these variables increase (that is, group cohesion and relevance of topic, as well as the degree of deviation on the topic). Notice also that in the most extreme case (the solid curved line at the top), the frequency of communication tends to diminish after about two-thirds of the 45-minute discussion (30 minutes). This leads us to believe that a certain amount of rejection or ostracism results if the deviant doesn't come around.

Although this study represents a quantitative analysis of a group discussion, Leavitt (1964) offers a qualitative analysis of the four stages of conformity pressure. The first stage might be called *reason*. We do not like hearing our ideas disconfirmed, but we are interested in logically convincing the deviant that he or she is wrong. Even at this stage, it is clear we expect the deviant to change to conform to the group and

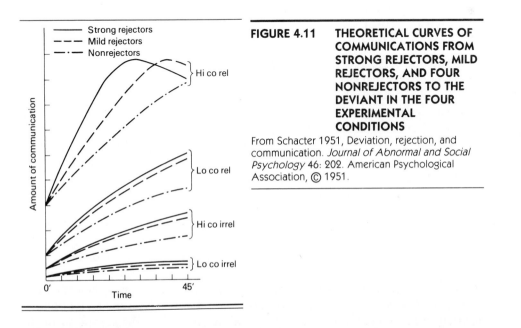

—— Strong rejectors
--- Mild rejectors
—·— Nonrejectors

Hi co rel

Lo co rel

Hi co irrel

Lo co irrel

Amount of communication

0'   45'
        Time

FIGURE 4.11   THEORETICAL CURVES OF COMMUNICATIONS FROM STRONG REJECTORS, MILD REJECTORS, AND FOUR NONREJECTORS TO THE DEVIANT IN THE FOUR EXPERIMENTAL CONDITIONS

From Schacter 1951, Deviation, rejection, and communication. *Journal of Abnormal and Social Psychology* 46: 202. American Psychological Association, © 1951.

not vice versa. The second stage is *seduction*. During this stage we attempt to appeal to the deviant's social needs. The comments begin to take on the tone of, "Aw, come on, be a sport, we know you don't want to put the whole group on the spot just for the sake of this little issue." It isn't long before the group enters stage three, which is *coercion*. During this stage the group members lose their smiles and good nature. The comments begin to take on the air of threat, something like, "Now look, this has gone far enough. If you won't play ball, then we are going to have to clip your wings but good the next time you want help from us." The fourth and final stage is *isolation*. At this point the group gives up on and ignores the deviant. This tactic may finally bring conformity if the ostracism is prolonged.

Leavitt (1964, pp. 273–274) summarized the four stages when he writes: "It's as though the members of the group were saying, 'Let's reason with him; if that doesn't work, let's try to tease him by emotional seduction; and if even that doesn't work, let's beat him over the head until he has to give up. Failing that, then we'll excommunicate him; we'll amputate him from the group; we'll disown him'." One student wrote of her experience with this conformity influence:

> As a high school band member I experienced all four of these stages when we were to march in the Apple Blossom Parade.
>
> The band master told everyone to wear saddle shoes. When I explained to him that I had none, he said, "Get some, since everybody needs to be dressed the same" (step 1). I told him I had no money. "Then borrow some," another band member suggested. "Come on, we need you" (step 2). I told them I couldn't borrow any because of an unusual foot size. "Then if you don't get them, you can't march in the parade," said someone else (step 3).
>
> I didn't; I hid when the band came down the street. I never returned to the band again. I felt alone, isolated, and ostracized (step 4), and that ended my musical career. Although it was over twenty years ago, it still hurts when I think about it.

On a more personal level, Williams (1989) reports that in spite of all the publicity regarding the dangers of contracting AIDS from unsafe sex, many young people today continue to engage in risky behaviors. She writes, "Even teen-agers who are not sexually active tend to see the matter as a personal choice, . . . and it seems clear that pressure from peers . . . has more impact on teen-agers generally." On the basis of over 900 surveys and interviews nationwide, she reports that, "Teen-agers say that social pressure is the chief reason why so many do not wait to have sexual intercourse until they are older. Both boys and girls say they are pressured by other teen-agers to go further than they wanted to" (p. A1).

Janis (1982, p. 9) has conducted a thorough investigation of the problems that conformity pressure brought to some major American historical events. He refers to the results as *groupthink*, which he defines as "a quick and easy way to refer to a mode of thinking that people engage in when they are deeply involved in a cohesive in-group, when the members' strivings for unanimity override their motivation to realistically appraise alternative courses of action." Janis cites several major political decisions that were characterized by groupthink, including the escalation of the

Vietnam war and the 1961 American invasion of Cuba (the Bay of Pigs). Although not included in his book, Watergate was another example that fits his definition. (The 1987 Iran-Contra arms scandal may also be another example.) Further studies (Whyte 1989) have cited the Watergate scandal, the decision to launch the space shuttle Challenger, and the Iran-Contra arms scandal all as disastrous examples of the groupthink phenomenon.

Groupthink tends to occur when several factors are operating at once. These are called the symptoms of groupthink, and they can occur in any group. The eight symptoms are summarized below.

Type I: Overestimations of the group—its power and morality

1. An illusion of invulnerability, shared by most or all of the members, which creates excessive optimism and encourages taking extreme risks.
2. An unquestioned belief in the group's inherent morality, inclining the members to ignore the ethical or moral consequences of their decisions.

Type II: Closed-mindedness

3. Collective efforts to rationalize in order to discount warnings or other information that might lead the members to reconsider their assumptions before they recommit themselves to their past policy decisions.
4. Stereotyped views of enemy leaders as too evil to warrant genuine attempts to negotiate, or as too weak and stupid to counter whatever risky attempts are made to defeat their purposes.

Type III: Pressures toward uniformity

5. Self-censorship of deviations from the apparent group consensus, reflecting each member's inclination to minimize to himself the importance of his doubts and counterarguments.
6. A shared illusion of unanimity concerning judgments conforming to the majority view (partly resulting from self-censorship of deviations, augmented by the false assumption that silence means consent).
7. Direct pressure on any member who expresses strong arguments against any of the group's stereotypes, illusions, or commitments, making clear that this type of dissent is contrary to what is expected of all loyal members.
8. The emergence of self-appointed mindguards—members who protect the group from adverse information that might shatter their shared complacency about the effectiveness and morality of their decisions. (Janis 1982, pp. 174–175)

For corrective measures for avoiding groupthink, see the article by Janis at the end of this chapter.

Certain groups are particularly vulnerable to groupthink. Those with members who are high in need for affiliation (see Chapter 2), those that are very cohesive (see

Chapter 7), or those that have an autocratic leadership style (see this chapter) are likely candidates. However, there are procedures that can be employed to minimize the possibilities of groupthink (Janis 1982, pp. 260–276). Some of these precautions are:

- Assign one member to be the "devil's advocate" or critical evaluator to allow disagreements and criticism of the leader.

- Leaders should not reveal their preferences to the group at the beginning of the discussion.

- Several groups with different leaders can work independently on common problems to offer different perspectives.

- Group members should discuss the group's processes with trusted friends and report their reactions to the group.

- Outside experts should be called in periodically as resource persons. They should be encouraged to disagree with the group's assumptions.

- Whenever issues involve relations with rival groups (e.g., labor and management) time should be spent discussing all warning signals from the rivals and hypothesizing alternative "scenarios of the rivals' intentions."

- After preliminary decisions have been reached, the group should adjourn and hold a "second chance" meeting at a later date to let their ideas "incubate."

Although these suggestions may not always be applicable (even if they are, they may not always work), they do offer a constructive alternative to reduce the dangers of groupthink.

In a more recent study, Whyte (1989) argued that the term "groupthink" is an incomplete explanation for such disastrous occurrences (decision fiascoes). Whyte's contention is that the way choices are "framed in a domain of losses" has more to do with risky "groupthink" decisions than actual group dynamics.

Whyte gave consideration to the events surrounding the space shuttle Challenger disaster to describe this phenomenon.

> This situation was the product of flawed decisions as much as it was a failure of technology. The pressures on the National Aeronautics and Space Administration (NASA) to launch a space shuttle at the earliest opportunity were intense, despite evidence that this course of action was inadvisable. A decision to delay the launch was undesirable from NASA's perspective because of the impact it would have on political and public support for the program. In contrast, a successful launch would have appeased the public and politicians alike, and would have amounted to another major achievement. NASA engineers claimed that pressure to launch was so intense that authorities routinely dismissed potentially lethal hazards as acceptable risks. . . .

A choice in the domain of losses was involved on either side of this decision. Had the launch of the Challenger been delayed any further, the space shuttle program would have undoubtedly suffered consequences. As it stands, the decision to launch the shuttle amounted in even dearer losses. Considerations in the Whyte study show that the phenomenon of "groupthink" is not a simple one.

GROUP DEVELOPMENT

A number of writers have been interested in the social influence process as it is manifested in different stages or phases of group development. Group development seems to be partly the result of individual psychological needs and partly the result of the social influences manifested in the group. The various theories on group phases are somewhat incompatible, in that some writers identify three phases and others identify four. Also, some writers identify the phases that occur during the course of one group discussion (Tuckman 1965, Fisher 1980), whereas others identify the phases that occur over the course of the life of a group, including several meetings (Bennis and Shepard 1956, Thelen and Dickerman 1949). Still another viewpoint is that the phases occur in each meeting and continue to occur throughout the group's life history (Schutz 1958, Bales and Strodbeck 1951). This last viewpoint seems the most profound in providing insight into the phenomenon of group development.

With these differing frames of reference in mind, let us look at the four group phases that seem representative of the literature. *Phase one* (orientation) seems to be a period in which group members simply try to break the ice and begin to find out enough about one another to have some common basis for functioning. It is variously referred to as a period of orientation, inclusion, or group formation. In this phase people ask questions about one another, tell where they are from, reveal what they like and dislike, and generally make small talk. An excerpt from a student paper reveals this:

> Even though we had a task to accomplish for the class, we began by talking about ourselves (one guy and girl found they both liked moto-cross racing, and two others found that they had both been to Daytona Beach last spring vacation). After we had a chance to "break the ice" we were more willing to throw out ideas on how to go ahead with the group project without being afraid of having our ideas shot down in flames.

Phase one seems to be characterized by the establishing of some minimal social relationship before group members feel comfortable getting down to work. However, some executives who have experienced many years of decision-making meetings may begin work with little or no social orientation and only the barest minimum of group orientation. With these exceptions, the vast majority of us feel better having some period to build relationships prior to launching into the group's work.

Phase two (conflict) is frequently characterized by conflict of some kind or another. After the orientation phase passes, the pressure to accomplish something sooner or later intensifies whatever differences may exist. This student's description illustrates the transition from phase one to phase two:

> We talked about personal interests until some common ground was established, then we found we could talk about the assignment more freely. But after talking about

nonsubject things, it was hard to keep the line of talk on the problems at hand. Some wanted to get the assignment accomplished while two guys in the group continually swayed the conversation to things that were easier to talk about, but had nothing to do with the subject (Howard has a big thing for John Deere farm machinery). At first we were constantly trying not to hurt anyone's feelings, so we let the conversation drift. We didn't question or reject each other's ideas, and I feel we often settled for less than we should have. The longer we were in the group together, the more we got to know each other and the more times we voiced our real opinions. That's when the tempers started to flare!

Typically, in phase two the group begins to thrash out decisions for procedures as well as for determining the solution to the group task. Conflict over procedures may be one way in which group members fight for influence or control in the group.

After a period of small talk in one middle-aged encounter group, one member suggested that they go around the group and introduce themselves in some detail, telling what their jobs were, what part of the country they were from, and so on. Just as they were about to begin, another member suggested that they *not* tell these things, to avoid the stereotyping that would inevitably result. A heated argument resulted. Eventually they decided to assume their fantasized identities—that is, they adopted nicknames and behaviors and job titles that represented the type of person they wished they could be. Much later in the group they decided that the new procedure had been much better in helping them to try out behaviors they normally would have been too inhibited to attempt. For example, one female psychiatrist assumed the identity of "Bubbles," a cocktail waitress, because she had always wondered what it would be like to be a sex object and get outside her role as a professional person. The conflict regarding procedures turned out to be very productive for the group in the long run.

Phase three (emergence) involves a resolution of the conflict experienced in phase two. Group cohesiveness begins to emerge, and the group settles into working more comfortably as a unit. This phase is described by three different sources in the following ways.

> Perhaps the major pitfall to be avoided at this point is that of glossing over significant differences for the sake of harmony . . . behavior is essentially a kind of polite behavior which avoids upsetting the group. (Thelen and Dickerman 1949)

> Resistance is overcome in the third stage in which ingroup feeling and cohesiveness develop, new standards evolve, and new roles are adopted. In the task realm, intimate, personal opinions are expressed. (Tuckman 1965)

> Social conflict and dissent dissipate during the third phase. Members express fewer unfavorable opinions toward decision proposals. The coalition of individuals who had opposed those proposals which eventually achieve consensus also weakens in the third phase. (Fisher 1974)

Phase four (reinforcement) is the phase of maximum productivity and consensus. Dissent has just about disappeared, and the rule of the moment is to pat each other on the back for having done such a good job. Group members joke and laugh and generally reinforce one another for having contributed to the group's success.

Student reactions to a group project in this phase include the following typical comments: "At first I thought this assignment would be a waste of time, but now I think it was the most worthwhile thing we have done in the course so far." "Everybody I have talked to feels like the group exercise was really good. We are looking forward to doing more of these."

Psychologically, we all need to feel that what we do is somehow justified or worthwhile (this is referred to in Chapter 3 as rationalizing or reducing cognitive dissonance). Thus, even if we have had bad experiences with a group, we tend to repress those and remember the good things we have experienced. The various group development theories are summarized in the chart in Figure 4.12 and in the following quotation from the earliest of the group development theorists (Thelen and Dickerman 1949, p. 316):

> Beginning with individual needs for finding security and activity in a social environment, we proceed first to emotional involvement of the individuals with each other, and second to the development of a group as a rather limited universe of interaction among individuals and as the source of individual security. We then find that security of position in the group loses its significance except that as the group attempts to solve problems it structures its activities in such a way that each individual can play a role which may be described as successful or not in terms of whether the group successfully solved the problem it had set itself.

Deadlines and time constraints sometimes offer more initiative than actual accomplishments. In a comprehensive study on models of group development, Gersick (1988) established that a group's progress is triggered more by the group members' awareness of time and deadlines than by completion of an absolute amount of work in a specific developmental stage.

Although Seeger (1983) argues that group phases do not really exist, Osborn and Harris (in Cathcart and Samovar 1984) conclude:

> The consensus of numerous systematic observations in . . . group dynamics is that phases or cycle regularities exist in the natural development of small groups. . . .
>
> It must be kept in mind that the phases are general patterns of development and not distinct stages neatly accomplished. In fact, it is frequently difficult to determine the end of one phase and the beginning of another. (p. 111)

THE SYSTEMS PERSPECTIVE

In this chapter we examined the complicated and fascinating questions of who influences whom and why. In the discussion of status and power we saw that the two go hand in hand; that is, high-status individuals tend to have more power. An obvious extension of this is the notion that because of differing group norms, different characteristics bring about status in different groups. On a football team, the best athlete has the most status. Among college professors, the smartest person usually has the most status. In street gangs, the toughest member typically has the highest status. And so it goes from one group to another.

FIGURE 4.12   SUMMARY OF LITERATURE ON GROUP PHASES

	Phase 1	Phase 2	Phase 3	Phase 4
Thelen and Dickerman (1949)	Forming	Conflict	Harmony	Productivity
Bennis and Shepard (1956, 1961)	Dependence	Interdependence	Focused work	Productivity
Tuckman (1965)	Forming	Storming	Norming	Performing
Fisher (1980)	Orientation	Conflict	Emergence	Reinforcement
Bales and Strodbeck (1951)	Orientation	Evaluation		Control
Schutz (1958)	Inclusion	Control		Affection

A major portion of this chapter dealt with the issues of leadership and followership. Although these two are not always discussed together, they are interrelated. Here the systems principle of *equifinality* applies. In other words, the leadership style that would be appropriate in one situation with one set of followers may not be the most appropriate in a different situation with a different set of followers. A great deal of study has led to the belief that the democratic leadership style is the most likely to get the best results in a great many cases. However, our systems perspective reminds us that some situations point to the authoritarian style as the most appropriate. In situations involving life-or-death decisions or in times of crisis requiring rapid decisions, the democratic approach may be too slow or simply impractical. As we saw earlier, two popular theoretical syntheses regarding leadership styles are offered by Fiedler (1967, 1974) and Hersey and Blanchard (1982). They each suggest a contingency theory of leadership. In other words, the best leadership style is one flexible enough to adapt to the situation. If asked which leadership style is best, they would answer, "It depends."

This chapter also dealt with the topics of social influence and conformity. Systems theory concepts are beautifully illustrated in this literature. Conformity pressure differs depending on the type of group (for example, military vs. the commune), the style of leadership (say, authoritarian vs. democratic), the personalities of the group members (dominant vs. acquiescent), and a number of other factors. We know from the research literature that conformity is more likely (1) in a group in which membership is highly valued by its participants; (2) among members with dependent, obedient, and acquiescent personalities; (3) when the leader is more authoritarian; (4) when the group is unanimously against the deviant member; and (5) to produce public compliance than actual private acceptance. Conformity is clearly dependent on an entire constellation of other variables.

One study analyzed conformity in a systems way (although the authors did not identify their analysis as a systems analysis). Rarick, Soldow, and Geizer (1976) looked at conformity as a result of the combination of the person's personality and the situation in which he or she is placed. The personality variable was self-confidence (they call it self-monitoring), and the situational variable was group size (dyad or three- to six-person group). They found that less confident people conform more in three- to six-person groups than highly confident people. This confirms numerous previous findings. However, they also found that in a dyad, confident people did not conform any more or less than those lacking in confidence. This study very nicely illustrates the systems perspective that all these variables (and others) simultaneously influence one another.

The last section of this chapter dealt with group development. We know that groups go through some fairly common phases, depending on the type of group. As we saw earlier, some writers assume that all the phases occur during the course of one group discussion. Other writers believe that these phases evolve slowly over the group's lifetime. However, the systems theory approach would agree with writers such as Schutz (1958) and Bales and Strodbeck (1951) that these phases are simply parts of a recurring *cycle* of events that probably occur during a single meeting and tend to be repeated throughout the group's lifetime, as well. This point of view seems to be the most theoretically valid and is supported by other authors who apply the systems approach to the analysis of small group interaction (see, for example, Fisher and Hawes, 1971).

EXERCISES

1. Leadership Case Studies

Break into small groups, and discuss one of the following leadership case studies. Attempt to reach agreement on the case. Have each group report its decision to the class and the reasons for the choice. What issues in leadership from Chapter 4 are illustrated in these cases?

Case A   In the men's sportswear department of the Arcade Department Store, two men and four women are employed regularly as sales personnel. In addition to salary, they receive a bonus determined by the amount by which the individual's daily volume of sales exceeds a quota. Mr. Stone, the buyer, is head of the department, but during his frequent absences, his assistant buyer, Mr. Jones, is in charge. In addition to the six regulars, the department also employs several extra salespersons during the summer. These are college students on vacation who have been given some training by the store's personnel department. They are eager beavers and often outsell the regulars. They also work for a salary plus a bonus.

During Mr. Stone's absence on a buying trip, the regulars complained to Mr. Jones that the extras were making it difficult for them to make their quotas, that they mixed up the stock and generally were a nuisance. Mr. Jones, a close personal friend of one of the regulars, ordered the extras to take care of the stock and to sell only when customers were waiting. On his return, Mr. Stone countermanded this order; he told the extras to get in there and sell or look for other jobs. A competitive spirit, he said, was good for the department. The regulars are now more resentful than ever; customers are beginning to notice the bad feeling, and some of them have taken their trade elsewhere.

Which one of the following comments on this situation seems to you most sound?

1. Mr. Stone should return to the position taken earlier by his assistant—that is, instruct the extras to work on stock and handle customers only when no regular is free to do so.

2. In addition to telling the extras to sell to the top of their capacity, Mr. Stone should call the regulars in, take a firm stand with them, and advise them to increase their sales or look elsewhere for work.

3. Mr. Stone is right; a competitive spirit is good for the department. Beyond making this point clear, he should continue to have a hands-off policy and let the situation work itself out.

4. Mr. Stone should put the extras on a straight hourly basis of compensation.

5. Mr. Stone should investigate the activities of the extras and the sales methods and compensation plan of all employees.

Case B   Mr. Welty, publisher of a newspaper, employs a total staff of about 200. He prides himself on the high morale among his employees and on their loyalty to him and to the paper. "You may call my kind of management paternalism," he once said, "but I know all of my employees personally and don't have to buy their friendship and loyalty." Though unaware that he had any personnel problem, Mr. Welty had a personnel consultant make a survey and evaluation of the organization.

To his astonishment, Mr. Welty learned that in the pressroom, morale was very low—that nearly all of the thirty-eight employees there had bitter feelings against the foreman, Harry Fitzpatrick. They considered him arbitrary, vindictive, and indifferent to their welfare. As evidence of this indifference, they pointed to the deplorable condition of the locker room. Six of the apprentices, former servicemen, were especially sour on Fitzpatrick. He was down on all ex-servicemen, they said, and constantly abused and insulted them.

Shocked by these disclosures, Mr. Welty toured the pressroom and locker room with Fitzpatrick, putting questions to some of the workmen. He then ordered the locker room repaired and cleaned up, and in a long talk with Fitzpatrick he reprimanded him sharply. After twenty-three years with the firm and thirteen as foreman, he insisted, Fitzpatrick should know better than to treat employees in that way.

A few months later, on again checking the situation in the pressroom, Mr.

Welty found no improvement in employee morale and no improvement in Fitzpatrick's relationship with the workmen. Obviously, something more drastic than a verbal reprimand was necessary. Reluctant to dismiss Fitzpatrick, Mr. Welty appointed an acting foreman for the pressroom and for a one-year period assigned Fitzpatrick to supervise the installation of new presses in another part of the plant. "This may be a cowardly decision," he admitted to himself, "but a lot can happen in a year, and I'll cross that bridge when I come to it a year from now."

How should Mr. Welty have handled this situation?

1. Exactly as he did. In the course of a year something may well happen to solve the problem.

2. He should have transferred Fitzpatrick for one year to the new job of installing presses but with the understanding that he would not again be foreman of the pressroom.

3. He should have transferred him to the new job for a year, trying in the meantime to help him improve as a foreman but leaving open the question of what to do with him at the end of the year.

4. He should have fired Fitzpatrick immediately on making the second checkup.

5. He should have kept Fitzpatrick as a journeyman printer, if he cared to stay, but should have relieved him of the foremanship.

Case C: Jacobs Furniture, Inc.   You are Bev Stone, manager of the Accounting Department of Jacobs Furniture. The entire company has about 1700 employees, 15 of whom are in your department. You have just returned from a meeting held by the general manager, Bill Keppler. In this meeting, Bill explained to all the department heads that there was an important task for them to accomplish. The local United Way drive is currently under way. Each year every organization in the city is asked to do what it can to donate money to the United Way, which supports many worthwhile, nonprofit agencies in the community.

Bill explained that last week the brochures and pledge cards had been sent to everyone in the company and that, to date, only 5 percent had responded. Then, Rick Adams, an engineer on loan to the United Way from a local computer company, gave a short presentation telling of the many worthwhile services the United Way provides. Bill Keppler then said that he wanted each department head to go back to his or her employees and see what could be done to raise the participation rate in each department.

You have mixed feelings about this assignment. On one hand, there is no doubt that the United Way is a deserving organization. On the other hand, because business has been very poor for the past few years, employees have had zero raises during that period. Morale is quite low, mostly because of economic pressures. There has been much complaining already about the increases in taxes resulting in less and less take-home pay. Also, with the cost of living on the increase, even the *same* amount of money wouldn't buy as much as it would have five years ago. With the taxes increasing, they have even *less* to spend than they did before. In this context, you feel awkward about asking people in your work group to donate more of their pay to charitable causes.

Your boss has made it clear that he supports this charity to a very strong degree. Therefore, you must do something. Decide what specific steps you will take in carrying out this task.

2. Interaction Analysis Exercise

Observe a group discussion, and try to use the Bales Interaction Process Analysis scoring sheet (Figure 4.13) to make your observations more systematic. Start by observing and recording only one person in the group. Simply place a check mark in the appropriate row when a person says something in the group. As you gain more experience, record two or three group members. You may also want to try having several people observe the same person to check the reliability of your observations.

3. Group Development Exercise

Observe a real-life problem-solving group. Listen carefully for statements that indicate the four phases of group development. You might take notes to record exact statements that illustrate the four phases. Notice also if the group does *not* seem to go through these four phases. Compare your observations with those of others who have observed different groups. Do most of the observations correspond to the research findings?

FIGURE 4.13   BALES INTERACTION PROCESS ANALYSIS SCORING SHEET

Scoring of Interaction (Bales)	Person 1	Person 2	Person 3	Row totals
1. *Seems friendly,* raises other's status, gives help, reward				
2. *Dramatizes,* jokes, laughs, shows satisfaction				
3. *Agrees,* shows passive acceptance, understands, concurs, complies				
4. *Gives suggestions,* direction, implying autonomy for other				
5. *Gives opinion,* evaluation, analysis, expresses feeling, wish				
6. *Gives information,* repeats, clarifies, confirms				
7. *Asks for information,* repetition, confirmation				
8. *Asks for opinion,* evaluation analysis, expresses feeling				
9. *Asks for suggestion,* direction, possible ways of action				
10. *Disagrees,* shows passive rejection, formality, withholds help				
11. *Shows tension,* asks for help, withdraws "out of field"				
12. *Seems unfriendly,* deflates other's status, defends or asserts self				
Column totals				

READINGS: OVERVIEW

In the first article, Hersey and Blanchard offer further elaboration on how to identify the maturity of group members, which influences the choice of an appropriate leadership style.

The second article, by Irving Janis, describes a classic social influence phenomenon. The description of the ways to prevent "groupthink" provide a bit more depth for ways in which groups can improve their performance.

Situational Leadership

Paul Hersey
Kenneth H. Blanchard

The need for a significant Situational Model in the leadership area has been recognized in the literature for some time.

A. K. Korman, in his extensive review of studies examining the Ohio State concepts of Initiating Structure and Consideration, concluded that:

> What is needed . . . in future concurrent (and predictive) studies is not just recognition of this factor of "situational determinants" but, rather, a systematic conceptualization of situational variance as it might relate to leadership behavior [Initiating Structure and Consideration].

In discussing this conclusion, Korman suggests the possibility of a curvilinear relationship rather than a simple linear relationship between Initiating Structure (task behavior) and Consideration (relationship behavior) and other variables. Situational Leadership, which is an outgrowth of our Tri-Dimensional Leader Effectiveness Model, has identified such a curvilinear relationship.

Situational Leadership is based on an interplay among (1) the amount of guidance and direction (task behavior) a leader gives; (2) the amount of socioemotional support (relationship behavior) a leader provides; and (3) the readiness ("maturity") level that followers exhibit in performing a specific task, function or objective. This concept was developed to help people attempting leadership, regardless of their role, to be more effective in their daily interactions with others. It provides leaders with some understanding of the relationship between an effective style of leadership and the level of maturity of their followers.

Thus, while all the situational variables (leader, follower(s), superior(s), associates, organization, job demands, and time) are important, the emphasis in Situational Leadership will be on the behavior of a leader in relation to followers. As Fillmore H. Sanford has indicated, there is some justification for regarding the followers "as the most crucial factor in any leadership event." Followers in any situation are vital, not only because as a group they actually determine whatever personal power the leader may have. . . .

When discussing leader/follower relationships, we are not necessarily talking about a hierarchical relationship, that is, superior/subordinate. The same caution will hold during our discussion of Situational Leadership. *Thus, any reference to leader(s) or follower(s) in this theory should imply potential leader and potential follower.* As a result, although our examples may suggest a hierarchical relationship, the concepts presented in Situational Leadership should have application no matter whether you are attempting to influence the behavior of a subordinate, your boss, an associate, a friend, or a relative.

Maturity of the Followers or Group

Maturity is defined in Situational Leadership as the ability and willingness of people to take responsibility for directing their own behavior. *These variables of maturity should be considered only in relation to a specific task to be performed.* That is to say, an individual or a group is not mature or immature in any *total* sense. All persons tend to be more or less mature in relation to a specific task, function, or objective that a leader is attempting to accomplish through their efforts. Thus, a saleswoman may be very responsible in securing new sales but very casual about completing the paperwork necessary to close on a sale. As a result, it is appropriate for her manager to leave her alone in terms of closing on sales but to supervise her closely in terms of her paperwork until she can start to do well in that area too.

In addition to assessing the level of maturity of individuals within a group, a leader may have to assess the maturity level of the group as a group, particularly if the group interacts frequently together in the same work area, as happens with students in the classroom. Thus, a teacher may find that a class as a group may be at one level of maturity in a particular area, but a student within that group may be at a different level. When the teacher is one-to-one with that student, he or she may have to behave very differently than when working with the class as a group. In reality, the teacher may find a number of students at various maturity levels. For example, the teacher may have one student who is not doing his work regularly; when he turns work in, it is poorly organized and not very academic. With that student, the teacher may have to initiate some structure and supervise closely. Another student, however, may be doing good work but is insecure and shy. With that student, the teacher may not have to engage in much task behavior in terms of schoolwork but may need to be supportive, to engage in two-way communication, and help facilitate the student's interaction with others in the class. Still another student may be psychologically mature as well as competent in her schoolwork, and thus can be left on her own. So leaders have to understand that they may have to behave differently one-on-one with members of their group from the way they do with the group as a whole.

Basic Concept of Situational Leadership

According to Situational Leadership, there is no one best way to influence people. Which leadership style a person should use with individuals or groups depends on the maturity level of the people the leader is attempting to influence, as illustrated in Figure 1.

Style of Leader versus Maturity of Follower(s)

The attempt in Figure 1 is to portray the relationship between task-relevant maturity and the appropriate leadership styles to be used as followers move from immaturity to maturity. As indicated, the reader should keep in mind that the figure represents two different phenomena. The appropriate leadership style (*style of leader*) for given levels of follower maturity is portrayed by the prescriptive curve going through the four leadership quadrants. This bell-shaped curve is called a *prescriptive curve* because it shows the appropriate leadership style directly above the corresponding level of maturity.

Each of the four leadership styles—"telling," "selling," "participating," and "delegating"—identified in Figure 1, is a combination of task and relationship behavior. . . . Task behavior is the extent to which a leader provides direction for people: telling them what to do, when to do it, where to do it, and how to do it. It means setting goals for them and defining their roles.

Relationship behavior is the extent to which a leader engages in two-way communication with people: providing support, encouragement, "psychological strokes," and facilitating behaviors. It means actively listening to people and supporting their efforts.

The maturity of followers is a question of degree. As can be seen in Figure 1, some bench marks of maturity are provided for determining appropriate leadership style by dividing the maturity continuum below the leadership model into four levels: low (M1), low to moderate (M2), moderate to high (M3), and high (M4).

The appropriate leadership style for each of the four maturity levels includes the right combination of task behavior (direction) and relationship behavior (support).

"Telling" Is for Low Maturity   People who are both *unable and unwilling* (M1) to take responsibility to do something are not competent or confident. In many cases, their unwillingness is a result of their *insecurity* regarding the necessary task. Thus, a directive "telling" style (S1) that provides clear, specific directions and supervision has the highest probability of being effective with individuals at this maturity level. This style is called "telling" because it is characterized by the leader's defining roles and telling people what, how, when, and where to do various tasks. It emphasizes directive behavior. Too much supportive behavior with people at this maturity level may

FIGURE 1   SITUATIONAL LEADERSHIP

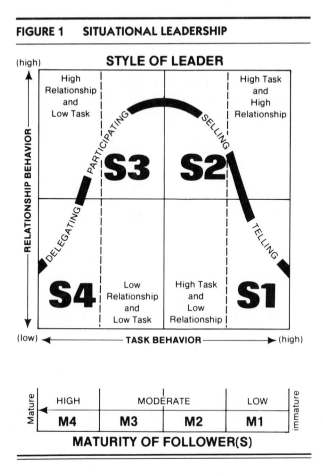

be seen as permissive, easy and, most importantly, as rewarding of poor performance. This style involves high task behavior and low relationship behavior.

"Selling" Is for Low to Moderate Maturity   People who are *unable but willing* (M2) to take responsibility are confident but lack skills at this time. Thus, a "selling" style (S2) that provides directive behavior, because of their lack of ability, but also supportive behavior to reinforce their willingness and enthusiasm appears to be most appropriate with individuals at this maturity level. This style is called "selling" because most of the direction is still provided by the leader. Yet, through two-way communication and explanation, the leader tries to get the followers psychologically to "buy into" desired behaviors. Followers at this maturity level will usually go along with a decision if they understand the reason for the decision and if their leader also offers some help and direction. This style involves high task behavior and high relationship behavior.

"Participating" Is for Moderate to High Maturity   People at this maturity level are *able but unwilling* (M3) to do what the leader wants. Their unwillingness is often a function of their lack of confidence or *insecurity*. If, however, they are competent but unwilling, their reluctance to perform is more of a motivational problem than a security problem. In either case, the leader needs to open the door (two-way communication and active listening) to support the follower's efforts to use the ability he already has. Thus, a supportive, nondirective, "participating" style (S3) has the highest probability of being effective with individuals at this maturity level. This style is called "participating" because the leader and follower share in decision making, with the main role of the leader being facilitating and communicating. This style involves high relationship behavior and low task behavior.

"Delegating" Is for High Maturity   People at this maturity level are both *able and willing, or confident,* to take responsibility. Thus, a low-profile "delegating" style (S4), which provides little direction or support, has the highest probability of being effective with individuals at this maturity level. Even though the leader may still identify the problem, the responsibility for carrying out plans is given to these mature followers. They are permitted to run the show and decide on the how, when, and where. At the same time, they are psychologically mature and therefore do not need above average amounts of two-way communication or supportive behavior. This style involves low relationship behavior and low task behavior.

It should be clear that the appropriate leadership style for all four of the maturity designations—low maturity (M1), low to moderate maturity (M2), moderate to high maturity (M3), and high maturity (M4)—correspond to the following leadership style designations: *telling* (S1), *selling* (S2), *participating* (S3), and *delegating* (S4). That is, low maturity needs a *telling* style, low to moderate needs a *selling* style, and so on. These combinations are shown in Table 1.

In using the shorthand designations (S1, S2, S3, S4) and labels ("telling," "selling," "participating," and "delegating") for leadership styles that are identified in Figure 1 and Table 1, one must keep in mind that they should only be used when referring to behaviors represented by the effective face of the Tri-Dimensional Leader Effectiveness Model. However, when discussing basic or ineffective styles, we shall refer to them only by quadrant number: Q1, Q2, Q3, or Q4. For example, when a low relationship/low task style is used appropriately with the corresponding maturity level M4, it will be referred to as S4 or "delegating." But when that same style is used inappropriately with any of the other three maturity levels, it will only be called Q4 and might be better described as abdication or withdrawal rather than "delegating."

Situational Leadership not only suggests the high probability leadership style for various maturity levels, but it also indicates the probability of success of the other style configurations if a leader is unable to use the desired style. The probability of success of each style for the four maturity levels, depending on how far the style is from the high probability style along the prescriptive curve in the style of leader portion of the model, is as follows:

M1   S1 high, S2 2nd, Q3 3rd, Q4 low probability

M2   S2 high, S1 2nd, S3 2nd, Q4 low probability

M3   S3 high, S2 2nd, S4 2nd, Q1 low probability

M4   S4 high, S3 2nd, Q2 3rd, Q1 low probability

In indicating the probability of success of each style above, in some cases the "S" designation was used for a style, and in other cases the "Q" designation was used. As discussed, the shorthand designations (S1, S2, S3, S4) and labels ("telling," "selling," "participating," and "delegating") should only be used when referring to behaviors represented by the effective face of the Tri-Dimensional Leader Effectiveness Model. Thus, the high probability style and the 2nd (secondary) styles were indicated by an "S" designation, while the 3rd and low probability styles were indicated by a "Q" designation. In most cases, there are at least two leadership styles in the effective range. At the same time, there are usually one or two leadership styles that are clearly in the less effective range.

TABLE 1   LEADERSHIP STYLES APPROPRIATE FOR VARIOUS MATURITY LEVELS

Maturity Level	Appropriate Style
M1 *Low Maturity* Unable and unwilling or insecure	S1 *Telling* High task and low relationship behavior
M2 *Low to Moderate Maturity* Unable but willing or confident	S2 *Selling* High task and high relationship behavior
M3 *Moderate to High Maturity* Able but unwilling or insecure	S3 *Participating* High relationship and low task behavior
M4 *High Maturity* Able/competent and willing/confident	S4 *Delegating* Low relationship and low task behavior

Preventing Groupthink

Irving L. Janis

1. *The leader of a policy-forming group should assign the role of critical evaluator to each member, encouraging the group to give high priority to airing objections and doubts. This practice needs to be reinforced by the leader's acceptance of criticism of his or her own judgments in order to discourage the members from soft-pedaling their disagreements.*

2. *The leaders in an organization's hierarchy, when assigning a policy-planning mission to a group, should be impartial instead of stating preferences and expectations at the outset. This practice requires each leader to limit his or her briefings to unbiased statements about the scope of the problem and the limitations of available resources, without advocating specific proposals he or she would like to see adopted. This allows the conferees the opportunity to develop an atmosphere of open inquiry and to explore impartially a wide range of policy alternatives.*

3. *The organization should routinely follow the administrative practice of setting up several independent policy-planning and evaluation groups to work on the same policy question, each carrying out its deliberations under a different leader.*

4. *Throughout the period when the feasibility and effectiveness of policy alternatives are being surveyed, the policy-making group should from time to time divide into two or more subgroups to meet separately, under different chairpersons, and then come together to hammer out their differences.*

5. *Each member of the policy-making group should discuss periodically the group's deliberations with trusted associates in his or her own unit of the organization and report back their reactions.*

6. *One or more outside experts or qualified colleagues within the organization who are not core members of the policy-making group should be invited to each meeting on a staggered basis and should be encouraged to challenge the views of the core members.*

7. *At every meeting devoted to evaluating policy alternatives, at least one member should be assigned the role of devil's advocate.*

8. *Whenever the policy issue involves relations with a rival nation or organization, a sizable block of time (perhaps an entire session) should be spent surveying all warning signals from the rivals and constructing alternative scenarios of the rivals' intentions.*

9. *After reaching a preliminary consensus about what seems to be the best policy alternative, the policy-making group should hold a "second chance" meeting at which the members are expected to express as vividly as they can all their residual doubts and to rethink the entire issue before making a definitive choice.*

Is a Little Knowledge of Groupthink a Dangerous Thing?

Even if we had more than a little knowledge of groupthink, my answer to this question would be a categorical "yes" if we have in mind a naive person in a position of power who might be led to believe that groupthink is the only major source of error in policy-making and therefore that decisions can be made better by just one man (notably himself) than by a group of colleagues. I would also answer "yes" if I thought that a substantial number of policy-makers might be misled into believing that preventing groupthink should be given high priority, so that all sorts of safeguards should be introduced into the decision-making process without regard for hidden costs. Finally, I would wearily say "yes" if I discovered that many executives were being subjected to a lot of nonsense from overly eager faddists on their staff who were taking up precious time trying to introduce some kind of group therapy in the conference room, like an earlier generation of faddists who tried to inflict parlor-room psycho-analysis on their friends.

But my answer is "no" for anyone who takes the trouble to examine the fragmentary evidence on which I have drawn inferences about the conditions that give rise to groupthink. My two main conclusions are that along with other sources of error in decision-making, groupthink is likely to occur within cohesive small groups of decision-makers and that the most corrosive effects of groupthink can be counteracted by eliminating group insulation, overly direc-tive leadership practices, and other conditions that foster premature consen-sus. Those who take these conclusions seriously will probably find that the little knowledge they have about groupthink increases their understanding of the causes of erroneous group decisions and sometimes even has some practical value in preventing fiascoes. (If I didn't think so, I wouldn't have bothered to write this chapter.)

A little knowledge of groupthink might be valuable for anyone who partici-pates in a group that makes policy decisions, whether it is the executive committee of an international organization, an ad hoc committee set up by a government agency, the steering committee of a local business, professional, or political organization, or a student committee at a college. Such knowledge can be especially useful if it inclines the participants to consider introducing antidote prescriptions, provided, of course, that they are aware of the costs in time and effort and realize that there are other disadvantages they must also watch out for before they decide to adopt any of them as a standard operating procedure.

Sometimes it may even be useful for one of the members of the group to ask, at the right moment, before a decision is definitely made, "Are we allowing ourselves to become victims of groupthink?" I am not proposing that this question should be placed on the agenda or that the members should try to conduct a group therapy session. Rather, I have in mind making salient the realization that the desire for unity within the group can be discussed frankly and that agreement within the group is not always desirable. This open acknowledgment may enable some members to adopt a psychological set that inclines them to raise critical questions whenever there are signs of undue complacency or a premature consensus. One such question has to do with the consensus itself. A leader or a member who is aware of the symptoms of groupthink, for example, might ask to hear from those who have not yet said anything, in order to get all points of view onto the table before the group makes a final decision. In addition to this common-sense application, some ingenious procedures may be worked out or spontaneously improvised so that the symptoms of groupthink are counteracted by participants who know about the groupthink hypothesis, without constantly reminding the group of it.

With these considerations in mind, I suggest that awareness of the shared illusions, rationalizations, and other symptoms fostered by the interaction of members of small groups may curtail the influence of groupthink in policy-making groups, including those that meet in the White House. Here is another place where we can apply George Santayana's well-known adage: "Those who cannot remember the past are condemned to repeat it." Perhaps a better understanding of group dynamics among government leaders will help them avoid being condemned to repeat the fiascoes of the recent past described in this book.

Communication Processes

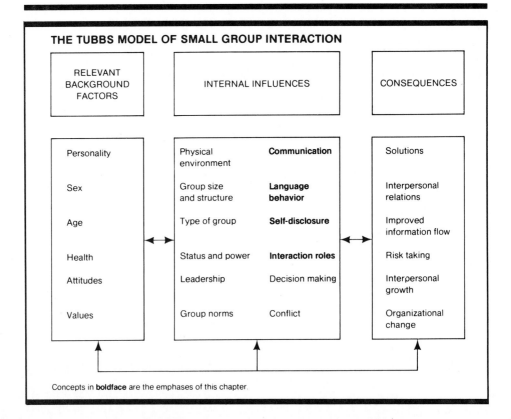

THE TUBBS MODEL OF SMALL GROUP INTERACTION

RELEVANT BACKGROUND FACTORS	INTERNAL INFLUENCES		CONSEQUENCES
Personality	Physical environment	**Communication**	Solutions
Sex	Group size and structure	**Language behavior**	Interpersonal relations
Age	Type of group	**Self-disclosure**	Improved information flow
Health	Status and power	**Interaction roles**	Risk taking
Attitudes	Leadership	Decision making	Interpersonal growth
Values	Group norms	Conflict	Organizational change

Concepts in **boldface** are the emphases of this chapter.

Chapter 5 continues with four more internal influences. Because communication is one of the most important aspects of group interaction, it is discussed thoroughly. It is first defined and then outlined into several different types. The topic of language behavior is presented, along with four specific problems that groups often confront. These are bypassing, inference making, polarizing, and signal reactions. In a group, one must also decide how much to share or contribute; therefore, self-disclosure is one of the four internal influences found in this chapter. Interaction roles is the last of the internal influences. One often establishes several roles in day-to-day living. Some examples of these are group task, group-building, and group maintenance roles.

GLOSSARY

Intentional-Unintentional Communication: Intentional communication occurs when we communicate what we mean to. Unintentional communication occurs when we communicate something different from what we intend, as when we accidentally offend someone.

Verbal-Nonverbal Communication: Verbal communication is the use of words to get across a message. Nonverbal communication is the use of physical actions, such as facial expression or tone of voice.

Defensive-Supportive Communication: Defensive communication occurs when a psychological barrier is created, known as a *defense mechanism*. This barrier acts to reduce effective communication. Supportive communication minimizes these types of problems.

Content and Process: Content of a group discussion includes comments about the *topic* of the discussion. Process is the *manner* in which the discussion is conducted.

Bypassing: Bypassing is a misunderstanding that occurs when "the sender and receiver miss each other with their meaning."

Inference Making: Inference making refers to going beyond observations and what we know. Inferences represent only some degree of probability of coming true.

Polarizing: Polarizing is the exaggeration that occurs when people attempt to make a point.

Signal Reactions: Signal reactions are learned responses to certain stimuli, such as emotional reactions to really offensive swear words or racial slurs.

Appropriateness: Appropriateness includes several factors that help determine the timing and extent of self-disclosure.

Group Task Roles: Group task roles are identifiable behaviors that are directed toward accomplishing the group's objective.

Group-Building and Maintenance Roles: Group-building and mainte-nance roles help the interpersonal functioning of the group and alter the way of working by strengthening, regulating, and perpetuating the group.

Individual Roles: Individual roles are roles that are designed to satisfy an *individual's* needs rather than to contribute to the needs of the group.

CASE STUDY: The Faculty Committee

A committee of university faculty members was deciding whom to have vote on an important new policy statement. It had worked for several months to develop and refine this policy statement, and it wanted to send a copy to all people in the university who would be affected by this policy. The committee had not anticipated any difficulty deciding whom to send the memo to. Then this problem occurred.

Prof. Brown: Now that we all have agreed on the final policy to be communicated, let's decide which method should be used to convey the policy.

Prof. Smith: Let's use an interorganization memo. (The group all agreed.) Let's send a ballot to each person through the faculty mail. (Again, general agreement.)

Prof. Brown: OK, the subject of the memo is adoption of the new faculty senate operating procedures, right? (General agreement.) All right, let's address this to all members of the faculty.

Prof. Jones: Whom are you including in the faculty?

Prof. Brown: That's obvious.

Prof. Jones: No, I don't think so. Are department chairmen included as faculty, or are they administrators?

Prof. Brown: Well, they teach, don't they?

Prof. Jones: Yes, but they also serve as administrators.

Prof. Brown: What does it matter what category they go by?

Prof. Jones: OK, let me put it this way. Do the deans and the president qualify as faculty or administrators?

Prof. Thomas: Well, they are listed in the catalog as faculty.

Prof. Jones: OK; however, this policy is the first major step in allowing greater *faculty* governance at this school. How can we get greater faculty governance if we include members of the administration in our definition of faculty?

Prof. James: Yeh. What if it's a close vote, and all the administrators vote as a block to defeat our new policy?

Prof. Brown: I still think we are making a mountain out of a molehill.

Prof. Jones: (Getting irritated.) We work for almost a year getting a faculty senate organized, and now you think it's a trivial matter whether or not the proposal gets defeated?

Prof. Brown: I didn't say anything of the kind. I only meant that I think it is unlikely that the administration has enough votes to make much difference no matter how we define the term "faculty."

Prof. Jones: Well, I strongly disagree. I think this is a *crucial* point. Are we, the faculty, going to have a hand in running this place once and for all, or are we going to let this little bit of progress be eroded by allowing administrators to vote on *our faculty senate?*

Prof. Smith: I'm afraid our time is running out for today's meeting. Since many of us have classes to go to, I think we should table this discussion until our next meeting. In the meantime, let's all try to rethink our positions on this.

Prof. Jones: I don't have to do any rethinking! If we are going to go back to being dictated to by the administration, I don't want any further part of this committee. I volunteered to be on this committee because I thought we had a chance to improve things around here. I can see now I have wasted my time.

Chairperson: Do I have a motion for adjournment?

Prof. Thomas: So moved.

Chairperson: Is there a second?

Prof. Smith: Second.

Chairperson: Meeting adjourned until next week.

1. What is the major problem for this group?

2. How could they have avoided this outcome?

3. If you could role play this discussion, what would you say to help resolve this situation?

This group discussion, which actually occurred, illustrates one type of problem groups may encounter: language-related problems and the relationship between language, thought, and behaviors. The committee members could not agree on how to interpret the word "faculty." This disagreement led to emotional reactions and eventually to one member's resignation. This problem is just one type of difficulty related to problems of communication. But before we go any further, let us stop and define *our* terms so we don't run into the same problem this committee did.

COMMUNICATION

Communication Defined

Communication within the small group is both similar to and different from communication in other settings. Group communication involves the process of creating meanings in the minds of others. These meanings may or may not correspond to the meanings we intend to create. Group communication involves the sending and receiving of messages between and among the participants. Group communication includes both verbal and nonverbal message stimuli. In all these ways, group communication is similar to communication that occurs in other contexts, such as interpersonal communication (informal communication between two or more people); public communication (between a speaker and an audience);

organizational communication (or communication in an organizational setting); or mass communication (in which a source attempts to communicate with large numbers of people, usually through some electronic or written medium). This chapter will focus on communication principles as they relate to the small group context.

Ruch and Goodman (1983, p. 133) argue persuasively that communication skills are the most important skills of all for managers and leaders. They write:

> Our advice to chief executive officers in any business is to never settle for anything less than the best in communication. Don't put in position second-rate managers as professional communicators. Find the bright stars and give them room to grow and be creative. And then back them up and follow their judgment and instincts within the framework of their professional expertise.

Communication among group members also may depend on the nature of the group. Some groups are highly structured. In such groups there is a leader, and there are followers. In an unstructured group the lines between leadership and followership are not so well defined. These various group environments have very different kinds of communication. A recent study (Courtwright, Fairhurst, and Rogers 1989) compared the communication between work groups in structured, "authority-based" plants and less-structured, "self-managing" plants.

Authority-based groups are highly structured. They are group environments that we think of as being "traditional." In an authority-based group, orders come from the top, and no one in the "lower ranks" questions the leader. In the first chapter we discussed mechanical and organic systems. Authority-based groups are mechanical systems. In a mechanical system, the communication moves in one direction, from leader to subordinate, and tends to be one-sided. In other words, "no questions asked."

Courtwright, Fairhurst, and Rogers (1989) confirmed such types of communication in their study. Words such as "initiate," "define," "structure," "dominate," and "inform" used by management were indicative of the authority-based, top-down direction of communication. This study also discovered competitive and argumentative communication to be common in such systems. Its findings reflect "a greater overall level of disagreement, conflict, and managerial attempts to dominate" (p. 797) in a mechanistic system.

Self-managing groups are organic systems. They are less structured, less traditional task groups. Communication in self-managing groups is more discussion-oriented, with more "question and answer interactions" occurring between group leaders and subordinates. According to Courtwright, Fairhurst, and Rogers (1989, p. 797), "The underlying theme of team self-management is that team members have a high level of decisional autonomy and control of activities previously reserved for management, such as selecting work procedures and varying work standards."

In organic systems, communication flows through a group like blood through the circulatory system of a living thing. This circulatory process is vital to the life of the group.

Intentional-Unintentional

Most of the time we communicate for a purpose. It may be to get our point across, to persuade another, to prompt action, or simply to have fun. These types of messages are known as *intentional;* that is, we intend to communicate in order to achieve our purpose. However, we also may transmit messages that are unintentional. The slip of the tongue, or Freudian slip, is one well-known phenomenon. On October 15, 1986, Vice-Admiral Poindexter of the U.S. Navy was interviewed by Bryant Gumbel on the *Today* show. Gumbel asked about the recent exposé on the so-called disinformation campaign to discredit Libya. Gumbel said: "Don't you think you have a credibility problem from this?" Admiral Poindexter replied: "I don't think I have any credibility at all." He obviously meant to say that he had no credibility *problem* at all. All of us can sympathize with a situation in which we say something quite different from what we had intended to say.

According to Freud, our id, or pleasure center, leads us to reveal what we really feel, whereas our ego, the rational data-processing part of our personality, tends to limit or censor what we utter. When the id forces win out over the rational ego forces, the Freudian slip results. Freud (Ruch 1972, p. 102) stated that such unintentional verbal messages more than likely result when we are "distracted, confused, embarrassed, or simply not psychically engaged [or] when the thought is insufficiently worked out or the problem particularly complicated."

Unintentional messages may be transmitted by action as well as by words. The person who crosses his arms in front of him while rearing back in his chair may be unknowingly communicating his disapproval of events occurring in a group discussion. Frequently, group members will direct their remarks (through eye contact) to those members that they prefer or that they feel have influence in the group. This is often done unconsciously and unintentionally.

The best-selling book *The Making of a Psychiatrist* (Viscott 1972) includes the description of a patient characterized by unintentional, compulsive gestures. Viscott (pp. 50–54) describes him in the following manner:

> "Mr. Parker, I'm going to be taking over from Dr. Meredith and I will try to be as helpful to you as I can. . . ." "Good, good," he said, reaching over and touching me on the knee with his hand, tapping me twice. . . .
>
> In order to control his inner world, Harold Parker had developed an intricate system of rituals which he repeated to ward off bad luck . . . he would touch something solid twice.
>
> "What do you think is going to happen with your company, Mr. Parker?" I asked.
>
> "I think things will turn out well, as they always do. It's a sound company." He tapped my desk twice again and smiled an artificial smile. . . .
>
> "I'm running it," said Harold Parker, tapping his right foot once. Once? Where's the second tap? I was pretty sure there would be another tap coming. There's *supposed* to be another tap coming. The first tap supposedly symbolizes a bad wish and the second supposedly erases it. Where was it? Maybe he didn't tap his foot magically at all. Maybe he just liked to tap his foot. Maybe I was reading a lot into all of this. Maybe this was all bullshit. Paying attention to so many details of a patient's behavior was trying.
>
> "You're running the company from here?"
>
> "I'm on the phone a couple of times a day to Edgar. He's my manager. That's how I'm running it." Mr. Parker tapped my desk twice.

This brief account illustrates one way in which actions can communicate without our even knowing it. This example also illustrates the potential pitfalls in trying to overinterpret, or read too much into, a person's verbal or nonverbal slips.

Communication is not one-way, especially in groups. Members react to messages. They respond to one another. This response is called *feedback*. Stech and Ratliffe (1985) say feedback is just as complicated as sending the message. Like the intended message, feedback also has content and relationship levels. Actually, when person 2 gives feedback to person 1, that feedback is actually person 2's intended message. In a continuing interaction, the two people continue to shift roles as sender and receiver, alternately providing each other with messages and feedback (p. 22).

Aronson (in Cathcart and Samovar 1984, p. 336) points out that the value of feedback is not limited to the recipient.

> Frequently in providing feedback, a person discovers something about himself and his own needs. If a person feels, for example, that it's wrong to experience anger, he may block out his awareness of this feeling. When the expression of such feelings is legitimized, he has a chance to bring them out in the open, look at them, and to become aware that his expression of anger has not caused the world to come to an end. Moreover, the direct expression of a feeling keeps the encounter on the up-and-up and thus helps to prevent the escalation of negative feelings.

Groups are one context in which we get feedback on behaviors that helps us eliminate unintentional cues. The gap between what we intend to communicate and what is actually received is called the *arc of distortion* (Bennis 1961). The larger the gap, the less effective we are in our relations with others. We can reduce the gap if we are receptive to feedback from others and if others are willing to share their impressions with us. In order for the arc to be reduced, the feedback must be of high quality. Miles (1967) suggests that effective feedback must "(1) be clear and undistorted, (2) come from a trusted nonthreatening source, and (3) follow as closely as possible the behavior to which it is a reaction."

Most practitioners of communication encourage clarity. When you want someone to understand and follow your instructions, you see to it that they are clear and concise. However, as Eric Eisenberg (1984) has pointed out, people, particularly in small groups and organizations, confront many different situational requirements, develop many different and often conflicting goals, and respond to one another with communication strategies that do not always minimize ambiguity but are still effective.

If this can occur, Eisenberg argues, perhaps ambiguity (the lack of specific detail, use of abstract language, and absence of a course of action) can be used in groups and organizations in a strategic sense. "Strategic ambiguity" is the purposeful use of ambiguity to accomplish goals. Ambiguity used strategically in an organization can result in promoting unified diversity, facilitating organizational change, and preserving privileged positions in the organization. For example, leaders often say that they stand for "a spirit of community," which is rarely defined but does tend to encourage people's cooperation. Eisenberg summarized the use of ambiguous strategy when he wrote "in turbulent environments, ambiguous communication is not a kind of fudging, but rather a rational method used by communicators to orient toward multiple goals. . . . The use of more or less ambiguity is in itself not good or bad, effective or ineffective; whether a strategy is ethical depends upon the ends to which it is used, and whether it is effective depends upon the goals of the individual communicators."

Verbal-Nonverbal

As indicated above, we communicate not only with words (verbal messages), but by nonverbal means as well. In Chapter 3 we discussed the importance of environmental influences on small group interaction. Later in this chapter we will discuss verbal cues under the heading "Language Behavior." In addition, visual and vocal nonverbal cues will vary as a part of the process of discussion and will influence the eventual results of the discussion.

Visual Cues

Visual cues are highly influential in interpersonal communication. *Facial expression* and *eye contact* are probably the two most important types of visual cues. Those who avoid looking at us communicate disapproval or disinterest. Those who look at us may still indicate a negative reaction on the basis of their facial expression. Probably the most rewarding cue is a smiling face and a head nod in combination with direct eye contact. From these and other cues we infer support, confirmation, and agreement. Knapp (1972, p. 119) emphasizes the importance of the face: "The face is rich in communicative potential. It is the primary site for communication of emotional states; it reflects interpersonal attitudes; it provides nonverbal feedback on the comments of others; and some say it is the primary source of information next to human speech." Barnlund (1968, p. 521) echoes this feeling: "Of all the features that identify a man, none is as differentiating as his face; of all the parts of the body, none is as richly expressive."

Although facial expression is usually a critical factor in nonverbal communication, there are some rare occasions in which other factors may take precedence. Note the following news item:

> Los Angeles (AP) The braless robber has struck for the second time in two days. . . . Police said the robber, wearing a sheer blue blouse without a bra, robbed a South Pasadena branch of the Bank of America of about $400 Tuesday. . . . On Monday, a person believed to be the same woman held up a Los Angeles savings and loan office and escaped with $2,600. Police said a red-faced teller was unable to describe the robber's face, noting only that she was braless under a light-colored blouse.

One study confirmed the finding that the general tendency to look into a person's eyes can be preempted by other factors. Wahlers and Barker (1973) conducted an interview study and found that braless women got significantly less eye contact from males than their bra-wearing counterparts.

Eye contact, however, is a powerful type of nonverbal cue. Argyle (1967) estimates that in group communication we spend between 30 and 60 percent of the time exchanging mutual glances with others. Many of these may last less than a second. He summarizes (pp. 115–116) several unstated rules about visual interaction:

a. A looker may invite interaction by staring at another person who is on the other side of a room. The target's studied return of the gaze is generally interpreted as acceptance of the invitation, while averting the eyes is a rejection of the looker's request.

b. There is more mutual eye contact between friends than others, and a looker's frank gaze is widely interpreted as positive regard.

c. Persons who seek eye contact while speaking are regarded not only as exceptionally well-disposed by their target, but also as more believable and earnest.

d. If the usual short, intermittent gazes during conversation are replaced by gazes of longer duration, the target interprets this as meaning that the task is less important than the personal relation between the two persons.

Several other principles have been borne out by experimental studies as well as by systematic observation of ongoing behaviors. For example, females consistently give more eye contact than males (Mehrabian 1969). Also, we are able to assert dominance over others almost exclusively with eye contact in a matter of seconds when we first encounter one another (Strongman and Champness 1968). We tend to direct our comments toward those from whom we expect or would like feedback (Kendon 1967). Conversely, avoiding eye contact is a way of protecting oneself from the contact of others. Argyle and Dean (1965) summarize the functions of eye contact by stating that it signals information seeking, openness to communication, concealment or exhibitionism, recognition of social relationships, and conflicts in motivation.

Facial expression, eye contact, and body positioning all reveal clear information about our present attitudes and feelings. We give approval and show disdain all without saying a word. Sometimes our nonverbal responses to people lead others to make decisions about those people. This is reflected in the body of research investigating group members' nonverbal responses to leaders. The data demonstrate the existence of a social mechanism leading to the devaluation of leadership. When some group members display unfavorable nonverbal responses to a leader, the remaining group members tend to rate that leader's contributions as less valuable. When favorable nonverbal cues are given, the leader's contributions are rated as higher (Brown and Geis 1984, Butler and Geis 1990). The latter study hypothesized and found that competent, assertive women in leadership roles elicit significantly more negative responses than men in the same positions. This is thought to be a result of female leaders breaking with the stereotypic submissive, "feminine" behaviors. When women served in stereotypic masculine roles (leadership), they received nonverbal disapproval from their peers. This disapproval was passed on to other group members, who assessed the female leaders as making less valuable contributions. This has much to do with the elements of social influence and conformity discussed in Chapter 4.

Hand gestures are another type of visual cue. Barnlund (1968) states, "Next to the face, the hands are probably the most expressive part of the human body." Entire books have been devoted to the study of the hands in oral communication. It was once thought that hand gestures could be taught as a means of developing greater expressiveness. For example, the outstretched hands with the palms up would indicate a request for help, whereas the clenched fist would indicate a threat. The study of gestures today is more descriptive and leans less in the direction of trying to prescribe which gestures should be used in certain situations.

In one company, for example, a union grievance was filed on the basis of a gesture of the employee's boss. The grievance charged: "Animus toward the grievant can be demonstrated by the Department Head's handling of the application. . . . The application was tossed across the desk by the Department Head in the direction of the grievant. The Department Head's manner was offensive, embarrassing and unprofessional to both the grievant and the [union president]" (1986). This grievance went through several steps of the grievance procedure and tied up dozens of hours of managerial time for the better part of a year. There were also threats of legal action.

Physical appearance includes facial attractiveness as well as body shape and size and styles of dress. In one study of physically attractive versus unattractive people, Widgery (1974) found that on the basis of faces alone, more attractive people are consistently assumed to have higher credibility than their homely counterparts. Walster et al. (1966) found that among 752 college students at a freshman dance, physical attractiveness was by far the most important factor in determining the extent to which a date would be liked by his or her partner. B. F. Skinner has argued that beauty is a form of reinforcer, because it encourages us to look once again. Certainly most fashion models of both sexes are reinforcing to look at!

As we saw in Chapter 4, body shape has been described in three basic categories by Sheldon (1954). The mesomorph is muscular and athletic looking and would be considered the most attractive. The ectomorph is tall, thin, and fragile looking. The endomorph is soft, round, and fat. Three representative examples of the respective body types would be Arnold Schwarzenegger, Pee Wee Herman, and John Candy. Our body shapes are usually some mixture of these three types. Jack Lalanne, the famous physical fitness personality, once said on a television show that if you raid the refrigerator every night, even if you are alone, your body itself communicates to everybody every day that you eat too much. So you're not fooling anybody.

Styles of dress also communicate about us. We are often judged as "straight" or "punkers" on the basis of our clothing choices. Lefkowitz, Blake, and Mouton (1955) conducted an interesting study of the influence of a person's dress on jaywalking behavior. They collected data on jaywalking on three different days for three different one-hour periods. They wanted to determine if pedestrians (these happened to be in Austin, Texas) would violate the "wait" signal more if they saw someone else violate it than if there were no violator. They were also interested in any differential effects that would result from differences in the violator's dress. The experimenters made use of a confederate who jaywalked while dressed one of two ways. First he dressed in a high-status manner, with a freshly pressed suit, shined shoes, white shirt, tie, and straw hat (Mr. Clean). The low-status dress consisted of an unpressed blue denim shirt, soiled and patched pants, well-worn shoes, and no hat (Mr. Dirty). Observations were made on 2103 pedestrians who crossed the intersection during the hours of the experiment.

The study revealed several interesting results. Ninety-nine percent of the pedestrians obeyed the "wait" signal when no confederate was present or when the confederate also obeyed. When "Mr. Dirty" jaywalked, 4 percent of the other pedestrians also violated the signal. When "Mr. Clean" jaywalked, 14 percent of the other pedestrians also disobeyed. Some students replicated this study in 1973 and found quite similar results. Although these studies are dated, it is still valid today that a person with multicolored hair or spiked hair and punk appearance would not get very far in a job interview in most companies.

To summarize, our appearance through facial attractiveness, body shape, and choice of clothing will determine to some extent our influence on others.

Body movements are also an influential type of nonverbal cue. Each of us can probably remember having someone say, "You seem kind of down today," as a reaction to our slumped shoulders and slightly bowed head. Probably one of Peter Falk's most memorable roles is his slouchy interpretation of the character Columbo. Although there are a wealth of other cues (gestures, raincoat, cigar), body movements stand out very vividly, as did John Wayne's swagger or Vanna White's walk.

Body orientation is an important factor in small group interaction. Knapp (1972, p. 97) defines body orientation as "the degree to which a communicator's shoulders and legs are turned in the direction of, rather than away from, the addressee." Mehrabian (1969) found that a seated communicator who leaned forward was perceived as having a more positive attitude than one who leaned backward and away from the person judging. Goffman (1961) noted that higher-status persons were more relaxed in staff meetings in a psychiatric hospital than lower-status individuals, who sat straighter in their chairs. Body position may also add to our perceiving a person as being "uptight." Schutz (1971, p. 212) describes this in the context of an encounter group.

> If a person is holding himself tight, I would either move on to someone else and count on the group interaction to loosen him up so that he can work better later, or perhaps choose to try to help him break through that defense. . . . A first step is to ask the person to relax by unlocking his arms and legs if he has them crossed, perhaps to stand up and shake himself loose, jiggle and breathe very deeply for several minutes.

Inclusiveness is another important aspect of body orientation. In a small group discussion, subgroups frequently form that are usually annoying to at least some in the group. Subgroups may be the result of one person directing comments to only one or two others. This term "directing comments" refers to body orientation and the direction of eye contact. Those who feel excluded from the discussion will sooner or later begin to withdraw their participation from the group, and the benefit of their contributions will be lost. Thus body orientation can be a potent factor in determining the discussion's outcome.

Vocal Cues

In addition to verbal messages and visual cues, vocal cues affect small group interaction. There is usually some confusion between the terms "vocal cues" and "verbal cues." Perhaps it would be helpful to remember that vocal cues are lost when a verbal (word) message is written down. Vocal cues include regional dialects, methods of pronunciation, and the five major factors of (1) volume, (2) rate and fluency, (3) pitch, (4) quality, and (5) inflection.

Try to imagine the sound of your voice saying, "Now that we are all here, we can get the meeting started." Now think of how it would sound as stated by Bill Cosby, Arsenio Hall, David Brinkley, Humphrey Bogart, W. C. Fields, Elizabeth Taylor, Mae West, Roseanne Barr, Bart Simpson, or some of your own friends. Each person's voice is unique; sometimes voice prints are used like fingerprints for identification. This individuality results from the complex combination of vocal cues mentioned above. Speaking with adequate *volume,* or loudness, is the first responsibility of any communicator. Conversely, the first responsibility of listeners is to let speakers know they can't be heard. Speakers should be asked to speak more loudly and to repeat the part that was missed (Tubbs and Moss 1991). This requires some tact, however. The intent should be to communicate, "I want to know what you're saying," rather than, "Listen, dummy, I'm important and you're not taking my listening convenience into sufficient account."

Groups tend to have more problems with adequate volume than, say, people involved in personal conversations. As the size of the group increases, the hearing difficulties may also increase, because there are more potential sources of interfering noise and the distance from the speaker to any given member in the group tends to be greater.

A second critical vocal cue is *rate and fluency*. Rate refers to words uttered per minute (WPM), and fluency refers to the lack of interruptions (which may influence the rate). We have all suffered the unpleasantness of listening to a person who injects long pauses in the middle of sentences or who frequently throws in such distracting verbal fillers as "ah," "um," "er," "why I," "and-uh," "like," among others. An average speaking rate is between 125 and 175 words per minute. If the person is able to articulate well—that is, to speak distinctly—a faster rate seems to be more interesting to listen to. Studies in listener comprehension indicate that we can understand rates two and three times the normal speed with little difficulty. In group discussion, the fluent speaker is usually more pleasant to listen to.

Vocal *pitch* refers to the frequency in cycles per second (CPS) of the vocal tones. Melanie Griffith and Dudley Moore have high-pitched (or high-frequency) voices; Sylvester Stallone and Bea Arthur have lower-pitched voices. There is probably no such thing as the perfectly pitched voice; however, most successful professional announcers seem to have lower-pitched voices (e.g., Merlin Olsen and Dick Enberg).

Vocal *quality* refers to the resonance of the voice. Different examples would include breathiness (Connie Stevens), harshness (George C. Scott), nasality (Sylvester Stallone), and huskiness (Deborah Winger). Vocal quality may determine the extent to which people may want to listen to us for any length of time. Johnny Carson's laugh was once described as being "like the sound of cracking plastic." The voice of comedian Don Adams was once compared to "the sound of scratching your fingernail across a blackboard." On the other hand, some people who try to make their voices sound more deep and resonant come across as phony and artificial.

Inflection refers to the relative emphasis, pitch changes, and duration in uttering different word parts in a sentence. The American southerner's accent is characterized by a drawn-out vowel sound—for example, Atlanta (northern pronunciation) versus Atlaaanta (southern pronunciation). Inflections also include the rise in vocal pitch at the end of an interrogative sentence:

Are you ^coming?

Probably the most critical thing to remember about vocal inflections is that they may indicate a lot of the emotional tone of a statement. The statement "Oh, great" can be said with true enthusiasm or great disgust. We can use our voices to indicate sarcasm, ridicule, and superiority, and what we convey may be counterproductive to the group's progress.

Leathers (1976) reports that several emotions can be reliably detected in most speakers. He has groups of students rate ten different vocal messages according to the emotions they convey. The rating instructions are as shown in Figure 5.1. Although Leathers's technique is for the purpose of research, the practical aspect is that vocal cues do accurately convey emotions. As we become more aware and in control of our nonverbal cues, we may improve our effectiveness in groups. For example, several students complained about a professor who was being quite abusive in his tone of voice to them. They were considering quitting his class because of this. When he was told, he was shocked. He had been unaware of the negative consequences his vocal tone had on his teaching effectiveness.

FIGURE 5.1   THE VOCALIC MEANING SENSITIVITY TEST
Source: Reprinted with permission of the author from Dale Leathers, *Nonverbal Communication Systems* (Boston: Allyn and Bacon, 1976).

The communicator you are listening to—either live or on tape recording—is attempting to communicate ten different classes or kinds of meaning to you. Each attempt to communicate a class of meaning will begin with the words, "This is vocal message number_____." You are to listen very carefully and place the number of the vocal message in the blank across from a word, such as disgust or happiness, which comes closest to representing the meaning which has just been communicated to you vocally. Follow the same procedure for each of the ten vocal messages.

Class of Vocalic Meaning	Number of Vocal Message
Disgust	_____
Happiness	_____
Interest	_____
Sadness	_____
Bewilderment	_____
Contempt	_____
Surprise	_____
Anger	_____
Determination	_____
Fear	_____

Clearly, not all the cues are exhibited in the small group setting. However, as we become more aware of our nonverbal behavior overall, we can begin to change some of these cues in situations that appear to need improvement. We can also begin to develop our sensitivities to the nonverbal behaviors of others. For example, if a meeting has been going on for a long time, you can detect tiredness and low levels of energy through bored facial expressions, yawns, or unenthusiastic vocal tones. These cues may indicate that the group needs to take a break in order to continue at peak efficiency. But the person not sensitive to these cues may try to keep pushing a tired group, only to accomplish less and less.

In summarizing this section on verbal and nonverbal cues, we need to point out that all these cues are perceived as a whole. We do not dissect them in reality as we have done in this analysis. For example, it has been found that when we say one thing but nonverbally indicate something else (for example, "I really appreciate that" spoken sarcastically), the *nonverbal* message is more likely to be believed (Keltner 1970). In this same context, subjects in one study who were told to lie showed several nonverbal changes. There were more errors in their speech, they had less direct eye contact, and they talked for shorter durations than they had when they were telling the truth (Mehrabian 1971). Obviously, nonverbal communication plays a significant role in small groups. As one source puts it, whether you talk or not, "You can't *not* communicate" (Watzlawick, Beavin, and Jackson 1967). Let us keep in mind the importance of both verbal and nonverbal messages.

Nonverbal communication takes a different form at the organizational level. Suzyn Ornstein (1989) asserted that people are often unaware of the nonverbal communication that results from the layout and decor of an office. Definite relationships have been established between office design and various organizational behaviors, attitudes, and impressions. An open-office layout, as opposed to the conventional, individual office design, is often conducive to communication in the workplace and can lead to greater employee satisfaction. If employees are comfortable in their office, they feel that their managers are concerned about their well-being, and they will be more satisfied in their jobs. Other elements of the workplace that affect employee behaviors and attitudes include seating arrangement, lighting, temperature, noise, and the presence of artwork. The decor and layout of corporate offices lead to the impressions that people have about that corporation. "Not only is office configuration important in conveying information about the organization's values, but the physical layout of the offices themselves . . . also serves to reinforce the company's values" (Ornstein 1989, p. 144).

Ornstein made some suggestions to managers about what they should consider when implementing changes in office layout: (1) Managers should seek input from employees who will be affected by the change; (2) Managers should thoroughly analyze the work to be performed in the space under consideration; (3) Managers should consider the values, goals, and behaviors they want to reinforce by their selection of office design; and (4) Managers should consider the influence office design has on outsiders who have cause to visit the facility.

Defensive-Supportive

For several years it has been an established fact that when someone threatens you psychologically, you react by throwing up a barrier against that threat. That barrier is referred to as a *defense mechanism*. Once that defensive barrier has been erected, effective communication is reduced. Thus it is valuable to learn how we can avoid arousing others' protective psychological shields. Gibb (1961) described six differences between what he called defensive and supportive communication climates. These six differences are:

Supportive Climates	Defensive Climates
Description	Evaluation
Problem orientation	Control
Spontaneity	Strategy
Empathy	Neutrality
Equality	Superiority
Provisionalism	Certainty

When we feel we are being evaluated, especially when someone is criticizing us, we are likely to rise to our own defense. However, when we feel that a person is objectively describing us without adding an evaluation, we are not as likely to become defensive. When someone tries to control or coerce us, we become more uncomfortable than when a person seeks to solve a problem without forcing us to go along with the solution. Then, too, a person who has a preset plan usually turns us off, as opposed to one who reacts spontaneously to situations. Strategy often implies a gimmick or some deception. Similarly, when a person is neutral toward us, as opposed to empathic or sympathetic, it usually makes us more defensive. When a person acts in a superior manner instead of treating us as an equal, we say that person is on an ego trip. Such superior behavior is deflating to our self-esteem and arouses our defenses. Finally, when someone acts as a "know-it-all," this attitude of certainty or dogmatism is less pleasant than when the person is willing to have an open mind and act with a degree of provisionalism. Gibb found that groups with defensive climates got more bogged down in worthless ego-protecting discussion and accomplished less than those with more supportive climates.

The notion of effectiveness in showing consideration and initiating structure is further supported by other prior research done on the communication of effective supervisors. Effective supervisors have been shown to: "(1) be more communication-oriented than the ineffective leader, (2) be receptive and responsive to subordinate inquiries, (3) tends to ask or persuade rather than to tell, and (4) gives advanced notice of changes and explains why" (p. 311). All of these sound like informative, content-oriented forms of communication that lead to a "leader role" designation for the communicator. At the same time, these messages show consideration for the persons receiving them. Such a style of communication helps to build effective working relationships between the leader and followers. "Interpersonal communication between supervisor and subordinate is both relational and content-oriented. Although supervisors may consider their primary communication goals as informational or content-oriented, it is clear that relational messages are also important" (Penley and Hawkins 1985, p. 324).

Sometimes it may become necessary to criticize a group member. This is difficult and embarrassing for everyone involved. In fact, Weisinger (1989, p. 245) described criticism within a group as "one of the most difficult criticism encounters." When one member of the group is criticized, the other members of the group are less likely to contribute, for fear of being put down. Weisinger (pp. 246–248) offered three strategies for criticizing group work or group members while still maintaining a supportive environment for the group.

1. Direct critical comments to the work, and not to the person who performed it.

2. Turn individual criticism into a group criticism by making the statement general.

3. Present the criticism in a way that forces the group members to come up with answers to the problem.

The first strategy depersonalizes the criticism by addressing it to the task rather than the person. It's the difference between saying, "This could use some more work," and "You did this wrong. You must redo it." The latter is more likely to bring about feelings of resentment and defensiveness than the first. The second strategy aims the criticism at the whole group, as a general request for change. Rather than saying, "You are not spending enough time on the project," comment that, "We could all stand to commit ourselves more to the project." There is a chance that the person for whom the comment was intended will miss it altogether. However, such a strategy maintains the supportive nature of the group and will help to encourage the other members of the group. The purpose of the third strategy is to involve the group members in the solution process. Instead of laying harsh criticism on the members of the group ("Your sales records are rotten! The company is ready to fold"), invite them to come up with a solution to the problem ("Sales are down throughout the company. Does anyone have any ideas on how to remedy the situation?").

A specific line of research on supportive versus defensive communication has been conducted along the lines of the confirming versus disconfirming aspects of communication. Sieburg and Larson (1971, p. 1) define these concepts in the following way: "confirmation, as used in an interpersonal sense, refers to any behavior that causes another person to value himself more. Its opposite, disconfirmation, refers to any behavior that causes another person to value himself less."

The confirmation/disconfirmation literature has expanded within recent years. Although the basic thrust of the theory remains the same—that is, that communication with others is potentially confirming or disconfirming—the role of such behavior in communication has been continually refined.

Dance and Larson (1972) divide communication patterns into four types:

1. explicit rejection (disconfirming)

2. implicit rejection (disconfirming)

3. explicit acceptance (confirming)

4. implicit acceptance (confirming)

Explicit rejection involves either a negative evaluation or an overt dismissal of the person or his message. For example:

A. "I can't understand how they can just sit on their duffs and not do anything about it. Time is running out."

B. "Yeah, well, I don't see you doing anything about it."

Implicit rejection involves four more subtle types of disconfirmation.

A. Interruptions—when a speaker cuts you off in mid-sentence

B. Imperviousness—When a speaker ignores what you say as if you had never said it

C. Irrelevant response—when the speaker starts off on a totally unrelated topic in response to your initial comment

D. Tangential response—when a person gives some acknowledgement to your initial comment but immediately launches off on a new irrelevant topic

Explicit acceptance involves a positive evaluation of either the person or his communication content. For example:

A. "So I just told him straight out that he wasn't going to pull that kind of stuff with me."

B. "That took guts."

Implicit acceptance involves either a direct acknowledgement of a person's remark, an attempt to clarify the remark by asking for more information, or an expression of positive feeling. For example:

A. "What I meant to say was that I've known him for a long time, and I've never seen him do anything like that."

B. "Oh, well, now I understand."

The importance of confirmation/disconfirmation literature lies in the specific identification of communication patterns that seem to help or hinder communication effectiveness in most situations. Cissna (1976), who summarized studies in widely differing situations, found that the only factor that appeared in all these studies was the confirmation/disconfirmation factor. Thus, this factor may be one of the most pervasive dimensions in human communication.

See also Cushman and Cahn (1985) and Cahn and Tubbs (1983). See the article by Gibb at the end of this chapter for a more complete description and for a good explanation of the use of the supportive style of communicating.

Content and Process

One rather difficult distinction to make about group discussion is the difference between the content of the discussion and the process. Suppose a group is discussing this topic: "How can political corruption in the United States be reduced?" When the discussion is over, the professor asks others in the class to comment on the discussion. Comments concerning the *content* of the discussion might include the following:

- I think political corruption will always be with us.

- I think politics are not more dirty now than in the past.

- The political system has shown its strength by catching its own offenders.

These comments are typical of an untrained observer. They all deal with the topic of the discussion, and the observer frequently gets into the heat of the discussion topic himself.

Comments regarding the *process* of the same discussion are quite different, as illustrated by the following:

- Joe dominated the group while the others couldn't get a word in edgewise.

- Most of your comments were based on opinions. Few actual facts were brought out.

- I think you got bogged down in defining the problem and never really got to any conclusion as to how to solve the problem.

These comments deal with the process or manner in which the discussion was conducted. This type of observation usually requires more insight into group interaction. Also, this type of comment allows both participants and observers to learn from one sample discussion some principles of group interaction that can be generalized to other discussions. Thus, it is important to be able to distinguish discussion content from the discussion process.

Notice the difference in the following two students' descriptions of a group discussion. They were asked to describe the group processes in their small group. (The topic was the ethics of cloning humans—exercise 3 in Chapter 1.)

Student 1

I feel a certain resentment toward the idea of *producing* life, which I consider cloning to be. I especially feel a resentment toward producing beings to act as slaves or to be used by us in any way. My group discussed the idea of controlling the traits of cloned human beings for specialized purposes. I do not feel that God appreciates his children tampering with the miracle of life.

Student 2

The group started with the usual "I guess we're supposed to's" and, after only a minimal amount of paper shuffling, got down to the subject at hand.

Of the five-person group, only four participated. It was interesting to note who assumed the leadership role, for how long, for what reasons, how effectively, etc. I feel that the member who occupied this role initially usually does not do so in other groups—that members who seemed to know something about this subject successfully opened the discussion and maintained it by asking others questions. What I looked for but did *not* see was direct eye contact, an authoritative tone of voice (I didn't say authoritarian), and backbone enough to justify occupying the leader's role. I think she was assuming this behavior to get a good grade.

Notice how student 1 discusses only the *topic* of the discussion content. Student 2, however, really discusses the group's *process,* or behavior, and therefore does a much better job of fulfilling the assignment.

Therapeutic-Pathological

We are more and more coming to realize that some communication patterns are psychologically more healthy or unhealthy than others. One popular way of determining the difference is called *transactional analysis*. This method is described in the best-selling book *I'm OK—You're OK,* by Thomas Harris (1967). A *transaction* is defined as when "I do something to you and you do something back" (pp. 11–12). Transactions can be analyzed in terms of three types of brain functions (called ego states)—namely, the Parent, Adult, and Child (P-A-C). For example, the child-child transaction is shown in Figure 5.2.

According to the theory, transactions that occur between the two participants' adult ego states are more likely to produce an I'm OK—You're OK, or a psychologically healthy, outcome. The adult ego state represents the rational, data-processing state of the brain. It is comparable to the *descriptive, provisional, problem-oriented,* and *equal* type of comment described by Gibb. The parent ego state is more like Gibb's *evaluative* comment and often implies *control, certainty,* and *superiority.* An example of a parent comment in a small group would be a participant's saying, while waving a pointed finger at the group, "You two are always goofing around; I want you to shape up!" This type of comment is likely to produce a response from the child ego state of those on the receiving end, which might be something like, "Oh yeah, well who's gonna make me?" or "What do I need with you and this dumb group anyway?"

The child ego state is defined as the location of feelings such as anger, happiness, fear, or love. Harris describes the four possible life conditions as: (1) I'm OK—You're OK, which is the desirable situation, basically a psychology of live and let live; (2) I'm Not OK—You're OK, the situation in which a person lacks self-esteem

FIGURE 5.2   CHILD–CHILD TRANSACTION

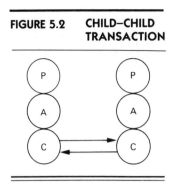

and considers others to be superior; (3) I'm OK—You're Not OK, wherein the person has feelings of superiority; and (4) I'm Not OK—You're Not OK, in which the person takes a pathological kill-or-be-killed position of defensiveness based on insecurity.

The objective of transactional analysis is to teach us the difference among these different types of transactions so that we can improve our communication effectiveness by keeping more of our transactions in the adult ego state. This, however, is often easier said than done. In one discussion a group member asked, "What's important here?" This question is usually generated from the adult ego state and is supposed to help group members focus their attention on the main issues before the group. However, in this case it was stated with an exasperated tone of voice and an angry facial expression. The comment did not help the group but made other group members feel "Not OK," actually diverting attention from the significant issue under discussion. Incidentally, transactional analysts would probably argue that the comment was an ulterior transaction (Figure 5.3) that on the surface was on the adult-adult level but that was really motivated by the critical parent to punish the child in the group who was holding up the group's progress. (See also Tubbs and Carter 1977.)

Literally thousands of discussions begin with an adult level of problem analysis and degenerate to something less productive. Let us look at a series of statements in two actual discussions. The first exemplifies a deterioration of exchanges between the participants' parent ego states to the point where they are playing the game "Ain't it awful?" (Berne 1964). The second series represents comments on the same topic that are reality-based and were generated from the participants' adult ego states. In both cases, the discussion topic was, "What can be done to create better job equality among the races?"

Discussion I (Parent Level: "Ain't It Awful?")

A: All I know is, racism is racism. A white male today is discriminated against in finding a job.

FIGURE 5.3 AN ULTERIOR TRANSACTION

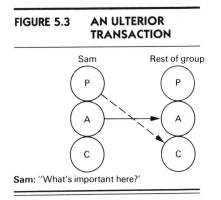

Sam: "What's important here?"

B: I know what you mean. I've heard of cases where entrance exam results are fudged so that minorities can get in.

C: It's always the way. You work your guts out trying to get ahead and what good does it do you?

D: You're right. There's no justice!

Discussion 2 (Adult Level: Rational Thinking)

A: Earlier in our discussion we defined job equality as an equal opportunity to obtain a job, assuming equal qualifications.

B: What about affirmative action programs designed to increase minority employment to a certain percentage of a work force within a certain time period—say, a year?

C: Does anybody have a thought on that?

D: Well, on one hand it does not meet our definition of equality in the short run, because some less-qualified person may be given an unfair advantage. But in the long run, it eradicates the effects of several years of discrimination in the other direction.

A: In other words, we need short-term inequality to bring about long-term equality?

C: I guess it's a little like procrastination in studying. If you ignore your homework for several weeks, you have to study extra hard to catch up and then maintain some moderate study effort from then on.

D: In other words, once the percentage of the work force in any given job reaches the percentage of that group in the general population, then "true equality" can be realized.

A: I think that makes sense.

B: It will be uncomfortable in the meantime, but it seems to be a desirable goal.

As you can see, the second discussion focuses on the issues and avoids generalizations or such platitudes as, "It's always the way. You work your guts out trying to get ahead and what good does it do you?" The second type of discussion leads to an action plan, whereas the first type often ends with nothing much accomplished and with final comments such as, "Well, it's a crazy world, but what can you do about it?"

As we conclude this section on communication, let us keep in mind that as hard as we try to avoid breakdowns, they are an inherent part of the process. Eisenberg (1984, p. 227) reminds us:

> People within organizations confront multiple situational demands and, therefore, develop multiple and conflicting goals and the resulting communicative strategies do not always minimize ambiguity, but are, however, effective. Strategic ambiguity is essential to organizing in that it: (1) promotes unified diversity, (2) facilitates organizational change, and (3) amplifies existing source attributions and preserves privileged positions.

LANGUAGE BEHAVIOR

The study of the interaction between verbal symbols and the thought patterns associated with them is referred to as *general semantics*. If you have ever become bogged down in a group discussion because of a difficulty in defining terms or dealing with any problems with language, as in the case study at the beginning of this chapter, you will immediately see the relevance of this topic to the study of small group interaction. In fact, some discussions may even have as their task the problem of choosing the appropriate verbal symbol to represent a concept. New products frequently have several proposed names that may be market-tested for consumer response. The intermediate-sized Ford Granada, for example, had several other potential names that apparently were not popular. According to Smith (1974): "Ford tested Eagle, Fairmont, Stallion, Lucerne, Gibraltar, Scandia, and many other monikers before selecting [the name] Granada for its new compact luxury car. Chrysler Corporation's design studies have flirted with special models carrying such names as Boca Raton, Gatsby, Gandy Dancer, Easy Rider and Magnum." Committees spend hours brainstorming possible names and then determining procedures for testing market reaction to the main contenders.

Although few of us will ever make decisions concerning product names, each of us will undoubtedly be involved with language problems of one sort or another in group discussions. Our discussion will focus on four specific problems that frequently plague groups: (1) bypassing, (2) inference making, (3) polarizing, and (4) signal reactions.

Bypassing

In January of 1990 an Avianca Airlines passenger plane crashed on Long Island, New York, killing seventy-three people. A subsequent investigation attributed the crash to a miscommunication between the pilots and the air traffic controllers. One report indicated that "Avianca pilots were not trained to use the term 'fuel emergency' . . . Controllers testified that the plane received no priority to land that night because the term 'fuel emergency' was not used" (Detroit Free Press, June 23, 1990, p. 4A).

This case illustrates a situation in which a misunderstanding occurred because of a language problem. This sort of misunderstanding is referred to as *bypassing*. It is defined as "the miscommunication pattern which occurs when the *sender* (speaker, writer, and so on) and the *receiver* (listener, reader, and so forth) *miss each other with their meaning*" (Haney 1986). In group discussions, the entire focus of the discussion may be diverted by a difference in interpretation of a given word. Note the incredible problems arising in one group as seen by one participant:

> At the start of our meeting I introduced a definition of communication (communication is an expression of ideas). Although the basics were appreciated, Ed and Al requested a revision, as the statement was too simple. They decided to drop the words "an expression of ideas." I didn't believe this was a very good revision and said so. A slight altercation developed lasting about five minutes. It was resolved that other ideas would be considered.
>
> After sufficient waiting (about thirty seconds), I realized no great ideas were forthcoming, so I subtly suggested that my idea be reconsidered. This time Pete and John were on my side. Still, my full idea could not survive Al and Ed, so it was given new form. . . . In the process of getting a communication definition, they had to satisfy me that their changes were justified, while I was attempting to show my original as the best. "Well, you haven't done any better," was surprisingly effective. While I had been using sword points, the best they could muster was a safety pin.
>
> After the mutilation of my last idea, I decided I would not volunteer any more material and thus "watch them squirm."

It seems hard to believe that such intense reactions could result from a difference of opinion over the definition of the term "communication." However, this reaction is more typical than atypical.

Ogden and Richards (1946) inspired the diagram in Figure 5.4, which helps us understand the relation between an object (or referent) and a symbol used to represent that object. As Figure 5.5 shows, the symbol may vary, but the object remains the same. The object has a word chosen to represent it, but that word and the object have no necessary inherent relationship. It is a little like selecting a name for a newborn baby. At first the choice seems arbitrary, but after a few years it seems impossible to think of that person having a different name. The relationship is indirect between symbol and referent; it exists only in the mind. Because each of us has a different brain and nervous system, the relationship between any given referent and any given word will vary to some extent from person to person.

Part of the bypassing problem is that we frequently assume words contain meaning. A different view is that words are symbols arbitrarily designated to represent concepts or referents. Over time, we begin to associate the word with its referent so strongly that they become inseparable. It is easy enough to say that the word is not the thing and that we should be able to separate the symbol from the referent, but it is difficult in practice not to respond emotionally when another person refers to us as a fascist pig, a nigger, a stupid hillbilly, or a honky.

FIGURE 5.4   THE RELATIONSHIP BETWEEN AN OBJECT AND THE SYMBOL FOR THE OBJECT

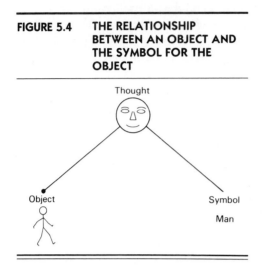

FIGURE 5.5   THE SAME OBJECT MAY BE REPRESENTED BY MORE THAN ONE SYMBOL

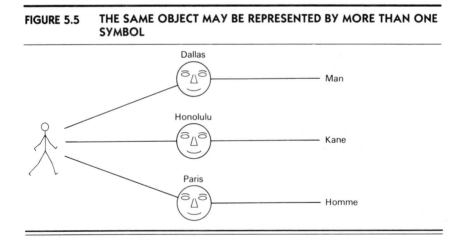

Two problems related to bypassing occur when (1) we use the same word to mean different things (dress "casually") or (2) different words are used to express essentially the same idea. For example, we may argue that company employees are not performing properly because of a "communication problem" as opposed to a "lack of motivation." It may be that we are really talking about related problems (that is, employees would be better motivated to perform [motivation problem] if they could suggest some new job procedures to their supervisors [communication problem]), but the issue may be clouded by arguments over the labels used to describe the problem.

Haney (1986) suggests two outcomes that can result from bypassing. On one hand, we may have apparent agreement when, in fact, we are calling different things by the same name (dressing casually). On the other hand, we may have actual agreement but apparent disagreement, as in the employee problem described above. Given these possible outcomes, here are some guidelines (slightly modified) that Haney (1986) suggests to remedy the potential difficulties.

- Be person-minded, not word-minded.
- Question and paraphrase.
- Be receptive to feedback.
- Be sensitive to contexts.

McCormack (1984), in his best-selling book *What They Don't Teach You At Harvard Business School,* confirms Haney's advice when he writes: "Insight demands opening up your senses, talking less and listening more. I believe you can learn almost everything you need to know—and more than other people would like you to know—simply by watching and listening, keeping your eyes peeled, your ears open. And your mouth closed. . . . Watch your listen/talk ratio" (pp. 8–9). These points also corroborate the ancient rhetorician who observed, "We have two ears and only one tongue, so that we might listen more than we speak."

In a nutshell, these guidelines focus on the idea that not all of us use words precisely the same way and that all words have the potential for multiple usage and interpretation. When you suspect that there may be a difference in word usage, ask questions, and be willing to try to restate or paraphrase the person's message. Remember to use different words in your restatement to see if the basic intent is understood. Also, be receptive to feedback. If we are too impervious or insensitive to allow for the possibility that we may not have stated something perfectly clearly, then we are unlikely to get much feedback to that effect. However, if we are willing to admit to fallibility, we invite feedback and can benefit from that information. Finally, we can often guess the intended meaning of a given statement on the basis of its use in a given context. For example, one supervisor frequently bade good-bye to his employees with the common phrase, "Well, take it easy now." It was quite obvious from the context that he meant this only as a casual expression. He did *not* intend employees to work less hard. By employing the four techniques mentioned above, we can reduce the frequency of bypassing.

Inference Making

Each of us makes numerous inferences every day. For example, we infer (1) that the sun will rise tomorrow; (2) that a chair won't collapse when we sit down; (3) that the sun is shining on the other side of town, because it is shining at our location; (4) that a car coming at us from a side street will stop at the stop sign and not run into the side of our car; and (5) that a person who consistently fails to show up for a group discussion is not committed to our group task. In each of these five cases, there is

FIGURE 5.6

Observational statements	Inferential statements
Approaching certainty	Approaching uncertainty

some probability that our inference will be borne out by the actual events. However, these five examples illustrate quite a range from most probable (number 1) to least probable (number 5).

Statements of inference go beyond what we know through observations. They represent only some degree of probability of coming true. This idea is illustrated in the diagram in Figure 5.6.

One of the major problems in groups is being able to recognize our own inference making. You can test your own ability on the following sample story. True (T) means that the inference drawn is definitely true on the basis of the information in the story. False (F) means that the inference is definitely wrong on the basis of the information in the story. A question mark (?) means that you cannot be certain of the inference on the basis of the story.

Sample Story
A customer handed the pharmacist a prescription for birth control pills. "Please fill this quickly. I have someone waiting in the car."

The pharmacist hurried to fill the order.

Statements about the Story
1. A woman was having a prescription filled
for birth control pills.   T F ?
2. She did not want to become pregnant.   T F ?
3. She was in a hurry to have the order filled.   T F ?
4. The pharmacist did his best to speed up the order. T F ?

If you answered T to any of the statements, you probably assumed or inferred that the customer and the pharmacist were female and male, respectively. Yet there is no statement in the story to support that assumption. Actually, a man is ordering birth control pills for his wife. The pharmacist, a female, cannot do "his" best to fill the order.

Another way of describing inference making is to say that it involves certain assumptions or conclusion drawing (sometimes jumping to the wrong conclusion). This becomes a problem in groups when we react to each other on the assumption that a person is behaving a certain way for the reason that seems obvious or apparent. However, the person may be acting that way for reasons other than the obvious. For example, a person may aggress against another by saying, "I'm sick and tired of your holding us back in our work." On the surface, this appears to be a comment intended to help the group get more accomplished. Beneath the surface, however, it may be part of an effort to undermine the other person's status in the group and may be a part of the struggle between the two for leadership in the group. These levels can

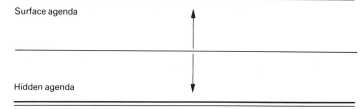

FIGURE 5.7   SURFACE AND HIDDEN AGENDAS COMPARED

Surface agenda

Hidden agenda

be diagrammed as shown in Figures 5.7 and 5.8. Although it is helpful to recognize that all behaviors are motivated and that they may be motivated by multiple causes, it is also dangerous to attempt to infer too much. Even if we make such an inference, we must recognize the possibility of error.

On the other hand, it is often difficult to analyze the group process without making some inferences. For example, one encounter group was having its last meeting, and the discussion somehow got around to the subject of death. After a somewhat extended discussion on this subject, the group leader intervened by saying, "I wonder if this discussion of death is motivated by the reluctance we are all feeling tonight about saying good-bye for the last time." Although this comment was initially rejected by the group, it turned out a lot of people were reluctant to end the friendships that had grown out of this group, and the topic of the discussion shifted to directly expressing and resolving those feelings.

Some inference making may be useful to the group, whereas at other times it may be harmful. A person who tries to read too much into behaviors may become a "psychopest" (Luft 1969). For example, a person crossing arms across the chest may do this for no reason but increased comfort. An overinterpretation might be that the person is becoming defensive and is trying to put up a barrier between self and others. In attempting to analyze behaviors, it is wise to recognize that analyses often involve inferences that go beyond what we have observed and involve some probability for error.

FIGURE 5.8

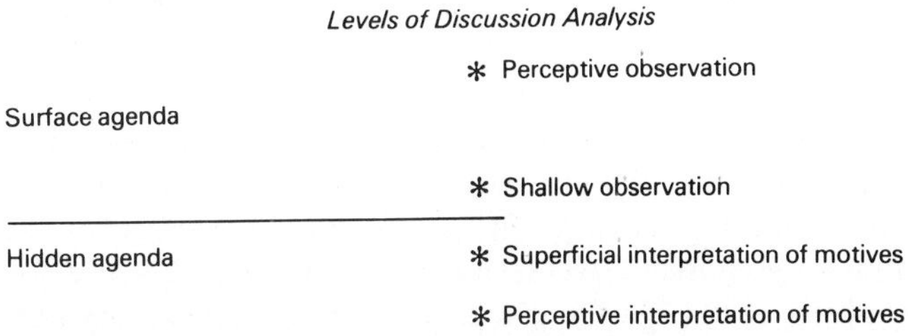

Levels of Discussion Analysis

＊ Perceptive observation

Surface agenda

＊ Shallow observation

Hidden agenda   ＊ Superficial interpretation of motives

＊ Perceptive interpretation of motives

Polarizing

Perhaps one of the most common problems in groups is polarization. It is difficult to exchange differences in viewpoint without tending to overstate or exaggerate to make our point. When this happens, it encourages the others to exaggerate a bit more in the opposite direction to make their point. Before long the sides are so far apart that constructive discussion of the issues is often discontinued for the time being. Consider the following example:

Kyle: I can't see why a woman should get a job just to avoid the boredom of housework, when a man who needs to support his family goes without a job.

Sue: Just because your masculinity is threatened is no reason to keep women out of work!

Kyle: My masculinity? You women's libbers are always hung up on trying to be the dominant sex!

Sue: You men are all alike. You can't stand being bettered by anyone, especially a woman. You want us to tell you how brilliant you are because you know what day of the week it is.

This exchange actually occurred in a student discussion. The topic was, "How can greater job equality be achieved in this country?" The discussion had been progressing well until this polarization occurred. Polarization has three distinct characteristics. First, the statements get more emotionally intense. Second, they go from being specific to being more general ("You men are all alike!"). Third, they tend to move away from the topic at hand (job equality) to other issues ("You can't stand being bettered by anyone").

A simple method usually nips polarization in the bud. It is described by Rogers and Roethlisberger (1952) in the following way:

The next time you get into an argument with . . . a small group of friends, just stop the discussion for a moment and, for an experiment, institute this rule. "Each person can speak up for himself only *after* he has repeated the ideas and feelings of the speaker accurately and to that speaker's satisfaction." You see what this would mean. It would simply mean that before presenting your own point of view, it would be necessary for you to achieve the other speaker's frame of reference—to understand his thoughts and feelings so well that you could summarize them for him. Sounds simple doesn't it? But if you try it, you will discover that it is one of the most difficult things you have ever tried to do.

After you have tried this restating exercise, notice the effects. First, the tendency for statements to gain emotional intensity is significantly reduced. The calmness is quite dramatic when compared with the interchange between Kyle and Sue above. Second, the discussion tends to stay with manageable specifics rather than moving to gross generalities that are quite frequently based on stereotypes (men are not all alike any more than women are all alike). Third, the discussion is more likely to remain focused on the group's discussion topic than to go off on a tangent that may be much less relevant to the group's task. This simple technique actually can be quite potent in reducing the problem of polarization.

Signal Reactions

Signal reactions are learned responses to certain stimuli. Perhaps the best-known example of a signal reaction is the salivation of Pavlov's dogs. Ivan Pavlov was a Nobel-prize-winning Russian physiologist. He accidentally stumbled on a very important concept of learning known as *classical conditioning.* He noticed that the carefully calibrated measurements of his test animals' salivation started to break down because his experienced dogs began to salivate in anticipation of the food when he opened the door to the room before he fed them. His coming in the door was the *conditioned stimulus*—the signal that triggered the salivation response. Eventually, he brought the salivation response under stimulus control by associating a bell with food so that the dogs learned to salivate at the sound of the bell even when the food was *not* present.

It is interesting that the founder of general semantics, Alfred Korzybski, wrote that the signal response was an animal-like response. He wrote (1948, p. 249):

> In Pavlov's experiments a dog is shown food and a bell rung simultaneously. At the sight of food, saliva and gastric juice flow. Associations soon *relate* the ringing of a bell and the food, and, later, simply the ringing of the bell will produce the flow. In another animal some other signal, a whistle, for instance, would produce similar effects. In different people, through experience, associations, relations, meanings, and s.r. [stimulus response] patterns are built around some symbol. Obviously in grown-up humans the identification of the symbol with the thing must be pathological.

Actually, Korzybski was a little extreme in saying that we are pathological to allow such strong connections between signal and response. One study showed that the repetitive sound of a gong produced marked emotional responses in former sailors (as measured by their perspiration levels) but very little emotional reaction among former soldiers. Edwards and Acker (1962) write: "This signal was used as a call to battle stations aboard U.S. Navy ships during the war, and it continued to elicit a strong autonomic response from the Navy veterans. Even though more than fifteen years had elapsed since this stimulus had signaled danger. . . ." Although this study did not involve reactions to verbal symbols, it does demonstrate the natural, not pathological, tendency toward strong signal reactions.

A study that directly tested emotional reactions to verbal symbols also proved that strong physiological reactions to symbols are typical rather than pathological. Subjects were exposed to various words on a screen, and their perspiration was measured as an index of their reactions. There were no significant differences between reactions to positive words such as *beauty, love,* and *kiss* and negative words such as *cancer, hate,* and *death.* However, some words did cause significant responses. These were referred to as "personal" words and included the person's first and last names, father's and mother's first names, major in school, year in school, and school name. Subjects were significantly aroused by these "personal" words (Crane, Diecker, and Brown 1970).

Certainly nobody would argue that these college students were pathological or that they "confused" their own name with themselves as physical beings. Yet these studies collectively indicate that all of us learn to react to certain verbal and nonverbal stimuli in some strong and predictable ways. When the response becomes habitual, it is like a reflex action. At this point, the so-called signal, or automatic response, may create problems.

A recent example of a signal reaction occurred in Sacramento, California. Holes in the pavement used to access utilities are commonly referred to as "manholes." However, because the Sacramento city council has a majority of women, the term "manholes" was thought to be sexist. A major contest was held to come up with a gender-neutral term. Some examples included, "sewer viewer," "peopleholes," and "peepholes." They finally decided on the term "maintenance hole." This appears to be a signal reaction to the term "manhole" (Associated Press 1990).

In group discussions, certain phrases may produce signal reactions that are counterproductive. Such phrases have been referred to as "idea killers" (Bittel 1956) or communication stoppers. They include, among others:

- "That's ridiculous."

- "We tried that before."

- "That will never work."

- "That's crazy."

- "It's too radical a change."

- "We're too small for it."

- "It's not practical."

- "Let's get back to reality."

- "You can't teach an old dog new tricks."

- "We'll be the laughingstock."

- "You're absolutely wrong."

- "You don't know what you're talking about."

- "It's impossible."

- "There's no way it can be done."

On the other hand, "igniter phrases" that seem to promote group productivity would include some of the following:

- "I agree."

- "That's good!"

- "I made a mistake. I'm sorry."

- "That's a great idea."

- "I'm glad you brought that up."

- "You're on the right track."

- "I know it will work."

- "We're going to try something different today."

- "I never thought of that."

- "We can do a lot with that idea."

- "Real good, anyone else?"

- "I like that!"

- "That would be worth a try."

- "Why don't we assume it would work and go from there."

Other specific terms that are likely to produce signal reactions are such words as "weirdo," "queer," "honky," "racist," "male chauvinist pig," and many swear words. In fact, even swear words have different levels of offensiveness that vary from culture to culture. Profane words have been classified as (1) religious, (2) excretory, and (3) sexual (Bostrom and Rossiter 1969). In our culture the sexual words are usually the most offensive; but in Italy, where the Roman Catholic Church is very strong, religious words are considered much more offensive, and in Germany excretory swear words are considered to be the worst. The 2 Live Crew album "As Nasty As They Wanna Be" was declared obscene by a federal court judge in Florida in part because of the use of swear words. This is a vivid example of the emotional impact created by language. One writer expressed her reaction by stating that, "But incitement to rape, even if it rhymes and has a rap beat, cannot be defended, whatever its rhythms. . . . Exhortations to sexual violence do not have to be tolerated" (Beck 1990, p. 7A). Several studies indicate that those who swear may reduce their credibility in the eyes of others (Bauduin 1971). It also seems advisable to avoid communication stoppers and idea killers whenever possible.

Because we know that words do have a great deal of potential for influencing thought and subsequent action, note the set of terms in Figure 5.9. Just pick any three-digit number at random, and pick the corresponding three words from the lists. These terms all have some relevance to small group interaction. If all else fails, they can be used for fun. For example, 2, 6, 9 would be "Machiavellian managerial transactions." Numbers 8, 4, 3 would be "stagnated interpersonal relations." So if you want to impress your friends with how much you have learned by reading this book, try the "SNOW" index.

SELF-DISCLOSURE

Perhaps one of the greatest dilemmas facing a group member is the choice between openly expressing his or her thoughts and feelings versus concealing or distorting inner feelings, thoughts, and perceptions. In a discussion on racial equality, we may not openly reveal our true feelings for fear of sounding like racists or bigots. Nobody wants to be labeled an Archie Bunker if it can be avoided! On the other hand, if every

FIGURE 5.9   SYSTEMATIC NEW ORDER (OF) WORDS

(SNOW INDEX)

0 external	0 bureaucratic	0 acceptance
1 authoritarian	1 group	1 solutions
2 Machiavellian	2 functional	2 consensus
3 energetic	3 logistical	3 relations
4 situational	4 interpersonal	4 commitment
5 socialized	5 instrumental	5 responsibility
6 systematic	6 managerial	6 development
7 dynamic	7 organizational	7 coordination
8 stagnated	8 executive	8 power
9 transparent	9 homogeneous	9 transactions

person in the group conceals his or her thoughts, there will be little said and, therefore, little accomplished. The question is not *whether* to reveal or conceal but *how much* to reveal or conceal. *Self-disclosure* has been defined by Tubbs and Baird (1980) as "a process, whereby an individual voluntarily shares information in a personal way, about his or her "self" that cannot be discovered through other sources."

You may wonder why a person should bother to let himself or herself be known to others. Jourard (1964) studied mentally disturbed individuals and concluded that a great deal of human energy is consumed in attempts to keep from being known by others. That energy could be used for other purposes, but neurotic individuals are so "wrapped up in themselves" that they are seldom able to devote sufficient energy to other problems (such as a group problem-solving discussion). All of us are periodically faced with such situations. When we get bad news from home or from a friend, it is much harder to concentrate on such mundane problems as how to budget our study time for tomorrow's exam. However, the mentally unhealthy person is habitually in this state of mind.

Part of returning to mental health involves sharing oneself with others. Jourard (1964, p. 24) states:

> Self-disclosure, or should I say "real" self-disclosure, is both a symptom of personality health . . . and at the same time a means of ultimately achieving healthy personality. . . . I have known people who would rather die than become known. . . . When I say that self-disclosure is a symptom of personality health, what I mean really is that a person who displays many of the other characteristics that betoken healthy personality . . . *will also display the ability to make himself fully known to at least one other significant human being.*

Perhaps a less self-centered motive for self-disclosure is the desire to improve the quality of communication within a group. Keltner (1970, p. 54) states:

We probably do not reveal enough of ourselves in speech-communication to enable our co-communicators to understand us better. The complexities of the world we live in demand better communication than we have known. *To communicate better, we must understand each other better. To understand each other better, we must reveal more of ourselves through speech and speech-communication events.*

Countless students in group discussion feel that they don't know what to contribute to a discussion. They often feel that they have no good or new ideas to add to what has already been said. Yet as we will see in the last section of this chapter, numerous roles may be adopted by group members, several of which involve some degree of self-disclosure. For example, if an idea is initiated by another, you may make a substantial contribution by offering your *reaction* to the idea (opinion giving)—by encouraging or showing agreement or disagreement. Counterproductive role behaviors may also involve self-disclosure (for example, aggressing, reporting a personal achievement, confessing a personal ideology that is irrelevant to the discussion topic, or seeking sympathy from the group).

Self-disclosure is not always desirable. An optimum amount of self-disclosure seems a desirable goal to achieve. Some of us are too closed (concealers); others of us "wear our hearts on our sleeves" (revealers). Culbert (1968, p. 19) describes the problem of overdisclosing rather vividly:

> The revealer is likely to react by immediately disclosing any self-information to which he has access. The revealer, too, is attempting to master the problem, but for him mastery seems to be attained by explicitly acknowledging and labeling all the relevant elements comprising the situation. While a concealer runs the risk of having insufficient external feedback, a revealer runs the risk of overlabeling the limited number of objective elements present or of labeling them so early that their usefulness in the relationship is nullified.

Encounter groups usually proceed under the assumption that people have learned to be too closed too often. Thus, participants are encouraged to share their feelings and perceptions as openly and honestly as they can. Much of the self-disclosure involves giving feedback to others concerning the ways in which they "come across." This feedback is often useful in reducing the size of the arc of distortion discussed earlier in this chapter.

The Johari Window

Perhaps the most useful model for illustrating self-disclosure in groups is the Johari window (named after its originators, Joe Luft and Harry Ingham) (Luft 1970). See Figure 5.10 for this model.

This window classifies an individual's relating to others according to four quadrants (or windowpanes). The size of each quadrant represents the person's level of self-awareness. Quadrant one, the open quadrant, represents our willingness to share with others our views on such things as current national or world events, current movies, sports, and what is generally referred to as "cocktail party" conversation.

The second quadrant is referred to as the blind quadrant or the "bad breath" area.

FIGURE 5.10   THE JOHARI WINDOW

From *Group Processes: An Introduction to Group Dynamics,* by Joseph Luft, by permission of Mayfield Publishing Company. Copyright © 1963, 1970 by Joseph Luft.

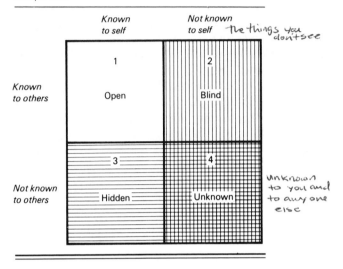

This area represents the things that others may know about us but that we do unintentionally and unknowingly. We may continually dominate meetings or bore people with long-winded accounts of how good our high school was. Conversely, we may annoy people by our silence, because they may feel that they have opened themselves up to the group while we have "played our cards pretty close to the chest" by revealing little. Group members seem to resent both those who talk too much and those who talk too little.

The third quadrant is the hidden area that is most likely to be changed (reduced) by self-disclosure. It represents the feelings about ourselves that we know but are unwilling to reveal to others. It may represent our greatest fears, some past experiences we would like to forget, or our secret sexual fantasies, among other things.

The fourth quadrant is called the area of the unknown. It represents all the areas of potential growth or self-actualization. This includes almost anything outside our experience, such as the sport we've never played, the places we have never seen, the hobby we haven't taken the time to try, the organization we have never joined, the style of behaving we have never been willing to risk, and others.

Luft advocates changing the shape of the window so that quadrant one enlarges while all the others become smaller. I once participated in an encounter group in which we tried to grow interpersonally along the lines suggested by this model. One participant introduced herself as "Mickey" and told us what city she was from, and so on. She was dressed in slacks and a sweater. Only after fifteen weeks did we find out that she was a nun. She had been trying to develop herself as a person without having the rest of us react to her role rather than to her. Thus, her unknown quadrant was diminished by her efforts to try new, less inhibited behaviors. She also reduced her blind quadrant by asking for interpersonal feedback. We might have been more inhibited in our feedback had we known she was a nun. She also destroyed the stereotypes most of us had toward nuns.

Luft illustrates the Johari window as it applies to groups in Figure 5.11. Each window represents a person.

More recently, Eisenberg and Witten (1987) have questioned the viability of widespread "open communication" policies among management and worker groups in a corporation. Open communication for many years has been regarded as the ultimate strategy for improving employee morale and productivity. In an "open communication" setting, superiors and subordinates talk with one another freely and openly about company goals, work stressors, and other job-related issues. Eisenberg and Witten, among others, contradict such a blanket statement about open communication. They argue that there are situations when managers and employees have successfully chosen to be more or less open. These decisions stem in part from concern for serving personal goals as well as those of the company.

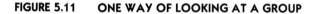

FIGURE 5.11   ONE WAY OF LOOKING AT A GROUP

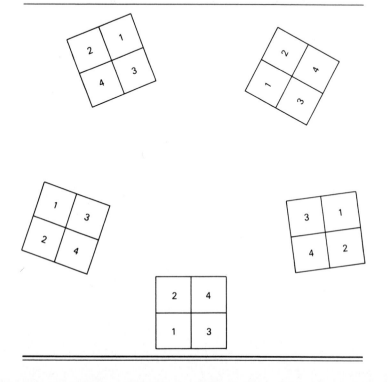

Appropriateness

Within this framework questions still arise as to the timing and extent of self-disclosure. Luft (1969, pp. 132–133) answers this question when he proposes the following guidelines designating situations in which self-disclosure is appropriate:

1. *When it is a function of the ongoing relationship.* What one shares with another belongs in the particular relationship; it is not a random or isolated act.

2. *When it occurs reciprocally.* This implies that there is some degree of interdependence and mutuality involved.

3. *When it is timed to fit what is happening.* The self-disclosure grows out of the experience that is going on between or among the persons involved. The timing and sequence are important.

4. *When it concerns what is going on within and between persons in the present.* Some account is taken of the behavior and feelings of the participants individually and of the persons collectively. There is a recognition of the relationship as an emergent phenomenon in addition to the individual selves.

5. *When it moves by relatively small increments.* What is revealed does not drastically change or restructure the relationship. The implication is that a relationship is built gradually except in rare and special cases.

6. *When it is confirmable by the other person.* Some system is worked out between the persons to validate reception of that which has been disclosed.

7. *When account is taken of the effect disclosure has on the other person(s).* The disclosure has not only been received; there is evidence of its effect on the receiver.

8. *When it creates a reasonable risk.* If the feeling or behavior were really unknown to the other, it may have been withheld for a reason bearing on differences which have yet to be faced by the participants.

9. *When it is speeded up in a crisis.* A serious conflict jeopardizing the structure of the relationship may require that more quadrant 3 material be quickly revealed to heal the breach or help in the reshaping of the relationship.

10. *When the context is mutually shared.* The assumptions underlying the social context suggest that there is enough in common to sustain the disclosure.

Probably the most difficult problem for members of encounter groups to resolve when they go "back home" is knowing how to apply what they have learned without overdoing it. One encounter group graduate said, "How do I use this openness with my boss when he hasn't read the book?" His concern was warranted. It may be quite difficult to put into practice any new behaviors when the others "back home" haven't changed and are still as closed and perhaps as devious as ever.

The most logical advice would be to try to use what you can, when you can. Not all of our learnings will be usable all the time. But certainly some new behaviors (such as increased openness and sensitivity) will be appropriate some, if not most, of the time. Experiences in groups frequently teach us lessons we can't possibly unlearn. Once we have experienced a greater level of personal intimacy with others, day-to-day superficiality may compare rather badly. Schutz (1971, p. 284) puts it this way:

Relating to people more honestly is certainly possible. Find someone you have withheld something from and tell it to him. See what happens. Next time you feel like touching someone, do it. Next time you are hurt or frightened, express it. When you catch yourself trying to protect an image, stop, and see if you can be real instead. If you're embarrassed to pay someone a compliment, do it anyway. If you want to know how people respond to you, ask them.

Another way to put it is that the competent communicator has a higher level of rhetorical sensitivity. That is, he or she learns when and with whom to disclose and when and with whom to refrain from disclosure (Hart and Burks 1972; Hart, Eadie, and Carlson 1975). Total disclosure at all times with all people is obviously not desirable.

INTERACTION ROLES

Each of us is required to enact multiple roles in our everyday living. Usually we are able to function effectively in these different roles, which require or expect certain behaviors. We are, at different times, student, son or daughter, friend, counselor, leader, or follower; some are spouses, parents, and employees as well. It is important to realize that roles are simply sets of identifiable behaviors. When we say that a person is assuming a role, this does not imply that he or she is faking it or acting in a way that is not within that person's true character. In fact, some writings (Hart and Burks 1972) indicate that the more interpersonally sensitive person is one who is able to develop a considerable degree of role flexibility. It is desirable to learn to widen our repertoire of roles and to discover those roles we most enjoy.

A student relatively new to the small group field indicated an awareness of a few interaction roles:

This group discussion was a real experience for me. I have never been mixed in with a complete group of strangers and have things work out so smoothly. In most groups you get a few quiet shy ones, who don't say anything, and opposed to them, there's usually one big mouth, normally found in a group, who says everything and has all of the ideas without giving anyone else a chance to give their opinion. It was good to work in a group that was well balanced and one in which everyone participated.

As we mentioned in the discussion of leadership, different functions can be performed by any group member. This is another way of saying that individuals assume different roles in helping the group move toward its goal. We discussed the task roles and socioemotional functions or roles in Chapter 3. Benne and Sheats (1948) proposed a classification of roles into three broad categories: (1) task roles, (2) group-building and maintenance roles, and (3) individual roles. Although other sets of categories have been developed for research purposes (McCroskey and Wright 1971, Leathers 1969), this time-tested approach is still one of the most useful for learning to identify roles and to develop role flexibility.

Group Task Roles

These behaviors are directed toward accomplishing the group's objective through the facilitation of problem solving.

- *Initiating-contributing:* Proposing new ideas or a changed way of regarding the group goal. This may include a new goal or a new definition of the problem. It may involve suggesting a solution or some way of handling a difficulty the group has encountered. It may also include a new procedure for the group to better organize its efforts.

- *Information seeking:* Asking for clarification, for authoritative information and facts relevant to the problem under discussion.

- *Opinion seeking:* Seeking information related not so much to factual data as to the values underlying the suggestions being considered.

- *Information giving:* Offering facts or generalizations based on experience or authoritative sources.

- *Opinion giving:* Stating beliefs or opinions relevant to a suggestion made. The emphasis is on the proposal of what ought to become the group's values rather than on factors or information.

- *Elaborating:* Expanding on suggestions with examples or restatements, offering a rationale for previously made suggestions, and trying to determine the results if a suggestion were adopted by the group.

- *Coordinating:* Indicating the relationships among various ideas and suggestions, attempting to combine ideas and suggestions, or trying to coordinate the activities of group members.

- *Orienting:* Indicating the position of the group by summarizing progress made and deviations from agreed-upon directions or goals or by raising questions about the direction the group is taking.

- *Evaluating:* Comparing the group's accomplishments to some criterion or standard of group functioning. This may include questioning the practicality, logic, or procedure of a suggestion.

- *Energizing:* Stimulating the group to action or decision, attempting to increase the level or quality of activity.

- *Assisting on procedure:* Helping or facilitating group movement by doing things for the group—for example, performing routine tasks such as distributing materials, rearranging the seating, or running a tape recorder.

- *Recording:* Writing down suggestions, recording group decisions, or recording the outcomes of the discussion. This provides tangible results of the group's effort.

Group-Building and Maintenance Roles

The roles in this category help the interpersonal functioning of the group. They help alter the way of working; they strengthen, regulate, and perpetuate the group. This is analogous to preventive maintenance done to keep a mechanical device such as a car in better working order.

- *Encouraging:* Praising, showing interest in, agreeing with, and accepting the contributions of others; showing warmth toward other group members, listening attentively and seriously to the ideas of others, showing tolerance for ideas different from one's own, conveying the feeling that one feels the contributions of others are important.

- *Harmonizing:* Mediating the differences among the other members, attempting to reconcile disagreements, relieving tension in moments of conflict through the use of humor.

- *Compromising:* Operating from within a conflict situation, one may offer a compromise by yielding status, by admitting a mistake, by disciplining oneself for the sake of group harmony, or by coming halfway toward another position.

- *Gatekeeping and expediting:* Attempting to keep communication channels open by encouraging the participation of some or by curbing the participation of others.

- *Setting standards or ideals:* Expressing standards for the group and/or evaluating the quality of group processes (as opposed to evaluating the content of discussion).

- *Observing:* Keeping a record of various aspects of group process and feeding this information, along with interpretations, into the group's evaluation of its procedures. This contribution is best received when the person has been requested by the group to perform this function. The observer should avoid expressing judgments of approval or disapproval in reporting observations.

- *Following:* Going along with the group, passively accepting the ideas of others, serving as an audience in group discussion.

Individual Roles

These behaviors are designed more to satisfy an individual's needs than to contribute to the needs of the group. These are sometimes referred to as self-centered roles.

- *Aggressing:* Deflating the status of others, disapproving of the ideas or values of others, attacking the group or the problem it is attempting to solve, joking maliciously, resenting the contributions of others and/or trying to take credit for them.

- *Blocking:* Resisting, disagreeing, and opposing beyond reason; bringing up dead issues after they have been rejected or bypassed by the group.

- *Recognition seeking:* Calling attention to oneself through boasting, reporting on personal achievements, acting in inappropriate ways, fighting to keep from being placed in an inferior position.

- *Self-confessing:* Using the group as an opportunity to express personal, nongroup-related feelings, insights, ideologies.

- *Acting the playboy:* Showing a lack of involvement in the group's task. Displaying nonchalance, cynicism, horseplay, and other kinds of "goofing-off" behaviors.

- *Dominating:* Trying to assert authority or superiority by manipulating others in the group. This may take the form of flattery, asserting a superior status or right to attention, giving directions authoritatively, and/or interrupting others.

- *Help seeking:* Attempting to get sympathy from other group members through expressions of insecurity, personal inadequacy, or self-criticism beyond reason.

- *Special interest pleading:* Speaking on behalf of some group such as "the oppressed," "labor," "business," usually cloaking one's own prejudices or biases in the stereotype that best fits one's momentary need. (Adapted from Schnake 1990.)

It is generally desirable to learn to perform the task roles and the group-building and maintenance roles and to avoid the individual roles. However, even the first and second sets of roles may be misused and abused. For example, there is a fine line between initiating and dominating, between encouraging and flattering, and between opinion giving and recognition seeking. The way in which the role is enacted can make a crucial difference in whether the behavior is viewed as constructive or self-serving. One student attempted to be a gatekeeper by asking silent members if they had any ideas they would like to contribute. After his attempts were rebuked, he wrote the following analysis of his behavior.

> On one occasion, I tried to involve another group member in the discussion against his will. The conflict was resolved in a later discussion, but my bad feelings during the intervening period made me realize that this was an area for attention. . . .
> This "expansiveness" and disregard for another person's feelings is an amazing trait to find in myself, because it is something I dislike in other people. It has caused me to resolve that (1) I will not be "overbearing" with quiet people, (2) I will listen more, (3) I will attempt to be more aware of the feelings of others.

Even behaviors motivated by the best intentions may go astray in producing a desired contribution to the group effort.

THE SYSTEMS PERSPECTIVE

In this chapter we examined some issues close to the hearts of many modern communication scholars. The chapter began with an analysis of five critical issues in the study of communication. We looked at the differences between intentional-unintentional, verbal-nonverbal, defensive-supportive, content-process, and therapeutic-pathological communication. Although these issues apply to all communication contexts, our examples and specific applications were focused on the small group context. These issues have considerable overlap with topics discussed in other chapters in this book. For example, how does one express leadership behavior, or establish a group norm, or manifest one's personality, or express one's values? All of these are manifested through behaviors that communicate to others in the group.

The systems perspective fits very well with the new emphasis in communication theory on the transactional model of communication. Writings of Sereno and Bodaken (1975), Wilmot (1975), and Tubbs (1976) stress that the participants in any communication event are highly dependent upon one another. They are simultaneously influencing one another and are both senders and receivers at all times. Wilmot goes so far as to state that "the process of your creating a message may affect you *more* than it does the person receiving it." The transactional point of view can be summarized by stating that a person's communication can be defined only *in relation* to some other or others.

In this chapter we discussed the verbal-nonverbal distinction in communication. The systems nature of this relationship is stressed by Barnlund (1968, p. 535): "In particular, Birdwhistell has emphasized that no physical motion is meaningless, but that its significance derives from the *interactional context* in which it is evoked. Persons are engaged in physical conversation even when verbally silent, modifying their positions continually in response to perceptible movements in others [emphasis added]." Knapp (1972, pp. 8–9) adds further support for this viewpoint: "We are constantly being warned against presenting material out of context. . . . There is a danger that the reader may forget that nonverbal communication cannot be studied in isolation from the total communication process. Verbal and nonverbal communication should be treated as a total and inseparable unit." We might add that each of the communication factors discussed in this chapter is, similarly, related to all the others.

In the second section of this chapter we looked at four issues related to language behavior—bypassing, inference making, polarizing, and signal reactions. Each of these factors is related to both the background factors of the individuals and the eventual consequences of group discussion. We saw that background factors were related to signal reactions in the study showing that former sailors experienced a physiological reaction to an alarm bell they had not heard for fifteen years. We also saw that similar reactions can be elicited by such verbal stimuli as our own names or our parents' names. The influence of language on group consequences was shown by the use of "idea killers" such as "It's impossible," "That's crazy," or "That will never work." The net effect of these types of statements is to reduce potential group productivity in terms of both idea production and interpersonal relations, as we saw in the case study at the beginning of this chapter.

The third section of this chapter dealt with the question, "How much should I reveal and how much should I conceal in a group?" The Johari window was offered as a helpful model for understanding one's relationship to others. Guidelines for appropriate self-disclosure were included. Obviously, appropriate self-disclosure will vary considerably from group to group. Probably high self-disclosure is appropriate in an encounter group with a highly supportive atmosphere and a norm of openness and trust. However, social groups, educational groups, work groups, and especially problem-solving groups are hardly the place for a high degree of very personal self-disclosure. Personality also interacts with self-disclosure. If we open up to those who are highly Machiavellian, they will turn around and use those revelations to benefit themselves and possibly to harm us. Appropriate self-disclosure, then, is very much contingent on a number of relevant variables. For this reason, Tubbs and Baird (1980) have developed a contingency model of self-disclosure that suggests how much to disclose and under what circumstances.

The final section discussed the issue of which roles members may adopt in groups. Task and maintenance roles were indicated as useful roles to learn and to use. Individual, or self-centered, roles were identified to help indicate communication behaviors that are typically *not* useful to the group. These roles undoubtedly interact with people's personality traits. For example, the person who is dominant and achievement-oriented will probably adopt the task roles quite comfortably. The affiliators will naturally gravitate toward the group maintenance roles. Finally, the hostile or acquiescent personality types will be tempted to adopt the self-centered roles of aggressing and blocking or help seeking and special interest pleading, respectively. One of the reasons for studying different types of roles is to increase our ability to adopt different roles in accordance with the demands of the situation. Barnlund (1968, p. 170) summarizes a great deal of literature on role taking:

> A number of studies show that role insight is associated with social maturity and a high level of general adjustment. Commenting on the close connection between role sensitivity and interpersonal effectiveness, Cameron has written, "To the extent that an individual, in the course of personality development, learns to take social roles skillfully and realistically, acquires an adequate repertory of them, and becomes adroit in shifting from one role to another when he is in difficulty, he should grow into a flexible, adaptive social adult with minimum susceptibility to behavior disorders."

The readings for this chapter deal with improving management communication skills and with defensive communication.

EXERCISES

1. Nonverbal Communication

(a) Eyelogue   Group members form two lines facing each other. Without talking, express your feelings for a few seconds to the person facing you. Then move one line so that each person is facing someone different. Repeat until you have expressed a feeling toward every person in the group.

(b) Group Grope   Have group members mill around the room encountering one another nonverbally while blindfolded. Afterward, discuss and have group members share their impressions.

(c) Nonverbal Sociogram   Have group members move around and stand near others to whom they feel psychologically close. One person may want to diagram the standing positions on the board for discussion.

(d) Hand-Holding Go-around   Stand in a circle with all group members holding hands with eyes closed. Have the instructor (or a volunteer) go around the outside of the circle putting his or her hands on each pair of clasped hands, one pair at a time. After the person has gone all the way around, discuss the impressions experienced.

2. Transactional Analysis Exercise

Observe any discussion in the class, and attempt to identify the ego states that seem to motivate various comments. Write down several representative comments for each of the three ego states (Figure 5.12).

3. Self-Disclosure Exercise

Pair off with someone you feel close to. Begin to talk about the topics listed below. Feel free to stop if you feel the topics are too close for comfort. Discuss the following by taking turns before moving to the next topic.

(a) Your hobbies and interests

(b) Your attitude toward your body—likes and dislikes

(c) Your family's financial status

(d) Attitudes toward your parents and others in your family

(e) Attitudes toward religion

(f) Your love life, past and present

(g) Personal problems that really concern you

(h) How you react to your partner on the basis of this exercise*

---

*The topics are similar to those developed by Sidney Jourard (1971) and published in *Self-Disclosure: An Experimental Analysis of the Transparent Self* (New York: Wiley), pp. 177–178.

FIGURE 5.12

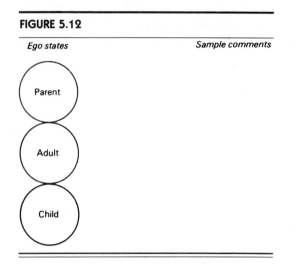

Ego states   *Sample comments*

4. Member Roles Exercise

Have a group discussion using the fishbowl format (a group of observers surrounding a group of discussants). Try to identify the roles each member plays by placing a check mark in the appropriate box in the chart shown in Figure 5.13. These observations should be fed back to the group members and discussed in a supportive way. For a variation, some group members can be briefed in advance to act out certain roles to test the observers' abilities to recognize the behavior.

FIGURE 5.13   MEMBER ROLES EXERCISE CHART

Roles Members	A	B	C	D	E	F	G	H
Group Task Roles								
1. Initiator-contributor								
2. Information seeker								
3. Information giver								
4. Coordinator								
5. Orientor								
6. Evaluator								
7. Energizer								
8. Opinion giver								
Group-Building Roles								
9. Encourager								
10. Harmonizer								
11. Compromiser								
12. Gatekeeper and exploiter								
13. Standard setter								
14. Follower								
Self-centered Roles								
15. Aggressor								
16. Blocker								
17. Recognition-seeker								
18. Playboy (playgirl)								
19. Dominator								
20. Help-seeker								

READINGS: OVERVIEW

Much has been written about the importance of developing a supportive style of personal communication in and outside small groups. In the first article, Tubbs and Dischner demonstrate the successes that occurred from teaching supervisors to use supportive communication and group participation in a General Motors plant.

Jack Gibb offers valuable insights in the second article, "Defensive Communication." Many discussions have gone astray because of this problem. Both articles go further into topics discussed in the body of the chapter.

From the Brink of Death

Stewart L. Tubbs and Ruth A. Dischner

In 1985 Bud Bartell took over the Buick-Oldsmobile-Cadillac Group's (BOC) Pittsburgh plant of General Motors. Although the plant had been built in 1950 and was not that old technologically, neither the pressroom nor the die-room had been modernized like many other similar GM plants.

The Pittsburgh team spent a year working to improve the existing operations. However, by 1986 the team came to the conclusion that major changes were needed to maintain the plant's very existence. That same year GM announced it was closing 11 of its operations within three years as part of a massive downsizing strategy. In addition, the company announced a plan to improve its competitive position by cutting costs and significantly reducing its salaried workforce.

Because of increasing global competition, it was apparent that a major turnaround at the Pittsburgh plant would be *required* to keep it from being idled.

The team's members immediately began to implement a "building-blocks" approach to changing the plant's culture. First, they instituted zero-based manpower planning, the objective of which was to increase operating efficiency.

Then they began exploring alternative business opportunities for the plant. Mr. Bartell and his staff put together a complete business plan to acquire the aftermarket production business for replacement parts such as fenders as a dedicated supplier to GM's Service Parts Organization. The plan called for a $32 million changeover to synchronous manufacturing with a just-in-time, zero-inventory system.

This would be a major undertaking since no other plant in the world, as far as the team knew, had ever accomplished this while still operating. The NUMMI (New United Motor Mfg. Inc.) plant in Fremont, Calif., GM's joint venture with Toyota, closed operations and then hired back the most capable workers. Saturn has been building its new organization by picking the best talent from all over GM. However, BOC-Pittsburgh would change over to a new business while still operating the old with the existing resources. Mr. Bartell believed that if the plan involved closing and then reopening the plant, it would never be approved.

As it was, Mr. Bartell discussed the proposal with Doug Tracey, the manufacturing manager for the Lansing Automotive Div. That division promotes decentralization. It encouraged the plant to go ahead with its plan. Mr. Bartell sold the idea that—with the plant's dedicated workforce, a good union/

From: Industry week, *May 21, 1990, 15–18. Reprinted by permission.*

management joint process in place, and a strong work ethic—he could make the plant competitive. But appropriate technological and human innovations would be required. The result was ultimate approval from the GM executive committee.

The plant was converted into a rapid die-change and die-storage operation. Now it manufactures 250-piece small-lot runs of fenders on one line. The plan is to expand to five lines and to manufacture hoods, deck lids, quarter panels, and doors for all of GM's aftermarket. The plant will be a dedicated supplier for the Service Parts Organization, formerly the GM Parts Div.

Simultaneous with these changes, like other GM facilities, the plant had to significantly reduce its salaried workforce. In the process, extensive training increased the flexibility of the existing supervisory force. An "area manager" concept was instituted to broaden the responsibilities of each supervisor, who was put through extensive training for several months.

The area manager's role differs from the "old" supervisory position:

- Instead of having employees from 12 different classifications reporting to several supervisors, each production area now has one area manager, with all classifications working in that area reporting to him or her.

- Responsibility and accountability for all activities within an area reside with one individual.

- Area managers are expected to supervise both technical and nontechnical functions. (Many of the new area managers had no experience directing technical functions and were dependent on their employees' knowledge.)

- The need for effective interpersonal skills is greater than ever.

The selection of appropriate employees to become area managers was seen as a key to the success of the entire change. Viewed as especially critical was the selection of the initial area managers who would truly be "pioneering" the new concept and, in a sense, "selling" it to the rest of the organization. The first candidates were selected because they possessed excellent interpersonal skills, in addition to having a sound technical knowledge base. Other criteria used in the selection process were: knowledge of manufacturing processes and procedures; a high level of oral and written communications skills; understanding of basic technology; knowledge of scheduling and management systems; a high level of analytical ability; and knowledge of quality-control procedures.

As openings developed, notices were posted and candidates nominated themselves for the area-manager positions.

The plant staff, in discussions with the salaried workforce, made it clear that any future promotions would be made from among the area managers. This resulted in a number of young, well-educated, high-potential employees applying and being selected for area management.

Two full-time coordinators were established. One was salaried and one represented the United Auto Workers (UAW). They worked closely in all phases of the project and acted as liaisons among top management, the new area managers, and an outside consultant.

A two-day seminar—"Improving Supervisory Management Skills"—was presented to 90 people from December 1985 to August 1987. The first session included several top-plant staff members, and subsequent sessions predominantly involved supervisors who were about to become area managers.

The general theme of the seminar was that the role of supervisors and managers today is inherently different from that of the past. Today's manager must rely more on the expertise of his or her subordinates and co-workers because of the increasing complexity of business. Therefore, managers must be more "developmental" than "heroic."

Upon completion of the seminar, the new area managers began a four-week "in-plant" training program that began by presenting the area managers with a listing of the expectations for their newly created roles. The training staff worked with the area managers in helping them understand the new role and identify where they would need training.

An individually tailored training program was developed for this four-week period for two reasons:

1. The candidates had varied work experiences. Some had production-supervision backgrounds, others came from engineering, and some were from the skilled-trade groups. Such varied backgrounds resulted in different training needs.

2. One of the primary mandates to the new area managers was that they would be held accountable for everything that happened within their areas. They would be expected to change from being "reactive" to being "proactive." No longer would upper management make all the decisions. This new philosophy of moving the decision-making down the organization might as well begin with the training, it was decided. Letting the area manager design his or her own training was thought to do two things. First, a sense of ownership in and commitment to the program would develop as a result of being able to participate in the design. Second, giving area managers control over how they spent their time for a four-week period would show that management trusted their judgment and wanted them to act on what they felt was most appropriate.

Although there were some differences in what different groups of area managers chose to do during their training periods, most of the area managers chose to:

- Review the concepts learned in the two-day seminar and discuss their applications.

- Jointly develop a "philosophy-of-management" statement with all the managers from a specific area.

- Seek staff clarifications as to the expectations of area managers.

- Identify their production areas' customers. Plan visits to clarify their customers' expectations.

- Meet with employees from other departments to discuss the implementation of the area-manager concept and establish a support system.

- Identify one's own training needs and arrange with the appropriate department for training.

- Meet with the area managers already "on-line" to discuss the "realities."

- Meet with the union officers and then with all area employees to discuss implementation.

Meanwhile, through the UAW/GM quality network effort, a joint labor-management approach was used to develop more viable working relationships.

In addition, a new effort was launched to negotiate more flexible labor classifications. This enabled the plant to have much greater worker utilization and job enrichment at the same time. Recently, 43 skilled and unskilled hourly employees were put through six weeks of training to create cross-functional work groups.

The results? Through continuous improvements in quality, the plant has earned the distinction of "No. 1 U.S. GM stamper." Uptime has improved from 26% to 65%. Changeover time for dies has dropped from 23 hours to $5^{1}/_{2}$ hours. Efficiency has increased 26% in the last 18 months.

Numerous changes continue within the social structure: combining job classifications, rearranging reporting structures, amending work rules, implementing participative-management styles, and changing the organizational culture through the introduction of a team approach to the organization of labor.

Defensive Communication

Jack R. Gibb

One way to understand communication is to view it as a people process rather than as a language process. If one is to make fundamental improvement in communication, he must make changes in interpersonal relationships. One possible type of alteration—and the one with which this paper is concerned—is that of reducing the degree of defensiveness.

Definition and Significance

Defensive behavior is defined as that behavior which occurs when an individual perceives threat or anticipates threat in the group. The person who behaves defensively, even though he also gives some attention to the common task, devotes an appreciable portion of his energy to defending himself. Besides talking about the topic, he thinks about how he appears to others, how he may be seen more favorably, how he may win, dominate, impress, or escape punishment and/or how he may avoid or mitigate a perceived or an anticipated attack.

Such inner feelings and outward acts tend to create similarly defensive postures in others; and, if unchecked, the ensuing circular response becomes increasingly destructive. Defensive behavior, in short, engenders defensive listening, and this in turn produces postural, facial, and verbal cues which raise the defense level of the original communicator.

Defense arousal prevents the listener from concentrating upon the message. Not only do defensive communicators send off multiple value, motive, and affect cues, but also defensive recipients distort what they receive. As a person becomes more and more defensive, he becomes less and less able to perceive accurately the motives, the values, and the emotions of the sender. The writer's analyses of tape-recorded discussions revealed that increases in defensive behavior were correlated positively with losses in efficiency in communication.[1] Specifically, distortions became greater when defensive states existed in the groups.

The converse, moreover, also is true. The more "supportive" or defense reductive the climate, the less the receiver reads into the communication distorted loadings which arise from projections of his own anxieties, motives, and concerns. As defenses are reduced, the receivers become better able to

Reproduced from The Journal of Communication, *Vol. 11, No. 3, Copyright, September, 1961, 141–148. Reprinted by permission of the International Communication Association.*

concentrate upon the structure, the content, and the cognitive meanings of the message.

Categories of Defensive and Supportive Communication

In working over an eight-year period with recordings of discussions occurring in varied settings, the writer developed the six pairs of defensive and supportive categories presented in Table 1. Behavior which a listener perceives as possessing any of the characteristics listed in the left-hand column arouses defensiveness, whereas that which he interprets as having any of the qualities designated as supportive reduces defensive feelings. The degree to which these reactions occur depends upon the personal level of defensiveness and on the general climate in the group at the time.[2]

Evaluation and Description

Speech or other behavior which appears evaluative increases defensiveness. If by expression, manner of speech, tone of voice, or verbal content the sender seems to be evaluating or judging the listener, then the receiver goes on guard. Of course, other factors may inhibit the reaction. If the listener thought that the speaker regarded him as an equal and was being open and spontaneous, for example, the evaluativeness in a message would be neutralized and perhaps not even perceived. This same principle applies equally to the other five categories of potentially defense-producing climates. The six sets are interactive.

Because our attitudes toward other persons are frequently, and often necessarily, evaluative expression which the defensive person will regard as non-judgmental are hard to frame. Even the simplest question usually conveys the answer that the sender wishes or implies the response that would fit into his value system. A mother, for example, immediately following an earth tremor that shook the house, sought for her small son with the question: "Bobby, where are you?" The timid and plaintive "Mommy, I didn't do it" indicated how Bobby's chronic mild defensiveness predisposed him to react with a projection of his own guilt and in the context of his chronic assumption that questions are full of accusation.

Anyone who has attempted to train professionals to use information-seeking speech with neutral affect appreciates how difficult it is to teach a person to say even the simple "who did that?" without being seen as accusing. Speech is so frequently judgmental that there is a reality base for the defensive interpretations which are so common.

When insecure, group members are particularly likely to place blame, to see others as fitting into categories of good or bad, to make moral judgments of their colleagues, and to question the value, motive, and affect loadings of the

TABLE 1   CATEGORIES OF BEHAVIOR CHARACTERISTICS OF SUPPORTIVE AND DEFENSIVE CLIMATES IN SMALL GROUPS

Defensive Climates	Supportive Climates
1. Evaluation	1. Description
2. Control	2. Problem orientation
3. Strategy	3. Spontaneity
4. Neutrality	4. Empathy
5. Superiority	5. Equality
6. Certainty	6. Provisionalism

speech which they hear. Since value loadings imply a judgment of others, a belief that the standards of the speaker differ from his own causes the listener to become defensive.

Descriptive speech, in contrast to that which is evaluative, tends to arouse a minimum of uneasiness. Speech acts which the listener perceives as genuine requests for information or as material with neutral loadings is descriptive. Specifically, presentations of feelings, events, perceptions, or processes which do not ask or imply that the receiver change behavior or attitude are minimally defense producing. The difficulty in avoiding overtone is illustrated by the problems of news reporters in writing stories about unions, communists, Negroes, and religious activities without tipping off the "party" line of the newspaper. One can often tell from the opening words in a news article which side the newspaper's editorial policy favors.

Control and Problem Orientation

Speech which is used to control the listener evokes resistance. In most of our social intercourse someone is trying to do something else—to change an attitude, to influence behavior, or to restrict the field of activity. The degree to which attempts to control produce defensiveness depends upon the openness of the effort, for a suspicion that hidden motives exist heightens resistance. For this reason, attempts of nondirective therapists and progressive educators to refrain from imposing a set of values, a point of view, or a problem solution upon the receivers meet with many barriers. Since the norm is control, non-controllers must earn the perceptions that their efforts have no hidden motives. A bombardment of persuasive "messages" in the fields of politics, education, special causes, advertising, religion, medicine, industrial relations, and guidance has bred cynical and paranoidal responses in listeners.

Implicit in all attempts to alter another person is the assumption by the change agent that the person to be altered is inadequate. That the speaker secretly views the listener as ignorant, unable to make his own decisions, uninformed, immature, unwise, or possessed of wrong or inadequate attitudes is a subconscious perception which gives the latter a valid base for defensive reactions.

Methods of control are many and varied. Legalistic insistence on detail, restrictive regulations and policies, conformity norms, and all laws are among the methods. Gestures, facial expression, other forms of nonverbal communication, and even such simple acts as holding a door open in a particular manner are means of imposing one's will upon another and hence are potential sources of resistance.

Problem orientation, on the other hand, is the antithesis of persuasion. When the sender communicates a desire to collaborate in defining a mutual problem and in seeking its solution, he tends to create the same problem orientation in the listener; and, of greater importance, he implies that he has no predetermined solution, attitude, or method to impose. Such behavior is permissive in that it allows the receiver to set his own goals, make his own decisions, and evaluate his own progress or to share with the sender in doing so. The exact methods of attaining permissiveness are not known, but they must involve a constellation of cues and they certainly go beyond mere verbal assurances that the communicator has no hidden desires to exercise control.

Strategy and Spontaneity

When the sender is perceived as engaging in a stratagem involving ambiguous and multiple motivators, the receiver becomes defensive. No one wishes to be a guinea pig, a role player, or an impressed actor, and no one likes to be the victim of some hidden motivation. That which is concealed, also, may appear larger than it really is with the degree of defensiveness of the listener determining the perceived size of the suppressed element. The intense reaction of the reading audience to the material in *The Hidden Persuaders* indicates the prevalence of defensive reactions to multiple motivations behind strategy. Group members who are seen as "taking a role," as feigning emotion, as toying with their colleagues, as withholding information, or as having special sources of data are especially resented. One participant once complained that another was "using a listening technique" on him!

A large part of the adverse reaction to much of the so-called human relations training is a feeling against what are perceived as gimmicks and tricks to fool or to "involve" people, to make a person think he is making his own decision, or to make the listener feel that the sender is genuinely interested in him as a person. Particularly violent reactions occur when it appears that someone is trying to make a stratagem appear spontaneous. One person has reported a boss who incurred resentment by habitually using the gimmick of "spontaneously" looking at his watch and saying, "My gosh, look at the time—I must run to an appointment." The belief was that the boss would create less irritation by honestly asking to be excused.

Similarly, the deliberate assumption of guilelessness and natural simplicity is especially resented. Monitoring the tapes of feedback and evaluation sessions in training groups indicates the surprising extent to which members perceive the strategies of their colleagues. This perceptual clarity may be quite shocking to the strategist, who usually feels that he has cleverly hidden the motivational aura around the "gimmick."

This aversion to deceit may account for one's resistance to politicians who are suspected of behind-the-scenes planning to get his vote, to psychologists whose listening apparently is motivated by more than the manifest or content-level interest in his behavior, or to the sophisticated, smooth, or clever person whose "oneupmanship" is marked with guile. In training groups the role-flexible person frequently is resented because his changes in behavior are perceived as strategic maneuvers.

In contrast, behavior which appears to be spontaneous and free of deception is defense reductive. If the communicator is seen as having a clean id, as having uncomplicated motivations, as being straightforward and honest, and as behaving spontaneously in response to the situation, he is likely to arouse minimal defense.

Neutrality and Empathy

When neutrality in speech appears to the listener to indicate a lack of concern for his welfare, he becomes defensive. Group members usually desire to be perceived as valued persons, as individuals of speech worth, and as objects of concern and affection. The clinical, detached, person-is-an-object-of-study attitude on the part of many psychologist-trainers is resented by group members. Speech with low affect that communicates little warmth or caring is in such contrast with the affect laden speech in social situations that it sometimes communicates rejection.

Communication that conveys empathy for the feelings and respect for the worth of the listener, however, is particularly supportive and defense reductive. Reassurance results when a message indicates that the speaker identifies himself with the listener's problems, shares his feelings, and accepts his emotional reaction at face value. Abortive efforts to deny the legitimacy of the receiver's emotions by assuring the receiver that he need not feel bad, that he should not feel rejected or that he is overly anxious, though often intended as support giving, may impress the listener as lack of acceptance. The combination of understanding and empathizing with other person's emotions with no accompanying effort to change him apparently is supportive at a high level.

The importance of gestural behavior cues in communicating empathy should be mentioned. Apparently spontaneous facial and bodily evidences of concern are often interpreted as especially valid evidence of deep-level acceptance.

Superiority and Equality

When a person communicates to another that he feels superior in position, power, wealth, intellectual ability, physical characteristics, or other ways, he arouses defensiveness. Here, as with the other sources of disturbance, whatever arouses feelings of inadequacy causes the listener to center upon the affect loading of the statement rather than upon the cognitive elements. The receiver then reacts by not hearing the message, by forgetting it, by competing with the sender, or by becoming jealous of him.

The person who is perceived as feeling superior communicates that he is not willing to enter into a shared problem-solving relationship, that he probably does not desire feedback, that he does not require help, and/or that he will be likely to try to reduce the power, the status, or the worth of the receiver.

Many ways exist for creating the atmosphere that the sender feels himself equal to the listener. Defenses are reduced when one perceives the sender as being willing to enter into participative planning with mutual trust and respect. Differences in talent, ability, worth, appearance, status, and power often exist, but the low defense communicator seems to attach little importance to these distinctions.

Certainty and Provisionalism

The effects of dogmatism in producing defensiveness are well known. Those who seem to know the answers, to require no additional data, and to regard themselves as teachers rather than as co-workers tend to put others on guard. Moreover, in the writer's experiment, listeners often perceived manifest expressions of certainty as connoting inward feelings of inferiority. They saw the dogmatic individual as needing to be right, as wanting to win an argument rather than solve a problem, and as seeing his ideas as truths to be defended. This kind of behavior often was associated with acts which others regarded as attempts to exercise control. People who were right seemed to have low tolerance for members who were "wrong"—i.e., who did not agree with the sender.

One reduces the defensiveness of the listener when he communicates that he is willing to experiment with his own behavior, attitudes, and ideas. The person who appears to be taking provisional attitudes, to be investigating issues rather than taking sides on them, to be problem solving rather than debating, and to be willing to experiment and explore tends to communicate that the listener may have some control over the shared quest or the investigation of the ideas. If a person is genuinely searching for information and data, he does not resent help or company along the way.

Conclusion

The implications of the above material for the parent, the teacher, the manager, the administrator, or the therapist are fairly obvious. Arousing defensiveness interferes with communication and thus makes it difficult—and sometimes impossible—for anyone to convey ideas clearly and to move effectively toward the solution of therapeutic, educational, or managerial problems.

Notes

1. J. R. Gibb, "Defense Level and Influence Potential in Small Groups," in L. Petrullo and B. M. Bass (eds.), *Leadership and Interpersonal Behavior* (New York: Holt, Rinehart and Winston, Inc., 1961), pp. 66–81.
2. J. R. Gibb, "Sociopsychological Process of Group Instruction," in N. B. Henry (ed.), *The Dynamics of Instructional Groups* (Fifty-ninth Yearbook of the National Society for the Study of Education, Part II, 1960), pp. 115–135.

Conflict Resolution and Decision-Making Processes

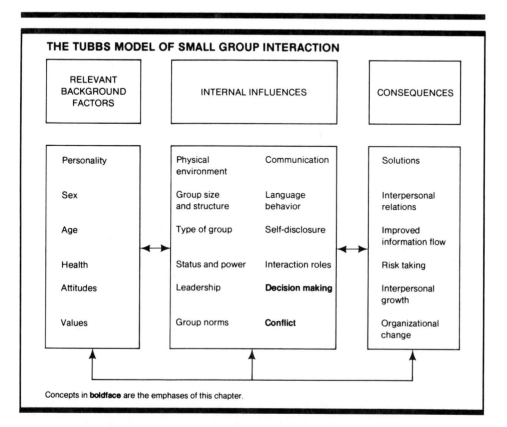

THE TUBBS MODEL OF SMALL GROUP INTERACTION

RELEVANT BACKGROUND FACTORS	INTERNAL INFLUENCES		CONSEQUENCES
Personality	Physical environment	Communication	Solutions
Sex	Group size and structure	Language behavior	Interpersonal relations
Age	Type of group	Self-disclosure	Improved information flow
Health	Status and power	Interaction roles	Risk taking
Attitudes	Leadership	**Decision making**	Interpersonal growth
Values	Group norms	**Conflict**	Organizational change

Concepts in **boldface** are the emphases of this chapter.

PREVIEW

The internal influences of the Tubbs Model of Small Group Interaction are concluded in Chapter 6. Several different decision-making processes are presented. The reflective thinking process, which is left-brain oriented, comprises several phases. The Kepner-Tregoe approach is based mainly on the criteria phase, such as musts and wants. The single question form, brainstorming, incrementalism, mixed scanning, and tacit bargaining are the other methods for decision making discussed in Chapter 6. The second part of Chapter 6 relates to conflicts, which arise often in groups. Sources and types of conflict are covered along with the undesirability of conflict. The final section places importance on working toward conflict resolution. The conflict grid is used as an illustration.

GLOSSARY

The Reflective Thinking Process: The reflective thinking process is a pattern for small group problem solving that includes six components:
(1) What is the problem?
(2) What are its causes and limits?
(3) What are the criteria for an acceptable solution?
(4) What are the available solutions?
(5) What is the best solution?
(6) How can it be implemented?

The Kepner-Tregoe Approach: This approach is a variation of the reflective thinking sequence. Its most important contribution is the way in which a group works through the criteria phase, differentiating between the musts and the wants of a solution.

The Single Question Form: The single question form is a brief method of group problem solving using the "single question" format.

Brainstorming: Brainstorming is a technique used to *generate* ideas. It emphasizes brain activity. It can be applied as part of the problem-solving process.

Incrementalism: Incrementalism is the process of making decisions that result in change.

Mixed Scanning: Mixed scanning is a decision-making strategy that combines examining a problem comprehensively (the rational approach) and part by part (the incremental approach).

Tacit Bargaining: Tacit bargaining is "bargaining in which communication is incomplete or impossible."

CASE STUDY: Herb Hamilton

The situation reported in this case occurred in a classroom of a large state university. Herb Hamilton was a 48-year-old high school biology teacher taking an evening graduate-level psychology course in stress management. Dr. Martin, the professor, was 37 years old, had been teaching for 15 years, and was an adjunct professor of psychology at the university (where he taught one night a week) and a full professor at a nearby engineering college. The class had 19 people in it ranging in age from 25 to 48. (Herb was the oldest member of the class.) This is Dr. Martin's account.

Our first class met on January 12. After covering the basic description of the course, assignments, etc., I began a lecture offering a brief overview of the major sources of stress. I mentioned job, family, and community. As I proceeded to discuss divorce statistics, Herb became very upset and said the following, as best I can recall, "It's easy for you to be smug. You have a job, you are married, and you don't know the first thing about what stress feels like. You can only talk about it in an intellectual vacuum!"

After finishing the class, I talked with Herb for about fifteen minutes. He revealed to me that he was under psychiatric care; had been through a very messy divorce during which his wife broke a milk bottle across his face; was currently on a disability leave from his teaching job after having suffered an emotional breakdown; and was the father of four children who "never bothered to call him unless they wanted some money." I tried to calm him down since he was shaking noticeably. I told him that the course was designed to help each of us cope more effectively with the stresses in our lives.

He continued to be disruptive, abusive, and insulting through the next several weeks of class. Several students complained privately that they couldn't believe how antisocial his behavior was and that he was violating their right to learn by his behavior.

Then, on the evening of March 2, Herb came to class smelling of alcohol. I was seated directly behind him. Two students were presenting a report on alcoholism. They began with a thirty-five item test of knowledge about alcoholism. Herb began criticizing the test by stating that he couldn't answer these items because they were statements, not questions. They explained that it was a true-false test and the items were intended to be statements of fact that could be indicated as true or false.

As one person began to read off the correct answers, Herb debated and criticized virtually every item's answer. After the first item, I asked Herb to let the students go on with the report and then we could discuss the entire report as a class. Herb continued to argue every point. Four or five times, other class members asked Herb to be quiet and quit interrupting the presentation. By the time we got to item 21 on the test, the entire class was getting upset.

The twenty-first item on the test stated that alcohol is a stimulant. The speaker said that this statement was false, that it was a depressant. This particularly upset Herb, who argued that it was a stimulant in small quantities and a depressant only in large quantities. I corroborated the speaker, explaining that alcohol depressed the inhibitory mechanisms in the central nervous system, which made it *appear* that the drinker was acting like he or she had been stimulated. Herb turned around to the rest of the class and said, "People, can we tolerate this? This is absolutely wrong. We aren't even getting the accurate facts in this class. We are getting garbage," or words very similar to those.

1. What should Dr. Martin do?

2. How could this conflict have been dealt with? In what ways could it have been avoided?

Perhaps one of the most frequent criticisms of committees is that they are a waste of time. By this people usually mean that groups often require a lot of effort without achieving any tangible results. Therefore it is important to note that several techniques have been developed that can help us get better results from the time we spend in problem-solving groups or committees.

DECISION-MAKING PROCESSES

To increase our understanding of organizational behavior in general, it is particularly important to concentrate on organizational decision making. The decision making of the organization is, in essence, its nucleus; it's what holds the organization together and makes it progress. The goals, tasks, and choices determining the organization's activities are highlighted, which broadly illuminates the dynamics of organizational life.

A majority of the really crucial events of the world are a consequence of the organizational decision-making process rather than isolated, individual decision making. An industrial example cited by Bass (1983) is the "delayed decisions by Detroit auto manufacturers to switch to production of small cars." He goes on to say that it can "only be understood in terms of consumer attitudes toward the small car (fostered by a generation of advertising), the gasoline crisis, political support for continued low gasoline prices, differential profitability of small and large autos, short public memory, and long lead times for investment turnarounds" (p. 2). The unanswered question is whether an understanding of better organizational decision-making processes could have produced a better decision under the conditions.

Decision-making processes are limited to our own ability to process information. As was discussed in Chapters 2 and 5, each of us, having our own background and experience, processes information in very exclusive ways. Walsh (1989) referred to these as "belief structures." In the past, belief-structures, although necessary for information processing to occur, were believed to limit capabilities to understand information and thus to greatly impact the quality of decision making. However, Walsh reports that information processing in decision making is not nearly so simple as was once thought.

As you no doubt know, decision making is hard work. Often the decision-making models in textbooks are extremely simplified compared to the actual cases that confront us in real life. Some fascinating material recently has been published that reveals that even within our own brains, we use two different models or methods for decision making. The left hemisphere of the brain is more prone to logical, factual, sequential, and systematic thinking and decision making. The right hemisphere tends to function more in a holistic, intuitive, emotional manner. For example, one recent advertisement for a new sports car stated that the left side of our brains would like its craftsmanship, good economy, and high resale value, and the right side of our brains would like the fact that it goes like a "bat out of hell."

The right side of the brain would enjoy pictures and cartoons, whereas the left side would like charts that organize concepts. The chart in Figure 6.1 compares the right and left brain functioning methods.

Simon (1987) discussed some of the terms that are used to describe the right brain and left brain decision-making processes. The term "rational" or "logical" is often applied to decision making that is consciously analytical, or what we have described as *left brain*. The term "irrational" is applied to decision-making behaviors that are more intuitive and respond to the emotions, as right brain processes have been described.

Simon went on to discuss nonrational decision making, which is both intuitive (right brain) and judgmental (left brain). This occurs when, under pressure, people arrive at accurate, analytical solutions for complex problems at the snap of a finger. The decision seems to have been made intuitively but is analytical in nature. Simon describes the expert problem solver, who will arrive at a problem diagnosis and decision quickly and intuitively without being able to report how he/she attained the result. This ability is best explained by a judgmental recognition and retrieval process that employs thousands of patterns stored in the long-term memory.

Think of, for instance, a champion chess player who can take up to thirty minutes to make a move in a tournament. Yet when, as part of a fund-raiser, these professionals go up against fifty opponents simultaneously, making a move every thirty seconds, their accuracy is only mildly reduced. As Simon argued, nonrational kinds of decision-making processes occur in both simple and complex decision making.

Gibson and Hodgetts (1986, pp. 155–156) identify four different kinds of creativity that may be applied to group problem solving:

> *Innovation* is original thinking. This is probably the most difficult since by definition it is something never created before. Reportedly, the flip top can was invented by a can opener company which was going broke and needed to think up a new product line.
>
> *Synthesis* is the combining of information from other sources into a new pattern. A kaleidoscope is somewhat like this. The colored pieces of glass are combined and recombined to make new patterns.
>
> *Extension* is the expansion of ideas beyond their current boundaries. McDonalds decided a few years back to add breakfast to their existing product lines. This increased their profits by 40 percent!
>
> *Duplication* is to copy good ideas. Japanese companies have become famous for taking original ideas from American companies and copying them and improving on them. The motorcycle, electronics, watch, and auto industries are but a few examples.

As you look at several decision-making models in this chapter, you will notice that implied in each approach is a bias toward the left brain or the right. It is probably good to remember that both sides of the brain should be used in concert, because their functions complement one another.

FIGURE 6.1   LEFT AND RIGHT BRAIN FUNCTIONS

	Left	Right	
1	Logical, more like a computer analyzing component bits of information in a systematic manner and sequence, then drawing a conclusion from the premises.	Intuitive, more like an artist looking for an *overall* image, concept, or Gestalt. The conclusions are often reached in a flash of insight, rather than in a systematic method.	1
2	Either/or thinking, one correct answer (such as in mathematics).	Many alternatives, numerous shades of gray, subtle gradations or nuances of meaning.	2
3	Precise, literal meaning, such as in legal documents.	Nonliteral comparisons, such as in metaphors and analogies. (For example, comparing a group's leader to a ship's rudder.)	3
4	Verbally oriented.	Nonverbally oriented, uses graphic or pictorial descriptions.	4
5	Explicit, carefully defined, and fully explained.	Implicit, impressionistic, like a sketch rather than a photograph.	5
6	Controlled, disciplined.	Emotional, sensual, like reacting to music or to fragrances or colors.	6
7	Pragmatic, very practical real-world orientation.	Imaginative, nontraditional, innovative, uses fantasy.	7
8	Dominant.	Passive.	8
9	Intellectual, cerebral.	Sensually oriented, prefers experiencing to intellectualizing.	9
10	Careful with time and the use of time.	Casual with time and the use of time.	10
11	Scientific.	Artistic.	11
12	Preprogrammed, organized.	Ambiguous, nebulous.	12
13	Objective, verifiable.	Subjective, personal, unique.	13
14	Skeptical, preferring evidence and factual proof.	Accepting, preferring intuition and gut-level impressions.	14
15	Comparison against standards of performance.	Comparison against internal private standards.	15

Finally, some of the following models are prescriptive—that is, they prescribe a desired way to solve problems. Other models are more descriptive and describe how we tend to solve problems rather than tell us how we should do it. Each model has some research evidence suggesting that it is helpful in improving the decisions that people make. However, our ability to solve problems will probably be helped most if we become familiar with several of these approaches and gain what we can from each instead of picking only one.

Best too use several approaches to problem solving Eclective approach

The Reflective Thinking Process

Systematic - left brain

Undoubtedly, the best-known pattern for small group problem solving is the reflective thinking sequence first proposed by John Dewey (1910). It emphasizes the left brain funtions. Although the method has several variations, the basic components are: (1) What is the problem? (2) What are its causes and limits? (3) What are the criteria for an acceptable solution? (4) What are the available solutions? (5) What is the best solution? and (6) How can it be implemented? A more detailed outline includes the following:

I. Problem Phase

   a. *Identification of problem area, including such questions as:*

      1. What is the situation in which the problem is occurring?

      2. What, in general, is the difficulty?

      3. How did this difficulty arise?

      4. What is the importance of the difficulty?

      5. What limitations, if any, are there on the area of our concern?

      6. What is the meaning of any term that needs clarifying?

   b. *Analysis of the difficulty*

      1. What, specifically, are the facts of the situation?

      2. What, specifically, are the difficulties?

   c. *Analysis of causes*

      1. What is causing the difficulties?

      2. What is causing the causes?

II. Criteria Phase

   a. What are the principal requirements of the solution?

   b. What limitations must be placed on the solution?

   c. What is the relative importance of the criteria?

III. Solution Phase

   a. *What are the possible solutions?*

1. What is the exact nature of each solution?

2. How would it remedy the difficulty? by eliminating the cause? by offsetting the effect? by a combination of both?

b. *How good is each solution?*

1. How well would it remedy the difficulty?

2. How well would it satisfy the criteria? Are there any that it would not satisfy?

3. Would there be any unfavorable consequences? any extra benefits?

c. *What solution appears to be best?*

1. How would you rank the solution?

2. Would some combination of solutions be best?

IV. Implementation Phase

What steps would be taken to put the solution into effect?

Although this sequence is well known and widely taught, other approaches that are of value also have been proposed.

The Kepner-Tregoe Approach   Systematic-Left brain

A variation of the reflective thinking sequence has been proposed by two business consultants (Kepner and Tregoe 1965). The overall format is similar to the reflective thinking sequence; however, the most important contribution seems to be the way in which a group works through the *criteria phase*.

Let's say that the group is trying to figure out how to cut its departmental spending by 10 percent. When we select the best solution, several criteria must be considered. There are certain required elements and other desired elements to any solution. Kepner and Tregoe refer to these as the *musts* and *wants*, respectively. For example:

Musts	**Wants**
The budget must be reduced by 10 percent.	We would like to avoid laying people off.
We must have it accomplished within a year.	Sooner would be better.
Any changes must be in line with existing company policies.	We would like to involve people in the decision.
Any changes must not violate our union contract.	We would like people to willingly cooperate.

If we use the method described above, the criteria for an acceptable decision could be assigned a numerical value and ranked in order of importance. Then a grid could be constructed on which you could evaluate different solutions against the relevant criteria.

More recently, Magner (1988) described the process the federal government used to decide which state received the multibillion-dollar contract for the Superconducting Super Collider (SSC), a high-powered atomic research facility. The exact same process was used as that described in this text. For example, the competing states (alternative solutions) were listed according to the major criteria and were evaluated along the scale Outstanding, Good, Satisfactory, and Poor. The actual ratings appear in Figure 6.2 (Magner 1988, pp. A1, A4). You can see why Texas won the competition.

The Single Question Form

Larson (1969, p. 453) has found that another, rather brief method is about as good as the methods already described. Larson studied the differences between high- and low-success individual problem solvers and derived a technique that could be used by groups. This method involves using the following format:

- What is the single question, the answer to which is all the group needs to know to accomplish its purpose?

- What subquestions must be answered before we can answer the single question we have formulated?

FIGURE 6.2   SSC RATINGS FOR COMPETING STATES

	Ariz.	Col.	Ill.	Mich.	N.C.	Tenn.	Texas
Geology	S	G	O	S	G	O	O
Reg. Resources	S	S	O	O	G	S	O
Environment	G	O	G	G	G	G	O
Setting	G	G	P	S	S	O	O
Reg. Conditions	S	O	G	O	G	O	G
Utilities	G	G	G	G	G	G	G

GEOLOGY: geologic suitability, operational stability, operational efficiency and construction risk.

O - outstanding	S - satisfactory
G - good	P - poor

REGIONAL RESOURCES: community resources, accessibility, industrial base and institutional support for the project.
ENVIRONMENT: environmental impacts, compliance with regulatory requirements and ability to mitigate any adverse impacts.
SETTING: real estate, flexibility for changes in site plan, and natural and man-made features.
REGIONAL CONDITIONS: vibrations, noise and climate.
UTILITIES: availability of electricity, water and other utilities.

- Do we have sufficient information to answer confidently the subquestions?

- What are the most reasonable answers to the subquestions?

- It we assume that our answers to the subquestions are correct, what is the best solution to the problem?

More direct approach This technique evolved out of an analysis of the basic differences in communication behaviors between successful and unsuccessful problem solvers studied by Bloom and Broder (1961). It seems that the successful problem solvers were more willing and more interested in getting at solutions; they avoided getting bogged down with the trivial detail of the discussion. Their attitudes seemed to be characterized as, "Let's assume for the moment a few things," rather than, "How can we be expected to solve this when those guys who gave us the problem can't solve their own problems?" In other words, there is an eagerness to make progress rather than to alibi out of making progress. Dance and Larson (1972, p. 128) summarize these two different sets of behaviors in Figure 6.3. Notice that this is a descriptive summary that has prescriptive implications.

Each of the problem-solving methods described thus far (that is, reflective thinking, the Kepner-Tregoe approach, or the single question form) will probably

FIGURE 6.3   SOME DIFFERENCES BETWEEN HIGH- AND LOW-SUCCESS PROBLEM SOLVERS

Used with permission of F.E.X. Dance, *Speech Communication: Concepts and Behavior* (New York: Holt, Rinehart and Winston, 1972), p. 128.

High Success	Low Success
1. Starting the attack on the problem	
Able to select some phrase or concept as a point of departure. Able to state a specific objective toward which to work.	Tried to change the problem to one which they could solve more easily. Tendency to disagree with the problem, for example, "This is a stupid problem."
2. Approach to basic ideas within the problem	
Used analogies and examples to help themselves understand the concepts within the problems. Considered more implications of the ideas which they came up with, such as, "What would result from . . ." "What causes . . ."	Did not attempt to arrive at an understanding of the problem, for example, "We haven't studied that yet." Used more unconnected series of thoughts.
3. General approach to problems	
Set up hypotheses about what the correct answer would do. If unfamiliar terms were used in the problem, made an assumption about the meaning and proceeded.	Selected answers on the basis of feeling and impressions (especially in social problems). Devoted little time to considering the nature of the problem.
4. Attitudes toward solving problems	
"You can figure it out if you try."	"You either know it or you don't." Easily discouraged. Avoided complex problems. Little confidence in their own reasoning abilities.

offer you and your group a way to get better results than if you used no systematic method at all. Try using each of these methods in solving some of the problem exercises in this book. Don't give up—most problems can be solved if we work at them long enough.

Brainstorming
Rightbrain

Another popular technique that can be applied to problem-solving is brainstorming (Osborn 1953). This technique is primarily used to generate ideas and can be applied as *part* of the problem-solving process. It emphasizes right brain activity. For example, groups frequently dwell on one or two proposed solutions to a problem, when many more solutions may be available. Brainstorming would be one way to help generate more alternative solutions for the group to consider.

Brainstorming can be applied to any of the phases of the reflective thinking sequence discussed earlier. The problem identification phase includes the need to determine the factors causing the problem; the criteria phase requires identification of the requirements for an appropriate solution; the solution phase requires some alternatives from which to choose; and the implementation phase requires creative application of the chosen solution. The guidelines (adapted from Osborn 1953) for using the brainstorming technique are listed below.

example in class – Problems for Research Paper

Rules for Brainstorming

1. *Put judgment and evaluation temporarily aside.*

   a. Acquire a "try anything" attitude.

   b. No faultfinding is allowed. It stifles ideas, halts association.

   c. Today's criticism may kill future ideas.

   d. All ideas are at least thought starters.

2. *Turn imagination loose, and start offering the results.*

   a. The wilder the ideas, the better.

   b. Ideas are easier to tame down than to think up.

   c. Freewheeling is encouraged; ideas can be brought down to earth later.

   d. A wild idea may be the only way to bring out another really good one.

3. *Think of as many ideas as you can.*

   a. Quantity breeds quality.

   b. The more ideas to choose from, the more chance of a good one.

   c. There is always more than one good solution to any problem.

   d. Try many different approaches.

4. *Seek combination and improvement.*

    a. Your ideas don't all have to be original.

    b. Improve on the ideas of others.

    c. Combine previously mentioned ideas.

    d. Brainstorming is a group activity. Take advantage of group association.

5. *Record all ideas in full view.*

6. *Evaluate at a later session.*

    a. Approach each idea with a positive attitude.

    b. Give each idea a fair trial.

    c. Apply judgment gradually.

Osborn offers a few additional tips to further stimulate the creation of ideas (ideation). After ideas are generated, think of adding, subtracting, multiplying, and dividing as ways of modifying the ideas you already have. Effective toothpaste was improved by adding fluorides. Portable radios were made portable by subtracting size through the use of printed circuits. The common razor blade market was revamped by the creation of a double-edged razor (multiplying). General Motors decided to divide up the production of the Oldsmobile Cutlass to several assembly plants, because the single plant at Lansing, Michigan, could not expand fast enough to keep up with demand.

Osborn's ideas have been updated by Sabatine (1989, p. 13), who suggests the following practical tips for creatively brainstorming solutions:

- The "PMI" method—The next time someone presents a new idea or solution to you, think of all the pluses (P) of the idea, then all of the minuses (M), and finally, what is interesting (I) about the idea.

- Using humorous metaphors and analogies when speaking and writing—"That's like trying to sell anabolic steroids to the Incredible Hulk."

- Engaging in athletic activities, games, and hobbies, especially with children (e.g., "Pictionary").

- Practicing relaxation techniques and simple meditation to reduce stress and anxiety.

- Taking long walks, mowing the grass (incubating).

- Taking notice and discussing your "gut" feelings with others.

- Reviewing your problems or ideas before you fall asleep.

- Carrying a small notebook and recording your insights.

- Daydreaming regularly, engaging in detailed fantasizing and visualizing.

- Drawing and doodling when working on a problem.

- Viewing mistakes as learning opportunities.

- Learning to laugh at yourself, not taking yourself too seriously.

One aspect of brainstorming that may be less obvious is the incubation of ideas—allowing ideas to develop during a period of relative relaxation. Sometimes allowing ideas to incubate, or "set," creates a new insight into a problem. Many company executives as well as important politicians prefer to be alone before making important decisions. This period of solitude may help you to let all the facts sink in before you commit yourself to a decision.

The brainstorming process has a success record that is hard to ignore. Cocks (1990) cites a well-known product innovation that resulted from brainstorming:

Brainstorming has a high success rate.

> In Minneapolis 3M encourages employees to devote about 15% of their work schedule to non-job related tasks, or doing "skunkworks" duty, as it's known around the office. One skunkworking engineer came up with the idea for those neat adhesive Post-it notes while letting his imagination roam. This and other employee-generated brainstorms, from three-dimensional magnetic recording tape to disposable masks, have encouraged 3M to set a goal of 25% in total revenues from new products developed in the past five years. Currently those revenues are running closer to 30%, and 3M figures that nearly 70% of its annual $12 billion in sales comes from ideas that originated from the work force.

Incrementalism

decision-making that results in change.

Right Brain

Braybrooke and Lindblom (1963) have pointed out that many economists, social scientists, political analysts, and other decision makers generally resort to a style of decision making that is far from the rational models described earlier in this chapter. They argue that numerous decisions concerning governmental policies such as welfare and social security are arrived at partially as a result of adapting to political pressure rather than as a result of rational analysis of the available alternatives. Because environmental obstacles frequently prevent groups from choosing a "best" alternative, other alternatives may result by default. A Supreme Court vacancy may be filled by a "compromise candidate," one who is clearly not the most outstanding contender but who is the only one upon whom the public can agree. This is an example of a nonrational decision.

non-rational

The term "incrementalism" refers to the process of making decisions that result in change. Some decisions result in vast amounts of change, whereas other decisions progress toward change by small bits, or *increments*. A second variable is the amount and quality of knowledge or understanding underlying a decision. When these two factors are taken in combination, the model in Figure 6.4 results.

Braybrooke and Lindblom's analysis is primarily centered on political decisions resulting in societal change. With respect to quadrant 1 in the diagram in Figure 6.4, the researchers contend that few decisions resulting in major social changes can be made with a high level of intellectual understanding of a problem. Numerous "think tanks" are devoted to analyzing what we should be doing to prepare ourselves for the year 2000 and beyond. Yet even the best estimates are "guesstimates" that must be continually revised on the basis of new data. The decision to enact forced busing of schoolchildren to achieve a racial balance in public schools was an attempt to bring about a major social change. Yet the magnitude of resistance to this move was severely underestimated. In another context, the decision to have year-round daylight saving time was implemented in an attempt to save fuel. However, because

decisions not based on rational thinking but on how society will react to the changes.

FIGURE 6.4   MODEL OF DECISION MAKING
Reprinted with permission of The Free Press, a Division of Macmillan, Inc. from *A Strategy of Decision* by David Braybrooke and Charles C. Lindblom. Copyright © 1963 by the Free Press of Glencoe.

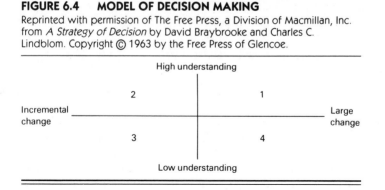

of the threat of children being run down by cars in the dark early-morning hours, more parents drove their children to school, thus using more energy than daylight saving time was saving. These decisions illustrate the point that attempts to make major changes are not always accompanied by a full realization of the consequences. Thus, the majority of decisions resulting in large changes would be depicted in Figure 6.4 as falling in quadrant 4.

Quadrant 2 refers to the daily decisions of most groups that result in relatively small changes. Decisions to change the prime lending rate of a bank, to increase social security benefits, or to add a few employees to a payroll are all examples of such decisions. Obviously, defining "small" changes is a matter of judgment. These types of decisions frequently result from the careful study of experts in costing, economics, and management. Thus, the chances are increased that the decision will be made with a high level of understanding of the problem. However, this may not always be the case. If the decisions result in unwanted or unanticipated problems such as inflation or unionization, the decision is defined as falling into quadrant 3. Braybrooke and Lindblom (1963, p. 73) offer the following explanation for the tendency toward incremental change:

> For a democracy like the United States, the commitment to incremental change is not surprising. Nonincremental alternatives usually do not lie within the range of choice possible in the society or body politic. Societies, it goes without saying, are complex structures that can avoid dissolution or intolerable dislocation only by meeting certain preconditions, among them that certain kinds of change are admissible only if they occur slowly. Political democracy is often greatly endangered by nonincremental change, which it can accommodate only in certain limited circumstances.

Their point of view is that we make group decisions on the basis of relatively limited information and understanding of the consequences of those decisions. By implication, it would seem that this calls for problem-solving strategies that are flexible and subject to change on the basis of feedback indicating the change is desirable. For example, the United States auto makers at one time committed large amounts of money to the development of a rotary engine as a possible alternative to the piston engine. However, when the demand for more energy-efficient engines became greater, the work on the rotary engine was permanently halted. This type of bit-by-bit planning is representative of the exploratory decision making sometimes required in a continually changing environment.

Mixed Scanning

combination of both rationalism & incrementalism (part by part approach)

Etzioni (1968) offers a decision-making strategy that he asserts is "neither rationalism nor incrementalism." Actually, it is a combination of the two approaches. Rather than examining a problem comprehensively (rational approach) or part by part (incremental approach), we can combine elements of both of these approaches into a so-called mixed-scanning strategy. Etzioni offers the following example (1968, p. 284) in support of this contention:

Balance between "the general" and "the specific or Detail" is a major factor in successful problem-solving

> Infantrymen taking positions in a new field in hostile territory scan it for hidden enemy troops. They are trained to scan a field. A rationalistic strategy is likely to be avoided because it would entail examining the whole field bit-by-bit, exhaustively, which would be dangerous and fatiguing and is likely not to be completed. Incrementalists would examine places in which enemy troops have been known to hide and some others near them or similar to them. Unlike the whole field, these places can be prodded by fire. Soldiers who are tired of marching and combat will sometimes follow this procedure. But armies known for their effectiveness train their soldiers in a different procedure. A major consideration in this regard is that accuracy of aim declines with distance. The infantrymen are taught first to scan the whole field in a rough, nondiscriminating way for some obvious sign of danger (a movement, an unnatural shadow, and so on).—If none is visible, they proceed with a bit-by-bit examination from the left to the right, beginning with subfields closest to them and moving outward to more distant ones. The assumption is that scanning is going to become more superficial the longer it is carried out, which is made to coincide with the scanning of the more remote, less dangerous subfields.

Mix Scanning

The basic idea is to combine an analysis of the "big picture" with an appropriate amount of attention to detail. In an employment decision, several candidates may be assessed according to specific ratings on several criteria relevant to the job. This would be an example of paying attention to detail. It may be that one person meets all the criteria very well, and he or she would be a strong replacement for the employee who is to be replaced. However, at the same time, perhaps a completely different level of scanning is needed to anticipate the type of employee that might be best several years from now. In one such case, a decision to replace a college debate coach resulted in hiring a professor in interpersonal and small group communication, because the debate program was getting smaller while the interpersonal and small group curriculum was increasing in size and scope.

A similar example of such a mixed-scanning model applies to the technique of efficient reading. The so-called SQ3R method of reading involves these five steps (Robinson 1961):

1. *Survey.* Glance at (or scan) the chapter outline and leaf through the pages to get a general idea of how much material is allotted to each topic in the outline.

2. *Question.* Begin to look more closely at the chapter and ask yourself questions about what the topics might be about.

3. *Read.* Read the chapter straight through once.

4. *Recite.* See how much of the material you can recite or explain to someone (or write down on a blank paper).

5. *Review.* Review the points you were able to recite and check the ones you were not.

This widely recommended study method contains elements of Etzioni's mixed-scanning model. It involves a general overview as well as an appropriate amount of attention to the necessary details. Etzioni urges that this alternating between levels of analysis enables us to "see the forest for the trees." Many groups seem to have trouble either getting down from the clouds of ambiguities and abstractions or getting up out of the quagmire of trivia long enough to see the overview. This ability to maintain a balance between attention to the general versus the specific appears to be a major factor in successful problem solving.

Tacit Bargaining   Negotiation Problem Solving

Still a third strategy for decision making that is considered an alternative to the rational-thinking approach is advanced by Schelling (1960). This strategy is referred to (p. 53) as "tacit bargaining," or "bargaining in which communication is incomplete or impossible." Examples of such situations (pp. 56–57) include the following:

1. Name heads or tails. If you and your partner name the same, you both win a prize.

2. Circle one of the numbers listed in the line below. You win if you all succeed in circling the same number.
   7   100   13   261   99   555

3. You are to divide $100 into two piles, labeled A and B. Your partner is to divide another $100 into two piles labeled A and B. If you allot the same amounts to A and B, respectively, that your partner does, each of you gets $100; if your amounts differ from his, neither of you gets anything.

In his research Schelling found that in the first problem, thirty-six participants chose heads and only six chose tails. In problem 2, the first three numbers got thirty-seven out of forty-one votes (seven got the most, then one hundred, then thirteen). In problem 3, thirty-six out of forty-one split the money into two equal piles of $50 each. The data suggest that people can cooperate fairly successfully in some problem-solving situations if it is to their advantage to do so. However, numerous situations exist in which the participants have divergent interests. For example, several fraternity representatives meet together on an interfraternity council; each member is interested in promoting the entire Greek system, but his primary loyalty is to his own fraternity. This divided loyalty creates an arena of "politicking" such that most members will choose *not* to communicate in a completely open and honest way.

This is often referred to as a "mixed-motive" situation, in which there is simultaneous pressure to cooperate and to compete. Thus, many proposed solutions are likely not to be prompted by the most honorable intentions but to be motivated by the interests of a single person. Similar situations exist in congressional committees, which often split according to partisan (Republican and Democrat) affiliations. In these situations, decisions are frequently based on compromises and a philosophy of "I'll support you on this issue, but you owe me support on the next issue." Rational and objective choices are less likely to prevail under these circumstances. These bargaining situations imply communication procedures that are distinctly different from those in other kinds of problem-solving situations.

Negotiations between union and management are often characterized by each side's making highly publicized statements of extreme positions in order to strengthen its respective bargaining position. Thus the union president will call for a minimum wage increase of 10 percent, and the company's representative will state flatly that 3 percent is all it can afford to give. In reality, both parties exaggerate their public position and privately acknowledge that a 6 or 7 percent agreement is what they are really trying to achieve. Keltner (1970) has graphically depicted this form of information exchange in Figure 6.5.

If we assume that in these bargaining situations it would be naive to advise participants to simply "give in," still some reasonable suggestions can be made to increase the effectiveness of communication as well as the quality of decisions made. A good negotiator should learn to master the following abilities (adapted from Keltner, pp. 241–242):

- He should be willing to face the issues directly and precisely.

- He should be convinced of the position he represents.

- He must have considerable self-confidence.

- He must be reasonably skeptical.

- He must inspire trust in his counterparts at the bargaining table.

- He desires respect rather than popularity.

In concluding this section on problem solving, we should point out that, to some extent, the situation will affect the strategy of decision making chosen. In some situations one of the rational thinking approaches will be most appropriate; in other, more tentative, situations, the incremental approach may be preferable. The mixed-scanning strategy seems to have application in most situations, and the tacit-bargaining strategy will be most likely in situations allowing little or no free communication among participants. In using any strategy you should know which one you are using and understand the underlying assumptions and requirements of each. You should also expect some problems with each and realize the communication requirements inherent in each. Also, as you attempt to make decisions, you will undoubtedly encounter many types of conflict, which is the subject of the next section.

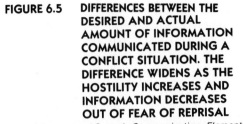

FIGURE 6.5   DIFFERENCES BETWEEN THE DESIRED AND ACTUAL AMOUNT OF INFORMATION COMMUNICATED DURING A CONFLICT SITUATION. THE DIFFERENCE WIDENS AS THE HOSTILITY INCREASES AND INFORMATION DECREASES OUT OF FEAR OF REPRISAL

From *Interpersonal Speech-Communication, Elements and Structures* by John W. Keltner. © 1970 by Wadsworth Publishing Company, Inc. Reprinted by permission of Wadsworth Publishing Company, Belmont, California 94002.

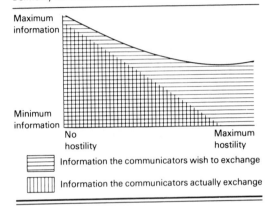

CONFLICT AND CONFLICT RESOLUTION

It has been said that conflict is an inevitable part of people's relating to one another. As Johnson (1973, p. 145) puts it, "A conflict-free relationship is probably a sign that you really have no relationship at all, not that you have a good relationship." It has also been said that where there is movement, there is friction, and where there is friction, heat is produced. Certainly many small groups involve movement, especially if their task is to solve and act on problems. It appears obvious that in such cases the heat referred to is the emotional heat that results from conflicts. "Group processes themselves do not insure that top managers will adequately explore available information. Groups frequently avoid uncertainty and prematurely smooth over conflict" (Brodwin and Bourgeois 1984, p. 167).

In our society, conflict is usually considered to be bad, that thing that results in wars, divorces, worker strikes, and bloody noses. However, most experts agree that conflict within and among groups has some *desirable* effects. Both the desirable and undesirable aspects of conflict will be discussed in this section. However, we look first at the sources from which conflicts arise.

Sources of Conflict

According to Deutsch (1969), conflict exists whenever incompatible activities occur. An incompatible action prevents, obstructs, interferes with, injures, or in some way reduces the effectiveness of the other action. Incompatible actions may occur within a single person (intrapersonal), a single group (intragroup), between two or more people (interpersonal), or between two or more groups (intergroup). Conflicts may originate from a number of different sources, including: (1) differences in information, beliefs, values, interests, or desires; (2) a scarcity of some resource, such as money, power, time, space, or position; and (3) rivalries in which one person or group competes with another (Deutsch 1969). To these sources could be added the difficulty of the task, the pressure to avoid failure, the relative importance of a group's or individual's decision, and differences in skill levels that may cause more skilled individuals to become irritated at the less skilled; this often leads to a reciprocal irritation. In an earlier chaper we discussed personality differences. These differences lead to incompatibilities among certain members of a group. Members may be incompatible because of their differences—or they may be incompatible because of their similarities, such as in the need to achieve or dominate others. All these factors tend to instigate conflict.

See also the article by Phillips at the end of this chapter for more on the constructive use of conflict.

Desirability of Conflict

As mentioned above, many writers believe that conflict in a group is desirable. For example, in Chapter 4 we discussed the very real problem of groupthink, which can occur in any group. Conflict helps eliminate or reduce the likelihood of groupthink. Furthermore, Deutsch (1971, pp. 42–55) cites Simmel (1955) in his argument that conflict has other desirable functions, such as preventing stagnation; stimulating interest and curiosity; providing a medium through which problems can be aired and solutions arrived at; causing personal and social change; being part of the process of testing and assessing oneself and, as such, being highly enjoyable as one experiences the pleasure of full and active use of one's capacities; demarcating groups from one another and thus helping to establish group and personal identities; fostering internal cohesion in groups involved in external conflicts; resolving tension among individuals and thus stabilizing and integrating relationships; eliminating sources of dissatisfaction in social systems by permitting immediate and direct resolution of rival claims; revitalizing existing group norms or helping the emergence of new norms in order to adjust adequately to new conditions; and ascertaining the relative strengths of antagonistic interests within a social system, thereby constituting a mechanism for the maintenance or continual readjustment of the balance of power.

Alfred Sloan was one of the early executives who helped make General Motors successful. He recognized the importance of idea conflict in decision making. Once, Sloan was chairing a meeting of the GM board of directors in which someone presented an idea for buying a small company. After the presentation Sloan asked each member around the table for an opinion. Not one gave an objection to the proposal; they all agreed the company should buy at the earliest possible moment. Finally, Sloan looked at the other board members and said: "Gentlemen, I don't see any reason not to adopt the idea either. Therefore, I suggest we postpone this decision for thirty days while we do some more thinking." Thirty days later the board decided against the plan—after finding out many negatives they had not known earlier (Cosier and Schwenk, 1990, p. 69).

Conflict clearly plays an important role in small group interaction. However, it is a double-edged sword, as we shall see.

Types of Conflict   *conflict of ideas vs conflict of feelings*

Many people fail to differentiate between two very different types of conflict—namely, conflict of ideas versus conflict of feelings (often called personality conflict). As we saw in the example above, Alfred Sloan recognized the importance of idea conflict in making a decision. If there is too little conflict of ideas, groupthink can occur, as we saw in Chapter 4. Idea conflict, however, can very easily turn into conflict of feelings. We can call this personal conflict. Notice the difference between the conflicts in these two conversations in a group discussion.

Conversation 1

> **Judy:** Why don't we have our next meeting at my sorority house?
>
> **Dave:** I think the campus center meeting room might have fewer interruptions. I know how hard it is to have meetings at my fraternity house.

Conversation 2

> **Judy:** Why don't we have our next meeting at my sorority house?
>
> **Dave:** And have people interrupting us all the time? No, thanks, I'd rather meet in the campus center.

In the first situation there was a conflict of ideas. In the second, the conflict could have escalated to the personal level, depending on Judy's reaction. The personal animosity that may have been created by Dave is the kind that tends to get in the way of group success. As shown in Figure 6.6, our goal in using conflict successfully is to avoid turning idea opponents into personal opponents.

Undesirability of Conflict

Our society frequently considers conflict to be undesirable. Millions of dollars are lost each year because of work stoppages and strikes. Thousands of divorces result from unchecked marital conflicts. And every once in a while a disaster like that at Kent State occurs as a result of conflict that has gotten out of control. Even in meetings, discussions, and conferences, conflict may cause reactions similar to that of one student who said, "I don't even want to go to publication council meetings

FIGURE 6.6   OPPOSITION AND SUPPORT

	Idea Supporter	Idea Opponent
Personal Supporter	1 + +	2 + −
Personal Opponent	3 − +	4 − −

AVOID TURNING IDEA OPPONENTS
INTO PERSONAL OPPONENTS

anymore. Every week it is just one hassle after another. Nothing ever gets accomplished because every time we end up arguing."

Conflicts are often hard to keep under control once they have begun. There is a definite trend toward escalation and polarization. Once conflict escalates to a point at which it is no longer under control, it almost always yields negative results. In this same vein, one conflict tends to lay the groundwork for further conflicts at a later time. Part of this is because of defensive reactions. Defensiveness leads us to distort our perceptions so that ambiguous acts are more frequently misconstrued as threatening when they may in fact not be intended that way. Watzlawick, Beavin, and Jackson (1967, pp. 103–104) cite the following example of developing trust in a risky situation:

> We have established a very interesting communication pattern for the establishment of trust between humans and bottle-nosed porpoises. While this may be a ritual developed "privately" by only two of the animals, it still provides an excellent example for the analogic communication of "not." The animals had obviously concluded that the hand is one of the most important and vulnerable parts of the human body. Each would seek to establish contact with a stranger by taking the human's hand into his mouth and gently squeezing it between his jaws, which have sharp teeth and are powerful enough to bite the hand off cleanly. If the human would submit to this, the dolphin seemed to accept it as a message of complete trust. His next move was to reciprocate by placing the forward ventral portion of his body (*his* most vulnerable part, roughly equivalent to the human throat) upon the human's hand, leg, or foot, thereby signaling his trust in the friendly intention of the human. This procedure is, however, obviously fraught with possible misinterpretation at every step.

Nye (1973) identifies three conditions that both cause and result from conflicts. First is *competition*. In many instances there is a win-lose arrangement so that both competitors cannot possibly win. Any athletic contest illustrates that fact. Similarly, several people may seek a promotion, although only one can actually be promoted. In politics one candidate must lose, and this often produces bitter feelings, as illustrated by Nixon's famous remark after the 1962 California gubernatorial election, "You won't have Dick Nixon to kick around anymore."

Second, *domination* is related to conflict. Zimbardo (1972) conducted an experiment in which about two dozen normal, well-adjusted college students acted as either guards or prisoners (half in each group) in a simulated prison. After only four days, three of the "prisoners" had to be released because they suffered such extreme depression and anxiety. At the end of six days, extreme hostility had developed between the prisoners and guards. Zimbardo (1972, p. 8) described the situation in the following way: "We were horrified because we saw some boys ('guards') treat others as if they were despicable animals, taking pleasure in cruelty, while other boys ('prisoners') became servile, dehumanized robots who thought only of escape, of their own individual survival, and of their mounting hatred of the guards."

The third factor is *provocation,* which Nye (1973, p. 8) defines as "intentional or unintentional harm to other persons or groups." This specific factor is most likely to promote further future conflicts. Harmful acts produce grudges that may last for years before conflict has a chance to resume. In any case, the three factors described above illustrate the negative side of conflict. The logical question that arises is, "How do we reduce conflict and keep it at a manageable level?"

Toward Conflict Resolution

A number of systems have been proposed for improving our abilities to resolve conflict. Two famous psychologists (Blake and Mouton 1970) have proposed a scheme whereby we can try to avoid win-lose situations and, when it is possible, apply a win-win approach. This can best be illustrated with their model, called the Conflict Grid® (Figure 6.7).

See the article by Roy Lewicki and Joseph Litterer at the end of this chapter for a further elaboration on conflict resolution.

The Conflict Grid clearly illustrates the possibility of having *both* concern for results and concern for people at the same time. Intuitively, it would seem difficult to "have your cake and eat it too" when it comes to conflict resolution. Alternative strategies of dealing with conflict are also depicted on the grid. Try to identify where your style would fit.

The 1,1 style is the "hands-off" approach. Neutrality is maintained with an attitude of, "the less said about it the better." The 1,9 position is excessively person oriented. Its goal is to maintain the *appearance* of harmony at all cost. In reality deep conflicts exist but are never dealt with. An uneasy state of tension exists, which is frequently characterized by lots of smiling and nervous laughter (but members avoid looking at each other). The 5,5 position represents the willingness to compromise. Although compromise may be a viable alternative in some cases, it should not be a chronic way of avoiding deeper levels of conflict resolution. The bullheaded approach is depicted by the 9,1 position. This style is even worse than the

FIGURE 6.7   BLAKE AND MOUTON'S CONFLICT GRID ®
Reproduced by permission from "The Fifth Achievement," Robert R. Blake and
Jane Srygley Mouton. *Journal of Applied Behavioral Science*, 6(4), 1970.

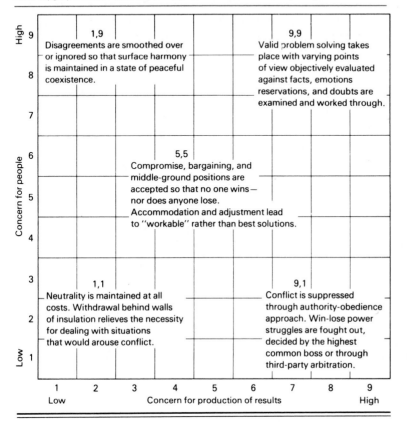

compromise. Because absolute stalemates often occur, a group full of these types may get nowhere fast.

The optimum style for reducing conflict is the 9,9 approach. Here the individuals attempt to be both person and results oriented. Conflicts are not ignored, but individuals don't go around with a chip on their shoulder either. Differences are discussed with such comments as, "I don't agree with the position that . . ." At the same time, personally insulting statements such as "Anybody who believes that is nuts" are avoided. Tubbs and Moss (1991, p. 223) offer four guidelines for implementing the 9,9 style:

- Make sure you agree on the use of your terms or definitions.

- Build on areas of mutual agreement.

- Determine the specific changes necessary for a satisfactory resolution of the issues.

■ Avoid personal attacks, and stick to the issues.

Savage, Blair, and Sorenson (1989) argue that the best strategy for conflict management (negotiation) depends on the desired outcome. "A systematic model of strategic choice for negotiation must account for both substantive and relationship outcomes." That is to say, substantial gains should be maximized while a working relationship is maintained. Strategies will differ according to the negotiation context.

Consideration is given to unilateral and interactive negotiation strategies. The unilateral negotiation strategies are not unlike those offered in the Blake-Mouton Conflict Grid. They include: (1) the trusting collaboration strategy, (2) the open subordination strategy, (3) the firm competiton strategy, and (4) the active avoidance strategy. The point of separation between the Blake-Mouton grid and the categories offered in the Savage and others study is the conscious change of terminology; "strategies" are preferred to "styles." For instance, the open subordination strategy is equivalent to the smoothing over of the Blake-Mouton 1,9 style. Savage, Blair, and Sorenson assert that an act of open subordination in negotiation sacrifices short-term substantive gains for the maintenance of a long-term relationship. It is a strategic move on the part of the negotiator, reflective of his or her substantive and relationship goals.

Interactive strategies take into account the substantive and relationship needs of both parties. The philosophy is that sometimes it is in the best interest of the manager to take the priorities of the other party into consideration. Interactive strategies are an elaboration of the unilateral strategies based on this consideration of priorities. Interactive strategies include: (1) trusting collaboration, (2) principled negotiation, (3) firm competition, (4) soft competition, (5) open subordination, (6) focused subordination, (7) active avoidance, (8) passive avoidance, and (9) responsive avoidance.

Most negotiation literature focuses on substantive outcomes without "systematically considering" the ways negotiations affect relationships. An interactive strategic approach can address both parties' substantive and relationship priorities.

A conflict-reducing method known as *principled negotiation* has been developed by researchers working on the Harvard Negotiation Project (Fisher and Ury 1981, Fisher and Brown 1988). The authors outline four principles that compose the method.

Separate the people from the problem. The natural tendency in any conflict situation is to get angry with the other party. A more effective method is to use the approach described as "hard on issues, soft on people." If possible, treat the other party with respect, and avoid sarcastic comments and nonverbal behaviors.

Focus on interests, not positions. I once had a disagreement with the full professors in a department that centered on which candidate to hire. They wanted Tom, and I wanted Harry. We absolutely could not agree. I wanted Harry because of his distinguished publication record, which would strengthen our position regarding reaccreditation. They did not like his personality. We focused on the common interest of reaccreditation. They agreed as a group (of twenty) to each publish one article in the next year, which would be more publications than Harry would have brought to our organization. I agreed to let them hire Tom, with the provision that if they did not live up to their promise of publishing twenty articles, I would select the next new hire. The agreement was satisfactory to all parties and was based on the common interest rather than on the position (in this case Tom or Harry). At the end of one year they had published ten articles (not twenty), so I selected a new professor to hire who had several high-quality publications. Again, all parties were satisfied, and the case for reaccreditation was strengthened. This example also illustrates the systems principle of equifinality discussed in Chapter 1.

Invent options for mutual gain. All the material discussed regarding brainstorming and creative problem solving applies here. For example, Consumers Power Corporation in Michigan established a joint venture with Oxford Energy in England. They built a plant in California that burns used automobile tires as a source of energy. With electrostatic precipitators, they also eliminate any air pollution. Tires contain so much petroleum that a ton of tires has more BTUs of energy than a ton of coal. This is an ingenious innovation to rid the overcrowded landfills of old tires and create clean, low-cost energy at the same time (Morris 1990).

Insist on objective criteria. The word "insist" is probably too strong a word, but striving for objective criteria is often useful. For example, in determining prices for houses, usually the bank will require an appraisal done by an objective third party. Part of the data in setting the value are the recent selling prices of several "comparables," which are other houses in a similar location with comparable features. This method of valuing a property is a common method of using objective criteria.

These steps represent an assertive way to manage conflict. However, many people run away from conflict. That can make the situation worse, because differences do not simply disappear with time; sometimes they get worse. It is important to confront conflict.

Tannenbaum and Schmidt (1972) propose that one frequent source of conflict is the leadership struggle between superior and subordinate in decision making. They argue that the leader has to be flexible enough to modify his or her decision-making style to fit the "followership" of the group. Their discussion focuses primarily on the business setting, but the implications are valid for any small group setting in which conflict arises from a leadership struggle. They propose a continuum of decision-making styles that can serve as a model for the leader (in conjunction with the group) so that the group can choose the style most appropriate for its situation and that would reduce unnecessary conflict. This model (Figure 6.8) has also been described as including four styles of decision making: (1) tells, (2) sells, (3) consults, and (4) joins.

A related system of conflict prevention through better decision making includes four other styles: (1) railroading, (2) teaming up, (3) majority vote, and (4) consensus. *Railroading* occurs when one or more group members force their will on the group. This technique is very likely to produce resentment and result in unnecessary conflict. *Teaming up* refers to a situation in which various minority members within a group form a coalition to help each other achieve mutually advantageous goals. This pattern is frequently used in Congress when politicians make trades through which they agree to support each other's bills. This may have short-term success but may also result in further conflict once the scheme is discovered. *Majority vote* represents the wishes of at least 51 percent of a group's

FIGURE 6.8   CONTINUUM OF LEADERSHIP BEHAVIOR

Reprinted by permission of the *Harvard Business Review*. An exhibit from "How to Choose a Leadership Pattern" by Robert Tannenbaum and Warren H. Schmidt (March/April 1958). Copyright © 1958 by the President and Fellows of Harvard College; all rights reserved.

Boss-centered leadership						Subordinate-centered leadership
Use of authority by manager						Area of freedom for subordinates
Manager makes decision and announces it	Manager "sells" decision	Manager presents ideas and invites questions	Manager presents tentative decision subject to change	Manager presents problem, gets suggestions, makes decisions	Manager defines limits; asks group to make decision	Manager permits subordinates to function within limits defined by superior

By permission of News America Syndicate

members. However, the remaining minority may be bitterly opposed to the outcome of the decision. This bitterness often results in conflict at a later time. *Consensus* denotes agreement among all members of a group concerning a given decision. Consensus is generally considered to yield the best resolution of conflict in a group decision. Few groups are as concerned as they should be about trying to reach consensus on decisions. Juries represent one of the few types of groups that are required to reach consensus. Those that don't—hung juries—are dismissed.

Consensus does not come quickly or easily. Agreement generally results from careful and thoughtful interpersonal communication between group members. If we are to achieve complete group consensus, some individual preferences of group members must be surrendered. The group as a whole must decide if consensus can be achieved. If several members are adamant in their positions and refuse to change their minds in agreement with the others, the group may decide that reaching complete consensus is not worth the effort. In this case it may be better to postpone the group decision—particularly if the group making the decision will also be implementing the decision. If several group members are not in favor of the solution, they will be less anxious to put it into practice.

Conflict resolution seems to improve as we engage in certain types of behaviors. These can be summarized as follows:

1. Focus on the problem, not on personalities.

2. Build on areas of agreement. Most groups have at least some positions or goals that are not mutually exclusive.

3. Attempt to achieve consensus. Try consensus testing by taking a nonbinding straw vote. Then discuss why the minority might be objecting to the decision.

4. Avoid provoking further conflict.

5. Don't overreact to the comments of others. Extreme statements on either side tend to destroy consensus and produce a "boomerang effect."

6. Consider compromise. This is often the best way to go from a win-lose to a win-win situation. (Borisoff and Victor 1989)

Although these are not hard-and-fast rules, and they may not work in all cases, they should improve a group's chances of keeping conflict at a manageable level so that the group can move forward toward its goal.

Diane Yale (1988), a practicing lawyer and mediator, suggested that the way we think about conflict has a tremendous effect on how we go about trying to resolve it. For instance, if we think about conflict and conflict resolution as a battle to be won or lost, then we go into the situation ready to fight or surrender (depending on our position). She outlined three approaches to conflict that occur in the form of metaphor: the competitive, adversarial metaphor; the problem-solving metaphor; and the creative orientation. In these metaphors, three different ways of thinking about and approaching conflict are presented.

The competitive, adversarial metaphor often results in a winner and loser in the resolution process. Yale developed this metaphor as follows: "If your thought . . . is that [conflict] is a battleground, . . . a place where combat or contest is enacted, then someone will be breathing fire, trying to engulf the process in that idiom, and trying to singe and consume us with flame" (p. 18). If group members approach conflict in this way, cohesiveness is likely to suffer. Group members will be at odds with one another.

The problem-solving metaphor can lead to frustration among group members. The resolution process can become a burden, and group members are less likely to be satisfied with the results. Yale developed the problem-solving metaphor in the following way: "Something that is problematic is something that is open to doubt, debatable, uncertain, difficult to solve. A problematist is one who is preoccupied with problems. . . . If your [conflict] is focused on problem-solving, everything that comes at you . . . is seen as a problem or a solution. Often your solutions create more problems. . . . In this metaphor, you work hard . . ." (p. 19).

The creative orientation, aside from being the preferred model of conflict, brings an innovative quality to group conflict resolution. The emphasis of creative orientation is to design a new reality consistent with the values of the group members and large enough to include the visions of all the parties involved. Yale's own metaphor for this approach to conflict is that of a garden. "If being in a garden were your metaphoric purpose, nurturing would be among the first thoughts that would come to mind—preparing the ground, planting seeds and seedlings, caring for them while they grow, blossom and mature. . . . You may have to prune away or pinch back or thin out so that you get sturdier, healthier lovelier growth. There is a cycle of growth and decay. You do not try to hold on to what is no longer in season, you go on to the next season" (p. 22).

Schweiger, Sandberg, and Ragan (1986) cite results of a laboratory study that compared the effectiveness of the dialectical inquiry, devil's advocacy, and consensus approaches to strategic decision making by groups:

> The following is a brief description of: dialectical inquiry and devil's advocacy: (consensus has already been defined).
>
> *Dialectical inquiry*—Relies on the use of constructive group conflict through debates between contrary sets of recommendations and assumptions. Formalized argumentation and debate among group members allow assumptions and recommendations to be systematically evaluated. The strengths and weaknesses of each is made explicit.
>
> *Devil's Advocacy*—Relies on the use of constructive group conflict through critiques on a single set of recommendations and assumptions.
>
> Results showed that both dialectical inquiry and devil's advocacy led to higher quality recommendations and assumptions than consensus. Dialectical inquiry was also more effective than devil's advocacy with respect to the quality of assumptions brought to the surface. However, subjects in the consensus groups expressed more satisfaction and desire to continue to work with their groups and greater acceptance of their groups' decisions than did subjects in either of the two other types of groups studied.

In a follow-up study, Schweiger, Sandberg, and Rechner (1989) found that there was virtually no difference between the dilactical inquiry and devil's advocacy approaches, which we can label the "conflict" approaches. However, there was significant difference between the conflict approaches and the consensus approach. The authors state that, "Compared to consensus groups, groups using [the conflict approaches] made significantly higher quality decisions. Members of such groups reported more reevaluation of their own assumptions and recommendations but lower acceptance of their group's decisions than members of consensus groups" (p. 745). Clearly, the most effective groups will be those which can balance the need for intellectual inquiry and mental accuity on one hand with the group's need for harmony and idea acceptance on the other.

Cosier and Schwenk (1990, p. 69) state that, "There is growing evidence that suggests conflict and dissent are what organizations really need to succeed. Decisions should be made after thoughtful consideration of counterpoints and criticism. People with different viewpoints must be encouraged to provide thoughts on important decisions. Widespread agreement on a key issue is a red flag, not a condition of good health." Unfortunately, there is often a tendency to avoid conflicting situations in groups. No one wants to "rock the boat," as it were. This is particularly true in a situation where subordinates are trying to make a good impression on a supervisor. People involved in various groups often share a common background and belief system. Coming to a consensus too quickly, before discussing the pros and cons, is a danger.

In their 1990 study, Cosier and Schwenk suggested two techniques for programming conflict into the decision-making process, thus dissolving the potential of groupthink. Outlines of the two programs, (1) the devil's advocate decision program and (2) the dialectic decision method follow.

The devil's advocate decision program:
1. A proposed course of action is generated.

2. A devil's advocate (individual or group) is assigned to criticize the proposal.
3. The critique is presented to key decision makers.
4. Any additional information relevant to the issues is gathered.
5. The decision to adopt, modify, or discontinue the proposed course of action is taken.
6. The decision is monitored.

The dialectic decision method:
1. A proposed course of action is generated.
2. Assumptions underlying the proposal are identified.
3. A conflicting counterproposal is generated based on different assumptions.
4. Advocates of each position present and debate the merits of their proposals before key decision makers.
5. The decision to adopt either position, or some other position, e.g., a compromise, is taken.
6. The decision is monitored. (pp. 72–73)

THE SYSTEMS PERSPECTIVE

In this chapter we have examined the very difficult task of improving our ability to make decisions. Most untrained groups do not follow a disciplined path toward a decision. Instead, we frequently find ourselves either off the track or bogged down in conflicts that keep us from accomplishing a task. The focus in this chapter has been biased toward problem-solving groups. However, other types of groups also have to make decisions and deal with conflicts. Certainly these issues arise for families, learning groups (as we saw in the case at the beginning of this chapter), social groups planning events, and work groups solving organizational problems. Conflict, too, is present in each of these types of groups.

It is probably apparent by now that the decision-making process in most groups can be improved. In this chapter we examined seven alternative problem-solving strategies: (1) the reflective thinking process, (2) the Kepner-Tregoe approach, (3) the single question form, (4) brainstorming, (5) incrementalism, (6) mixed scanning, and (7) tacit bargaining. You might want to become familiar enough with all of these methods so that you would be able to use whichever one seems most appropriate for a given problem and a given group. Again, this illustrates the systems principle of *equifinality* in that several alternative methods may be used to reach the same desired end result—namely, the solution to the group's problem.

By now you may have wondered how one *does* decide which of the seven problem-solving strategies to use. Should you use a rational strategy, such as the reflective thinking process or brainstorming, or should you use incrementalism or tacit bargaining? The systems perspective suggests that the appropriateness of any method will depend on the demands of the specific situation. Therefore we need to be familiar with all the alternatives in order to increase our tool kit of behavioral science "tools."

The rational problem-solving methods work well in most cases but seem particularly suited to an autonomous group trying to satisfy its own needs while being allowed to do so by a democratic leader. By comparison, governmental groups are not autonomous and must answer to the taxpayers. Thus incrementalism may be appropriate, because major changes may be demanded without the luxury of enough time to gather exhaustive amounts of data on the problem. It's a little like the old story that when you are up to your hips in a swamp full of alligators, you don't want a systematic estimate of the probability of danger; you want somebody to throw you a rope!

Tacit bargaining seems to be primarily appropriate in the mixed-motive situations we described earlier. Notice the assumptions and viewpoints expressed in the following quotations. Karrass (1970, p. 4), in his book on negotiating, writes, "In a successful negotiation both parties gain, but more often than not one party wins more than the other." In a similar vein, Korda (1975, p. 4) writes, "No matter who you are, the basic truth is that your interests are nobody else's concern, your gain is inevitably someone else's loss, your failure someone else's victory." The viewpoint expressed in these two quotations indicates some of the attitudes and values relevant to the mixed-motive situation. These statements also describe the outcomes or consequences of bargaining types of problem-solving situations. Obviously, these types of competitive situations suggest very different communication behaviors and skills than would the encounter group, which stresses trust, mutual self-disclosure, and risk taking. Thus the demands of the situation will play a great part in suggesting which problem-solving strategy we will want to employ.

The second part of this chapter dealt with conflict and conflict resolution. It should be emphasized that conflict may have some desirable consequences for the group. However, conflict that gets out of control may be destructive. Also, conflict between ideas is usually more productive than conflict between personalities.

In terms of personality and its relation to conflict, we would expect more conflict-producing behaviors from those high in aggression, dominance, and need for autonomy. Conversely, we would expect less conflict and more conflict-resolving attempts from those high in need for affiliation and nurturance. Other background factors that would probably relate to conflict include the degree of differences or heterogeneity in group members' ages, sex, values, attitudes, and beliefs. Consistency theories would lead us to believe that the greater and more numerous these differences, the greater the group conflict and the lower the satisfaction level resulting from the discussions.

Perhaps one of the most important factors related to conflict is the style of leadership and the resulting group norms regarding conflict. In this chapter we examined Blake and Mouton's (1970) Conflict Grid and Tannenbaum and Schmidt's (1972) tells, sells, consults, and joins model. Both models seem to suggest practical methods for developing some leadership expertise in resolving conflicts.

1. Problem–Solving Discussion Assignment

Each group should decide on a topic and should formulate a discussion question that cannot be answered yes or no. A sample question would be "What can be done about the problem of current marijuana laws?" This form of discussion question is preferable, because it poses a problem to be answered by the group. A less desirable discussion question would be: "Should marijuana be decriminalized?" Notice that this question can be answered yes or no and is less open ended and, therefore, less helpful in prompting discussion.

Each group may want to gather some preliminary information on the topic. (This is optional.) Select a moderator, and work up an agenda for your discussion, including the following:

(a) Define the nature and limits of the problem. *Analyze* causes and important aspects of the problem.

(b) Determine the criteria by which to judge an acceptable solution to the problem.

(c) Identify several alternative solutions to the problem.

(d) Decide which is the best solution (on the basis of the criteria you have identified).

(e) How might this solution be implemented?

The discussion will be approximately thirty minutes long. Moderators will be responsible for introducing and concluding the discussion as well as for moving the group along their agenda.

As a guide, you may want to review the following questions, which show in greater detail the various issues to be encountered at each phase of the agenda. Application of this pattern depends upon such factors as:

(a) Whether the discussion is one of fact, value, or policy

(b) The general scope of the problem

(c) The amount of time available

(d) The knowledge of the participants

   I. Problem Phase

      A. *Identification of problem area, including questions:*

         1. What is the situation in which the problem is occurring?

    2. What, in general, is the difficulty?

    3. How did this difficulty arise?

    4. What is the importance of the difficulty?

    5. What limitations, if any, are there on the area of our concern?

    6. What is the meaning of any terms that need clarifying?

  B. *Analysis of the difficulty:*

    1. What, specifically, are the facts of the situation?

    2. What, specifically, are the difficulties?

  C. *Analysis of causes:*

    1. What is causing the difficulties?

    2. What is causing the causes?

II. Criteria Phase

  A. What are the principal requirements of the solution?

  B. What limitations must be placed on the solution?

  C. What is the relative importance of the criteria?

III. Solution Phase

  A. *What are the possible solutions?*

    1. What is the exact nature of each solution?

    2. How would it remedy the difficulty? by eliminating the cause? by offsetting the effect? by a combination of both?

  B. *How good is each solution?*

    1. How well would it remedy the difficulty?

    2. How well would it satisfy the criteria? Are there any that it would not satisfy?

    3. Would there be any unfavorable consequences? any extra benefits?

  C. *Which solution appears to be best?*

    1. How would you rank the solution?

    2. Would some combination of solutions be best?

IV. Implementation Phase

What steps would be taken to put the solution into effect?

2. Adjunct of Exercise 1

In conjunction with Exercise 1, some members of the class may want to fill out the evaluation forms (Figures 6.9 and 6.10) on the discussion group. These forms can serve as the basis of a postdiscussion feedback session by which the group can analyze its own strengths and weaknesses in conducting their assignment.

3. Brainstorming Exercise

Utilizing the rules for brainstorming given in Chapter 6, try to answer the following question: How can we limit growth in population, industrial productivity, pollution, and use of natural resources in such a way as to ensure the preservation of the human race?

FIGURE 6.9   JUDGE'S EVALUATION REPORT ON THE LEADER

Name of leader _____

Evaluator _____

Assign for each criterion one of the following ratings:

5—Superior
4—Excellent
3—Average
2—Below average
1—Poor

	Criteria	*Rating*
1.	*Attitude.* Impartiality, fairness; ability to help group maintain discussion attitude.	_____
2.	*Knowledge.* Understanding of the problem. Knowledge of discussion method.	_____
3.	*Thinking.* Ability to think quickly, to see relationships.	_____
4.	*Introducing.* Skill in getting the discussion off to a good start.	_____
5.	*Speaking.* Ability to express ideas clearly, rephrase unclear contributions.	_____
6.	*Guiding.* Ability to keep discussion "on the track"; maintain progress; make internal summaries.	_____
7.	*Regulating.* Ensuring evenness of contribution, maintaining equanimity.	_____
8.	*Ending.* Summarizing group effect.	_____

General comments

FIGURE 6.10   JUDGE'S EVALUATION REPORT ON PARTICIPANTS

Name of participant _____

Evaluator _____

Assign the participant for each criterion one of the following ratings:

5—Superior
4—Excellent
3—Average
2—Below average
1—Poor

Criteria	Rating
1. *Attitude*. Objectivity, open-mindedness; willingness to modify views in light of new evidence.	_____
2. *Knowledge*. Information on the problem.	_____
3. *Thinking*. Analysis, ability to reason about the problem.	_____
4. *Listening*. Ability to understand and interpret view of others.	_____
5. *Speaking*. Ability to communicate ideas clearly and effectively; adaptation to the speaking situation.	_____
6. *Consideration for others*. Tact, courtesy, cooperation, evenness of contribution.	_____

General comments

For further practice, try brainstorming other topics for further brainstorming practice discussions.

4. Conflict Resolution Exercise: "Win as Much as You Can"

Directions   For ten successive rounds you and your partner will choose either an X or a Y. The "payoff" for each round is dependent upon the pattern of choices made in your cluster.

Strategy   You are to confer with your partner on each round and make a joint decision. Before rounds 5, 8, and 10 you confer with the other dyads in your cluster.

FIGURE 6.11   "WIN AS MUCH AS YOU CAN" TALLY SHEET

Round	Strategy						
	Time allowed	Confer with	Choice	$ Won	$ Lost	$ Balance	
1	2 min.	partner					
2	1 min.	partner					
3	1 min.	partner					
4	1 min.	partner					
5	3 min. + 1 min.	cluster partner					Bonus round: pay is multiplied by 3
6	1 min.	partner					
7	1 min.	partner					
8	3 min. + 1 min.	cluster partner					Bonus round: pay is multiplied by 5
9	1 min.	partner					
10	3 min. + 1 min.	cluster partner					Bonus round: pay is multiplied by 10

Instructions for participants

1. This is a learning exercise. In it, there are ten rounds and there are other teams with which you are playing.

2. The purpose of the exercise is to win as much as you can.

3. When the timekeeper says, "Begin round 1," your team will decide on its vote for the first round. Your vote may be either X or Y and should be reported secretly on a small piece of paper. The payoff for each round will be determined by how your team's vote is related to the votes of all the other teams. The payoff possibilities are shown at the top of the tally sheet (Figure 6.11).

4. When all votes are collected, the timekeeper will announce the total vote but *will not* disclose how each individual team voted.

5. As shown on the tally sheet, you will have two minutes to cast your vote for the first round. For all the other rounds, you will have one minute to cast your vote, except for Rounds 5, 8, and 10, which are bonus rounds.

6. During each bonus round your team will select as many representatives as it wishes to send to a meeting of the teams. The representatives from

all teams will then meet separately for three minutes to discuss their strategy.

7. After the representatives have met, you team will then have one minute to make its final decision about your vote. At the end of each round, when all the votes are in, you will be told the total outcome of the vote (2 X's, 2 Y's, or 4 Y's, and so on).

8. There are three key rules to keep in mind.
   (a) You are not to talk to the other teams or signal them in any way. You may communicate with them but only during Rounds 5, 7, and 10 through your representatives.
   (b) All members of your team should agree on your team's vote or at least be willing to go along with it.
   (c) Your team's vote must be reported on a small slip of paper when it is called for at the end of each round.

4 X's:	Lose	$1.00 each
3 X's:	Win	$1.00 each
1 Y:	Lose	$3.00
2 X's:	Win	$2.00 each
2 Y's:	Lose	$2.00 each
1 X:	Win	$3.00
3 Y's:	Lose	$1.00 each
4 Y's:	Win	$1.00 each

5. Conflict Resolution Exercise: "The Babysitter Case"

Mr. and Mrs. Todd have been using Paula Moore (age 17) as their regular babysitter every since their son Brad was born two years ago. Paula has always been competent and responsible while in the Todd's home. The Todds have a policy that Paula is not to have any visitors while she is babysitting. This is consistent with the policies of other families in the neighborhood where Paula lives and babysits.

Paula babysat for the Todds on Saturday night, and everything seemed routine. However, the next morning Mr. Todd's neighbor from across the street told him that two young men and Paula's 16-year-old sister had arrived in a customized van the night before, and the three young people had gone into the Todd's house. The neighbor couldn't say how long the three had been in the house, because he had left shortly after they arrived.

Mr. Todd checked with another neighbor and had the story confirmed. The second neighbor said that the three people had been in the Todd's house. He also added, "We don't use the Moore girls anymore for our kids. They are too boy crazy."

The Todds became quite upset, because this appeared to be a clear violation of their no-visitor policy for their babysitters. The situation is further complicated by the fact that Paula lives only a few houses down the street from the Todds and Mr. Moore (Paula's father) works in the same office with Mr. Todd. Thus the Todd and Moore families are in the same neighborhood group, and Mr. Todd and Mr. Moore are in the same work group. What should the Todds do?

READINGS: OVERVIEW

Probably one of the most troublesome issues in small group interaction is how to resolve conflicts. In the first article Phillips discusses five levels of conflict that can destroy an organization. However, trying to change conflict from a destructive to a constructive force in group activities takes some doing.

The second article, by Lewicki and Litterer, offers several methods for improving conflict-reduction skills. In this article, they show how conflict can be managed more effectively. Both articles provide a useful extension of the ideas presented in the chapter.

Manage Differences Before They Destroy Your Business

Ronald C. Phillips

How does a simple difference escalate into all-out war? The answer is "very quickly" if management is not aware of how conflict grows and what can be done to stop it.

Take the example of a company we'll call Software, Inc., which was in the process of developing a new product. It had completed a marketing study that concluded a certain packaging approach would be best. Wanting a second opinion, Software, Inc., retained an outside firm, which we'll call Market Services, to study the market independently in order to obtain as accurate a picture as possible. The result was a "disagreement" between the external firm and Software's marketing department.

Change Breeds Conflict

Most organizational conflict begins with disagreements such as that hypothesized above. These disagreements begin as differences in the facts, methods, goals, or values held by the parties involved. How these disagreements are dealt with determines the quality of the result, its timeliness, and its costs to the company. Company management must be concerned, therefore, that such disagreements be resolved with the best solution possible, in a timely manner, and with as little expense as possible. We can call this process the management of differences.

Managing differences has always been an important and formidable task for organizations, and it has become increasingly so with the accelerating changes occurring in the economy, government regulation, competition, workforce, and technology. With such change also comes an increasing number of disagreements as to what an organization's goals should be and how they are best accomplished. Change and conflict go hand in hand. It is imperative, therefore, that today's managers understand how simple disagreements can turn into wasteful and debilitating power struggles and what they can do to turn organizational conflict from a liability into an asset.

To help in this complex task of managing differences, I have identified five levels of conflict: differences, disputes, contentions, limited war, and all-out

From: Training & Development Journal, *September, 1988, 66–71. Reprinted by permission.*

war. I partially derived these levels from a paper by Helen Weingarten and Speed Leas titled "Levels of Marital Conflict," but I have modified and further elaborated each conflict level as it applies to the corporate environment.

To illustrate each conflict level, I shall go back to the Software, Inc. analogy. For each conflict level, I first will provide a description of the level of involvement between the disagreeing parties; I call this self-esteem. Second, I will describe how the goals of each level change. Third, I will describe some of the characteristic behaviors at each level as well as the options available to managing these differences. And finally, I will show how each conflict escalates to an ever-widening and more debilitating conclusion.

Level I: Differences

At the very beginning of the difference between Software, Inc. and Market Services things seemed to be going well. In general the mood was one of wanting to figure out why there are differences. This first level of conflict is where people most effectively deal with conflict.

Self-Esteem

At this juncture neither the people at Software nor at Market Services had invested their worth as professionals in the "superiority" of one report over another. They were puzzled at these differences and were intent upon uncovering how they came to be. When people approach differences in such an exploratory manner they don't focus on the end results—the conclusions—but rather on the reasons for the differences and how they resulted.

Goal

The goal of parties at Level I is to resolve the differences in order to answer the fundamental question at hand. In this case the question was, "What packaging approach will best suit the market population?" The underlying assumption at this level is that the resolution of differences will lead to a benefit for all parties concerned. For example, if the professionals involved in the two marketing studies found it important to figure out how two studies could reap such very different results, then both would not only be able to arrive at a satisfactory result for the organization but also advance their skills and knowledge of market research.

Key Behaviors

In the resolution of differences at Level I, there is a free exchange of undistorted information among participants. Perceptions, information, expertise, and values of each party are respected as needing exploration and study.

Hypotheses are generated and tested. There is a genuine search for mutually acceptable solutions, and each party seeks to measure the value of solutions based upon objective standards. In short, behaviors reflect a well-documented and effective problem-solving process.

Emotional Tone

During the Level I resolution process, parties feel anticipation, trust, and confidence in their capacity to arrive at a satisfactory conclusion. They sense that they could gain a great deal and lose little by exploring each other's points of view.

Third Parties

Level I parties view people not directly involved in the situation to be resolved as resources, consultants, and—perhaps—advisors to the resolution process. The parties welcome outside expertise and contributions.

Managing Differences

As described, the resolution of differences needs no deliberate intervention. The process is working. In general, Level I conflict needs to be nurtured by a knowledgeable manager to ensure that:

- the parties involved clearly understand it is their responsibility to resolve the differences and arrive at a conclusion that effectively responds to the question at hand—in this case, what kind of packaging best fits the client profile;

- provocations that lower the level of confidence and trust among the parties are eased;

- the resolution process is protected from external parties who would intentionally or unwittingly provoke a distrustful environment;

- the resources required for effective resolution are made available;

- positive reinforcement is provided for both the quality and value of the process.

Escalation Factors

Escalation of Level I differences into Level II disagreements comes about because of the provocative behaviors of parties involved or of "outsiders." This occurs if one party discounts the worth of a value, a fact, a method used or suggested, a personal or group characteristic, or a goal of the differing party.

In the marketing example, Software's marketing director called into question the experience of Market Services's staff. The discount was subtle, as they usually are in polite interchange. The director questioned, "How many other companies like ours have you done analyses for?" The director already knew the answer, but she wanted to make a point. Because the outside firm had only done one other such analysis, their work was questionable. It was a subtle way of putting the report down, not by questioning the merits of its facts, methods, or goals, but by questioning the competence of the people who did the work.

Escalation can also result from "outside" influence. This can occur when a third party makes statements to one of the other two parties; this tends to erode the level of trust and confidence of differing parties. In the marketing example, not only was there subtle discounting between the two differing parties, but Software's manager of sales also intimated his own company's marketing people were of little help. He said, "Looks to me like they're going down the same path they did on the KV project." The KV project was a dismal failure from a sales point of view. This comment inserted in casual conversation with one of Market Services's analysts provided one more provocation, which eroded trust and confidence between the differing parties.

Within two meetings the conflict had escalated into a dispute.

Level II: Dispute

Self-Esteem

At Level II one or all parties to a disagreement have assumed that their worth as persons or professionals is somehow measured by the level of acceptance of their position. The questioning of the competence of the outside firm was enough to push them to defend their analysis because it now was associated with their professional competence. Egos are now attached to the resolution.

Goal

At Level II there is a fundamental shift in resolution goals. Whereas the goal of Level I was to find mutual gain through the resolution process, the goal of Level II conflict is to resolve the dispute with as little loss as possible. Hence, the fundamental assumption underlying Level II conflict is that no mutually beneficial solution is possible. The best hope is a resolution that will do as little harm as possible to all concerned. Both Software and Market Services people were aware that the relationship was damaged, so the goal shifted from responding to the original problem of what kind of packaging is necessary to how they could stop the dispute without causing more harm.

Key Behaviors

During Level II dispute resolution, exchange of information is guarded. When information is exchanged it tends to be general rather than specific. Questions and answers are vague in order to give the appearance of and opportunity for agreement; in disputes the parties avoid any appearance of confrontation. Parties often state their positions and then rapidly move toward a compromise solution or, sometimes, toward an out-and-out accommodation without exploring the differences in depth. Before the parties communicate with one another, they often prepare calculated responses. If the parties are groups rather than single individuals, each party usually has a gripe session to determine what they want to communicate to the other side.

During Level II conflict, then, the parties aim to minimize their differences and to "give away" as little as possible. The best solution at this point is a compromise.

Emotional Tone

In Level II conflict, an outsider would seldom guess there are fundamental differences unless he or she was particularly sensitive to the emotional tone. Generally this tone takes the form of forced politeness and anxious impatience. The parties want to come to a resolution quickly because they don't want to risk further embarrassment.

Third Parties

The two differing parties now view people on the outside with caution because they believe that third parties don't understand the situation. The conflicting groups avoid outsiders because they don't want to disrupt a delicate situation by "opening up a can of worms." If outsiders are accepted at all, they usually are viewed as deal makers—people who can help both sides see that they need to give a little or stand the chance of losing a lot.

Managing Disputes

Well-trained negotiators who refuse to be baited by discounts can move Level II conflict from deal making to inquiry and discovery. Negotiators in a Level II conflict must have a high degre of self-confidence and must be respectful, assertive, and persistent enough to stick to the issues of the dispute. The facilitator should also be someone respected by the parties involved and who is reasonably skilled in mediating differences.

A skillful manager or other staffperson may be able to facilitate the negotiations as well as someone from the outside. A staffperson will have greater chance of success, of course, if he or she isn't connected to the disputing parties. This permits the parties to accept responsibility without appearing weak or incapable in the presence of a power figure.

The Harvard Negotiation Project has researched the key elements of conflict negotiation, and these elements are documented in the book *Getting to Yes* by Roger Fisher and William Ury. The basic mediation skills are

- helping parties separate people from the problem;
- staying focused on the needs of the parties and the organization, rather than on positions;
- helping the parties develop options for mutual gain;
- searching for objective standards to judge fair and effective solutions.

Escalating Factors

Parties to a Level II dispute can escalate the dispute to a Level III conflict—contention—by real or implied threats to take something valuable from a disputing party. In the case of the marketing conflict, after Market Services offered to resurvey certain market segments—which was a compromise from their perspective—Software's marketing director decided to withhold payment on the contract until the "mistakes" had been rectified. She also sent a letter to that effect to her vice president and to the project manager of Market Services. Obviously, Market Services felt that they "had been had." The issues that began as simple differences now have turned into a win-lose contest.

Level III: Contention

Self-Esteem

In Level III conflict the parties believe they are or will be valuable as a result of winning a contest with another party. In the marketing example, the gauntlet had been dropped. Letters had gone out. Significant others are now focusing their attention on the dispute, and reputations are at stake. The question of who is right and who is wrong now could mean something for people's careers.

Goal

The goal of Level III conflict is no longer to find a mutually acceptable level of gain or loss—it is to win. For example, if Software's marketing department can convince upper management to choose its analysis over Marketing Services's then the marketing department may believe they will gain important influence or a heftier budget allocation.

In Level III conflict a very important metamorphosis of goal focus occurs. In Level I the goal was to find the best solution to a problem, while in Level II the goal had changed to finding a solution that wouldn't embarrass the disputing parties. At Level III the goal becomes being "top dog."

Key Behaviors

At Level III conflict the disputing parties clearly draw their positions and behave as contenders. They don't exchange information for the purpose of resolving the problem, but when they do present information it is for the purpose of proving something. The parties defend their positions so strongly that the only option becomes adjudication. Information, facts, goals, methods, and values are polarized into right or wrong, black or white. Emphasis is upon strategy, argument, persuasion, and using the rules to one's favor.

It isn't unusual for parties to begin unfair tactics, particularly if they view themselves in a less powerful position. Such socially acceptable "dirty tricks" involve, for example, bringing up issues that have nothing to do with the real issues of the conflict. In the marketing example, Software's marketing director accused Market Services of overcharging, intimating there were discrepancies in the billings, and asked purchasing to audit the work. Note that this behavior is no longer centered on the fundamental issue from which it all began: the packaging of the new product.

Emotional Tone

Level III conflict is stressful. Exchanges are provocative and heated because the parties fear losing. Trust, long gone among the contenders, now reaches a low point even among the members of each team. As a result leaders often become dogmatic and rigid, expressing a high need to keep people in their place. In the later stages, parties are deeply frustrated and resentful towards the contender and, often, toward their own partners.

Third Parties

The two primary parties put people not in "power positions" into two camps: for us or against us. They look with suspicion upon people who try to stay neutral. Persons in power positions are courted as judges who are challenged to pick the winners and losers, while people attempting to defuse the situation are viewed as intruders.

Managing Contention

Level III conflicts are usually resolved by third-party adjudication; a person in authority finally picks a winner and a loser. For example, in the marketing situation a vice president could very well tire of the situation and, based upon some criteria often not at all related to the issues such as the amount of time and money wasted on this problem, select either the internal marketing department or the external research firm's report.

While Level III conflict doesn't lead to the bitter wounds that characterize Level IV conflict, it is still an extremely difficult deadlock. Because parties to a Level III conflict want a winner and loser rather than a negotiated or mediated solution, they often design their strategies to "play" to the authorities they believe will make the final judgment. Management has four intervention options at this point:

- **Adjudication.** The problem with adjudication—calling in a neutral third party to help solve the problem—is that it seldom resolves the conflict. The conflict often will resurface in future encounters over very different issues. If such contentions continue—particularly in ongoing, interdependent relationships—management eventually will have to reorganize or in some other way remove one or both parties from the relationship.

- **Enforced negotiation.** A second option is to make it clear that adjudication isn't an option and to force the involved parties to resolve the issue themselves. If the parties know that management is serious about this, they will come to some resolution. But while the outcome is an end to the contention, this solution seldom renders either a creative solution or a more productive working relationship between the parties. The parties will wait for a better opportunity finally to win.

- **Managerial mediation.** Management can make it clear that adjudication isn't an option, and the manager in charge can try to mediate the conflict. This methodology recently has been promoted as an important managerial skill. Though attractive, it has some serious flaws in dealing with Level III conflicts.

  The main problem with this option is that the conflicting parties view the mediator as an arbiter. In fact, however, the manager is accountable for the problem in the first place. He or she will feel pressured to push for a conclusion that best suits his or her particular needs. In other words, the manager is not a "disinterested" party, and the disputing groups will play their cards accordingly. Hence, what appeared to be a solution may actually be nothing other than a tabling of the conflict to await another day in court.

- **Enforced third-party mediation.** Once again, management can eliminate adjudication as an option and may require involuntary mediation by a neutral third party skilled in mediation. In this intervention, the manager uses his or her power only to require the contentious parties to negotiate the best solution with the aid of the third party.

  The advantages of this process are that it avoids adjudication and provides the parties with the help they need to deal with the underlying assumptions and behaviors that created the impasse. This method effectively forces the contentious parties to deal with their own assumptions, feelings, and behaviors. Through this tough, confrontational mediation, parties can accept responsibility for their own actions and once again focus on the original question of what is the best packaging method.

While enforced mediation has many advantages, it does have a few drawbacks. Though the results are usually superior in the long run, enforced third-party mediation takes time. Second, some managers consider adjudication as what they are paid to do—make the final decision. Finally, a mediator also presents a political problem. What does it indicate to upper management, for example, if a manager seeks an outside person to help resolve a dilemma? Some managers are afraid that upper management will see this alternative as a sign of their weakness.

Escalation

Unless it is heavily refereed, as in the regulated environment of the courtroom or collective bargaining, Level III conflict will move toward Level IV, or limited warfare. What causes this escalation is one party's perception that the other is out not just to win, but to win at the opposition's expense.

In the marketing case example, Software's marketing director convinced her vice president to put pressure on Market Services to remove their project manager.

Level IV: Limited Warfare

Self-Esteem

In limited warfare there is a significant change in the relation of self-worth to the conflict. It is no longer a matter of psychological well being: real and tangible harm is possible. The issue now is personal security.

Goal

The goal of limited warfare is to diminish the adversary's power sufficiently so he or she is no longer a threat. In this sense, conflict that began as differences in opinion has now become a power struggle.

Key Behaviors

The parties to the conflict are no longer contestants playing to managerial judges, they are now adversaries. The fundamental assumption is that the opposing party is out to harm and to undo one's security and career. Both parties begin actively to seek out powerful allies within the organization and to align themselves with these sources of power.

At this point whatever facts, methods, values, or goals were originally at issue are completely obscured. The fight has taken on a life of its own. It no longer makes a difference what issues were at stake.

The one element that makes the behaviors of Level IV conflict different from Level V is balance of power. Both parties want the other to stop harming their position. This means that an observer will witness attacks only up to a point. Neither party wants all-out war unless the balance of power is clearly seen in one adversary's favor in our marketing example, Software's director just wanted to remove Marketing Services's project manager, not the firm itself.

Emotional Tone

Hurt, anger, and disgust are the most predominate emotions of Level IV conflict.

Managing Limited Warfare

It is important to recognize that in Level IV conflict neither party's goal is to win a total victory. Rather each wants a limited victory in the sense of getting the adversary off its back. Both parties recognize that the time and resources going into the fight are taking away from their image with the rest of the company as well as their own sense of accomplishment and well being. There is no question at this level of conflict that the battle is costing everyone, including the organization, more than they wish to expend. But management also must recognize that the adversaries aren't going to back down—it's a matter of honor and justice, if not survival.

There is a second complicating factor: seldom is Level IV conflict a matter of just two individuals or singular issues. The conflict at this point involves groups of employees and diverse issues. The organization itself tends to be partially polarized. Everyone has their opinion of who is right and who is wrong; some as well fear becoming involved in the feud.

For these reasons there are only three options left to managers who have not yet been pulled into the war:

- **Enforce a truce.** A truce means stopping the gunfire. It is a good first step, but it will hold only if management takes further action to address the underlying causes of the war itself.

- **Eliminate one of the adversaries.** Traditionally this is the course most companies choose. The problem with this method is that the surgery itself is as costly and damaging as the cure. Management may eliminate the leadership of one warring faction, but the war usually continues to smolder in the rank and file. Often wounds remain open and the functioning of the entire organization suffers.

- **Enforced mediation and reconstruction.** At Level IV enforced mediation becomes more complex and is more encompassing. There are two problems: the warring parties and the dysfunction that they have created within the organization. Management must address both of these issues.

  First, enforced mediation requires a skilled mediator from outside the organization and a strong, decisive management on the inside. The parties involved have to be "handcuffed" to the mediation table because this is the last thing they want. In their minds they have tried mediation, and they don't want to struggle through it again.

  Second, enforced mediation at this level must address the social dysfunction the conflict has created. As I said before, Level IV conflict normally involves multiple parties and multiple issues. The task is not only to address the current issues of the conflict but to begin to reconstruct positive relationships throughout the damaged organization. It will take someone who is expert in mediation as well as in organization behavior to accomplish this task.

Escalation

Level IV conflict is more sensitive to power, and that is precisely why enforced mediation will work. If one adversary should be or become less powerful than the other, only mercy will restrain the empowered party from going for the throat. What maintains a limited war is the perception of cost and benefit. It is the fear of the adversary's power or third-party power that keeps attacks somewhat restrained. Take away that threat, and the outcome is all-out war.

In Level IV conflict aligned power groups are demanding victory. In the marketing case, the president of Market Services was incensed at the request to remove one of his most experienced and knowledgeable employees. He had been convinced by his own people that Software had been dealing with them unjustly. Furthermore, he had concluded his people had been attacked by a contentious, power-hungry female who wouldn't know marketing if she fell over it. His answer was, "I'll see you in court."

As for Software, the vice president, who is a financial expert, had aligned himself with the only thing he knew best. He wasn't going to let some outside consulting firm provide what his marketing director was calling a second-rate product and then try to sneak through overcharges. "We'll not only meet you in court," he retorted, "you'll never get another contract in this industry," was his retort.

Level V: All-Out War

All-out war means that all parties in power positions are polarized. There are at least two warring camps, each with the objective of eliminating the other. It is a pure and simple power struggle. Who gets hurt or how much is no longer of any consequence. In an all-out organizational war, cultural inhibitions and mores are dropped. Feelings are numbed. Cost no longer is a concern. Victory and justice are equated.

There is little need to describe organizational war in detail. There is nothing to be managed. The war will end of its own doing either through attrition or the intervention of a more powerful group such as stockholders or government. The key is not to let conflict escalate into organizational war.

How did Software and Market Services resolve their dispute? It is on the docket and, according to the attorneys, will remain there for approximately four more years. Civil courts are inundated with such business-to-business disputes.

If this had been an in-house conflict, we can only guess at the potential consequences. Organizational war threatens the existence of the business itself. Such wars are not at all uncommon: Steve Jobs versus John Scully at Apple Computer, Thomas Rattigan versus Irving Gould at Commodore International, and Henry Ford versus Lee Iacocca at Ford Motor Company, for example.

For this reason, it is imperative that managers learn to recognize and address conflicts at their earliest levels of dispute. This management of differences becomes especially important in times of significant upheaval, common in today's business environment. Managers who can manage differences are a particularly important asset for the enterprise.

Converting Win/Lose to Win/Win: The Tactics of Conflict Resolution

Roy J. Lewicki and Joseph A. Litterer

. . . [I]ntegrative bargaining, leading to a win/win outcome, is a very attractive process. For each party, it holds out the prospect of a larger, more satisfactory gain than might be realized through distributive bargaining. Further, by establishing a cooperative rather than a competitive relationship, integrative bargaining supports many societal expectations and values. In Chapter 5, we discussed the strategies and tactics of integrative bargaining that may be used once commitment to the process is established. In this chapter, we address ways to convert a win/lose relationship into a win/win relationship; that is, getting out of distributive bargaining and into integrative bargaining.

Let us begin by reviewing the structure of distributive and integrative bargaining (Table 1). The difference between the two processes is substantial. The primary concern is how to convert distributive bargaining into integrative given this difference. Distributive bargaining begins with a fundamental conflict over the allocation of limited resources; the accompanying tension, hostility, defensiveness and distrust perpetuates and magnifies the conflict even further. For productive negotiating to occur, this conflict must be handled in a way that arrests the escalation, reduces conflict, opens lines of communication, and increases trust and cooperativeness.

Put simply, in order to successfully convert a win/lose to a win/win situation, we must effectively deal with the dynamics of escalating, polarizing conflict. In this chapter, we will explore a variety of approaches and techniques that can be used to put derailed negotiations back on the track. Many of these techniques are applicable to a broader range of conflict settings than negotiation. Some of the approaches are predominantly directed at reducing the level of emotional tension and hostility; others are designed to enhance accurate communication between the parties, and still others help to create new alternatives for agreement on the substantive issues. Initially, we will discuss all of these techniques as actions that the parties themselves can take to move from unproductive polarization to productive deliberation. However, as we shall also point out, it is often difficult for negotiators to initiate these actions "in the heat of battle." Under conditions of high mistrust and suspicion, overtures of cooperation and conflict reduction are frequently seen as strategic ploys, tricks to lure the other

From Roy J. Lewicki and Joseph A. Litterer. Negotiation (Homewood, Ill.: Irwin, 1985), pp. 279–280, 290–299.

TABLE 1

	Distributive Bargaining	Integrative Bargaining
Pay-off structure	Fixed amount of resources to be divided.	Variable amount of resources to be divided.
Primary motivation	Gains of one will be the sacrifices of the other.	Parties concerned about maximizing joint outcomes.
Interests	Diametrically opposed.	Convergent or congruent.
Relationships	Short term relationship; people do not need to work together in the future.	Long term relationship; parties expect to work together in the future.

party into a false sense of trust and vulnerability. As a result, intervention by neutral third parties is often necessary. At the end of the chapter, we will examine the approaches that third parties traditionally take in breaking negotiation deadlocks. . . .

Controlling Issues

. . . [A] third major difficulty that inhibits parties from resolving conflict is that as conflict intensifies, the size and number of the issues expand. As conflict escalates, it snowballs; bits and pieces of other issues are accumulated in a large, unmanageable mass. While smaller conflicts can be managed one at a time, each in a way satisfactory to the details of the incident, larger conflicts become unwieldy and less amenable to any easy resolution. The problem for negotiators in escalated disputes, therefore, is to develop strategies to contain issue proliferation, and reduce the dispute to manageable proportions.

Roger Fisher has been a major advocate of strategies of issue control in negotiation, particularly in international affairs. In a well-known article on *fractionating conflict,* Fisher suggests six major approaches for reducing a large conflict into smaller parts:

1. Reduce the Number of Parties on Each Side.   When conflict escalates, each side seeks to build alliances for strength, or to bring their constituencies into the dispute; either they increase the number of parties at the negotiation or they bring more clout to the table. Additional parties, such as lawyers, expert witnesses, etc. are often brought into negotiations for the information they can provide. Rather than having them present their testimony and leave, however, experts often remain on the scene to provide additional input. Since the sheer number of parties at the table can make negotiations considerably more complex (more parties = more perspectives on the issues, more time needed to hear each side, more opportunities for disagreement, etc.), groundrules are needed for ways to limit the number of parties. One way to control conflict size is to return the dispute to the original negotiating parties. The fewer the actors present, or the more the conflict can be limited to two individuals, the more likely the parties will be to reach a favorable settlement.

2. Control the Number of Physical Issues Involved.

A second way to control the size of a conflict is to keep the number of issues small enough to manage. When conflict escalates, the size and number of issues proliferate. Some conflicts escalate to the point where there are too many issues to constructively manage. At the same time, keeping negotiations limited to a very few issues also raises problems. Single issue conflicts are frequently harder to manage because they quickly lead to win-lose polarization over the issue. Achieving a win-win solution requires a negotiating situation where all parties can win. In such circumstances, it is often desirable to expand the number of issues, in order to permit each side to view itself as having gained. This can be done by (a) defining the issue more broadly so that resolution can benefit both sides, or (b) coupling the issue with another issue so that two issues are involved, and each party can receive a preferred settlement on one of the issues. Small packages of two or three issues are frequently easier to resolve because multiple issues facilitate packaging and trading off on concessions.

3. State Issues in Concrete Terms Rather Than as Principles.

A third way that conflict issues become difficult to control is when events or issues are treated as matters of "principle." Small conflicts can rapidly become intractable disputes when their resolution is *not* treated as an isolated event, but instead must be consistent with a broader "policy" or "principle." Since any deviation from policy is viewed as a threat to that policy, and since broad policy is far more difficult to change than a concession on a single issue, negotiations are immediately problematic. For example, a union may request binding arbitration of grievances in a labor dispute; management not only does not want to grant the request, but states that the request is inconsistent with management's rights to handle discipline cases. "It's a matter of principle," they assert. Resorting to arguments of "principles" and "policies" is often a strategic defense by high power parties against any change from the status quo; the more arguments are conducted at that level alone, the less likely those disputes can be successfully resolved.

There are, of course, times when a single event is properly seen as an indicator of new principles or policy. That being the case, the negotiations should be arranged to specifically address the policy or principle. Many times, people are reluctant to do this, because they know negotiations over principles are difficult and lengthy. However, to attempt to negotiate a concrete issue when the negotiation is really on the "hidden agenda" of a major principle only results in frustration. If this is occurring, it is wise to face the issue and raise it directly. There are at least two strategies:

- Question whether the issue needs to be addressed at the principle or policy level. Ask with which established policy or principle the issue is closely connected. If none exists, and one party wants to look at the matter from a policy or principle level, suggest that the immediate concrete issue be handled and discussed separate from the underlying principle or policy. If need be, the parties can agree that the concrete issue can be settled in this instance, with no expectation as to how the policy will later be established.

- Point out that exceptions can be made to all policies, and that principles and policies can be maintained even if minor deviations are permitted to exist. For example, while "honesty is the best policy," there are often times when we know what deviations from the truth may be necessary. The parties may be willing to agree that this might be one of those times.

4. Restrict the Precedents Involved—Both Procedural and Substantive.   The final type of issue magnification is that the parties treat concessions on a single issue as violations of some substantive or procedural precedent. When a substantive precedent is at stake, one party will imply that to concede on this issue at this time will render him vulnerable to conceding on the same issue, or a similar issue, in the future. "If we give one inch on a cost-of-living clause this year," management argues, "you will be back wanting a foot next year." In contrast, procedural precedents are at stake when parties agree to follow a process they haven't followed before. For example, a procedural precedent may be set when the parties agree to negotiate in a relationship that previously has not been characterized by negotiation, and/or one has more power than the other. Parents are confronted by their children, who no longer wish to "obey orders;" teachers find their authority challenged by students. Belief in the domino theory is strong. The high power party, who supports the precedent, believes that if he/she negotiates now, rather than "quelling the rebellion," there will be no end to the number and types of demands in the future.

Issues of precedent are usually as thorny to control as issues of principle. Once again, a negotiator trying to move a conflict toward de-escalation and resolution should try to keep single issues from becoming translated into major questions of precedent. Focus the dialogue on the key issue, and persist in arguments that concessions on *this* issue at *this* time do not necessarily dictate any precedents—substantive or procedural—for the future.

5. Search for Ways to "Fractionate" the Big Issues.   Fisher calls these "salami tactics"—ways to slice a large issue into smaller pieces. Issues that can be expressed in quantitative terms are easy to slice—wage demands, for example, can be cut down to pennies per hour increment, or lease rates can be sliced down to pennies per square foot. When trying to fractionate issues of principle or precedent, use time horizons (when the principle goes into effect or how long it lasts) and the number of different applications of the principle as ways to slice the issues. Thus, a cost-of-living escalator may seem like an all-or-nothing issue. However, a cost-of-living escalator can be "sliced" according to *when* it is introduced, or to the *number of different worker classifications* to which it applies.

6. Issues Are Resolved Quickly When They Are "Depersonalized,"— Separated from the Parties Who Are Advocating Them.   The most common approach to negotiation—positional bargaining—tends to create conflict over both the issues and the relationship between negotiators. People become identified with positions on issues, and vice versa. Effective negotiation requires separating the issues from the parties, not only by working to establish a productive relationship between the parties (leaving only the issue conflict at stake), but by trying to resolve the issues without regard to the people.

Establish Commonalities

As we noted earlier, escalated conflict tends to magnify (in the parties' eyes) their perceived differences and to minimize their perceived similarities. The parties tend to see themselves as farther apart and having less in common than may be true. Therefore, a fourth major action that parties can take to de-escalate conflict is to establish commonalities or focus on common objectives. Several approaches are possible.

Superordinate Goals

Superordinate goals are common goals; they are desired by both parties and require the cooperation of both parties to achieve. In a corporation, for example, people do different jobs (e.g., marketing, manufacturing) which have different objectives, yet they must work together in some basic ways (for example, to get the product to the customer) or the corporation will not survive. A local city council and community members may disagree as to the ways to spend limited funds for community development; however, they may be able to agree if it is possible for them to write a joint grant proposal that will provide enough money to meet all objectives. Two negotiators may be in a heated conflict over how to resolve an issue, but if they share the common objective of completing negotiations by a certain deadline, then the deadline will increase the likelihood of concession making.

In order to have significant impact on negotiations, superordinate goals must be jointly desired by both sides, and must not be seen as benefiting one side more than the other. In a research study, Johnson and Lewicki showed that superordinate goals which were closely related to the issues of the conflict, and which were introduced by one party in the dispute, often became caught up in the conflict dynamics and lost their effectiveness. Random events (under neither party's control) or events created by neutral third parties, are frequently better superordinate goals than those which are searched for and planned by the parties. For example, natural disasters such as floods, storms, blackouts, fires, etc. bring divisive people and communities together in a common purpose of survival; the same impact can be seen in negotiations.

Common Enemies

A common enemy is a negative form of superordinate goal. The parties find new motivation to resolve their differences in order to avoid intervention by a third party, or to pool resources to defeat a common enemy. Political leaders of all persuasions have often provoked outside enemies to attack in order to bring their own constituencies together. Managers who are in conflict are sometimes told by their superiors that if they do not reach agreement, someone else will make the decision for them. Labor and management may behave more collaboratively when threatened with binding arbitration or government intervention in their dispute.

Agreement on the Rules and Procedures

A third way parties can establish commonalities is by mutual agreement on the rules by which negotiations will be conducted. Escalated conflict tends to exceed its bounds; as parties become more upset, they may be more likely to resort to any and all tactics to defeat their opponents. Efforts at effective conflict de-escalation and control may require that the parties rededicate themselves to basic ground rules for how they will manage their dispute. These include:

- Determining a site for a meeting. Changing the site or finding "neutral turf" may be helpful to get things moving again.

- Setting a formal agenda as to what may be discussed, what may *not* be discussed, and agreeing to abide by that agenda.

- Determining who may attend the meetings. Changing key negotiators or representatives may be a "signal" of intention to change negotiation approach or tactics.

- Setting time limits for the individual meeting, and for the overall negotiations session. As we have pointed out, progress in negotiation is paced according to the time available; therefore, setting limits is likely to create more progress than if no limits are set.

■ Setting procedural roles—who may speak, how long they may speak, how issues will be approached, what facts may be introduced, how records or "minutes" will be kept, how agreements will be affirmed, what clerical or support services are required, etc.

Finally—and perhaps a very radical step for some negotiators—the parties may agree to set aside a short period of time during negotiations for the expressed purpose of critiquing *how they are doing*. This mechanism effectively designates a selected time for the parties to critically evaluate their own progress in negotiation, and to suggest a time when groundrules may be reevaluated, procedural mechanisms changed, or perhaps even changing negotiator behavior. This "process orientation" may provide the opportunity for the parties to self-correct the procedural mechanisms that will allow them to make greater progress on their substantive disagreements.

Integrative Frameworks

Superordinate goals, common enemies and mutual commitment to rules are factors *outside* the boundaries of the dispute; they transcend the specific issues and bring the parties together in unified action. However, superordinate goals and common enemies do not establish the foundation for long-term cooperation; when the common goal or common enemy is removed, the parties may find that they have no greater basis for resolving their dispute than they did before. Hence, other mechanisms must be pursued to establishing a common ground for deliberation.

There are two primary vehicles for developing commonalities in disputes: first, by focusing on similarities between the parties rather than on differences; and second, by searching for cognitive ways to redefine the dispute such that all parties' interests may be accommodated.

Maximizing similarities is simply a process of refocusing the parties' attention on what they have in common, rather than where they disagree. As noted earlier, conflict processes tend to highlight perceived differences and magnify the importance of these differences. The longer the parties are in dispute, the more they quibble about the differences, and the more they recognize other differences that are then drawn into the dispute. One way to control this escalation is to re-emphasize what the parties have in common—objectives, purposes, overall philosophies and viewpoints, long-range goals, styles of operation, etc. Another is to review what they have accomplished together. Reemphasizing the commonalities tends to put the differences back into their proper perspective, and de-emphasizes this importance. This process either defuses the emotionality tied to the differences, or creates a positive emotional bond based on similarities that will allow differences to be bridged.

Integrative frameworks are ways of redefining the issues to create a common perspective from which initial positions appear more compatible. Eiseman refers to this process as creating an integrative conceptual framework, while

Fisher and Ury state that successful negotiators focus on *interests,* not positions. By defining negotiated issues in terms of positions—my position on this issue is X—parties tend to treat complex phenomena by simplistically defining a single point, and then refusing to move from it. In order to create movement, parties must establish ways of redefining the conflict so that they can explore compatible interests. Fisher and Ury use the simple example of two women quarreling in a library. One wants the window open and the other wants it closed. They bicker back and forth about how much to leave it open: a crack, halfway, three quarters of the way. No solution satisfies them.

Enter the librarian. She asks one why she wants the window open: "To get some fresh air." She asks the other why she wants it closed: "To avoid the draft." After thinking a minute, she opens a window in the next room, bringing in fresh air without a draft.

Eiseman notes that there are several ways to create integrative frameworks out of polarized positions:

1. Dimensionalize the Problem.   Instead of treating the conflict as distinctly different categorical viewpoints, treat it as points along a continuum. In the above example, the parties were in dispute about whether the window would be open or closed. In fact, there are amost an infinite number of degrees that the window can be open, from very slightly to a great deal. Once the parties redefine the issue as the amount it will be open, they can then "negotiate" more easily over the size of the opening.

2. Increase the Number of Dimensions.   The successful intervention of the librarian in the above example is predicated on her imaginative solution, that fresh air and no draft can be accommodated if one does not restrict the solution to opening a window in the same room. Multiple dimensions allow one party to "win" on one dimension and the other to "win" on the second. Increasing dimensions allows for the possibility that an additional dimension can be identified on which the parties can more easily reconcile their differences. It may also provide an entirely new way of looking at the problem, so that both sides can now recognize degrees, shades, and variations that may satisfy all parties.

3. Construct an "Ideal Case."   Sometimes parties are in dispute because each is proposing a solution which meets only his/her own needs but not those of the other side. One way to break this deadlock is to construct an ideal case that would meet the needs of both sides. In the above example, the librarian did this by saying to herself, "Ideally, how can one party get fresh air while the other avoids a draft?" Negotiating parties can construct ideal solutions by creatively devising ways that both parties could ideally have their needs met, and then determining how that ideal scenario might be attained.

4. Search for Semantic Resolutions.   Particularly in cognitive conflicts, where parties are negotiating over contract language, setting policy or establishing memoranda of agreement, conflict frequently intensifies over key words, phrases and expressions. Sometimes this conflict can be reduced to irrelevant hairsplitting, yet to the parties the wording has significance in its meaning and intent. Discovering how parties attach different meanings to some words, or exploring language that can accommodate both sides, is another alternative for achieving an integrative framework.

Make Preferred Options More Desirable to the Opponent

A final alternative method that parties can use to increase the likelihood of agreement is to make their desires and preferences more palatable to their opponent. We have noted that as conflict escalates, the parties become more locked into defining their *own* position on an issue. Moreover, as this position is formulated over time, negotiators try to remain consistent with the original position—that is, to establish clearcut "policy" which applies in all circumstances. Because these policies are designed to apply to a variety of circumstances, of necessity they become broader rather than more specific. If the other does not readily comply with a negotiator's position or policy, the negotiator's tendency is to escalate and rigidify his demands, or increase the magnitude of the threat for noncompliance. These actions heighten conflict.

Roger Fisher suggests that most influence situations can be characterized by a "demand" (what we want), and offers and threats that state or imply the consequences of meeting or not meeting the demand. The basic dynamics of this process are depicted in Table 2.

Fisher suggests that this emphasis is greatly misplaced and self-destructive. Rather than focusing on their own positions, demands, and threats, negotiators should direct their effort to the following question: how can we get them (our opponents) to make a choice which is best for us, given that our interests diverge? This approach is largely a matter of perspective-taking—focusing on the other's interests rather than one's own. Like role-reversal, it requires negotiators to focus less on their own position, and more on a clear understanding of opponent's needs. Moreover, once those needs are understood, parties should invest their efforts *not* in the tactics of getting the opponent to come to us, but in the ways we can move toward them. Several alternatives can be pursued to accomplish this objective:

1. Give Them a Yesable Proposal.   Rather than increasing the emphasis on *our* position, a negotiator's efforts should be directed at creating a position that *opponents* will find acceptable. Rather than stating our position and letting *them* suggest alternatives which we may approve or overrule, a negotiator should give attention to understanding *their* needs and devising a proposal which will meet those needs. Fisher terms this a "yesable" proposal—one to

TABLE 2

	Demand	Offer	Threat
	The decision desired by us	The consequences of making the decision	The consequences of not making the decision
Who?	Who is to make the decision?	Who benefits if the decision is made?	Who gets hurt if the decision is not made?
What?	Exactly what decision is desired?	If the decision is made, what benefits can be expected? —what costs?	If the decision is not made, —what risks? —what potential benefits?
When?	By what time does the decision have to be made?	When, if ever, will the benefits of making the decision occur?	How soon will the consequences of not making the decision be felt?
Why?	What makes this a right, proper, and lawful decision?	What makes these consequences fair and legitimate?	What makes these consequences fair and legitimate?

Every feature of an influence problem can be located somewhere on this schematic map. The nature of a given problem can be discovered through estimating how the presumed adversary would answer the above questions.

which their only answer can be, "yes, it is acceptable." To succeed, however, this approach requires a negotiator to begin to think about what the other party would want or would agree with, rather than exclusively considering his own goals and needs.

2. Ask for a Different Decision.   Rather than making demands more general, to fit with our "position" or "policy," negotiators should endeavor to make demands more specific. Negotiators must determine what specific elements of the demands are most palatable or offensive to the opponent, then use this information to *refine the demand.* "Ask for a different decision," asserts Fisher. Reformulate, repackage, reorganize, rephrase. Fractionate, split, divide, make more specific. Making demands more specific is not making them more rigid; they *would* be rigid if it were the *only* demand to be made. Rather, specific demands which can be reformulated are easier to recast to meet the other's needs.

Fisher and Ury describe an analogous procedure in their recommendation that successful negotiators be skilled at inventing options for mutual gain. This principle has already been discussed several times in our review of integrative bargaining. By inventing and refining ways that both parties can succeed, and by providing a variety of these options to the opponent, the likelihood that both parties can select a desirable option is greatly enhanced.

3. Sweeten the Offer Rather Than Intensifying the Threat. Negotiators can also make options more palatable by enhancing the attractiveness of accepting them. Again, this is a matter of placing the emphasis on the positive rather than the negative; in the traditional "carrot and stick" tactics of managerial motivation, it is making the carrot more attractive rather than enlarging the stick. Promises and offers can be made more attractive in a variety of ways: maximizing their attractive qualities and minimizing their negative ones, showing how they meet the opponents' needs, reducing the disadvantages to them of accepting an offer, making offers more credible (i.e., that it will actually be given if they accept), or setting deadlines on offers so that they expire if not accepted quickly. Many would argue that these are common "sales tricks" akin to rebates, "two for the price of one" offers, "today only" sales, "extra added attraction" elements, etc. They are. The same techniques that salesmen use to move their products can and should be used by negotiators to get their position accepted by an adversary. Many of these techniques were described in the chapter on persuasion.

4. Use Legitimacy or Objective Criteria to Evaluate Solutions. Finally, negotiators may insist that alternative solutions and settlements be evaluated by "objective" criteria that meet the test of fairness and legitimacy. Each side should be able to demonstrate that its "demands" are based on sound facts, calculations and information, and that preferred solutions are consistent with those facts and information. This procedure will frequently require disclosing and sharing facts, rather than disguising and distorting them. "Here's how we arrived at our proposal. Here are the facts we used, the cost data we estimated, the calculations we made. You can verify these by the following procedures." The more this data is open to public verification, and demonstrated to be within the bounds of fairness and legitimacy, the more convincing will be the position "independent" of the negotiator who advocates it, and the more persuasive it will be in achieving a settlement. . . .

Consequences

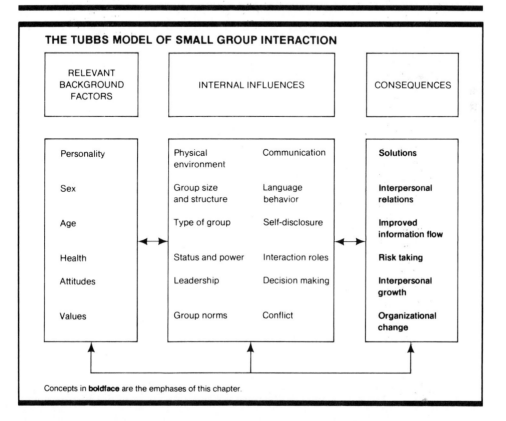

THE TUBBS MODEL OF SMALL GROUP INTERACTION

RELEVANT BACKGROUND FACTORS	INTERNAL INFLUENCES		CONSEQUENCES
Personality	Physical environment	Communication	**Solutions**
Sex	Group size and structure	Language behavior	**Interpersonal relations**
Age	Type of group	Self-disclosure	**Improved information flow**
Health	Status and power	Interaction roles	**Risk taking**
Attitudes	Leadership	Decision making	**Interpersonal growth**
Values	Group norms	Conflict	**Organizational change**

Concepts in **boldface** are the emphases of this chapter.

PREVIEW

Chapter 7 is devoted entirely to the consequences section of the Tubbs Model of Small Group Interaction. These consequences are potential outcomes or end results. One consequence (solutions to problems) is discussed, along with the quality and acceptance of solutions. Another end result of group communication is the improvement of intergroup relations. This is often a way of clearing up and reducing misunderstandings. An improvement in information flow often results from group discussion. As with information flow, risk taking also increases. It is related to the tendency that the threat of responsibility is lessened in a group setting. A great deal of interpersonal growth and organizational change also can be found under the consequences section. Each of these has several different methods to enhance their values.

GLOSSARY

Acceptance of Solutions: There are three different types of solutions for problem situations: (1) high quality, low acceptance; (2) high acceptance, high quality; (3) high acceptance, low quality.

Quality of Solutions: Groups have potential to make better-quality decisions than the same individuals would make if working alone.

CASE STUDY: XYZ Fraternity

Dave King is president of XYZ fraternity, which has sixty members living in the house. The house has room to sleep seventy-five; but membership has declined somewhat in recent years, and several rooms in the house are unfilled.

The fraternity house is located near a river that periodically floods its banks. When this happens, one room of the house gets water-soaked. This room has four members residing in it at the present time. These four have put a sign on the door of their room calling themselves the "swamp rats" and labeling the room "the Riverfront Apartment."

Dave and the other fraternity officers (vice-president, treasurer, and house manager) decided in an executive council meeting to use some of the unoccupied rooms in the house by letting the "swamp rats" move to drier quarters. They announced this plan at a chapter meeting on a Tuesday evening. That night, several members went to the "swamp rats" room to help them move out. The "swamp rats" had barricaded themselves in their room by placing their mattresses against the inside of the locked door. When Dave and the others tried to reason with the "swamp rats" to move out of the water-soaked room, the "swamp rats" opened the door, and a fight broke out. The "swamp rats" insisted that they did not want to be evicted from their "riverfront apartment." Now there is a high degree of hard feelings among the fraterniity members, and two factions have emerged. One group backs the officers, who feel that they were only trying to help. The other group backs the "swamp rats," who feel that the officers are overstepping their authority in trying to move them out of their room.

1. What should Dave have done differently?

2. How would you go about correcting the situation as it now exists?

This case study points to the fact that not all problem-solving attempts have positive outcomes or consequences. Dave King found out the hard way that even well-intentioned leaders sometimes live to see their best efforts backfire. This chapter deals with the potential outcomes or consequences of group interaction. These are sometimes referred to as the *end results*. However, our systems theory perspective reminds us that groups are ongoing and that today's end results are simply the new *inputs* for tomorrow's activities. The consequences of this particular decision eventually led to the deterioration of Dave's effectiveness as fraternity president. The interactions among the fraternity members led to increased polarization between the two factions. This problem eventually resolved itself when the senior class graduated and a river flood control program eliminated the flooding problem altogether. Now the fraternity is troubled with a whole set of new problems, and so it goes with the ongoing cycle of small group events.

After wading through six chapters on small group interaction, you should be able to answer such questions as, "Why use groups anyway? Wouldn't it be easier to just do the job yourself?" Certainly by now you are more aware of the many difficulties and complexities involved with group behavior. Before you throw up your hands and give up, read this chapter. At this time we will begin to elaborate upon the advantages of group interaction by determining the end results or potential consequences of group discussion. In this chapter we will examine six of these end results: (1) solutions to problems, (2) changes in interpersonal relations, (3) improved information flow, (4) increased risk taking, (5) interpersonal growth, and (6) organizational change.

SOLUTIONS TO PROBLEMS

Quality of Solutions

A clear result of small group research is that groups have the potential to make better-quality decisions than the same individuals would make if working alone. Group performance does not always surpass individual performance, but in those instances the group *process* has been counterproductive. This is supported by studies on communication in project groups (Zenger and Lawrence 1989). Reports have generally agreed that frequent communication among colleagues both inside and outside their project group is vital to high project performance. This notion has been stated in the following formula (Steiner 1972, p. 9):

Actual productivity = potential productivity − losses due to faulty process

Although people working in groups can often be more productive than one person working alone, people also may find it easy not to work in groups. This has come to be known as social loafing. In a recent study (Sheppard and Wright 1989), subjects were asked to work on a task either alone or in a group. Half of the subjects were offered a modest incentive for a good performance, and the other subjects were not. As the researchers predicted, people in groups tended to emit social loafing behaviors except when they were given sufficient reasons for performance.

When the group process is functioning well, group productivity tends to be as good or better than the individual's productivity. In an early test, Shaw (1932, p. 492) studied the relative effectiveness of individuals and groups in solving this problem (see if you can solve it):

> On one side of a river are three wives and three husbands. Get them all across the river by means of a boat carrying only three at a time. No man will allow his wife to be in the presence of another man unless he is also there.

Shaw found that 60 percent of her groups were able to determine the correct solution, whereas only 14 percent of the individuals were able to. In a related study, Maier and Solem (1952, p. 280) asked individuals and groups to solve this task:

> A man bought a horse for $60 and sold it for $70. Then he bought it back for $80 and again sold it for $90. How much money did he make?

About 45 percent of individuals solved the problem; 72 percent solved it in a leaderless group discussion, and 83 percent solved it in a discussion group with a leader who encouraged discussion and raised questions that promoted the group effort. Thus the study indicated that the groups surpassed the efforts of individuals, and that a leader helped improve the group effectiveness.

In addition to the type of tasks described above, some studies have examined tasks that could be subdivided (for example, assembly line production), tasks that involved guessing the number of objects in a jar, and tasks in which individuals compared the length of lines. Other studies have examined the effect of the presence of onlookers on a person's performance. It was found that some people are encouraged by the presence of others, whereas others are stimulated negatively, and some are unaffected. It has also been found that groups are better at solving complicated tasks requiring reasoning and elimination of poor solutions. In addition, it would seem that simply having several individuals solving a problem would increase the probability that a good solution would emerge. In other words, "two (or more) heads are better than one." Luft (1970, p. 30) summarizes the issue of group versus individual productivity: "Problems calling for a wide variety of skills and information or the cross-checking of facts and ideas seem to call for a group approach. Feedback and free exchange of thinking may stimulate ideas that would not have emerged by solo effort."

A good example of this type of decision is in the work of credit committees in lending institutions such as banks and credit unions. These committees are made up of individuals who have a high degree of technical knowledge—yet the committee must meet to consider all applications for loans larger than a certain dollar amount. Another good example would be surgical teams in hospitals. Here again, each person is highly educated, yet the collective wisdom of the group is superior to any one of the members acting alone. Finally, most large corporations are run by executive committees comprised of top-level executives. Here again, the reason is that committees make more effective decisions than individuals.

One ancient author stated the point eloquently when he wrote:

> Nowadays I make it a practice to call my workers into consultation on any new work . . . I observe that they are willing to set about on a piece of work on which their opinions have been asked and their advice followed. (Columella, 100 A.D.)

Finally, Collins and Guetzkow (1964, p. 55), summarizing the research on this issue, state: "Group members may collectively achieve more *than the most superior members are capable of achieving alone*" (emphasis added).

As we saw in Chapter 6, there are four methods for reaching decisions: (1) railroading, (2) teaming up, (3) majority vote, and (4) consensus. Consensus typically is the best method, because it optimizes good-quality decisions as well as a high degree of acceptance.

Acceptance of Solutions

The plant manager of a large manufacturing plant decided that his supervisors were using far too many pens and that this was an unnecessary cost. He wrote a memo to all supervisory personnel indicating that each one would have to turn in a completely empty pen to an assistant plant manager in order to get a new pen. The intent was to save money. Actually, the pens cost about 50 cents apiece, and the supervisor's salary figured out to about $20 per hour, so if a foreman had to spend more than six minutes searching for the assistant plant manager, the cost was actually *greater* than if the foreman had just gotten a new pen from the immediate area. The foremen determined that it usually took them about thirty minutes to find the assistant plant manager. Thus, under the new policy, the cost of replacing the pen had increased by twenty times. An even greater cost was the foremen's loss of positive attitude toward the plant. They felt that they were being treated like children, and several foremen went out of their way to do a poor job in retaliation. After less than one month, the plant manager rescinded his new policy in favor of the old practice of replacing pens.

A university department that moved into new offices encountered the same sort of problem. Professors were allocated offices by a combination of rank and seniority. The full professors got first pick in order of seniority, then the associate professors, by seniority, then the assistant professors, and so on. One associate professor ended up with one of the few offices without a window. He went into the department chairman's office to complain and commented that although he had over twenty years seniority, some of the full professors, who were considerably younger, had window offices. As he continued to plead his case for a window office, he began to get angry. He said he felt he had given the best years of his life to the school. He had even won an outstanding teaching award once. But because he had not published much, he had not received the promotion to full professor. As badly as the chairman felt, and as much as he sympathized with the professor, it was too late to rectify the situation without evicting someone else from a new office and making the other person feel cheated. Because acceptance or satisfaction with the decision was the key criterion for effectiveness in this decision, how could this situation have been avoided?

These cases illustrate one of the most common problems suffered by organizations—namely, employees rejecting solutions to problems. For solutions to be effective, they must be of high quality and they must be accepted by those who must carry them out. If a solution is weak on either of these two dimensions, its overall effectiveness is reduced. Maier (1963, p. 5) offers the following formula and explanation for determining a decision's effectiveness:

$$ED = Q \times A$$

where ED represents effective decision, Q represents quality, and A represents acceptance.

Three types of problem situations can be identified from this frame of reference. The first includes problems requiring a high quality but low acceptance. These problems are best solved by persons with a high level of technical knowledge and expertise. They might include important financial decisions involving setting prices, determining expenditures, and so on.

Second, some solutions require high acceptance but low quality. These might include fair ways of distributing new equipment, vacation schedules, undesirable work assignments, new offices or office equipment, or a new vehicle such as a truck.

Decisions such as these may include all individuals who may be affected by the results of the decision.

Third, some decisions require both high quality and high acceptance. It would appear that the majority of problems fall into this category. Because this is the case, Maier recommends that problem-solving groups rather than isolated individuals be used, because the acceptance of the solution is likely to be higher when people are involved in formulating a solution and because we have already seen that groups tend to produce better-quality solutions than individuals.

Participative decision making (PDM) not only can result in high-quality decisions and increased acceptance of the solutions, but it also may result in increased levels of satisfaction, commitment, and loyalty to the solution and to the group. Let us return to the pen replacement problem. The chances are that if the foremen were made aware of the problem and were asked to help find a way to reduce it, several things would occur. First, they might suggest a good solution. Second, they would be more likely to accept the new solution. Third, they probably would use peer pressure on one another to see that the new solution was followed. In each case, the result might have been better than what actually happened.

See the article at the end of this chapter in which Norman Maier more fully explains the use of the ED = Q × A formula. This article also shows the relevance of small group interaction to organizations and their effectiveness.

During World War II a group of social scientists was assigned to persuade housewives to serve more kidneys, beef hearts, and sweetbreads to their families, thus better utilizing the scarce supply of meat. Six groups of housewives were studied. Three groups heard a persuasive lecture showing how the use of these foods at home would help the war effort and would still be nutritious and tasty for their families. The other three groups were drawn into discussions of the difficulties of using these meats and ways of overcoming these difficulties. In both sets of groups, the housewives were asked to indicate (by a show of hands) how many thought that they would actually serve these meats in the upcoming week. A follow-up study revealed that 3 percent of the women in the lecture groups actually served the unfamiliar meats, whereas 32 percent of the discussion group members actually served the meats (Lewin 1953). Although this study had some methodological defects, it has become a classic in that it demonstrated the dramatic increase in commitment to an action plan that resulted from participating in a group discussion compared to listening to a persuasive speech. Many other studies have confirmed this powerful phenomenon (Tubbs and Carter 1977).

More recently, Moskal (1990) reported that the exact same technique was part of a major turnaround at Buick City. The Japanese Andon system was used, which gives the line worker the responsibility and authority to stop the assembly line when a problem occurs. Workers were able to stop production whenever they thought the product wasn't perfect. However, this happened so often that productivity was not maintained. "The word perfect was the problem . . . we redefined 'perfect' to mean 'meeting customer expectations and engineering specifications.' Plant brass also modified the 'Stop' concept to include a yellow cord at many operations that now alerts a team coordinator to a potential problem without actually stopping the assembly line" (p. 26). The results are that Buick LeSabre is now rated second highest in quality out of 154 makes of cars. Five years ago, it was second from the bottom (p. 22).

These studies indicate two things. First, people generally are resistant to changes that affect their lives, especially if these changes are initiated by others. Second, group decision making and "people involvement" can be powerful assets in increasing satisfaction and overcoming resistance to change. Let us look at each of these in more detail.

Resistance to change is a phenomenon that some would argue begins with the so-called birth trauma in which the fetus resists being plucked from the warm, dark security of the womb only to be exposed to the shock of the cold, bright, noisy world outside. Over time and experience, most of us develop a "separation anxiety" when we are forced to leave (or be separated from) any place or set of circumstances in which we feel comfortable. Each time we move or change schools or jobs, a certain amount of this is experienced. Try to remember how threatening your first day of high school (or college) was compared to the comfortable security of your immediate past. Resistance to change is normal and tends to increase when we do not understand the need for change or if we are not instrumental in bringing about the change.

More recently, many major American companies have increased their use of quality circles to increase both their product quality and worker involvement and commitment. A quality circle is simply a small group of employees (usually ten to fifteen) who get together on company time to talk about how they can do their jobs better. Main (1981, p. 76) quotes one top executive in Westinghouse as saying:

> The point is, we are making much better decisions than before . . . we are getting a contribution and commitment from larger numbers of people. The management team becomes excited and it works. When participative management catches on, . . . decisions are carried out by enthusiasts who have helped shape them, who feel they "own" the decisions, rather than by unwilling subordinates who have simply been told what to do without really knowing why.

In a study conducted by Brockner and Hess (1986) it was found that "the mean self-esteem level of the individuals in each quality circle was highly predictive of the group's task performance. Successful and unsuccessful circles did not differ in their size, longevity or organizational function. Moreover, self-esteem was uncorrelated with group size, longevity, or function, thereby discounting the possibility that the relationship between self-esteem and performance was a spurious function of any of these variables" (p. 620).

The results of the study do not indicate any cause of the relationship between self-esteem and the quality circles. The first possibility is that self-esteem caused the performance; second, performance within the quality circle caused the high self-esteem; or third, self-esteem and performance are related because of their common covariation with other factors.

Beebe (1986) cites three of the hundreds of companies that are successfully using quality circles to overcome resistance to change:*

> Problem: A mountain of paperwork was building on desks at CH2M Hills Boise office last year. Employees were slow to file reports and other documents in loose-leaf binders favored by the consulting engineering firm. The forms were not pre-punched.
>
> Solution: A volunteer group of workers suggested to the company that it switch to pre-punched forms. Doing so would relieve employees of an annoying chore and speed filing, they said.
>
> Savings: Pre-punched forms save the Boise office 60 man-days a year, Edward Sloan, CH2M Hill's district coordinator of construction management services said. Companywide it probably saves 2,400 man-days, he said.
>
> Problem: It took 15 to 20 minutes to unload each potato truck that entered the Ore-Ida Foods Inc. processing plant at Ontario, Ore. Employees estimated hundreds of hours were being wasted as potatoes moved down truck-mounted conveyors into the building.
>
> Solution: A group of Ore-Ida workers in Ontario last year recommended to managers that belly-dump trucks should be used to haul potatoes to the plant. Potatoes could be unloaded into bays in only a few minutes.
>
> Savings: Within one year, Ore-Ida realized $130,000 in labor savings and lost time, said John Walhof, the company's productivity manager.
>
> Problem: Could the error rate of machines that place electrical components on printed circuit boards at Hewlett-Packard Co.'s disc memory division in Boise be improved?
>
> Solution: The employees who operate the machines thought so. One group suggested a series of modifications that improved the manufacturer's error rating of its machines from 3,000 improperly mounted components per million to 500 parts per million, a sixfold improvement.
>
> Benefit: Far fewer components are being mounted incorrectly. Board rejection rates are down and employee morale is up, said Jim Stinehelfer, manufacturing manager in H-P's disc memory division.

Ore-Ida and CH2M Hill teams consist of six to ten people who meet once a week. Hewlett-Packard quality circles contain up to thirty people. Most of the groups are comprised of workers from the same area of the company. "We wanted to create an environment where employees are free to offer suggestions about their working environment, ideas on ways our products are produced, new products," said Ore-Ida's productivity manager of the company's People—Excellence—Products program. Ore-Ida has organized 138 PEP teams in all of its U.S. operations, including 35 at its Ontario plant and 35 at its Burley plant. Teams tackle everything from safety issues to product quality. Hewlett-Packard spokesmen have said their company has seen big increases in morale and productivity that can be related to quality circles. Line inspectors have been eliminated in many areas, because employees now monitor the quality of their work. The manufacturing manager of Hewlett-Packard stated the fundamental reason for the quality circles was to "make the people on the lines feel responsible for the quality of the product. The best way to have them feel that responsibility is to give it to them."

---

*By Paul Beebe; reprinted with permission of *The Idaho Statesman.*

There are several important factors to remember in *overcoming resistance to change*. First, people will accept changes that they have a part in planning. Obviously, it is much easier to live through the trauma of going to college if we choose to go and if we like the college or university than if we are forced by our parents to go or to go someplace we don't like. Second, changes will be accepted if they do not threaten our security. Many office work groups resist innovations such as computer systems for fear that the computer will eventually take away some of their jobs. Third, changes will be more readily accepted when people are involved in gathering facts that indicate the need for change. Farmers who notice decreasing crop yields will be more receptive to farming innovations than those who are prospering. Finally, greater acceptance and commitment will result when the changes are kept open to further revision based on the success or failure of the new procedures. None of us is very enthusiastic about adopting changes for a lifetime. However, if we feel the changes are on a trial basis, subject to modification, we are usually more willing to give them a try. Obviously, to the extent that these conditions are *not* met, resistance to change will be increased.

Many firms are beginning to take a step beyond quality circles with the self-managing work team concept. Sims and Dean (1985, p. 26) consider self-managing work teams the logical extension of quality circles: "Operating under several labels—self-managing work groups, autonomous work groups, and sometimes simply 'teams'—this organizational innovation has as its fundamental theme the attempt to place a remarkably high degree of decision making responsibility and behavior control in the hands of the work group itself."

A self-managing team usually elects its own leader, and often management appoints an external leader who acts as a coordinator/facilitator rather than a supervisor. Teams frequently take on responsibilities that have not traditionally been the topic for work groups in the past. Some of these include: (1) preparation of the annual budget, (2) timekeeping functions, (3) recording of quality control statistics, (4) solving technically related problems, (5) adjusting production schedules, (6) modifying or redesigning production processes, and (7) setting team goals and assessing internal performance.

For long-term success, teams must function in a responsible manner, and management must possess a high degree of trust and confidence in the system. To help ensure successful teams, organizations typically design them with "well defined physical and task boundaries, sometimes using socio-technical design concepts to ensure an appropriate match between technical systems and the conventions, rules, and norms governing interaction. Task interdependence within teams is usually higher than between teams." Sophisticated computerized information systems are frequently used in measuring inputs and outputs across team boundaries. This provides extensive and rapid feedback about the quantity and quality of team performance while reducing secrecy between teams. Teams are provided with as much information as possible.

Management typically initiates the self-managing work concept while striving for additional productivity, improving quality, reducing overhead, and reducing conflict. For the employee, the concept provides the opportunity to exercise more control over aspects of daily work life. Are these teams successful? There is no single conclusive answer to this question, but according to Sims and Dean (1985, pp. 26–27):

> The consensus of many managers is that self-managing teams provide a 20% to 40% productivity edge over the traditional system. Savings come about not because employees are working harder, but because they require less surveillance (therefore, there is less overhead), and scrap, lost time, and poor-quality products are significantly reduced. The old cliché "working smarter, not harder" seems to hold true.

Many other benefits of the team approach seem to manifest themselves. Teams become very flexible and adapt well to changing conditions and new start-ups. Also, plants with the team concept generally have very high responses to job satisfaction and attitude surveys.

Sims and Dean report that an informal estimate of plants in the United States using the self-managing team concept was over 200. The question to be asked is, Why hasn't the use of this innovation been more widespread? Sims and Dean report several reasons: "Managers, particularly middle managers, feel highly threatened by the concept because they believe it will reduce their power and influence. Perhaps an even more important reason is that startup costs for the team concept can be significant, and patience—a typical wait is 18 months to two years—is required before the rewards of successful implementation can be reaped." Furthermore, union support has not been uniform; some unions have seen the concept as a potential threat to their power. Finally, there has been little media attention given to the teams. Some companies consider this team concept an advantage over competitors and are therefore extremely secretive about their experiences.

Franecki, Catalanello, and Behrens (1984, p. 69) state that participative management (PM) techniques are becoming increasingly popular: "PM techniques . . . range from the more basic ones, such as joint setting of job-performance goals by supervisor and subordinate, to more elaborate ones, such as establishing work teams whose employee-members assign job tasks, acquire new members, and set quality standards." A field survey of 200 private-sector employers was conducted to analyze the use and benefits of the PM techniques. In general it was found that "respondents to the survey use a variety of employee committees, and they perceive positive effects for their firms: cost savings, improved operating statistics, and better employee relations were all reported. It also appears that employees approve of committees . . . This conclusion is significant because participation has sometimes resulted in overly high expectations by those it serves."

CHANGES IN INTERPERSONAL RELATIONS

Probably the most notable difference between a television interview with a professional golfer who has just won a major tournament and a baseball team that has won the World Series (or a football team that has won the Super Bowl) is the tremendous amount of energy, enthusiasm, and esprit de corps of the group versus the low-keyed response of the lone golfer. The backslapping, hugging, and champagne splashing of the group are some of the most obvious signs that interpersonal relations are an important by-product of group activity. Sensitivity training groups frequently provide powerful emotional experiences for group members. One group participant wrote of his experience (Tubbs and Moss 1974, p. 243), "I thought we had a good meeting. Afterward several people came up and we walked across campus together, which made me feel that they weren't resentful about my getting emotional. . . . I am feeling happier about myself in the group."

In Chapter 6 we examined the positive and negative aspects of conflict. Group discussion may improve interpersonal relations through the successful resolution of conflict. Conflict may be intragroup or intergroup. In either case, resolving conflict tends to affect interpersonal relations favorably.

A common technique for improving intergroup relations is to have members of each group get together and write down their perceptions of (1) themselves, (2) the others, and (3) how they think the others view them. Production and service groups in manufacturing plants frequently need to have such meetings to coordinate their activities more effectively. The production groups frequently feel that a service department (such as maintenance) does not act quickly enough to get defective machinery working. On the other hand, maintenance people feel as if they are always put under unreasonable pressures, because every time a piece of machinery breaks down, each production supervisor wants immediate attention to his or her problems, even though several machines require repair simultaneously.

Meetings designed to share perceptions of one another and to inform each other of particular problems can potentially clear up and reduce areas of misperception and misunderstanding. After one such meeting, one man said to another from a different department, "After drinking coffee with you and hearing your side of the story, it's going to be hard for me to cuss you out tomorrow the way I usually do." This comment is typical of the increased quality of interpersonal relations that can come out of group problem solving conducted in an atmosphere of support and mutual gain. However, if the meetings are conducted in an atmosphere of blame placing and faultfinding, the relations are likely to be even worse than if the meetings had not been held. In other words, the intermediate influences discussed in Chapters 5 and 6 have a significant influence on the end results.

A subset of interpersonal relations is group cohesion. *Cohesiveness,* according to Schachter et al. (1968, p. 192): "has been defined variously as referring to morale, 'sticking together,' productivity, power, task involvement, feelings of belongingness, shared understanding of roles, and good teamwork." This definition covers a lot of territory and can be further clarified by the definition offered by Cartwright (1968, p. 91): "Most agree that group cohesiveness refers to the degree to which the members of a group desire to remain in the group." Group cohesion can also be a by-product or end result of group activity. Generally, a prestigious or successful group is more attractive to belong to and results in higher levels of cohesion. The Boston Celtics basketball team and the Los Angeles Raiders football team are two examples of successful groups that could be expected to have high levels of cohesion.

Cohesion is a result of group interaction, but it in turn influences other things. As we saw in Chapter 4, cohesive groups tend to have stricter norms and tolerate smaller amounts of deviance from the group values. Cohesive groups may have high or low productivity, depending on the group norm regarding productivity. Cohesiveness increases the loyalty of each member to that particular group but frequently breeds deeper cleavages *between* groups. This may become a problem if the groups happen to be part of a single organization in which integration of several groups is necessary. In a study on predictors of performance in project groups (Keller 1986), group cohesiveness was found to be the strongest predictor of the project groups' performance both initially and over time. The findings suggested that, "cohesive project groups were able to achieve high project quality and meet their goals on budgets and schedules."

As with so many topics in this book, cohesiveness has been identified as one type of variable (consequence). However, it also has an influence on other variables. Cartwright (1968, pp. 106–107) describes the complexity of classifying cohesiveness:

> In our attempt to discover some theoretical order among the many findings related to group cohesiveness, we have identified certain factors as determinants and others as consequences of cohesiveness. . . . Factors that increase cohesiveness lead to consequences that, in turn, lead to greater cohesiveness. Several examples . . . come readily to mind. Similarity of beliefs and values tend to generate interpersonal attractions among members, and the resulting cohesiveness gives the group power to influence members toward greater similarity. As a group becomes more cohesive its ability to satisfy the needs of members increases, thereby raising the incentive value of the group. And cohesiveness tends to generate frequent interaction among members, which, under certain conditions at least, heightens interpersonal attraction and thus cohesiveness.

Cartwright goes on to say that the opposite spiral may also occur—that is, negative experience may lead to negative attitudes, which in turn may cause more negative experiences.

In summary, it is important to note that small group interaction has the potential of increasing interpersonal relations and cohesiveness. The great emphasis on "team building" in management training illustrates the usefulness of this concept. In terms of learning theory, the behaviors of talking and cooperating rather than avoiding and competing with one another have been reinforced, and the cooperating behaviors are, therefore, more likely to occur again. Thibaut and Kelley (1986, p. 12) put it this way: "The selectivity observed in interaction reflects the tendency for more satisfactory interactions to recur and for less satisfactory ones to disappear. The consequences of interaction can be described in many different terms, but we have found it useful to distinguish only between the rewards that a person receives and the costs he incurs." The critical element in improving interpersonal relations through group interaction is to make the experience as rewarding as possible. (See also Varney 1989.)

Team Building

Note the following analogy between a typewriter and a team. Xvxn though this typxwritxr is old, it works wxll xxcxpt for onx kxy. I havx wishxd many timxs that it workxd pxrfxctly. It is trux that thxrx arx forty-onx kxys that function wxll xnough. But just onx kxy not working makxs thx diffxrxncx.

Somxtimxs an organization or community is likx this typxwritxr—all thx pxoplx but onx arx working propxrly. You may say to yoursxlf, "Wxll, only onx won't makx to brakx a projxct." But it doxs makx a diffxrxncx. Any projxct, to bx xffxctivx, nxxds thx participation of xvxry mxmbxr.

So thx nxxt timx you think you arx thx "only onx" and that your xfforts arxn't nxxdxd, rxmxmbxr this typxwritxr and say to yoursxlf, "I am an important pxrson in thx organization and community, and I am nxxdxd vxry much." (Source Unknown)

The analogy above touches on a special case of group interpersonal relations referred to as team building. Dyer (1985) traces the team-building concept back to the late 1920s and early 1930s and the now classic Hawthorne studies conducted by researchers from Harvard Business School studying workers at the Hawthorne, Illinois, plant of the Western Electric Company. Although the research first focused on the relationship of lighting to worker productivity, the focus soon changed to studying the social relations between and among workers. They accidentally found the latter to be far more powerfully related to productivity than the level of lighting in the workplace. Since that time, the team concept has continued to grow in importance.

Larson and LaFasto (1989) report the results of their research investigating over thirty leaders of such high-performance teams as:

the Boeing 747 project team

the IBM PC team

the Rogers Commission (Challenger Disaster Investigation)

Cardiac surgical teams

the 1986 Mt. Everest expedition

the Centers for Disease Control epidemiology teams

New York stage production teams

the McDonald's Chicken McNuggets team

Championship football teams

On the basis of their fascinating research, eight dimensions of team excellence emerged.

1. CLEAR, ELEVATING GOAL   For example, the purpose of the Rogers Commission was to determine the causes of the Challenger disaster within 120 days. Paul Lazarus, a Broadway producer, is quoted as saying that, "It is better to have a clear idea and have it fail than to be unclear in conception, because you can learn from a failure and go on to the next clear idea" (p. 29).

2. RESULTS DRIVEN STRUCTURE   The Mt. Everest team had as its objective getting one or two team members to the top of the mountain. The group's structure was to use the other members strictly as support for getting the one or two strongest members to the summit. The McDonald's Chicken McNuggets team was purposely

structured as a separate entity from the rest of the company and reported directly to Bud Sweeney, the project director. The purpose was to cut through the corporate bureaucracy.

3. COMPETENT TEAM MEMBERS   The team members for the Centers for Disease Control are selected for their outstanding talent along the following dimensions: (1) technically competent, (2) friendly and outgoing, (3) politically astute, (4) willing to subordinate his or her own interests in favor of the group goal, (5) willing to spend a lot of time on the task, (6) imaginative, (7) honest, and (8) interested in challenge (p. 60).

4. UNIFIED COMMITMENT   Dr. Don Wukasch, a member of both the famous Michael DeBakey and Denton Cooley cardiac surgical teams, described his level of dedication to his teams: "Nothing was as important for me as being on that team and making it through the 10 years to get there. It was total commitment, and when I got married, that was part of the deal with my marriage. We looked at it and never had any questions as to what came first. It was the job" (p. 74).

5. COLLABORATIVE CLIMATE   Working well together is the basic building block of teamwork. Trust turns out to be the main ingredient. Anthony Rucci, a Baxter-Travenol Corporation team leader, states, "You need to clearly define the expectations, leaving people with the sense that you trust them enough to do things on their own, that you trust their judgment enough to let them take some personal initiative, that you are not looking over their shoulder. That is the quickest way that I know of for a manager of a team to demonstrate trust and to build a climate of trust" (p. 87).

6. STANDARDS OF EXCELLENCE   Director Paul Lazarus describes the level of excellence exemplified by one Broadway star: "Angela Lansbury did one song, and yet she requested more rehearsal time than anybody else simply because she would not go out on the stage unless she was prepared within an inch of her life . . . She rehearsed 'Send in the Clowns' . . . once a week for 10 weeks. We could have done it in one rehearsal, but that's the kind of perfectionism that someone like that strives for, and that's why Angela Lansbury is a major star" (p. 102).

7. EXTERNAL SUPPORT AND RECOGNITION   Emotional support from top leaders above the team followed by financial incentives are the strongest combination to ensure that the team continues to give its best.

8. PRINCIPLED LEADERSHIP   Although leadership has been discussed in Chapter 4, suffice it to say that Larson and LaFasto (1989) identify effective leaders as those who, (1) establish a vision, (2) create change, and (3) unleash talent (p. 121).

In case you are wondering how to develop this high level of team spirit, Huszczo (1990) identifies the ten pitfalls common to team building.

1. Confusing team building with teamwork

2. Viewing teams as if they are "closed systems"

3. Not using a systematic model to plan the team development

4. Starting team training without assessing team needs

5. Sending team members to team training individually rather than collectively

6. Treating team building as a Japanese management technique

7. Assuming that teams are all basically alike

8. Counting on training alone to develop effective teams

9. Treating team training as a program rather than a process

10. Not holding teams accountable for using what they learn in team training

Although all of these are important misconceptions to consider when examining a group-building communication process, I think it important to emphasize one particular misconception—that of viewing the group as if it were a closed system. A group's performance is a function of its collective abilities, motivations, and opportunities. It is important for group members to improve how they relate with each other, the roles they play, the relationships between these roles, and the norms that help the group members work effectively.

Quite often, group members forget that they are part of a larger system (an organization), which itself can define roles, goals, and norms for the group. At times, changes in an organization will create changes in a group that make it difficult for the group to work effectively. An effective group will create constructive external relationships with its broader system. Group members will have an understanding of the group's role in the organization and learn to recognize threats and opportunities from the larger system.

IMPROVED INFORMATION FLOW

Communication in small groups also can result in an increased knowledge level and increased coordination among group members based on the sharing of information. Information may be distorted severely if passed along serially from one person to the next through ten people. However, the distortion will be significantly decreased if the same ten people hear the information simultaneously in a meeting. In addition, active discussion by participants will help them remember the information better than if they heard an announcement or read it in a memo.

Another factor is the tendency for subgroups to form so that information that passes *between* groups is restricted. This is especially true in complex organizations. Lawrence and Lorsch (1969) have referred to problems of this nature as differentiation-integration problems. On one hand, organizations require specialization (differentiation) in order to operate effectively. Thus, different groups become specialists in such departments as production, finance, legal, research and development, data-processing inspection, master mechanics, engineering, accounting, sales, or personnel. At the same time, these groups must cooperate and coordinate their efforts to keep from working at cross purposes and generally harming organizational success. Lawrence and Lorsch (1969, pp. 54–55) summarize the results of one such set of four interdepartmental meetings:

> The managers and scientists were generally enthusiastic about what the program had accomplished. They reported that as a result of the program they had developed a more concerted effort to coordinate all of their research activity. . . . They were also using a new set of decision criteria to evaluate research and development projects. This was a direct result of their effort and according to them had facilitated the resolution of conflict. . . . Finally, the members of the integrating group indicated that they were devoting more time to working with other functional groups, enabling research to get a unified new product effort. According to organizational members, all of this added up to improved organizational integration without sacrificing differentiation.

Coordination problems certainly occur among members of a single group as well as among multiple groups in an organization. Almost invariably, groups of students assigned to work on class projects have at least some difficulty in finding (1) each other, (2) a free hour in common in which to meet, (3) the materials necessary to conduct the research for their assignments, and sometimes (4) a suitable place in which to conduct their discussion. In addition, group members may forget that they were supposed to meet, or they may get too busy to prepare for the meeting. A host of other tangential problems may add to the coordination difficulties. Not all of these problems will be solved by group discussions, but they will probably at least be reduced. In some circles it is known as "letting the right hand know what the left hand is doing."

Likert (1967) also points out that group decision making tends to lead to a different type of solution than person-to-person decision making. In the one-on-one setting, the focus of the solution is on the person perceiving an individual problem. In an organization, this approach frequently solves one person's problem while *creating* new problems for others. Suppose that five supervisors all want to take their vacations in June and July. Assuming that all of them cannot be absent at once, any decision regarding one person's vacation will potentially influence the vacation plans of the others. It may be that one person's plan is flexible and could be modified in light of the situations of the others in the group. The group method then focuses on coordinating the best solution for all, considering the limitations of the job demands.

In addition to offering better decisions for more people, the group decision-making method reduces the jealousy and hostility that frequently accompany the person-to-person method. When individuals are awarded decisions in their favor without others knowing the circumstances surrounding the decision, the others frequently feel that "special deals" have been made, and the superior is accused of playing favorites. However, this reaction is drastically reduced when all interested parties are witness to the decision and the surrounding circumstances. Although the group method may be time-consuming, the end results of increased knowledge level and increased coordination are frequently worth the time spent. In fact, the total time expenditure may be less, because the related problems of jealousy and resentment do not occur as much and do not have to be solved as offshoots of the original problem.

INCREASED RISK TAKING

Imagine the following situation (Wallach, Kagan, and Bem 1962):

> An engaged couple must decide, in the face of recent arguments suggesting some sharp differences of opinion, whether or not to get married. Discussions with a marriage counselor indicate that a happy marriage, while possible, would not be assured.

In questions such as this, as well as those dealing with career choices, military decisions, decisions regarding one's health, and other decisions, it has been found that groups tend to take bigger risks than individuals. This concept was first proposed by Stoner (1961) and has become a heavily researched topic known as the *risky shift phenomenon.*

Several theories have been proposed to account for such an occurrence. The "leadership hypothesis" holds that the influence of the group's leader causes the shift. The "diffusion of responsibility" hypothesis argues that because nobody in the group feels as much personal responsibility or accountability for the decision, more risk is taken. The "rationality hypothesis" argues that greater risk is simply a better choice with a greater likelihood of payoff. The "conformity hypothesis" posits that people take more risk as a result of buckling to pressure from others in the group. Finally, the "risk value" hypothesis holds that risk is generally admired or valued in our culture, and this value is reinforced in the group setting.

There is a great deal of contradictory evidence on each of these hypotheses, but some consistent trends can be identified. First, the risky shift itself is a fairly predictable phenomenon. Teger and Pruitt (1970, p. 72) state: "The difference between the mean level of risk taken initially by the individuals and the mean of their later group decisions is termed a 'shift.' If there is a change toward greater risk, it is termed a 'risky shift.' A risky shift is almost always found."

Second, the "leadership hypothesis" seems to have at least some limitations, because not all leaders encourage risk and because some studies show that risky choices are made even before the leader says anything.

The "diffusion of responsibility" hypothesis has the most intuitive appeal for many. It seems that people would feel more security in numbers and less fear of personal harm if they made decisions as part of a group. However, a summary of the literature on this view indicates that the hypothesis has serious shortcomings (Clark 1971).

The "rationality hypothesis" also has been seriously questioned, because several studies have shown what we might intuitively expect—that not all risky decisions are the better rational choices, and in some cases the groups actually choose the riskier choices that lead to worse consequences (Malmuth and Feshbach 1972).

The "conformity hypothesis" has also been criticized, because not all groups exert pressure toward risk. The "risk value" hypothesis seems to be one of the most popular views. Brown (1965) argues that our culture values risk and that this value causes group members to want to avoid being seen as "chicken," which results in their making riskier choices. However, Clark (1971) has argued that even this is not always the case. Several other conditions affect the occurrence of the risky shift. In his summary of the literature (1971, p. 264) he identifies four such conditions. The group must (1) actually discuss risk-relevant topics, (2) not have severe consequences for failure, (3) have members who vary in initial riskiness, and (4) have individuals who perceive themselves as being at least as willing to take risks as others in the group.

In your own group experiences you should be aware that groups do tend to cause individuals to take greater risks than they might take as individuals. In some cases this may be good, but in other situations excessive risks might result.

INTERPERSONAL GROWTH

Although we can probably learn to improve our interpersonal skills by observing our behavior and the behavior of others in any group, the encounter group or the sensitivity training group has this as one of its major objectives. Instead of focusing on problem solving (for example, how can we solve the problem of evaluating student performance in a communication course), encounter groups focus on improving interpersonal skills. The Johari window discussed in Chapter 5 is one model used for bringing about greater interpersonal growth.

In order to change a person's interpersonal behavior, a three-phase process must be undertaken. These phases are (1) unfreezing, (2) change, and (3) refreezing (Bennis et al. 1968). In order to better visualize this process, let us look at two actual individuals and their experiences in an encounter group.

The Case of Jim

Jim was a 28-year-old man who worked as a statistician in a manufacturing plant. He explained on the first evening of class that he wanted to be a supervisor and that he wanted a $200,000 home by the time he was 30. He and his wife had no children and lived in an apartment.

In the first class period, the leader stated that the experience would be unconventional and unstructured, with a lot of group discussion and few lectures. Within minutes, Jim began to criticize the leader by asking such questions as, "What are you getting paid for if you aren't going to teach us anything?" and, "Why should we do your job for you?"

The leader responded by saying, "I think it is interesting that you feel that learning can occur only if I lecture to the group. Do you think that it is possible for us to learn together rather than me trying to tell you the 'answers'?" A lively discussion followed in which the assumptions of traditional methods of education and leadership were discussed.

Over several weeks Jim criticized each of his bosses and former bosses and indicated that he had a record of quitting jobs because of conflicts with his supervisors. In each case, the problem (according to Jim) was that the supervisor did not adequately recognize his worth. Each week Jim would criticize the leader in class. Criticisms included the following:

I think you wear striped shirts because you like to get attention.

When are you going to tell us what we are supposed to be getting out of this class? I suggest if Frank won't tell us what to do, we start for ourselves. Let's go around the room and have everybody tell us one observation he has had about this group so far.

Over time, others in the group commented that Jim's criticism of the leader irritated them, and that they thought that the class procedures were worthwhile. Then one night the leader asked, "Jim, do you see any connection between your dissatisfaction with my leadership and your dissatisfaction with each of your bosses on your jobs?" Jim's face lighted up and he said, "I never thought of that!" Over several weeks Jim began to see that he was struggling for control with leaders and vacillated between exerting control (initiating an exercise in group observation skills) and requesting control ("When are you going to tell us what we should be learning?").

Over time, Jim was encouraged to try leadership behaviors in the group and was encouraged not always to expect the leader to have to lead. At the end of the term, Jim told the group that he felt that he had learned a lot about his problems of relating to authority figures and that he even felt more comfortable with his boss at work.

The Case of Wendy

Wendy was a 19-year-old college sophomore majoring in philosophy. On the first day of class she said that she had been valedictorian of her class and was currently into Nietzsche and nihilism. According to a sociogram taken in class, she was the least popular person in the class. She asked for feedback as to why, and she was told that "she seemed too condescending, cold, and generally snotty." She participated in an exercise called the "trust fall" in which she allowed herself to fall into the arms of a circle of her classmates.

Afterwards the exercise was discussed, and she said that she felt that she did not have to try to impress everybody with her superior intellect just to be accepted. Over the course of the term, she was gently reminded when she slipped back into her "superiority complex." For several years after the course, I would see her on campus, and she seemed to have retained her new warmth and approachability.

Jim and Wendy had different problems, but the same procedures were used to help them learn to improve their interpersonal skills. In both cases, an *unfreezing* occurred in which the assumptions about how to behave were questioned. Jim assumed that a leader had to be perfect and had to be strong and decisive to be of any value. Wendy assumed that she had to impress people with her intellect to be accepted. Both learned through feedback that their assumptions were not always correct.

The *change* phase came when both people were encouraged to adopt new behaviors that they typically would not have been willing to try. Jim tried leading the group himself, and Wendy tried to drop her façade and let people accept her for more reasons than just her brains.

The *refreezing* came when the group tried over time to reinforce or encourage Jim and Wendy's new behaviors. This trial-and-error learning over time, followed by feedback, tends to increase the likelihood that the new behaviors will be retained after the encounter group experience is over.

As we have said, acquisition of these new interpersonal skills follows the sequence of unfreezing, change, and refreezing. Schein (1987, p. 93) breaks it down a bit more.

A Three-Stage Model of the Change Process

Stage 1. *Unfreezing:* Creating motivation and readiness to change through
   a. Disconfirmation or lack of confirmation
   b. Creation of guilt or anxiety
   c. Provision of psychological safety

Stage 2. *Changing through Cognitive Restructuring:* Helping the client to see things, judge things, feel things, and react to things differently based on a new point of view obtained through
   a. Identifying with a new role model, mentor, etc.
   b. Scanning the environment for new relevant information

Stage 3. *Refreezing:* Helping the client to integrate the new point of view into
   a. The total personality and self-concept
   b. Significant relationships

It is quite general and vague to say that encounter groups provide an experience for interpersonal growth. Some more specific ways of identifying such growth have been presented by Egan (1973). He states (p. 23):

I grow interpersonally if

- I am freer to be myself in my interactions with others,

- I manage interpersonal anxiety more effectively,

- I learn how to show greater concern for others,

- I can take initiative in contacting others more easily,

- I can share myself more openly and deeply with the significant others in my life,

- I can be less fearful in expressing feelings and emotions in interpersonal situations,

- I can step from behind my façade more often,

- I can learn to accept myself and deal with my deficits in the community of my friends more often,

- Intimacy frightens me less,

- I can endure concerned and responsible confrontation more,

- I can learn to confront those who mean something to me with care and compassion,

- I can come to expect myself and others to work on the phoniness in their lives,

- I can commit myself more deeply to others without fear of losing my own identity,

- I can come to know who I am a bit more in terms of my personal goals and the direction of my life.

Although these goals may not be achieved by all encounter group participants, they are potential outcomes for some.

Numerous studies have been conducted to test empirically the extent to which the goals mentioned above are actually accomplished in encounter groups. An excellent review of these has been published by Cooper and Mongham (1971). Statistically significant positive changes have been documented in a number of studies, including

Miles (1965); Bunker (1965); Valiquet (1968); Underwood (1965); Lieberman, Yalom, and Miles (1973); and Burke and Bennis (1961). On the other hand, some writers have shown either no significant changes or some negative changes as a result of encounter groups.

Campbell and Dunnette's (1968) well-known article indicates some areas of weakness in encounter group research. They acknowledge the point that studies have shown that encounter groups do seem to bring about generally desirable results in line with their goals. However, they also point out that more specific behavioral measures should be used to determine success. They call for more research to indicate which *specific* encounter group practices (such as methods of giving feedback) are constructive and which are potentially destructive. They also indicate that encounter groups used for management training do not show any necessary improvement in specific indices of job performance.

Undoubtedly smarting from the sting of such critics as Campbell and Dunnette, Lieberman, Yalom, and Miles (1973) published an extensive volume of encounter group research. Eighteen different student groups at Stanford were studied in several different varieties of encounter group experiences, each lasting thirty hours. As a result of the experiences, of the total of 206 students who initially participated, 28 changed greatly, 40 changed moderately, 78 were unchanged, 17 changed negatively, 16 were casualties, and 27 dropped out (Lieberman, Yalom, and Miles 1973, p. 118). The results seem to represent moderate support in favor of encounter groups. The 16 casualties were concentrated for the most part in the groups whose leaders were more aggressive and confrontive. Also, the casualties had lower self-esteem and a more negative self-concept prior to the experience.

ORGANIZATIONAL CHANGE

On the basis of a rapidly increasing rate of change, modern organizations have been put under greater and greater pressure to adapt or go under. Certainly the policies and practices of colleges and universities have to be different today than they were five years ago. Numerous attempts have been made to help "ease the squeeze" felt by organizations. These attempts usually fall under the general label *organization development* (OD), which is another name for planned organizational change.

Over forty years ago, Kurt Lewin (1951) wrote about the problem of trying to get people to change. He called his analysis *force field analysis,* and it states basically that any situation occurs as a result of the combination of various competing forces. If you have ever tried to live up to your New Year's resolutions, you have experienced this. Figure 7.1 illustrates the concept further. Your motivation to live up to your New Year's resolutions represents one of the arrows labeled "driving forces." If you are thinking about exercising more or losing some weight, several arguments can add to your motivations (better-fitting clothes, more dates, better health). The restraining forces would be all the reasons why you don't live up to your resolutions (it's fun to eat, it's too cold to exercise, you hate to exercise alone).

Just as this force field analysis can be applied to individuals, it can be applied to groups and to organizations. In groups, some members may want to get the job accomplished (task-oriented behavior), whereas others may be much more interested in socializing with an attractive group member of the opposite sex. In fact,

FIGURE 7.1

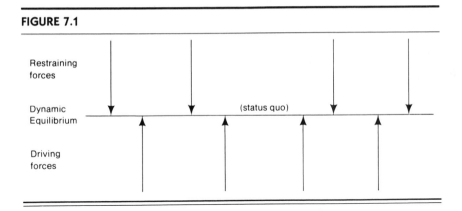

they may have joined the group just to meet that person. How much work actually gets accomplished is the status quo where these competing sets of forces meet. If the socializing couple leaves, the restraining forces will go up. Change can occur through either a reduction in the restraining forces or an increase in the driving forces, or both. Various methods of organizational development are designed to move the status quo in the more positive direction.

Although OD methods vary, most writers in the field would agree that various group methods play an important part in the process. Argyris (1962) contends that holding encounter groups with top administrators is the most effective tactic for promoting organizational change. Beckhard (1969) uses small groups as the basis of a "confrontation meeting" in which differing factions within an organization are brought together to resolve their mutual differences. Lorsch and Lawrence (1972) focus their OD attempts on diagnosing the problems within and between groups in their differentiation-integration approach discussed earlier. Likert (1967) has shown that group decision making is one of the basic methods of effective management and that organization development can occur through the use of small groups discussing survey feedback with their supervisors.

In a study of eleven successful and six unsuccessful change efforts, Greiner (1970) found that the successful efforts involved what he called *shared power approaches* (including group problem solving and group decision making). These were found to be more effective than either the *unilateral approaches* (including change by decree, by personnel replacement, or by structure) or the *delegated authority approaches* (including case discussion and encounter group sessions). Greiner (p. 217) describes the shared power approaches as follows:

> More toward the middle of the power distribution continuum, as noted earlier, are the shared approaches, where authority is still present and used, yet there is also interaction and sharing of power. This approach to change is utilized in two forms.

> *By Group Decision Making* Here the problems still tend to be defined unilaterally from above, but lower level groups are usually left free to develop alternative solutions and to choose among them. The main assumption tends to be that individuals develop more commitment to action when they have a voice in the decisions that affect them. The net

result is that power is shared between bosses and subordinates, though there is a division of labor between those who define the problems and those who develop the solutions.

By Group Problem Solving This form emphasizes both the definition and the solution of problems within the context of group discussion. Here power is shared throughout the decision process, but, unlike group decision making, there is an added opportunity for lower level subordinates to define the problem. The assumption underlying this approach is not only that people gain greater commitment from being exposed to a wider decision-making role, but also that they have significant knowledge to contribute to the definition of the problem.

Schein and Bennis (1965), in an early work entitled *Personal and Organizational Change through Group Methods,* describe in detail the reasons why groups are so potent in changing organizations. Changes occur in three ways. First, individuals gain an increased *awareness* of problems of which they are a part. This represents an intellectual or cognitive change in their amount of information. Second, there tends to be a change in *attitude* toward the problems. Individuals may be more willing to become a part of the solution rather than expending all their effort trying to place the blame for the problem. This part of the change process is more emotional, or gut level. Third, group experiences tend to produce a change in *behavior* that goes beyond the change in knowledge level or attitude.

Schein and Bennis (1965, p. 37) refer specifically to these behavioral changes as "increased *interpersonal competence;* i.e., skill in handling interpersonal and group relationships toward more productive and satisfying relationships." It is perhaps this threefold form of individual change that accounts for the tremendous potential groups have for bringing about organizational change. (See also the Maier and Kotter et al. articles that follow this chapter.) Main (1981, p. 93) quotes William Coates, executive vice-president of Westinghouse, as stating that organizational change is best achieved through the group participation method. Although it eats up many hours, Coates says that lost time is recovered later. "We spend a lot of time trying to get a consensus, but once you get it, the implementation is instantaneous." The company has already saved millions of dollars of expenses that would otherwise have to be added to their product costs.

Team building that emphasizes team problem solving is an organizational development tool used in today's business world. Organizational development as defined by Huse and Cummings (1985) is "the deliberate, reasoned, introduction, establishment, reinforcement and spread of change for the purpose of improving an organization's effectiveness and health. Effectiveness refers to setting and attaining appropriate goals in a changing environment; health refers to the motivation, utilization, and integration of human resources within the organization."

David Kearns (1990), Chief Executive Officer of Xerox Corporation, writes about a major organizational change in his company. He writes that between 1960 and 1975, Xerox had fallen from the dominant position in its industry. The company organized its workers into quality-of-work-life circles. All employees were trained in interpersonal skills, group dynamics, and problem-solving techniques. This went on for several years. He writes,

In 1983, we introduced what we call our Leadership Through Quality process—a management system that depends heavily on employee involvement and focuses the entire company on the achievement of total quality. We altered the role of first-line management from that of the traditional, dictatorial foreman to that of a supervisor functioning primarily as a coach and expediter. (p. 87)

Still more training was conducted in three-and-one-half-day offsite programs. Emphasis was on identifying quality problems, determining their causes, developing solutions, and implementing them—in other words, the reflective thinking process discussed in Chapter 6. The result was a 90 percent reduction in defects and a return to the top of the industry.

Excellence comes in all sizes. Not only giant corporations such as Xerox can benefit from using principles of group dynamics. Fernco, Inc., of Davison, Michigan, is an example of a small company that is also benefitting from these innovations (Davis 1990). Fernco manufactures plastic pipe products and employs 100 people. Three years ago they began to implement an employee involvement program based on the principles in this book. Your author was asked to design and conduct the program. We began by measuring employee attitudes with a survey to diagnose the strengths and weaknesses in the organization. Several offsite training programs were held with all the company management and the employees who volunteered to join the TAG Teams, as they became known. A set of company guidelines was developed in collaboration with an advisory committee made up of managers and employees. Four TAG Teams were formed to work on problems of their choice. After one year, employee attitudes showed significant improvement, and the teams had proposed numerous innovations that management strongly supported and quickly implemented. The company is the leader in their industry and is widely recognized in the region as an outstanding organization in which to work. They have almost no turnover, and there is a long waiting list to get a job there. This is but one more example of the use of groups to improve an already excellent organization (p. D6).

Meyer and Goes (1988) have advanced a three-part model for the assimilation of innovations by an organization. The three factors leading to these organizational changes are: (1) *contextual attributes* (the characteristics of environments, organizations, and leaders); (2) *innovation-decision attributes* (characteristics of innovation-context interactions); and (3) *innovation attributes* (characteristics inherent in the innovations themselves). When the model was applied to a practical setting, it was found that the model offered reasonably good predictions of the extent to which an organization will assimilate a given change. The findings also suggested that an organization's assimilation of a new policy or product is highly dependent on the attributes of that particular item.

See the article by Kotter, Schlesinger, and Sathe at the end of this chapter for a comprehensive discussion of the methods for accomplishing organizational change.

THE SYSTEMS PERSPECTIVE

This chapter dealt with the consequences of group interaction. In Chapter 1 our model indicated that all the other variables tend to culminate in these consequences. However, in ongoing groups, the outcomes or consequences of earlier group interactions tend to have a continuing influence on subsequent activities. Take the fraternity case study at the beginning of this chapter. As a result of the conflict over the "swamp rats," the fraternity developed two subgroups. This cleavage led to a deterioration over time of the entire fraternity's ability to work and play as a team. This example illustrates the systems concepts of *input* and *throughput* resulting in *output* that is fed back into the group as new *inputs,* because many groups represent ongoing *cycles* of events.

In this chapter we looked at six potential consequences of group interaction: (1) solutions to problems, (2) changes in interpersonal relations, (3) improved information flow, (4) increased risk taking, (5) interpersonal growth, and (6) organizational change. Each of these potential consequences may vary considerably depending on the particular combination of the other variables depicted in the model. For example, the quality and acceptance of solutions will vary depending on the degree of group member participation.

A great deal of material has been written about member acceptance of group-derived solutions. The term "consensus" is typically used in this context. Consensus means unanimous agreement with the solution. Conceptually, consensus and acceptance of the solution appear to be roughly equivalent. Gouran (1969) found that consensus is related to fewer opinionated statements (that is, fewer statements that express feeling, belief, or judgment when the factual basis for the statement is not apparent). Knutson (1972) found that groups containing individuals engaging in "high orientation behavior" will be more likely to reach consensus. Orientation behavior was defined (Knutson 1972, p. 160) as "Behavior which reflected an attempt on the part of the individual to resolve conflict, facilitate achievement of a group's goal, make helpful suggestions, or lessen tension."

Hill (1976) conducted a follow-up study on the question of the relationship of opinionatedness and leadership to group consensus. He found two interesting interrelationships—first (p. 257), that "leadership behavior characterized by moderately opinionated or unopinionated communication will be associated with groups which come closer to total consensus than groups with manifestly opinionated leaders." The second finding was that "group leaders who behave in an opinionated manner will be perceived by their fellow group members as significantly less competent than will be unopinionated leaders, and they will also be perceived as significantly less objective than either moderately opinionated or unopinionated leaders."

All the studies cited above confirm our thesis that small group interaction must be viewed as a system of interrelated variables in which a change in any one variable creates changes in the other variables in the system.

The second section of this chapter dealt with interpersonal relations. We saw that group member relations may be improved as a result of group interaction. However, groups comprised of members with highly incompatible personalities or value systems may, in fact, become even more polarized as a result of small group interaction. This outcome would depend on the style of leadership and quality of conflict resolution in the group. Information flow may also be improved as a result of interaction; but with a highly structured communication network and authoritarian leadership, communication flow might actually diminish. Similar points also can be made regarding risk taking, interpersonal growth, and organizational change. Each of these potential consequences depends to a considerable degree on the quality of the mix of other relevant variables in the model.

What we have attempted to do in this chapter and throughout the book is to indicate ways to better understand and improve your functioning in small groups. There are no guarantees that these improved consequences will occur. However, considerable research cited earlier leads us to believe there is a distinct probability that you can and will become a more effective group participant if you are able to implement the ideas we have discussed.

The readings for this chapter help show how you can improve several small group consequences. Directly or indirectly, these articles touch on how to improve all six consequences discussed in this chapter. The article by Norman Maier even suggests a contingency model consistent with systems theory that suggests which types of problems are more likely to be solved using group decisions and which types of problems can be solved by the leader acting alone.

EXERCISES

1. Getting the Car Home

Divide the class in half. Let one half attempt to solve this problem individually, with no conversation allowed between and among participants. Record the number who solve the problem correctly as well as the average amount of time taken to solve it (sum the times of each person and divide by the number of persons). Have the other half of the class form into groups of four or five people. Record how many groups correctly solve the problem and the average length of time taken per group.

Problem: You are stranded with a flat tire. In attempting to change the tire, you step on the hubcap containing the lug nuts (which hold the wheel on), and all five nuts are lost down a storm sewer. How do you get the car home?

2. Personal Feedback Exercise

On the basis of in-class experiences this term, answer the questions in Figure 7.2 for each person in the class (while every other person in the class does the same thing). Ultimately you will receive feedback from every other class member. These can be anonymous, or you may sign your name if you wish.

FIGURE 7.2   PERSONAL FEEDBACK EXERCISE FORM

Comments for _____

Following are some general impressions I have formed of your performance over the course of the semester.

1. In the task or problem-solving areas, you seem to have the following strengths:

    weaknesses:

2. In terms of your ability to *communicate clearly and effectively* on an interpersonal level, you seem to have the following strengths:

    weaknesses:

3. In terms of your ability to *work with others on a social-emotional level,* you seem to have the following strengths:

    weaknesses:

4. In the following areas you seem to have improved during the semester:

5. Additional comments:

Most of us who work in small groups are interested to one extent or another in getting results. In the first article, Norman Maier offers a very practical discussion of the formula $ED = Q \times A$ briefly described in this chapter. This article also bridges the gap between communicating in small groups and applying those concepts and skills to meeting the needs of an organization.

In the final article, Kotter et al. offer a comprehensive spectrum of seven methods for bringing about organizational change.

Improving Decisions in an Organization

Norman R. F. Maier

The Pragmatic Test of Decisions

Most management situations are sufficiently complex so that solutions to problems or decisions that are to be made cannot be classified into correct and incorrect categories. Rather the alternative possibilities have relative merits, and the standards by which they are to be judged are not agreed upon. Frequently the criteria for judging them are unclear, or there is a lack of agreement on the correct standards to use. People may favor certain decisions because they fit the facts, because they like them, because they get support from those who must execute them, because they are the only ones that came to mind, because making a change in preference may cause them to lose face, because they like the person who suggested a particular decision, because the alternative favored is their brain child, because they participated in reaching it, and for a variety of other reasons. Some of these reasons may be of assistance in the reaching of effective decisions while others may be a hindrance.

Regardless of why people favor certain solutions or decisions over others, the test of a decision's value is quite a different matter. If the pragmatic test is to be used, an effective decision would be the one that produced the desired objectives most completely, achieved the desired objective most efficiently (costwise, energywise, and with the least undesirable side effects), and carried with it the most valuable by-products. These three measures of success might sometimes be in conflict, but in any event they would all be dependent on the outcome of the decision.

In other words, decisions can best be evaluated in terms of subsequent events, and unfortunately it is then too late to change the decision. For example, General Eisenhower's decision to invade the French coast at a time when the weather report was doubtful is regarded as a good one because it turned out that the weather did not interfere with the plans. Had the weather turned out to be sufficiently unfavorable and created great losses, his decision would have been open to criticism. In this instance the weather information indicated that invasion was risky on the date set for the invasion. However, the

From Norman R. G. Maier, Problem-Solving Discussions and Conferences (New York: McGraw-Hill, 1963), pp. 1–9. Reprinted by permission of the estate of Norman R. F. Maier.

alternative was to set another date and go through the costly preparation process again.

Decisions of this sort may be regarded as lucky, or we might suppose that the decision maker has some kind of intuition, some special wisdom, or some special information that guides him. Regardless of how we view such decisions, the factor of chance plays a part. Some people are wealthy because their ancestors happened to settle along a river bank that later became a thriving city. Even if we view the ancestors as having the intuition to settle at the right place, the payoff on these decisions did not occur in their lifetimes. It seems unlikely that potential real estate values were factors influencing these decisions, and hence it would be more appropriate to attribute the successes of the decisions to luck than to wisdom.

Granting that chance plays a part in successful decisions, we also must concede that some people seem to be lucky more often than others and that the difference exceeds what one would expect from the laws of probability. Some executives seem to have an uncanny way of making decisions that turn out to be highly successful; others may go through several bankruptcies. Although the borderline between luck and decision-making aptitude may sometimes be narrow, it is important to do what we can to reduce the chance factors to their bare minimum if we are to examine the factors that make for decision-making ability.

Since the final evaluation of the decision is only possible some time after the decision has been made, and since the evaluation of alternatives is often not available, we must confine our speculation to the ingredients of decision that have high probabilities for success. In examining alternate decisions we may appraise them from the point of view of their probable effectiveness.

For example, if a first-place baseball team is to play the seventh-place team, an even-money bet placed on the first-place team would be wiser, even if it turned out that the seventh-place team won. One cannot take unknowns into account in appraising decisions before the actual test. However, failure to consider all the factors and influences that are available before the decision is made will reduce its possibility for success. Thus the illness of two star players on the first-place team should not be overlooked.

The Dimensions of Effective Decisions

Two different dimensions seem to be relevant in appraising a decision's potential effectiveness. One of these is the objective or impersonal *quality* of the decision; the other has to do with its *acceptance* or the way the persons who must execute the decision *feel* about it. The usual conception of effective decisions has emphasized the quality dimension. This approach leads to a careful consideration of the facts of the case. The advice is to "get the facts; weigh and consider them; then decide." It is this emphasis that causes one to assume that there is a correct answer to a problem, a right decision to make. Although this position is sound in technological matters that do not involve people, one cannot assume that it is universally sound. It is this position that causes us to concentrate on getting more information and to assume that when decisions do not work out there must have been some oversight. Thus nations may debate peace plans for the world, attempting to improve the decision, when the fault may lie elsewhere. It is quite possible that any number of plans would be adequate if they received international acceptance. As soon as the behavior of people is involved, opinions and feelings introduce a second dimension.

It is important to clearly separate these two dimensions since, as we shall see, the ways for dealing with them are very different. Failure to differentiate the dimensions leads to complications in discussion because one person may be using terms such as "good" to describe the quality of the decision, another to describe its acceptability; and a third may be thinking in terms of the outcome, which depends on both.

Decisions may have varying degrees of acceptance by the group which must execute them; and it follows that, quality remaining constant, the effectiveness of decisions will be a function of the degree to which the executors of the decision like and believe in them.

For example, let us suppose that there are four ways to lay out a job and that the quality of these methods, from best to poorest, is in the following order: method A, method B, method C, and method D. Suppose further that the persons who must use these methods have a preference order as follows: method D, method B, method C, and method A. It is conceivable under these circumstances that method B would yield the best results even though it is not the decision of highest objective quality. Naturally one must consider the degrees of difference between each alternative; nevertheless, the fact remains that an inferior method may produce better results than a superior one, if the former has the greater support.

The formula for an effective decision (ED) therefore would require consideration of two independent aspects of a decision: (1) its purely objective or impersonal attributes, which we are defining as quality (Q); and (2) its attractiveness or desirability to persons who must work with the decision, which we are defining as acceptance (A). The first depends upon objective data (facts in the situation); the second on subjective data (feelings which are in people). Simply stated, the relationship may be expressed as follows:

$$ED = Q \times A$$

This separation of quality and acceptance somewhat alters the meaning of such expressions as "good" decisions and "correct" decisions. The term "goodness" might be used to describe degrees of quality, acceptance, or effectiveness and hence has little meaning when applied to decisions. The term "correct" similarly has different dimensions and in addition is limited because it is an absolute term and suggests that there are no moderately effective decisions, medium-quality decisions, and partially acceptable decisions.

It must also be recognized that the effect of acceptance on performance will vary from one problem to another. It is clear that when the execution of a decision is independent of people, the need for acceptance is less than when the execution is influenced by the motivations and attitudes of the people who must carry it out. Nevertheless, a respect for acceptance may be a worthwhile consideration in all group problem solving since a concern for a participant's satisfaction may influence his motivations and attitudes, which in turn would influence his contributions. For example, a marketing plan may have high quality and still have poor acceptance by a group of persons involved in designing the visual appearance of a package. Since the execution of the design and its reception by the public are independent of the initial planning group, it can be assumed that the success of the decision will be independent of the degree of acceptance of the decision-making group. However, what effect will such a decision have on a group if it has been railroaded through? If some members of the planning group are dissatisfied with the decision, may not this make them less valuable participants in the future? When we take the long-range point of view, dissatisfaction with a perfectly good decision can depress a group's future performance; whereas, high satisfaction with a decision may serve to upgrade future performance.

If we can assume the position that the acceptance of a decision by the group that must implement it is a desirable ingredient, what are the problem issues? First of all, we must examine how this ingredient is related to the other desired ingredient—quality.

It is one thing to say that in striving for effective decisions two criteria must be satisfied, but can one achieve both of these objectives simultaneously? High-quality decisions, on the one hand, require wisdom, and wisdom is the product of intelligence and knowledge. Decisions of high acceptance, on the other hand, require satisfaction, and satisfaction is the product of participation and involvement in decision making. Thus the method for achieving *quality* differs from the method for achieving *acceptance;* as a matter of fact they are in conflict.

Figure 1*A* describes this basic problem in aiming at two objectives. If we aim for both objectives, we may achieve neither. The traditional leadership approach is to aim for quality first, as in Fig. 1*B*. This means that the man responsible for decisions uses whatever resources he feels are needed in obtaining facts and opinions, and he may make free use of experts or consultants. However, the actual decision-making function resides in the leader who finally weighs the evidence and decides. Once a satisfactory quality has been achieved, the next step in this process is to obtain acceptance of the decision.

Traditional methods for achieving this secondary objective have ranged through (1) imposing the decision on subordinates who must execute it (dictatorial methods, using the motivation of fear); (2) playing the father figure and gaining acceptance through a sense of duty and trust (paternalistic methods, using the motivation of loyalty); (3) using persuasion types of approach which explain the virtues of the decision (selling methods, in which personal gains are stressed); and (4) using participative approaches which encourage discussion of decisions by subordinates but leave the final decisions to the superior (consultative management, in which the motivation is based on a limited degree of participation in which there is opportunity to discuss but no

FIGURE 1   QUALITY AND ACCEPTANCE AS TARGETS

(A) Aiming at both objectives achieves neither. This is particularly true when the aim is good. As one moves from right to left and approaches the objectives, the directions in which they lie become farther apart. When one is next to them, they lie in opposite directions.(B) The traditional approach is to aim at quality and so assure achieving it. Once this is accomplished, concern turns to acceptance, which thereby becomes a secondary objective.

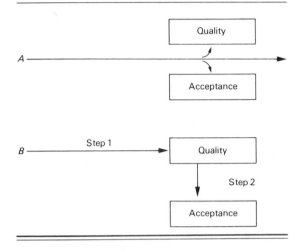

right to make a decision). Although this evolution of the decision-making process reveals improvement, the change has been confined to the aspect that is concerned with obtaining acceptance of decisions by subordinates. Throughout the history of the decision-making process, the quality ingredient has remained in the hands of the top man or group leader. Management philosophy is that the person held accountable for the decision should be the one who makes it. The fact that changes in methods for obtaining acceptance have occurred, however, suggests that the adequacy of the acceptance ingredient still leaves something to be desired. Patching up an old method may improve things, but it lacks elegance.

Suppose for the moment we make a fundamental change in our thinking and regard acceptance as the initial objective. This approach is shown in Fig. 2. To ensure success with this objective it is necessary to share the decision making with the subordinates who must execute the decision. Group decision, a method in which problems are solved and group differences are resolved through discussion, now emerges as the appropriate approach. It immediately becomes apparent that in attempting to be sure of obtaining acceptance, one risks the ingredient of quality. At least, that is the first concern of leaders and superiors when the question is raised. This notion of group decision becomes even more threatening when the leader discovers that he is to be held responsible for decisions made by his immediate subordinates. It is for this reason that he wishes to retain a veto power; yet such a safeguard tends to destroy the value

FIGURE 2   ACCEPTANCE AS PRIMARY OBJECTIVE

When acceptance is the initial target and is thereby assumed, concern for quality is the major worry. Will quality suffer if it is made the secondary objective?

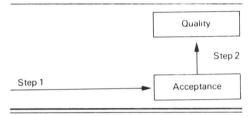

of group problem solving. Yes-men are the products of a superior's tendency to disapprove of decisions made by subordinates.

It appears then that the second objective is endangered whenever the appropriate method for obtaining the first is used. If this conflict is inevitable, it may be well to conclude that there is no one best approach to the problem of effective decision making. Perhaps problems, as well as approaches, should be analyzed. It is possible that the best approach may be a function of the nature of the problem.

Basic Differences in Problems

Problems may be examined with respect to the degree in which quality and acceptance are implicated. For example, in pricing a product it is apparent that a price may be so low that the loss will increase with the volume of business, or it may be so high that the company will be priced out of business. These two fates are possible, regardless of how acceptable the price is to the persons who make or sell the product. Establishing a proper price, therefore, is an illustration of a problem where the quality of the decision is a prime consideration. Although acceptance may influence the manufacture or sale of the product, it is quite clear that satisfaction with company decisions would not depend primarily upon problems of this type.

In contrast, let us select a problem involving the issue of fairness. What is fair is largely a matter of feeling, and it would be difficult for anyone to find an objective criterion that would ensure the achieving of fairness in a group. For example, when a new typewriter is introduced into an office group to replace an old one, who should get it? Should it be the person whose typewriter is replaced, the person with most seniority, the person who is most skilled, the person who is least skilled, the person who does the most work, or should some other criteria be found? Each member of the group might advocate a different scale of values, and invariably the criterion proposed is found to favor the person who advocated it. Thus when people want something, they select the facts and the values that tend to favor their feelings.

If a problem of this kind were solved by group decision, the supervisor would hold a meeting and conduct a group discussion to determine the fair way to introduce the new typewriter into the group. Usually this type of discussion resolves itself into a reshuffling of typewriters so that several persons stand to gain. Furthermore, different groups will solve the same problem in different ways, and each group will be most satisfied with its own solution. Solutions of this kind cannot be generalized, and their merit lies in the fact that they are tailored to fit the groups who make them.

The question of quality is a minor one in such instances. The supervisor need not be concerned with which of several possible solutions is objectively the best; his primary concern is to have a decision that is acceptable. Future performance of the group will depend more upon the way the members accept decisions on such matters than upon their objective qualities. As a matter of fact, it might be difficult to find measures of quality that would be acceptable to everyone.

If we follow this approach to distinguishing between problems, the first step in decision making is to analyze the problem in terms of the important objective—quality or acceptance. Three classifications of problems would seem to emerge.

High-Quality, Low-Acceptance Requirement

These are problems in which the quality of the decision is the important ingredient and the need for acceptance is relatively low. Such problems can be solved effectively by the leader with the aid of experts. The ingredient of acceptance should come up for consideration only after concern with the quality of the decision has been satisfied. Thus the procedure for obtaining acceptance may be regarded as secondary, though necessary.

We shall see later that the quality of decisions often can be improved by the effective use of group participation. This use of the group has additional objectives and raises new problems. For the present we will confine the discussion to the types of problems that can adequately be solved by experts and do not create major acceptance problems. These include:

Decisions regarding expansion, new products, decentralization, plant sites, etc.

Problems concerned with setting prices, determining costs, etc.

Decisions regarding the purchase of materials

Solutions to problems requiring specialized or technical knowledge

Although persons may disagree on the relative importance of the *quality* and *acceptance* requirements, this evaluation must be made by the person who is responsible for the decision. If he feels that a particular decision is required, he is in no condition to permit participation without directly or indirectly imposing his views. In this state of mind he is in a better condition to supply the solution and make acceptance the secondary objective. When the leader strongly favors a particular decision, he is a more effective persuader than conference leader. Thus, regardless of whether quality is the most important factor in a decision or whether the leader thinks it is the most important, the procedure is the same—protecting quality by the effective utilization of the knowledge and intelligence of the decision maker.

Certain decisions that involve acceptance but for which there are no acceptable solutions may also be included in this classification of problems. For example, an airline had the problem of choosing a uniform for stewardesses when the company's new jet plane was introduced. The solution to this problem involves a quality aspect in that the uniform should artistically conform to the design of the plane's interior, and it involves an acceptance decision from the stewardesses, who would have to wear the uniforms. In this instance, the reaction of the stewardesses to the company-imposed decision was quite unfavorable, so that it seemed that the approach used may have been a poor one. On the other hand, could stewardesses have agreed on a solution even if effort had been made to hold group meetings with such a large population?

If we assume that blondes, brunettes, and redheads are favored by different color combinations, it is quite unlikely that all girls would be satisfied with the same uniform, so that any group decision would tend to favor the predominant group. Would such an outcome be a good group decision? Until we know more, it might be best to confine the group decision method to situations that permit a resolution of differences. However, it is important not to assume that all conflicts in a group resist resolution. It is conceivable that if group discussion had been used the girls would have:

1. Evolved a compromise that was artistic

2. Adopted a uniform that permitted variation in some part (such as a scarf) so that complexion differences would have been recognized

3. Been more satisfied because of having had some opportunity to influence the decision

Whether the cost of such meetings would offset the cost of the discontent, which would be temporary, is a decision that the responsible person must make.

High-Acceptance, Low-Quality Requirement

These are problems in which poor acceptance can cause a decision to fail and in which the judgment of quality is influenced by differences in position, experience, attitudes, value systems, and other subjective factors. Problems of this type can best be solved by group decision.

An illustration of a problem falling into this group arose when a supervisor needed two of the three girls in his office for work on a Sunday. He asked them individually, and each claimed that she had made a date that she could not break. The fact that Sunday work paid double did not interest them.

He decided to try the group decision method he had just learned about in the company training program. He asked the girls to meet in his office on Friday morning and told them about the emergency job. Since he needed the help of two of them, he wondered what would be the fairest way to handle it. The girls readily entered into the discussion. It turned out that all had dates, but one had a date with some other girls, and all three agreed that a date with other girls was not a "real" date. Thus this girl agreed that it was only fair that she should work.

One more girl was needed. Further discussion revealed that one girl had a date with the man to whom she was engaged, and the third had a date with a new boyfriend. All girls agreed that a date with a fiancé was a real date, but it was not a "heavy" date. It was decided that the third girl, who had the date with a new conquest, should be excused from Sunday work. Thus she was not required to work, even though she had least seniority, because this was considered fair.

The quality issue does not enter into this problem for two reasons: (1) All girls were qualified to do the work. Had this not been true, the supervisor might have been more reluctant to try out this method. However, it remains to be seen whether the girls would have placed an incompetent girl on the job. (2) The problem was stated in such a way as to limit it to the matter at stake. Had he posed the problem in terms of whether or not anyone should be forced to work on Sunday, the answer might have been "no." We shall see later that a problem should be so stated as to keep it within the bounds of the supervisor's freedom of action. If he has no authority to set such matters as pay rates, he cannot expect the group to solve this type of problem through group decision.

In using group decision the superior serves as the discussion leader and presents the problem to his subordinates. His objective is to have the group resolve their differences through discussion while he remains neutral. He confines his activities to clarifying the problem, encouraging discussion, promoting communication, supplying information that may be at his disposal, and making appropriate summaries. His objective is to achieve unanimous agreement on a decision that is the product of the interaction in a group discussion.

Problems that fall into the high-acceptance category have to do with:

The fair way to distribute something desirable, be it a typewriter, a truck, office space, office furniture

The fair way to get something undesirable accomplished, be it unpleasant work, unattractive hours or shifts

The scheduling of overtime, vacations, coffee breaks, etc.

The fair way to settle disciplinary problems that involve violations of regulations, lack of cooperation, etc.

High-Acceptance, High-Quality Requirement

These are the problems that do not fall into the other two categories. At first this may seem to be the largest category of all, so that little seems to have been achieved by extracting the other two. However, in working with group problem solving, it soon becomes apparent that group decisions are often of surprisingly good quality. It is not uncommon for a supervisor to volunteer the information that the group's solution surpassed not only what he had expected, but what he could have achieved by himself. The fear that group decisions will be of poor quality appears to be greater than the hazard warrants. However, if the supervisor is anxious about the outcome, he is likely to interfere with the problem-solving process, rather than facilitate it. For this reason this category of problems should be handled by group decision only when the leader is experienced. Thus it is a category for which either group decision or leader decision is recommended, depending upon the supervisor's skills.

The fears of people frequently determine the motives they ascribe to others, particularly if they are members of an opposition group. For example, if a manager fears a drop in production, he unjustly assumes that his employees are motivated to produce less. Actually the motivational forces in employees form a complex pattern. They include not only what the employees want, but ways of protecting themselves from what they fear management wants to accomplish. With fear removed by the opportunity to participate, the outcome of a discussion often differs greatly from what is anticipated. Obstacles that seem insurmountable frequently disappear in thin air.

The Dynamics of Group Problem Solving

In order to illustrate the types of forces at work in a problem-solving interaction, it may be best to describe a case in the use of group decision. Specific incidents serve to bring theories and generalizations in closer contact with reality.

This case is selected because it is characteristic of the manner in which men solve problems involving attitudes toward prestige and seniority rights. At the same time it illustrates how the men on the job are aware of company objectives and do not take advantage of the company or of each other when the need for protective behavior is removed.

The problem arose because repair foremen in the telephone industry had a persistent problem in getting their men to clear "wet-weather drops."[1] A wet-weather drop is a defective line that runs from a pole to a building. These lines have to be replaced from time to time because water can seep through a break in the insulation and create a short. After a heavy rain there are reports of trouble, but since the difficulty is present only when the line is wet, the problem is a purely temporary one. During periods of expansion or when replacement material is at a minimum, many lines suffer from this wet-weather difficulty. If a station is out of order for this reason, the loss of service corrects itself and is not as serious as if the station were completely out of order. Hence the company, as well as the men, regards wet-weather drops to be minor and routine jobs in contrast to emergency jobs. Furthermore, repair men do not like to do this unimportant work, and they feel that anyone can do it without thinking. As a consequence, the men make little effort to get these jobs done. If the foreman decides to pressure men into bringing in a few wet-weather drops, he finds himself at a disadvantage. The men may promise to pick up one or two and then fail to do so. When asked why, they claim that they ran into extra difficulty on an emergency job and say, "You wanted me to do a good job on the other first, didn't you, boss?" Although the foreman may know the men are shirking, he never knows on what occasion the excuse is justified. It thus comes about that wet-weather drops are a headache to the foreman. When he gets far enough behind, he puts one man on the job full time and lets him clear wet-weather drops. The man in question feels degraded and wonders why he is picked on. To be as fair as possible, this job is usually given to the man with the least seniority. He may complain violently, but invariably the man with least seniority is in the minority. Among supervisory groups this practice is considered the fairest way to handle the situation, and they believe that the men want seniority to be recognized this way. They are completely unaware of the fact that this practice turns an undesirable job into one that has low status as well.

In a particular crew of twelve men the number of wet-weather drops was gradually increasing, and the time was approaching when something would have to be done about the matter. The foreman decided that this was a good problem on which to try group decision. He told his men that he realized no one liked to clear wet-weather drops and that he wanted to have their reactions on how the problem should be handled.

Of interest is the fact that no one in the group felt that the man with the least seniority should do the whole job. The man with most seniority talked against the idea of picking on the fellow with least seniority, saying that he had hated being stuck with the job when he had the least seniority and that he couldn't see why everybody shouldn't do a share of it. It was soon agreed that the job should be evenly divided among the crew. This crew divided up the job by assigning a work area for each man. In this way each man was to be responsible for the wet-weather drops in his area, and he was to be given a list of those. Each morning the local test desk was to designate for each man the wet-weather drop most in need of replacement. It was understood that he was to clear this one, if at all possible. This condition took care of clearing up the drops that were most essential from the point of view of the office. In addition, all agreed that each man should clear as many additional drops as his load permitted. However, when a man had cleared up all the wet-weather drops in his area, it was specifically understood that he should not be asked to help out another. This last condition clearly reveals an attitude built up over the years. It is evident that the reluctance to clear wet-weather drops hinged on the idea that when a man was conscientious, advantage was taken of him. Soon he got to be the "sucker" in the group or perhaps the foreman's pet. It was evident that all men were willing to do their parts but they did not wish to run the risk of being made a sucker. (Other foremen have testified that this defensive reaction made sense from the manner in which the job is frequently handled. The foreman wants to get the job done, and he begins to rely on those individuals who have cooperated in the past. Soon these men find they are doing all the undesirable jobs. It is just a matter of how long it takes a man to find out that he is losing out with the group.)

The results of this solution were immediately apparent. During the three-month period previous to the discussion, a total of eighty wet-weather drops had been cleared; during the week following the discussion, seventy-eight wet-weather drops were cleared and without any letup on the rest of the work. Within a few months the problem was practically nonexistent. The reaction of the men also bore out the effectiveness of the decision. Men discussed the number of drops they had cleared and showed a friendly competitive spirit. They discussed the time when they expected to be caught up and would only have to take care of wet-weather drops as they arose.

It should be noted that the men's notion of fairness was quite different from what the supervisor had anticipated. Although men strongly urge seniority privileges, they do not wish to give junior men a hard time. Rather, advantage is taken of junior men only when seniority rights are threatened. It is of special interest to note the protective reactions against the possibility that cooperation will lead to abuse. Once the protection was ensured, the men considered customer service. This recognition of the service is apparent from the fact that the crew wanted to clear the drops in the order of their importance. With defensive behavior removed, it is not uncommon for good quality solutions to emerge.

Dependence of the Solution's Quality on the Leader's Skills

The quality of group decisions can further be enhanced by improving the skills and the attitude of the discussion leader. Even with a minimum of skills the group decision approach can be effective with problems such as the following:

Setting standards on tardiness and absenteeism

Setting goals for production, quality, and service

Improving safety, housekeeping, etc.

Introducing new work procedures, changing standards, introducing labor-saving equipment, etc.

It is apparent that both quality and acceptance are needed in solving problems of this type, and for this reason they are the areas of greatest conflict in labor-management relations. However, the requirement of skill is more than methodology because it is something that cannot be decided, adopted, or purchased. It requires additional training in conference leadership, and this means an increase in a company's investment in management talents.

Conclusions

Problems may be divided into the following three types:

Type 1. Q/A problems: those for which the quality of the decision is clearly a more important objective than its acceptance. These may be successfully solved by the leader.

Type 2. A/Q problems: those for which acceptance of the decision is clearly a more important objective than its quality. These may be successfully handled by the group decision method in which the decision is made by the subordinates with the superior serving as a discussion leader.

Type 3. Q-A problems: those for which both quality and acceptance of the decision become major objectives. These problems may be handled in either of two ways, each requiring a different set of skills on the part of the leader. The alternatives are as follows:

Leader decision *plus* persuasive skills to gain acceptance or

Group decision *plus* conference leadership skills to gain quality.

The emphases in this book are on the second alternative because conference skills permit the effective use of a greater range of intellectual resources, thereby achieving high-quality decisions as a by-product.

Note

1. Taken from N. R. F. Maier, *Principles of Human Relations*, Wiley, New York, 1952.

Organizational Change Strategies and Tactics

John P. Kotter, Leonard Schlesinger, and Vijay Sathe

Solving and avoiding organizational problems inevitably involve the introduction of organizational change. When the required changes are small and isolated, they can usually be accomplished without major problems. However, when they are large and involve many people and subunits, they can often bring about significant problems.

The following scenario illustrates a common pattern in the process of organizational change:

1. Some factors in a business situation change over a period of time.

2. A number of aspects of the organization that once fit the situation and worked well no longer are appropriate.

3. Organizational problems begin to surface.

4. Managers become aware of the problems and attempt to take some corrective actions.

5. The management initiative runs into resistance.

6. The managers eventually overcome the resistance, but at a large cost to the organization (and often to themselves).

Though managers may encounter many potential problems while initiating an organizational change, the one that seems to emerge most often is related to human resistance.[1] To understand how managers can successfully manage organizational change, we must begin by examining this central problem area.

From John P. Kotter, Leonard A. Schlesinger, and Vijay Sathe, Organization: Text, Cases, and Readings on the Management of Organizational Design and Change, *2nd ed. (Homewood, Ill.: Irwin, 1986), pp. 349–362.*

[1]See Jay Lorsch, "Managing Change," in *Organizational Behavior and Administration,* ed. Paul Lawrence, Louis B. Barnes, and Jay Lorsch (Homewood, Ill.: Richard D. Irwin, 1976), pp. 669–72.

Human Resistance to Change

Human resistance to change takes many forms, from open rebellion to very subtle, passive resistance. And it emerges for many reasons—some of which are rational and some of which are not. Some reasons are primarily self-centered; others are relatively selfless.

Politics and Power Struggles

One major reason that people resist organizational change is that they see they are going to lose something of personal value as a result of the change. Resistance in these cases is often called "politics" or "political behavior," because people are focusing on their own best interests and not that of the total organization.[2]

After a number of years of rapid growth, for example, the president of one organization decided that its size demanded the creation of a new staff function—new-product planning and development—to be headed by a vice president. Operationally, this change eliminated most of the decision-making power that the vice presidents of marketing, engineering, and production had over new products. Inasmuch as new products are very important in this organization, the change also reduced the status of the marketing, engineering, and production VPs. Yet status was important to those three vice presidents. During the two months after the president announced his idea for a new-product vice president, the existing vice presidents each came up with six or seven reasons why the new arrangement might not work. Their objections grew louder and louder until the president shelved the new job idea.

In another example, a manufacturing company had traditionally employed a large group of personnel people as counselors, "father confessors," and friends to its production employees. This group of counselors exhibited high morale because of the professional satisfaction they received from the "helping" relationships they had with employees. When a new performance appraisal system was installed, the personnel people were required to provide each employee's supervisor with a written evaluation of the employee's emotional maturity, promotion potential, etc., every six months. As some of the personnel people immediately recognized, the change would alter their relationship with most employees—from a peer/friend/helper to more of a boss/evaluator. Predictably, they resisted the new system. While publicly arguing that the new system was not as good for the company as the old one, they privately put as much pressure as possible on the personnel vice president until he significantly altered the new system.

---

[2]For a discussion of power and politics in corporations, see Abraham Zaleznik and Manfred F. R. Kets De Vries, *Power and the Corporate Mind* (Boston: Houghton Mifflin, 1975), chap. 6; and Robert H. Miles, *Macro Organizational Behavior* (Santa Monica, Calif.: Goodyear Publishing, 1978), chap. 4.

Political behavior emerges in organizations because what is in the best interests of one individual or group is sometimes not in the best interests of the total organization or of other individuals and groups. The consequences of organizational change efforts often are good for some people and bad for others. As a result, politics and power struggles often emerge throughout these change efforts.

While this political behavior sometimes takes the form of two or more armed camps publicly fighting it out, it usually is much more subtle. In many cases, it occurs completely under the surface of public dialogue. In a similar way, although power struggles are sometimes initiated by scheming and ruthless individuals, they more often are fostered by those who view their potential loss as an unfair violation of their implicit, or psychological, contract with the organization.[3]

Misunderstanding and a Lack of Trust

People also resist change when they incorrectly perceive that it might cost them considerably more than they will gain. Such situations often occur when people are unable to understand the full implications of a change or when trust is lacking in the change initiator–employee relationship.[4]

For example, when the president of a small midwestern company announced to his managers that the company would implement a flexible working schedule for all employees, it had never occurred to him that he might run into resistance. He had been introduced to the concept at a management seminar and decided to use it to make working conditions at his company more attractive, particularly to clerical and plant personnel. Shortly after the announcement to his managers, numerous rumors began to circulate among plant employees—none of whom really knew what flexible working hours meant and many of whom were distrustful of the manufacturing vice president. One rumor suggested that flexible hours meant that most people would have to work whenever their supervisors asked them to—including weekends and evenings. The employee association, a local union, held a quick meeting and then presented the management with a nonnegotiable demand that the flexible hours concept be dropped. The president, caught completely by surprise, decided to drop the issue.

Few organizations can be characterized as having a high level of trust between employees and managers; consequently, it is easy for misunderstandings to develop when change is introduced. Unless misunderstandings are surfaced and clarified quickly, they can lead to resistance.

---

[3]Edgar Schein, *Organizational Psychology* (Englewood Cliffs, N.J.: Prentice-Hall, 1965), p. 44.

[4]See Chris Argyris, *Intervention Theory and Method* (Reading, Mass.: Addison-Wesley Publishing, 1970), p. 70.

Different Assessments of the Situation

Another common reason people resist organizational change is that their own analysis of the situation differs from that of those initiating the change. In such cases, their analysis typically sees more costs than benefits resulting from the change, not only for themselves but for their company as well.

For example, the president of one moderate-sized bank was shocked by his staff's analysis of their real estate investment trust (REIT) loans. Their complex analysis suggested that the bank could easily lose up to $10 million and that possible losses were increasing each month by 20 percent. Within a week, the president drew up a plan to reorganize that part of the bank that managed REITs. However, because of his concern for the bank's stock price, he chose not to release the staff report to anyone except the new REIT section manager. The reorganization immediately ran into massive resistance from the people involved. The group sentiment, as articulated by one person, was "Has he gone mad? Why in God's name is he tearing apart this section of the bank? His actions have already cost us three very good people [who quit] and have crippled a new program we were implementing [which the president was unaware of] to reduce our loan losses."

Those who initiate change sometimes incorrectly assume that they have all the relevant information required to conduct an adequate organizational analysis. Further, they often assume that those who will be affected by the change have the same basic facts, when they do not. In either case, the difference in information that groups work with often leads to differences in analysis, which in turn can lead to resistance. Moreover, insofar as the resistance is based on a more accurate analysis of the situation than that held by those initiating the change, that resistance is obviously good for the organization, a fact which is not obvious to some managers who assume that resistance is always bad.[5]

Fear

People sometimes resist change because they know or fear they will not be able to develop the new skills and behaviors required of them. All human beings are limited in their ability to change their behavior, with some people much more limited in this respect than others.[6] Organizational change can inadvertently require people to change too much, too quickly. When such a situation occurs, people typically resist the change—sometimes consciously but often unconsciously.

---

[5]See Paul R. Lawrence, "How to Deal with Resistance to Change," *Harvard Business Review*, May–June 1954.

[6]For a discussion of resistance that is personality based, see Goodwin Watson, "Resistance to Change," in *The Planning of Change*, ed. Warren Bennis, Kenneth Benne, and Robert Chin (New York: Holt, Rinehart & Winston, 1969), pp. 489–93.

Peter Drucker has argued that the major obstacle to organization growth is managers' inability to change their attitudes and their behaviors.[7] In many cases, he points out, corporations grow to a certain point and then slow down or stop growing because key managers are unable to change as rapidly as their organizations. Even if they intellectually understand the need for changes in the way they operate, they sometimes are unable to make the transition.

In a sense, all people who are affected by change experience some emotional turmoil, because change involves loss and uncertainty—even changes which appear to be positive, or "rational."[8] For example, a person who receives a significantly more important job as a result of an organizational change will probably be very happy. But it is possible that such a person feels uneasy. A new and very different job will require new and different behavior, new and different relationships, as well as the loss of some current activities and relationships that provide satisfaction. It is common under such circumstances for a person to emotionally resist giving up certain aspects of the current situation.

Still Other Reasons

People also sometimes resist organizational change to save face; to go along with the change would be, they think, an admission that some of their previous decisions or beliefs were wrong. They may resist because of peer group pressure or because of a supervisor's resistant attitude. Indeed, there are many reasons why people resist change.[9]

Because of all the possible reasons for resistance to organizational change, it is hardly surprising that organizations do not automatically and easily adapt to environmental or technological or strategic changes. Indeed, organizations usually adapt only because managers successfully employ strategies and tactics for dealing with potential resistance.

Tactics for Dealing with Resistance

Managers may use a number of tactics to deal with resistance to change. These include education/communication, participation, facilitation and support, negotiation, co-optation, coercion, and manipulation.[10]

---

[7] *The Practice of Management* (New York: Harper & Row, 1954).

[8] See Robert Luke, "A Structural Approach to Organizational Change," *Journal of Applied Behavioral Science,* 1973.

[9] For a general discussion of resistance and reasons for it, see Gerald Zaltman and Robert Duncan, *Strategies for Planned Change* (New York: John Wiley & Sons, 1977), chap. 3.

[10] Conceptually, there are a number of ways that one can label change tactics. This list of seven tactics is one useful approach. Other writers on this subject have used different variations on that list.

Education/Communication

One of the most commonly used ways of dealing with resistance to change is education and communication. This tactic is aimed at helping people see the need for the logic of a change. It can involve one-on-one discussions, presentations to groups, or memos and reports. For example, as a part of an effort to make changes in a division's structure, measurement system, and reward system, the division manager put together a one-hour audiovisual presentation that explained the changes and the reasons for the changes. Over a four-month period, he made this presentation no less than a dozen times to groups of 20 or 30 corporate and divisional managers.

Education/communication can be ideal when resistance is based on inadequate or inaccurate information and analysis, especially if the initiators need the resister's help in implementing the change. But this tactic requires at least a minimally good relationship between the initiators and the others, or the resisters may not believe what they hear. It also requires time and effort, particularly if a lot of people are involved.

Participation

Participation as a change tactic implies that the initiators involve the resisters or potential resisters in some aspect of the design and implementation of the change. For example, the head of a small financial services company once created a task force to help design and implement changes in the company's reward system. The task force was composed of eight second- and third-level managers from different parts of the company. The president's specific request to them was that they recommend changes in the company's benefits package. They were given six months and were asked to file a brief progress report with the president once a month. After making their recommendations, which the president largely accepted, they were asked to help the firm's personnel director implement them.

Participation is a rational choice of tactics when change initiators believe they do not have all the information they need to design and implement a change or when they need the wholehearted commitment of others in implementing a change. Considerable research has demonstrated that participation generally leads to commitment, not just compliance.[11] But participation does have its drawbacks. Not only can it lead to a poor solution if the process is not carefully managed, but it also can be enormously time consuming.

---

[11]See, for example, Alfred Marrow, David Bowers, and Stanley Seashore, *Management by Participation* (New York: Harper & Row, 1967).

Facilitation and Support

Another way in which managers can deal with potential resistance to change is through facilitation and support. As a tactic, it might include providing training in new skills, giving employees time off after a demanding period, or simply listening and providing emotional support.

For example, one rapidly growing electronics company did the following to help people adjust to frequent organizational changes. First, it staffed its human resource department with four counselors, who spent most of their time talking to people who were feeling "burned out" or who were having difficulty adjusting to new jobs. Second, on a selective basis, it offered people "minisabbaticals," which were four weeks in duration and which involved some reflective or educational activity away from work. And finally, it spent a great deal of money on education and training programs conducted in-house.

Facilitation and support are best suited for resistance due to adjustment problems. The basic drawback of this approach is that it can be time consuming and expensive, and still fail.[12]

Negotiation

Negotiation as a change tactic essentially involves buying out active or potential resisters. This could mean, for example, giving a union a higher wage rate in return for a work rule change, or it could involve increasing an individual's pension benefits in return for an early retirement.

Effective use of negotiation as a change tactic can be seen in the activities of a division manager in a large manufacturing company. The divisions in this company were very interdependent. One division manager wanted to make some major changes in the division's organization. Yet, because of interdependencies, she recognized that she would be forcing some inconvenience and change on other divisions. To prevent top managers in other divisions from undermining her efforts, she negotiated with each division a written agreement that promised certain positive outcomes (for them) within certain time periods as a result of her changes and, in return, specified certain types of cooperation expected from the divisions during the change process. Later, whenever other divisions began to complain about the changes or the change process itself, she pulled out the negotiated agreements.

Negotiation is particularly appropriate when it is clear that someone is going to lose out as a result of a change and yet has significant power to resist. As a result, it can be a relatively easy way to avoid major resistance in some instances. Like the other tactics, negotiation may become expensive—and a

---

[12]Zaltman and Duncan, *Strategies for Planned Change*, chap. 4.

manager who once makes it clear that he or she will negotiate to avoid resistance opens up the possibility of being blackmailed by others.[13]

Co-optation

A fifth tactic managers use to deal with potential or actual resistance to change is co-optation. Co-opting an individual usually involves giving him or her a desirable role in the design or implementation of the change. Co-opting a group involves giving one of its leaders, or someone it respects, a key role in the design or implementation of a change. A change initiator could, for example, try to co-opt the sales force by allowing the sales manager to be privy to the design of the changes and by seeing that the most popular salesperson gets a raise as part of the change.

To reduce the possibility of corporate resistance to an organizational change, one division manager in a large multibusiness corporation successfully used co-optation in the following way. He invited the corporate human relations vice president, a close friend of the president's, to help him and his key staff analyze some problems the division was having. Because of his busy schedule, the corporate VP was not able to do much of the actual information gathering or analysis himself, thus limiting his own influence on the diagnoses. But his presence at key meetings helped commit him to the diagnosis and the solution the group designed. The commitment was subsequently very important because the president, at least initially, did not like some of the proposed changes. Nevertheless, after discussion with his human resource VP, he did not try to block them.

Co-optation can, under certain circumstances, be a relatively inexpensive and easy way to gain an individual's or a group's support (less expensive, for example, than negotiation and quicker than participation). Nevertheless, it has its drawbacks. If people feel they are being tricked into not resisting, they obviously may respond negatively. And if they use their ability to influence the design and implementation of changes in ways that are not in the best interests of the organization, they can obviously create serious problems.

Manipulation

Manipulation, in this context, refers to covert influence attempts. In a sense, therefore, co-optation is a form of manipulation. Other forms do not have specific names but involve, for instance, the selective use of information and the conscious structuring of events so as to have some desired (but covert) impact on the participants.

---

[13]For an excellent discussion of negotiation, see Gerald Nierenberg, *The Art of Negotiating* (New York: Cornerstone, 1974).

Manipulation suffers from the same drawbacks as co-optation, but to an even greater degree. When people feel they are not being treated openly or that they are being lied to, they often react negatively. Nevertheless, manipulation can be used successfully—particularly when all other tactics are not feasible or have failed.[14] With one's back to the wall, with inadequate time to use education, participation, or facilitation, and without the power or other resources to use negotiation, coercion, or co-optation, a manager might resort to manipulating information channels to scare people into thinking there is a crisis coming which they can avoid only by change.

Coercion

The seventh tactic managers use to deal with resistance is coercion. Here they essentially force people to accept a change, explicitly or implicitly threatening them with the loss of jobs or promotion possibilities or raises or whatever else they control. Like manipulation, coercion is a risky tactic because people strongly resent forced change. Yet coercion has the advantage of overcoming resistance very quickly. And in situations where speed is essential, this tactic may be one's only alternative.

For example, when assigned to "turn around" a failing division in a large conglomerate, the chosen manager relied mostly on coercion to achieve the organizational changes she desired. She did so because she felt, "I did not have enough time to use other methods, and I needed to make changes that were pretty unpopular among many of the people."

Using Change Tactics

Effective organizational change efforts are almost always characterized by the skillful use of a number of these change tactics. Conversely, less effective change efforts usually involve the misuse of one or more of these tactics.

Managers sometimes misuse change tactics simply because they are unaware of the strengths and limitations of each tactic (see Figure 7–1). Sometimes they run into difficulties because they rely only on the same limited number of tactics regardless of the situation (e.g., they always use participation and persuasion, or coercion and manipulation).[15] Sometimes they misuse the tactics simply because they are not chosen and implemented as a part of a clearly considered change strategy.

---

[14]See John P. Kotter, "Power, Dependence, and Effective Management," *Harvard Business Review*, July–August 1977, pp. 133–35.

[15]Ibid., pp. 135–36.

FIGURE 7–1 TACTICS FOR DEALING WITH RESISTANCE TO CHANGE

Tactic	Best for:	Advantages	Drawbacks
Education/ communication	Resistance based on lack of information or inaccurate information and analysis.	Once persuaded, people will often help with the implementation of the change.	Can be very time consuming if large numbers of people are involved.
Participation	Situations in which initiators do not have all the information needed to design the change and where others have considerable power to resist.	People who participate will be committed to implementing change. And any relevant information they have will be integrated into the change plan.	Can be very time consuming. Participators could design an inappropriate change.
Facilitation and support	Dealing with people who are resisting because of adjustment problems.	No other tactic works as well with adjustment problems.	Can be time consuming, expensive, and still fail.
Negotiation	Situations where someone or some group will clearly lose out in a change and where they have considerable power to resist.	Sometimes is a relatively easy way to avoid major resistance.	Can be too expensive in many cases. Can alert others to negotiate for compliance.
Co-optation	Very specific situations where the other tactics are too expensive or are infeasible.	Can help generate support for implementing a change (but less than participation).	Can create problems if people recognize the co-optation.
Manipulation	Situations where other tactics will not work or are too expensive.	Can be a relatively quick and inexpensive solution to resistance problems.	Costs initiators some of their credibility. Can lead to future problems.
Coercion	When speed is essential and the change initiators possess considerable power.	Speed. Can overcome any kind of resistance.	Risky. Can leave people angry with the initiators.

hange Strategies

In approaching an organizational change situation, managers explicitly or implicitly make strategic choices regarding the speed of the effort, the amount of preplanning, the involvement of others, and the relative emphasis of different change tactics. Successful change efforts seem to be those in which these choices both are internally consistent and fit some key situation variables.

The strategic options available to managers can be usefully thought of as existing on a continuum (see Figure 7–2).[16] At one end of the continuum, the strategy calls for a very rapid implementation of changes, with a clear plan of action and little involvement of others. This type of strategy mows over any resistance and, at the extreme, would involve a fait accompli. At the other end of the continuum, the strategy would call for a much slower change process that is less clearly planned from the start and that involves many people in addition to the change initiators. This type of strategy is designed to reduce resistance to a minimum.[17]

With respect to tactics, the farther to the left one operates on the continuum in Figure 7–2, the more one tends to use coercion and the less one tends to use the other tactics—especially participation. The opposite is true the more one operates to the right on the continuum—the less coercion tends to be used and the more the other tactics tend to be used.

Exactly where a change effort should be strategically positioned on the continuum in Figure 7–2 seems to be a function of four key variables.

1. *The amount and type of resistance that is anticipated.* The greater the anticipated resistance, other factors being equal, the more appropriate it is to move toward the right on the continuum.[18] The greater the anticipated resistance, the more difficult it is to simply overwhelm it and the more one needs to find ways to reduce some of it.

2. *The position of the initiator vis-à-vis the resisters, especially with regard to power.* The greater the initiator's power, the better the initiator's relationships with the others; and the more the others expect that the initiator might move unilaterally, the more one can move to the left on the continuum.[19] On the other hand, the weaker the initiator's position, the more he or she is forced to operate to the right.

3. *The locus of relevant data for designing the change and of needed energy for implementing it.* The more the initiators anticipate they will need

---

[16]See Larry E. Greiner, "Patterns of Organizational Change," *Harvard Business Review,* May–June 1967; and Larry E. Greiner and Louis B. Barnes, "Organizational Change and Development," in *Organization Change and Development,* ed. Gene Dalton and Paul Lawrence (Homewood, Ill.: Richard D. Irwin, 1970), pp. 3–5.

[17]For a good discussion of an approach that attempts to minimize resistance, see Renato Tagiuri, "Notes on the Management of Change," Working Paper, Harvard Business School.

[18]Jay Lorsch, "Managing Change," pp. 676–78.

[19]Ibid.

FIGURE 7-2   STRATEGIC OPTIONS FOR THE MANAGEMENT OF CHANGE

Rapid changes	Slow changes
Clearly planned	Not clearly planned initially
Little involvement of others	Lots of involvement of others
Attempt to overcome any resistance	Attempt to minimize any resistance

Key Situational Variables

- The amount and type of resistance that is anticipated.
- The position of the initiators vis-á-vis the resisters (in terms of power, trust, etc.)
- The locus of relevant data for designing the change and of needed energy for implementing it.
- The stakes involved (e.g., the presence or absence of a crisis, the consequences of resistance and lack of change)

---

information from others to help design the change and commitment from them to help implement it, the more they must move to the right.[20] Gaining useful information and commitment requires time and the involvement of others.

4. *The stakes involved.* The greater the short-run potential for risks to organizational performance and survival, the more one must move to the left.

Organizational change efforts that are based on an inconsistent strategy, or ones that do not fit the situation, tend to run into predictable problems. For example, an effort that is not clearly planned but is quickly implemented will almost always run into unanticipated problems. Efforts that attempt to involve large numbers of people and at the same time try to move quickly will virtually always end up sacrificing either speed or involvement. Efforts in which the change initiators do not have all the information they need to correctly design a change but which nevertheless move quickly and involve few others sometimes encounter enormous problems.

Implications for Managing Organizational Change

Organizational change efforts can be greatly aided by an analysis and planning process composed of the following three phrases:

---

[20]Ibid.

1. Conducting a thorough organizational analysis—one which identifies the current situation, any problems, and the forces which are possible causes of those problems. The analysis must clearly specify:

   a. The actual significance of the problems.

   b. The speed with which the problems must be addressed if additional problems are to be avoided.

   c. The types of changes that are generally needed.

2. Conducting a thorough analysis of factors relevant to implementing the necessary changes. This analysis focuses on questions of:

   a. Who might resist the changes, why, and to what extent.

   b. Who has information that is needed to design the change and whose cooperation is essential in implementing it.

   c. The position of the change initiator vis-à-vis other relevant parties in terms of power, trust, and normal modes of interaction, etc.

3. Selecting a change strategy based on the analysis in Phases 1 and 2, and a set of change tactics, and then designing an action plan that specifies:

   a. What must be done.

   b. By whom.

   c. In what sequence.

   d. And within what time frame.

When initiating and managing an organizational change, it is conceivable that some or all of these steps will need to be repeated if unforeseen events occur or if new and relevant information surfaces. At the extreme, in a highly participative change, the process might be repeated a dozen times over a period of months or years. The key to successful organizational change is not whether these steps are repeated once or many times but whether they are done competently and thoroughly.

References

Adams, W. Clifton, 1972. The interrelationship among need for social approval, persuasibility, and activation. *Central States Speech Journal* **23:** 188–192.

Adler, Alfred, 1956. *The individual psychology of Alfred Adler.* Heinz and Rowena Ansbacher (eds.). New York: Basic Books.

——, 1964. *Superiority and social interest by Alfred Adler.* Heinz and Rowena Ansbacher (eds.). Evanston, Ill.: Northwestern University Press.

Adorno, T. W., Else Frenkel-Brunswik, Daniel Levinson, and R. Nevitt Sanford, 1950. *The authoritarian personality.* New York: Harper & Row.

Albanese, Robert, and David VanFleet, 1985. Rational behavior in groups: the free-riding tendency. *The Academy of Management Review* **11:** 244–255.

Alexander, David C., 1988. Managing technical change. In Klaus M. Blache. *Success factors for implementing change.* Dearborn, Mich.: Society of Manufacturing Engineers.

Allport, Floyd, 1924. *Social psychology.* Boston: Houghton Mifflin.

Allport, Gordon W., 1967. Attitudes. In Martin Fishbein (ed.). *Readings in attitude theory and measurement.* New York: Wiley, pp. 3–13.

Altman, Irwin, 1975. *The environment and social behavior.* Monterey, Calif.: Brooks/Cole.

Ancona, Deborah Gladstein, 1990. Outward bound: strategies for team survival in an organization. *Academy of Management Journal* **33:** No. 2, 334–365.

Applbaum, Ronald, Edward Bodaken, Kenneth Sereno, and Karl Anatol, 1974. *The process of group communication.* Palo Alto, Calif.: Science Research Associates.

Argyle, Michael, 1967. *The psychology of interpersonal behavior.* Baltimore: Penguin.

——, and J. Dean, 1965. Eye-contact, distance, and affiliation. *Sociometry* **23:** 289–304.

Argyris, Chris, 1962. *Interpersonal competence and organizational effectiveness.* Homewood, Ill.: Irwin.

Aronoff, Joel, and Lawrence A. Messe, 1971. Motivational determinants of small-group structure. *Journal of Personality and Social Psychology* **17:** 319–324.

Aronson, Elliot, 1984. Characteristics of effective feedback. In Robert S. Cathcart and Larry Samovar. *Small group communication: a reader* (4th ed.). Dubuque, Iowa: Wm. C. Brown, pp. 336–341.

———, 1973. The rationalizing animal. *Psychology Today* **6:** 46–52.

———, and Judson Mills, 1959. Effect of severity of initiation on liking for a group. *Journal of Abnormal and Social Psychology* **59:** 177–181.

Asch, Solomon, 1952. *Social psychology.* Englewood Cliffs, N.J.: Prentice-Hall.

———, 1955. Opinions and social pressure. *Scientific American* **193:** 31–35.

———, 1956. Studies of independence and conformity: a minority of one against a unanimous majority. *Psychological Monographs* **70:** No. 9 (Whole No. 416).

Associated Press, 1990. Bay area delivers flood of "quake babies." *Ann Arbor News,* July 12: A1.

Associated Press, 1990. City manages to get itself out of a (man) hole. *Ann Arbor News,* June 23: A2.

Atkinson, John W., 1966. Notes concerning the generality of the theory of achievement motivation. In John W. Atkinson and Norman T. Feather (eds.). *A theory of achievement motivation.* New York: Appleton-Century-Crofts, pp. 163–168.

Avianca pilots not trained to say "fuel emergency," 1990. *Detroit Free Press,* June 23: 4A.

Bach, George, and Peter Wyden, 1968. *The intimate enemy.* New York: Morrow.

Bales, Robert F., 1950. *Interaction process analysis.* Reading, Mass.: Addison-Wesley.

———, 1954. In conference. *Harvard Business Review* **32:** 44–50.

———, 1970. *Personality and interpersonal behavior.* New York: Holt, Rinehart and Winston.

———, and Fred Strodbeck, 1951. Phases in group solving. *Journal of Abnormal and Social Psychology* **46:** 485–495.

Ballen, Kate, 1988. The no. 1 leader is Petersen of Ford. *Fortune,* October 24: 69–70.

Barnlund, Dean, 1962. Consistency of emergent leadership in groups with changing tasks and members. *Speech Monographs* **29:** 45–52.

———, 1968. *Interpersonal communication: survey and studies.* Boston: Houghton Mifflin.

———, and Franklyn Haiman, 1959. *The dynamics of discussion.* Boston: Houghton Mifflin.

Barol, Bill, 1990. Anatomy of a fad. *Newsweek,* September: 40–41.

Barrett, Marty W., and Thomas A. Carey, 1989. Communicating strategy: the best investment a CEO can make. *Mid-American Journal of Business* **4:** No. 1, 3–6.

Bass, B., C. Wurster, P. Doll, and D. Clair, 1953. Situational and personality factors in leadership among sorority women. *Psychological Monographs* **67:** No. 16 (Whole No. 366).

Bass, Bernard M., 1983. *Organizational decision making.* Homewood, Ill.: Richard D. Irwin.

Batchelor, James, and George Goethals, 1972. Spatial arrangements in freely formed groups. *Sociometry* **35:** 270–279.

Bauduin, E. Scott, 1971. Obscene language and source credibility: an experimental study. Paper presented at the annual conference of the International Communication Association. Phoenix, Arizona.

Bay, Christian, 1967. Political and apolitical students: facts in search of a theory. *Journal of Social Issues* **23:** 76–91.

Beck, Joan, 1990. 2 Live Crew is more offensive than obscene. *Detroit Free Press,* June 25: 7A.

Beckhard, Richard, 1961. The confrontation meeting. In Warren Bennis, Kenneth Benne, and Robert Chin (eds.). *The planning of change.* New York: Holt, Rinehart and Winston, pp. 478–485.

Beebe, Paul, 1986. Going in circles. *The Idaho Statesman,* May 11.

Beebe, Steven A., and John T. Materson, 1986. *Communicating in small groups* (2nd ed.). Glenview, Ill.: Scott, Foresman.

Benne, Kenneth D., and Paul Sheats, 1948. Functional roles of group members. *Journal of Social Issues* **4:** 41–49.

Bennis, Warren, 1961. Interpersonal communication. In Warren Bennis, Kenneth Benne, and Robert Chin (eds.), *The planning of change.* New York: Holt, Rinehart and Winston.

———, and Herbert Shepard, 1948. A theory of group development. *Human Relations* **1:** 314–320.

———, and Herbert Shepard, 1961. Group observation. In Warren Bennis, Kenneth Benne, and Robert Chin (eds.). *The planning of change.* New York: Holt, Rinehart and Winston, pp. 743–756.

———, and Burt Nanus, 1985. *Leaders: the strategies for taking charge.* New York: Harper & Row.

———, Edgar Schein, Fred Steele, and David Berlew, 1968. Personal change through interpersonal relationships. In *Interpersonal dynamics: essays and readings on human interaction.* Homewood, Ill.: Dorsey, pp. 333–369.

Berelson, Bernard, and Gary Steiner, 1964. *Human behavior: an inventory of scientific findings.* New York: Harcourt, Brace and World.

Berg, David, 1967. A descriptive analysis of the distribution and duration of themes discussed by task-oriented small groups. *Speech Monographs* **34:** 172–175.

Berg, I. A., and B. Bass (eds.), 1961. *Conformity and deviation.* New York: Harper & Row.

Berne, Eric, 1964. *Games people play.* New York: Grove.

Bilodeau, J., and H. Schlosberg, 1959. Similarity in stimulating conditions as a variable in retroactive inhibition. *Journal of Experimental Psychology* **41:** 199–204.

Bird, G., 1940. *Social psychology.* New York: Appleton-Century-Crofts.

Bird, Lee, 1974. The Nixon years. *Flint Journal,* August 18:D1–D2.

Bittel, Lester R., 1956. Brainstorming. *Factory Management and Maintenance* **114:** 107.

Blache, Klaus M., 1988. What does it all mean? In Klaus M. Blache. *Success factors for implementing change.* Dearborn, Mich.: Society of Manufacturing Engineers.

Blair, Gwenda, 1988. *Almost golden: Jessica Savitch and the selling of television news.* New York: Simon and Schuster.

Blake, Robert, and Jane Mouton, 1970. The fifth achievement. *Journal of Applied Behavioral Sciences* **6:** 413–426.

Bloom, Benjamin S., and Lois J. Broder, 1961. Problem-solving processes of college students. In Theodore L. Harris and Wilson E. Schwahn (eds.). *Selected readings in the learning process.* New York: Oxford University Press, pp. 31–79.

Blotnick, Srully, 1986. Survey: women say affairs of the heart thrive at workplace. *The Idaho Statesman,* March 19: 2.

Borisoff, Deborah, and David A. Victor, 1989. *Conflict management: a communication skills approach.* Englewood Cliffs, N. J.: Prentice-Hall.

Bormann, Ernest, 1969. *Discussion and group methods.* New York: Harper & Row.

———, 1970. The paradox and promise of small group research. *Speech Monographs* **37:** 211–216.

Bostrom, Robert, 1970. Patterns of communicative interaction in small groups. *Speech Monographs* **37:** 257–263.

———, and Charles Rossiter, 1969. Profanity, justification, and source credibility. Paper presented at the annual conference of the International Communication Association, Cleveland, Ohio.

Bowers, D. G., and S. E. Seashore, 1966. Predicting organizational effectiveness with a four factor theory of leadership. *Administrative Science Quarterly*, pp. 238–265.

Bradford, David L., and Allan R. Cohen, 1984. *Managing for excellence: the guide to developing high performance in contemporary organizations.* New York: Wiley.

Bradley-Steck, Tara, 1987. High overhead: tall and thin executives receive fatter paychecks, university study reports. *Ann Arbor News*, March 3: A1.

Braybrooke, David, and Charles E. Lindblom, 1963. *A strategy of decision.* New York: Free Press.

Brilhart, John K., and Gloria J. Galanes, 1989. *Effective group discussion* (6th ed). Dubuque, Iowa: Wm. C. Brown Publications.

Brock, A. J. (trans.), 1952. Galen, on the natural faculties. In R. M. Hutchins (ed.). *Great books of the western world.* Chicago: Encyclopaedia Britannica **10:** 163–215.

Brockner, Joel, and Ted Hess, 1986. Self-esteem and task performance in quality circles. *Academy of Management Journal* **29:** 617–623.

Brodwin, D. R., and L. J. Bourgeois, 1984. Five steps to strategic action. In G. Carroll and D. Vogel (eds.). *Strategy and organization: A West Coast perspective.* Boston: Pitman, pp. 167–181.

Brown, Roger, 1965. *Social psychology.* New York: Free Press.

Brown, V., and Florence L. Geis, 1984. Turning lead into gold: evaluations of men and women leaders and the alchemy of social consensus. *Journal of Personality and Social Psychology* **46:** 811–824.

Bruskin, R. H., 1973. Fear. Reported in *Spectra* **9:** 4.

Buchholz, Steve, 1985. *The positive manager.* New York: Wiley.

Bunker, Douglas, 1965. Individual applications of laboratory training. *Journal of Applied Behavioral Science* **1:** 131–147.

Burgoon, Michael, 1971(a). Amount of conflicting information in a group discussion and tolerance for ambiguity as predictors of task attractiveness. *Speech Monographs* **38:** 121–124.

———, 1971(b). The relationship between willingness to manipulate others and success in two different types of basic speech communication courses. *Speech Teacher* **19:** 178–183.

———, Gerald R. Miller, and Stewart L. Tubbs, 1972. Machiavellianism, justification, and attitude change following counterattitudinal advocacy. *Journal of Personality and Social Psychology* **22:** 366–371.

Burke, Richard, and Warren Bennis, 1961. Changes in perception of self and others during human relations training. *Human Relations* **14:** 165–182.

Butler, Dore, and Florence L. Geis, 1990. Nonverbal affect responses to male and female leaders: implications for leadership evaluations. *Journal of Personality and Social Psychology* **58:** No. 1, 48–59.

Bynner, Witter (trans.), 1944. *The way of life according to Lao-tzu.* New York: John Day, Saying 17.

Byrd, Lee, 1989. Who to blame in Washington for everything: committees. *Ann Arbor News*, December 8: B1, B2.

Cahn, Dudley D., and Stewart L. Tubbs, 1983. Management as communication: performance evaluation and employee self worth. *Communication*, December, pp. 46–54.

Camp, Richard, P. Nick Blanchard, and Gregory E. Huszczo, 1986. *Toward a more organizationally effective training strategy & practice.* Englewood Cliffs, N.J.: Prentice-Hall.

Campbell, John, and Marvin Dunnette, 1968. Effectiveness of T-group experiences in managerial training and development. *Psychological Bulletin* **70:** 73–104.

Cartwright, Dorwin, and Alvin Zander, 1953. *Group dynamics: research and theory.* New York: Harper & Row.

———, 1968. The nature of group cohesiveness. In D. Cartwright and A. Zander (eds.). *Group dynamics* (3rd ed.). New York: Harper & Row, pp. 91–109.

Cathart, Robert S., and Larry A. Samovar, 1988. *Small group communication.* (5th ed.). Dubuque, Iowa: Wm. C. Brown.

Champness, Brian, 1969. Communication: what's in a glance? *Time,* October 17: 74.

Christie, Richard, and Florence L. Geis, 1970. *Studies in Machiavellianism.* New York: Academic Press.

Cissna, Kenneth, 1976. Interpersonal confirmation: a review of current theory and research. A paper presented at the annual convention of the Central States Speech Association, Chicago, April.

Clark, Russell III, 1971. Group induced shift toward risk: a critical appraisal. *Psychological Bulletin* **76:** 251–270.

Cocks, Jay, 1990. Let's get crazy. *Time,* June 11: 40–41.

Collins, Barry, and Harold Guetzkow, 1964. *A social psychology of group processes for decision making.* New York: Wiley.

Conger, Jay A., 1989. Leadership: the art of empowering others. *The Academy of Management Executive* **3:** No. 1, 17–24.

Cooley, Charles, 1918. *Social process.* New York: Scribner's.

Cooper, Gary, and Iain Mongham, 1971. *T-groups: a survey of research.* New York: Wiley-Interscience.

Cosier, Richard A., and Charles R. Schwenk, 1990. Agreement and thinking alike: ingredients for poor decisions. *Academy of Management Executive* **4:** No. 1, 69–74.

Couch, A., and K. Keniston, 1960. Yeasayers and naysayers: agreeing response set as a personality variable. *Journal of Abnormal and Social Psychology* **60:** 151–174.

Courtright, John A., Gail T. Fairhurst, and L. Edna Rogers, 1989. Interaction patterns in organic and mechanistic systems. *Academy of Management Journal* **32:** No. 4, 773–802.

Cousins, Norman, 1980. *Anatomy of an illness.* New York: Norton.

Crane, Loren, Richard Dieker, and Charles Brown, 1970. The physiological response to the communication modes: reading, listening, writing, speaking, and evaluating. *Journal of Communication* **20:** 231–240.

Crockett, Walter H., and Thomas Meidinger, 1956. Authoritarianism and interpersonal perception. *Journal of Abnormal and Social Psychology* **53:** 378–380.

Crowne, D. P., and D. Marlowe, 1964. *The approval motive.* New York: Wiley.

Crutchfield, Richard, 1959. Personal and situational factors in conformity to group pressure. *Acta Psychologica* **15:** 386–388.

Culbert, Samuel A., 1968. *The interpersonal process of self-disclosure: it takes two to see one.* New York: Renaissance Editions.

Cushman, Donald P., and Dudley D. Cahn, 1985. *Communication in interpersonal relationships.* Albany, N.Y. SUNY Press.

Cyert, R. M., and J. G. March, 1963. *A behavioral theory of the firm.* Englewood Cliffs, N.J.: Prentice-Hall.

Dance, Frank E. X., 1972. The centrality of the spoken word. *Central States Speech Journal* **23:** 197–201.

———, and Carl E. Larson, 1972. *Speech communication: concepts and behavior*. New York: Holt, Rinehart and Winston.

Davis, Lisa J., 1990. Fernco, employees utilize Japanese-style openness. *The Flint Journal*, February 5: D6.

Davis, Sammy Jr., and Jane and Burt Boyar, 1989. *The Sammy Davis, Jr. story: why me?* New York: Warner Books.

Delbecq, André L., Andrew H. Van de Ven, and David H. Gustafson, 1975. *Group techniques for program planning: a guide to nominal group and Delphi processes*. Glenview, Ill.: Scott, Foresman.

DePree, Max, 1989. *Leadership is an art*. New York: Doubleday Publishing Group.

Deutsch, Morton, 1969. Conflicts: productive and destructive. *Journal of Social Issues* **25:** 7–43.

———, 1971. Toward an understanding of conflict. *International Journal of Group Tensions* **1:** 42–55.

———, and Leonard Solomon, 1959. Reaction to evaluations by others as influenced by self-evaluations. *Sociometry:* 93–111.

Dewey, John, 1910. *How we think*. New York: Heath.

Dill, W. R., 1965. *Decision making: sixty-third yearbook of the National Society for the Study of Education, Behavioral Science and Educational Administration:* 200–202.

Drucker, Peter, 1990. The emerging theory of manufacturing. *Harvard Business Review*, May–June: 94–102.

Dumaine, Brian, 1990. Who needs a boss? *Fortune*, May 7: 52–60.

Dunegan, Kenneth J., and Dennis Duchon, 1989. Gender, task complexity and risk taking: catch 22 for women. *Mid-American Journal of Business* **4:** No. 1, 23–32.

Dyer, William G., 1985. *Team building: issues and alternatives* (2nd ed.). Reading, Mass.: Addison-Wesley.

Eakins, Barbara W., and R. Gene Eakins, 1978. *Sex differences in human communication*. Boston: Houghton Mifflin.

Edwards, Allen, 1953. *The Edwards personal preference schedule*. New York: Psychological Corporation.

———, and L. E. Acker, 1962. A demonstration of the long-term retention of a conditioned galvanic skin response. *Psychosomatic Medicine* **24:** 459–463.

Egan, Gerard, 1973. *Face to face: the small group experience and interpersonal growth*. Monterey, Calif.: Brooks/Cole.

Ehninger, Douglas, and Wayne Brocriede, 1963. *Decision by debate*. New York: Dodd, Mead.

Ehrlich, H. J., and Dorothy Lee, 1969. Dogmatism, learning, and resistance to change: a review and a new paradigm. *Psychological Bulletin* **71:** 249–260.

Eisenberg, Eric M., 1984. Ambiguity as strategy in organizational communication. *Communication Monographs* **51:** 227–239.

Eisenberg, Eric M., and Marsha G. Witten, 1987. Reconsidering openness in organizational communication. *Academy of Management Review* **12:** No. 3, 418–426.

Etzioni, Amatai, 1964. *Modern organizations*. Englewood Cliffs, N.J.: Prentice-Hall.

———, 1968. *The active society*. New York: Free Press.

Ewbank, Henry, and Jeffrey Auer, 1946. *Discussion and debate*. New York: Crofts.

Exline, Ralph, John Thibaut, Carole Hickey, and Peter Gumpert, 1970. Visual interaction in relation to Machiavellianism and an unethical act. In Richard Christie and Florence L. Geis. *Studies in Machiavellianism*. New York: Academic Press, pp. 53–75.

Faris, Ellsworth, 1932. The primary group: essence and accident. *American Journal of Sociology* **28:** 41–50.

Feinstein, Selwyn, 1990. Labor letter. *The Wall Street Journal,* July 10: A1.

Festinger, Leon, 1954. A theory of social comparison processes. *Human Relations* **7:** 117–140.

———, 1957. *A theory of cognitive dissonance.* Stanford, Calif.: Stanford University Press.

———, and Elliot Aronson, 1968. Arousal and reduction of dissonance in social contexts. In Dorwin Cartwright and Alvin Zander (eds.). *Group dynamics: research and theory* (3rd ed.). New York: Harper & Row, pp. 125–136.

Fiedler, F. E., 1958. *Leader attitudes and group effectiveness.* Urbana: University of Illinois Press.

Fiedler, Fred, 1967. *A theory of leadership effectiveness.* New York: McGraw-Hill.

———, and Martin Chemers, 1974. *Leadership and effective management.* Glenview, Ill.: Scott, Foresman.

Filley, Alan C., 1975. *Interpersonal conflict resolution.* Glenview, Ill.: Scott, Foresman.

Fisher, B. Aubrey, 1970. Decision emergence: phases in group decision making. *Speech Monographs* **37:** 53–66.

———, 1974. *Small group decision making: communication and the group process.* New York: McGraw-Hill.

———, and Leonard C. Hawes, 1971. An interact system model: generating a grounded theory of small groups. *Quarterly Journal of Speech* **57:** 444–453.

———, 1980. *Small group decision making* (2nd ed.). New York: McGraw-Hill.

Fisher, James L., and Marthy W. Tack, 1990. The effective college president. *Educational Record,* Winter: 6–10.

Fisher, Roger, and Scott Brown, 1988. *Getting together.* Boston: Houghton-Mifflin.

———, and William Ury, 1981. *Getting to yes.* Boston: Houghton-Mifflin.

Fiske, Edward, 1990. Of learning and college: how small groups thrive. *The New York Times,* March 5: A1.

Folger, Joseph P., and Marshall Scott Poole, 1984. *Working through conflict: a communication perspective* Glenview, Ill.: Scott, Foresman.

Following the leader: sometimes it's folly to go along with the boss, 1985. *Science,* October 18.

Footlick, Jerrold K., 1990. What happened to the family? *Newsweek,* Winter/Spring: 15–20.

Fox, William, 1987. *Effective group problem solving.* San Francisco: Jossey-Bass.

Franecki, Dennis J., Ralph F. Catalanello, and Curtiss K. Behrens, 1984. Employee committees: what effect are they having? *Personnel,* July–August: 67–73.

French, John, and Bertram Raven, 1959. The bases of social power. In Dorwin Cartwright (ed.). *Studies in social power.* Ann Arbor: Institute for Social Research, pp. 150–167.

Freud, Sigmund, 1960. The psychopathology of everyday life. In the *Complete Works,* Vol. 6. London: Hogarth Press.

Ganeen, Harold, and Alvin Moscow, 1984. *Managing.* Garden City, N.Y.: Doubleday.

Gardner, Eric, and George Thompson, 1956. *Social relations and morale in small groups.* New York: Appleton-Century-Crofts.

Gardner, John W., 1990. *On leadership.* New York: The Free Press.

Geier, John, 1967. A trait approach to the study of leadership. *Journal of Communication* **17:** 316–323.

Gelman, David, 1990. A much riskier passage. *Newsweek,* September: 10–17.

Gersick, Connie J. G., 1988. Time and transition in work teams: toward a new model of group development. *Academy of Management Journal* **31:** No. 1, 9–41.

Gibb, Jack, 1961. Defensive communication. *Journal of Communication* **11:** 141–148.

Gibson, Jane Whitney, and Richard M. Hodgetts, 1986. *Organizational communication: a managerial perspective.* New York: Academic Press.

Giffin, Kim, and Kendall Bradley, 1969. Group counseling for speech anxiety: an approach and rationale. *Journal of Communication* **19:** 22–29.

——, and Shirley Masterson Gilham, 1971. Relationship between speech anxiety and motivation. *Speech Monographs* **38:** 70–73.

——, and Bobby Patton, 1974. *Personal communication in human relations.* Columbus, Ohio: Charles Merrill.

Goffman, Erving, 1961. *Encounters.* Indianapolis: Bobbs-Merrill.

Goldberg, Alvin, and Carl Larson, 1975. *Group communication.* Englewood Cliffs, N.J.: Prentice-Hall.

Goldhaber, Gerald, 1971. Communication and student unrest. Unpublished report to the president of the University of New Mexico.

——, 1990. *Organizational communication* (5th ed.). Dubuque, Iowa: Wm. C. Brown.

—— et al., 1979. *Information strategies: new pathways to corporate power.* Englewood Cliffs, N.J.: Prentice-Hall.

Goldhamer, E., and E. Shils, 1939. Types of power and status. *American Journal of Sociology* **45:** 171–182.

Golembiewski, Robert, and Arthur Blumberg, 1970. *Sensitivity training and the laboratory approach.* Itasca, Ill.: Peacock.

Gordon, Thomas, 1955. *Group-centered leadership.* Boston: Houghton Mifflin.

Gouran, Dennis, 1969. Variables related to consensus in group discussions of questions of policy. *Speech Monographs* **36:** 387–391.

——, 1973. Group communication: perspectives and priorities for future research. *Quarterly Journal of Speech* **59:** 22–29.

——, 1974. *Discussion: the process of group decision making.* New York: Harper & Row.

Greenberg, Alan, 1990. Pistons' whole greater than the sum of their parts. *Ann Arbor News,* June 17: C3.

Greenhaus, Jeffery H., Saroj Parasuraman, and Wayne Wormley, 1990. Effects of race on organizational experiences, job performance evaluations, and career outcomes. *Academy of Management Journal* **33:** No. 1, 64–86.

Greiner, Larry, 1970. Patterns of organizational change. In G. Dalton, P. Lawrence, and L. Greiner (eds.). *Organizational change and development.* Homewood, Ill.: Irwin, pp. 213–229.

Gross, Bertram M., 1964. *Organizations and their managing.* New York: Free Press.

Grove, Andrew S., 1983. *High output management.* New York: Random House.

Gulley, Halbert, 1968. *Discussions, conferences, and group processes.* New York: Holt, Rinehart and Winston.

Hailey, Arthur, 1971. *Wheels.* Garden City, N.Y.: Doubleday.

Haiman, Franklin, 1963. Effects of training in group processes on open-mindedness. *Journal of Communication* **13:** 236–245.

——, 1951. *Group leadership and democratic action.* Boston: Houghton Mifflin.

Hain, Tony, 1972. *Patterns of organizational change.* Flint, Mich.: General Motors Institute.

Hall, Edward T., 1959. *The silent language.* Garden City, N.Y.: Doubleday.

Halpin, A. W., and J. Winer, 1957. A factorial study of the leader behavior description questionnaire. In R. Stogdill and A. Coons (eds.). *Leader behavior: its description and measurement.* Research Monograph No. 88. Columbus, Ohio: Bureau of Business Research, Ohio State University, pp. 6–38.

Haney, William V., 1986. *Communication and organizational behavior* (4th ed.). Homewood, Ill.: Irwin.

Hare, A. Paul, 1962. *Handbook of small group research.* New York: Free Press.

———, and Robert Bales, 1963. Seating position and small group interaction. *Sociometry* **26:** 480–486.

Harkins, Stephen G., and Kate Syzmanski, 1989. Social loafing and group evaluation. *Journal of Personality and Social Psychology* **56:** No. 6, 934–941.

Harkins, Stephen G., 1987. Social loafing and social facilitation. *Journal of Experimental Social Psychology* **23:** 1–18.

Harnack, Victor, and Thorrel B. Fest, 1964. *Group discussion, theory and technique.* New York: Appleton-Century-Crofts.

Haroldson, Tom, 1989. Stress: for kids 10–14, it's fact of life, study finds. *Ann Arbor News,* September 6: B4.

Harris, Thomas A., 1967. *I'm OK—you're OK.* New York: Harper & Row.

Hart, Roderick P., and Don M. Burks, 1972. Rhetorical sensitivity and social interaction. *Speech Monographs* **39:** 75–91.

———, William F. Eadie, and Robert E. Carlson, 1975. Rhetorical sensitivity and communicative competence. Paper presented at the annual convention of the Speech Communication Association, December, Houston.

Harvey, Jerry, and C. Russell Boettger, 1971. Improving communication within a work group. *Journal of Applied Behavioral Science* **7:** 1964–79.

Harvey, O. J., and C. Consalvi, 1960. Status and conformity to pressures in informal groups. *Journal of Abnormal and Social Psychology* **60:** 182–187.

Hatvany, Nina, and Vladimir Pucik, 1981. Japanese management practices and productivity. *Organizational Dynamics,* Spring: 5–21.

Hayes, Donald, and Leo Meltzer, 1972. Interpersonal judgments based on talkativeness: fact or artifact? *Sociometry* **35:** 538–561.

"He who runs may read," 1975. *Notes and Quotes,* July–August.

Hearn, G., 1957. Leadership and the spatial factor in small groups. *Journal of Abnormal and Social Psychology* **54:** 269–272.

Heider, Fritz, 1958. *The psychology of interpersonal relations.* New York: Wiley.

Hendrix, Kathleen, 1990. What do gangs, yuppies have in common? anthropologist sees same human drives. *Ann Arbor News,* June 27: B5.

Hersey, Paul, and Kenneth H. Blanchard, 1982. *Management of organizational behavior* (4th ed.). Englewood Cliffs, N.J.: Prentice-Hall.

Hill, Timothy, 1976. An experimental study of the relationship between opinionated leadership and small group consensus. *Communication Monographs* **43:** 246–257.

Holloman, Russ, 1990. Toward a management counter culture. *Journal of Management in Practice* **2:** 17–23.

Homans, George C., 1961. *Social behavior: its elementary forms.* New York: Harcourt.

Howell, William, and Donald Smith, 1956. *Discussion.* New York: Macmillan.

Huse, E. F., and T. G. Cummings, 1985. *Organization development and change* (3rd ed.). St. Paul, Minn.: West Publishing.

Huse, Edgar F., and James L. Bowditch, 1973. *Behavior in organizations: a systems approach to managing.* Reading, Mass.: Addison-Wesley.

Huszczo, Gregory E., 1990. Training for team building: how do you avoid the 10 common pitfalls of team-training approaches? *Training and Development Journal,* February, 37–43.

Jablin, F. M., 1979. Superior-subordinate communication: the state of the art. *Psychological Bulletin* **86:** 1201–1222.

Janis, Irving, 1971. Groupthink. *Psychology Today,* November, 43–46.

———, 1982. *Victims of groupthink* (2nd ed.). Boston: Houghton Mifflin.

Jarobe, Susan P., 1988. A comparison of input-output, process-output, and input-process-output models of small group problem-solving effectiveness. *Communication Monographs* **55**: 121–142.

Jennings, Helen Hall, 1950. *Leadership and isolation: a study of personality in interpersonal relations* (2nd ed.). New York: Longmans, Green.

Jemmott, John B. III, and Elida Gonzales, 1989. Social status, the status distribution, and performance in small groups. *Journal of Applied Social Psychology* **19**: No. 7, 584–598.

Johnson, David W., 1972. *Reaching out: interpersonal effectiveness and self-actualization.* Englewood Cliffs, N.J.: Prentice-Hall.

———, 1973. *Contemporary social psychology.* New York: Lippincott.

Jones, Richard P., 1981. Nude sunbathing. *Flint Journal,* September 6: c6.

Jourard, Sidney M., 1964. *The transparent self: self-disclosure and well-being.* Princeton, N.J.: Van Nostrand.

Kanter, Rosabeth Moss, 1983. *The change masters: innovation and entrepreneurship in the American corporation.* New York: Simon & Schuster.

Karlins, Marvin, and Edyth Hargis, 1988. Inaccurate self-perception as a limiting factor in managerial effectiveness. *Perceptual and Motor Skills* **66**: 665–666.

Karrass, Chester L., 1970. *The negotiating game.* New York: T. Crowell.

Kast, Fremont E., and James E. Rosenzweig, 1970. *Organization and management: a systems approach.* New York: McGraw-Hill.

Katz, Daniel, and Robert Kahn, 1978. *The social psychology of organizations* (2nd ed.). New York: Wiley.

Kearns, David T., 1990. Leadership through quality. *Academy of Management Executive* **4:** 86–89.

Kearney, William, and Desmond Martin, 1974. Sensitivity training: an established management development tool? *Academy of Management Journal* **17:** 755–760.

Keller, MaryAnn, 1989. *Rude awakening: the rise, fall, and struggle for recovery of General Motors.* New York: Morrow.

Keller, Robert T., 1986. Predictors of the performance of project groups in R & D organizations. *Academy of Management Journal* **29:** No. 4, 715–726.

Kelly, Francis J., and Heather Mayfield Kelly, 1986. *What they really teach you at the Harvard Business School.* New York: Warner Communications.

Keltner, John, 1970. *Interpersonal speech communication.* Belmont, Calif.: Wadsworth.

Kendon, A., 1967. Some functions of gaze-direction in social interaction. *Acta Psychologica* **26:** 22–63.

Keniston, Kenneth, 1967. The sources of student dissent. *Journal of Social Issues* **23:** 108–137.

Kepner, Charles H., and Benjamin B. Tregoe, 1965. *The rational manager: a systematic approach to problem solving and decision making.* New York: McGraw-Hill.

Kibler, Robert, and Larry Barker, 1969. *Conceptual frontiers in speech communication.* New York: Speech Association of America.

———, Larry Barker, and Donald Cegala, 1970. Effect of sex on comprehension and retention. *Speech Monographs* **37:** 287–292.

Kiesler, Charles, and Sara Kiesler, 1969. *Conformity.* Reading, Mass.: Addison-Wesley.

Kinch, John W., 1974. A formalized theory of the self-concept. In Jean Civikly (ed.). *Messages: a reader in human communication.* New York: Random House, pp. 118–126.

Kinkade, Kathryn, 1973. Commune: a Walden-two experiment. *Psychology Today,* January 6: 35–38.

Kinzel, Augustus, 1969. Toward an understanding of violence. *Attitude,* Vol. 1.

Kline, John, 1970. Indices of orientation and opinionated statements in problem-solving discussions. *Speech Monographs* **37**: 282–286.

Knapp, Mark L., 1972. *Nonverbal communication in human interaction.* New York: Holt, Rinehart and Winston.

Knutson, Thomas J., 1972. An experimental study of the effects of orientation behavior on small group consensus. *Speech Monographs* **39**: 159–165.

Korda, Michael, 1975. *Power! How to get it, how to use it.* New York: Random House.

Korn, Lester, 1988. *The success profile.* New York: Simon and Schuster.

Korzybski, Alfred, 1948. *Selections from science and sanity: an introduction to non-Aristotelian systems and general semantics.* Lakeville, Conn.: Institute of General Semantics.

Kotter, John P., 1986. *Power and influence: beyond formal authority.* New York: Free Press.

Kreps, Gary L., 1986. *Organizational communication.* White Plains, N.Y.: Longman.

Kretch, D., R. Crutchfield, and E. Ballachey, 1962. *Individual in society.* New York: McGraw-Hill.

Kriesberg, M., 1950. Executives evaluate administrative conferences. *Advanced Management* **15**: 15–17.

Labich, Kenneth, 1988. The seven keys to business leadership. *Fortune:* October 24: 58–66.

Lakin, Martin, 1972. *Interpersonal encounter: theory and practice in sensitivity training.* New York: McGraw-Hill.

Larson, Carl E., 1969. Forms of analysis and small group problem solving. *Speech Monographs* **36**: 452–455.

———, and Robert D. Gratz, 1970. Problem-solving discussion training and T-group training: an experimental comparison. *Speech Teacher* **19**: 54–57.

Larson, Carl E., and Frank M. J. LaFasto, 1989. *Teamwork.* Newbury Park, Calif.: Sage Publications.

Latané, B., K. Williams, and S. Harkins, 1979. Many hands make light the work: the causes and consequences of social loafing. *Journal of Personality and Social Psychology* **37**: 823–832.

Lawrence, P., and D. Dyer, 1983. *Renewing American industry.* New York: Free Press.

Lawrence, Paul, and J. Lorsch, 1969. *Developing organizations: diagnosis and action.* Reading, Mass.: Addison-Wesley.

Leana, Carrie R., Edwin A. Locke, and David M. Schweiger, 1990. Fact and fiction in analyzing research on participative decision making: a critique of Colton Vollrath, Ioggatt, Lengnick-Hall, and Jennings. *Academy of Management Review* **15**: No. 1, 137–146.

Leary, Timothy, 1957. *Interpersonal diagnosis of personality.* New York: Ronald Press.

Leathers, Dale, 1969. Process disruption and measurement in small group communication. *Quarterly Journal of Speech* **55**: 287.

———, 1970. The process effects of trust-destroying behaviors in the small group. *Speech Monographs* **37**: 180–187.

———, 1976. *Nonverbal communication systems.* Boston: Allyn and Bacon.

Leavitt, Harold, 1951. Some effects of certain communication patterns on group performance. *Journal of Abnormal and Social Psychology* **46**: 38–50.

———, 1964. *Managerial psychology* (2nd ed.). Chicago: University of Chicago Press.

Lefkowitz, M. R. Blake, and J. Mouton, 1955. Status factors in pedestrian violation of traffic signals. *Journal of Abnormal and Social Psychology* **51**: 704–706.

———, 1938. The conceptual representation and measurement of psychological forces. *Contributions to Psychological Theory* **1,** No. 4: 62.

Levinson, Elliot, 1988. The line manager and systems- induced organizational change. In Klaus M. Blache. *Success factors for implementing change.* Dearborn, Michigan: Society of Manufacturing Engineers.

Lewin, Kurt, 1948. *Resolving social conflicts.* New York: Harper.

———, 1951. *Field theory in social science.* New York: Harper & Row.

———, 1953. Studies in group decision. In Dorwin Cartwright and Alvin Zander (eds.). *Group dynamics.* Evanston, Ill.: Row, Peterson.

———, Ronald Lippitt, and Ralph White, 1939. Patterns of aggressive behavior in experimentally created "social climates." *Journal of Social Psychology* **10:** 271–299.

Liddell, William W., and John W. Slocum, 1976. The effects of individual-role compatibility upon group performance: an extension of Schutz's FIRO theory. *Academy of Management Journal* **19:** 420.

Lieberman, Morton, Irwin Yalom, and Matthew Miles, 1973. *Encounter groups: first facts.* New York: Basic Books.

———, Irvin Yalom, and Matthew Miles, 1972. The impact of encounter groups on participants: some preliminary findings. *Journal of Applied Behavioral Science* **8:** 29–50.

Likert, Rensis, 1961. An emerging theory of organization, leadership, and management. In Luigi Petrutto and Bernard Bass (eds.). *Leadership and interpersonal behavior.* New York: Holt, Rinehart and Winston, pp. 290–309.

———, 1961. *New patterns of management.* New York: McGraw-Hill.

———, 1967. *The human organization.* New York: McGraw-Hill.

Locke, Michelle, 1989. Poll finds meaning of "family" evolving. *Ann Arbor News,* October 10: C-1.

Loden, Marilyn, 1990. Feminine leadership: or how to succeed in business without being one of the boys. In Jon L. Pierce and John W. Newstrom (eds.). *Manager's bookshelf.* New York: Harper & Row, pp. 295–301.

Lomranz, Jacob, Martin Lakin, and Harold Schiffman, 1972. Variants of sensitivity training and encounter: diversity or fragmentation. *Journal of Applied Behavioral Science* **8:** 399–420.

Lowell, Jon, 1985. Saturn. *Ward's Auto World,* February: 35–37.

Luchins, A. R., 1942. Mechanization in problem solving. *Psychological Monographs* **54:** No. 6 (Whole No. 248).

Lorsch, Jay, and Paul Lawrence, 1972. *Managing group and intergroup relations.* Homewood, Ill.: Irwin.

Luft, Joseph, 1969. *Of human interaction.* Palo Alto, Calif.: National Press.

———, 1984. *Group processes: an introduction to group dynamics* (3rd ed.). Palo Alto, Calif.: National Press.

McCall, Morgan W. Jr., Michael M. Lombardo, and Ann M. Morrison, 1988. *The lessons of experience: how successful executives develop in the job.* Lexington, Mass.: Lexington Books.

McClelland, David C., 1961. *The achieving society.* Princeton, N.J.: Van Nostrand.

——— (ed.), 1955. *Studies in motivation.* New York: Appleton-Century-Crofts.

———, J. W. Atkinson, R. A. Clark, and E. L. Lowell, 1953. *The achievement motive.* New York: Appleton-Century-Crofts.

McCormack, Mark H., 1984. *What they don't teach you at Harvard Business School.* New York: Bantam Books.

McCroskey, James, 1971. Human information processing and diffusion. In Larry Barker and Robert Kibler (eds.). *Speech communication behavior: perspectives and principles.* Englewood Cliffs, N.J.: Prentice-Hall, pp. 167–181.

————, Carl Larson, and Mark Knapp, 1971. *An introduction to interpersonal communication*. Englewood Cliffs, N.J.: Prentice-Hall.

————, and David W. Wright, 1971. The development of an instrument for measuring interaction behavior in small groups. *Speech Monographs* **38**: 335–340.

McGrath, Joseph E., and Irwin Altman, 1966. *Small group research: a synthesis and critique of the field*. New York: Holt, Rinehart and Winston.

McKeachie, W., 1952. Lipstick as a determiner of first impressions of personality: an experiment for the general psychology course. *Journal of Social Psychology* **36**: 241–244.

McLaughlin, David, and Jay Hewitt, 1972. Need for approval and perceived openness. *Journal of Experimental Research in Personality* **6**: 255–258.

Magner, Mike, 1988. Geology blamed for state's loss of atom smasher. *Ann Arbor News*, November 11: A1, A4.

Maier, Norman R. F., 1963. *Problem-solving discussions and conferences*. New York: McGraw-Hill.

————, and A. R. Solem, 1952. The contributions of a discussion leader to the quality of group thinking: the effective use of minority opinions. *Human Relations* **5**: 277–288.

Main, Jeremy, 1981. Westinghouse's cultural revolution. *Fortune*, June 15: 74–93.

Maineiro, Lisa, 1990. The new sexual revolution: love in the workplace. *Fairfield Business Review*, Spring: 4–15.

Malmuth, Neil M., and Seymour Feshbach, 1972. Risky shift in a naturalistic setting. *Journal of Personality* **40**: 38–49.

Manz, Charles C., and Henry P. Sims, 1990. *Super leadership: leading others to lead themselves*. New York: Berkeley Books.

Markham, Steven E., Fred Dansereau, Jr., and Joseph A. Alutto, 1982. Group size and absenteeism rates: a longitudinal analysis. *Academy of Management Journal* **25**: 921–927.

Maslow, Abraham, 1970. *Motivation and personality* (2nd ed.). New York: Harper & Row.

————, and N. Mintz, 1956. Effects of esthetic surroundings: I. initial effects of three esthetic conditions upon perceiving "energy" and "well-being" in faces. *Journal of Psychology* **41**: 247–254.

Mayo, Elton, 1933. *The human problems of an industrial civilization*. New York: Macmillan.

Mead, Margaret, 1934. *Sex and temperament in three primitive societies*. New York: Dell.

Meerloo, Joost, 1956. *The rape of the mind*. New York: Grosset and Dunlap.

Mehrabian, Albert, 1956. Significance of posture and position in the communication of attitudes and status relations. *Psychological Bulletin* **71**: 359–372.

————, 1971. Nonverbal betrayal of feeling. *Journal of Experimental Research in Personality* **5**: 64–73.

Meyer, Alan D., 1988. Organizational assimilation of innovations: a multilevel contextual analysis. *Academy of Management Journal* **31**: No. 4, 897–923.

Michaelson, Larry K., 1985. Introduction to the special issue on using groups in teaching. *Organizational Behavior Teaching Review*, Fall: 1–2.

Mikol, Bernard, 1960. The enjoyment of new musical systems. In Milton Rokeach (ed.). *The open and closed mind*. New York: Basic Books, pp. 270–284.

Miles, Matthew B., 1965. Changes during and following laboratory training: a clinical-experimental study. *Journal of Applied Behavioral Science* **1**: 215–242.

————, 1967. *Learning to work in groups*. New York: Teacher's College Press, Columbia University.

Milgram, Stanley, 1974. *Obedience to authority: an experimental view*. New York: Harper & Row.

Miller, Gerald R., and Paula Bacon, 1971. Open and closed-mindedness and recognition of visual humor. *Journal of Communication* **21**: 150–159.

Miller, Katherine I., and Peter R. Monge, 1985. Social information and employee anxiety about organizational change. *Human Communication Research* **11:** 365–386.

Mills, Judson, and Elliot Aronson, 1965. Opinion change as a function of the communicator's attractiveness and desire to influence. *Journal of Personality and Social Psychology* **1:** 73–77.

Mills, Theodore, 1967. *The sociology of small groups.* Englewood Cliffs, N.J.: Prentice-Hall.

Miner, John B., 1988. *Organizational behavior: performance and productivity.* New York: Random House.

Mitroff, I. I., 1982. Dialectic squared: a fundamental difference is perception of the meanings of some key concepts in social science. *Decision Sciences* **13:** 222–224.

———, and R. O. Mason, 1981. The metaphysics of policy and planning: a reply to Cosier. *Academy of Management Review* **6:** 649–651.

Mohr, William L., and Harriet Mohr, 1983. *Quality circles: changing images of people at work.* Reading, Mass.: Addison-Wesley.

Morris, Charles, and J. Richard Hackman, 1969. Behavioral correlates of perceived leadership. *Journal of Personality and Social Psychology* **13:** 350–361.

Morris, Michael. Training's role for Consumer's Power Co.—1990. Keynote speech at the Consumer's Power Instructor Conference, Midland, Michigan, May 17, 1990.

Morrison, Ann M., Randall P. White, and Ellen Van Velsor, 1990. Breaking the glass ceiling: can women reach the top of America's largest corporations? In Jon L. Pierce and John W. Newstrom (eds.). *Manager's Bookshelf.* New York: Harper & Row, pp. 289–294.

Mortenson, C. David, 1970. The status of small group research. *Quarterly Journal of Speech* **56:** 304–309.

Mosca, Joseph, 1990. A profile of the 21st century employee. *Journal of Management in Practice* **2:** 9–15.

Moseley, Ray, 1974. Soviet monkey business: aping American execs. *Flint Journal,* January 13: A-8.

Moskal, Brian S., 1990. The wizards of Buick City. *Industry Week,* May 7: 22–28.

Mossholder, Kevin W., Arthur G. Bedian, and Achilles A. Armenakis, 1982. Group process–work outcome relationships: a note on the moderating impact of self-esteem. *Academy of Management Journal* **25:** 575–585.

Mosvick, Roger, 1971. Human relations training for scientists, technicians, and engineers: a review of relevant experimental evaluations of human relations training. *Personnel Psychology* **24:** 275–292.

Murray, Henry, 1938. *Explorations in personality.* New York: Oxford University Press.

Mydans, Seth, 1990. Academic success seen as selling out, study on blacks says. *San Francisco Chronicle,* April 25: B6.

Mydans, Seth, 1990. Wanna-be's: youth gangs spread from the inner city. *Ann Arbor News,* May 6: B1, B4.

Myers, Gail E., and Michele Tolela Myers, 1973. *The dynamics of human communication.* New York: McGraw-Hill.

Nadler, E. B., 1959. Yielding, authoritarianism, and authoritarian ideology regarding groups. *Journal of Abnormal and Social Psychology* **58:** 408–410.

Naisbitt, John, 1982. *Megatrends: ten new directions transforming our lives.* New York: Warner Books.

New tuck program teaches group skills, (1990). *Tuck News,* Dartmouth College Alumni Magazine, Hanover, New Hampshire, January: 33.

Newcomb, Theodore, 1943. *Personality and social change.* New York: Dryden.

———, 1963. Persistence and regression of changed attitudes: long-range studies. *Journal of Social Issues* **19:** 3–14.

Nicholas, John M., and Marsha Katz, 1985. Research methods and reporting practices in organization development: a review and some guidelines. *The Academy of Management Review* **10:** 737–749.

Nye, Robert, 1973. *Conflict among humans.* New York: Springer.

Ober, Nelson, and Fred E. Jandt, 1973. Students' self-concepts and evaluations of discussion instruction. *Speech Teacher* **22:** 64–66.

Ogden, Charles K., and I. A. Richards, 1946. *The meaning of meaning.* New York: Harcourt, Brace.

Organ, Dennis W., and Thomas Bateman, 1986. *Organizational behavior* (3rd ed.). Plano, Tex.: Business Publications, Inc.

Ornstein, Suzyn, 1989. The hidden influences of office design. *The Academy of Management Executive* **3:** No. 2, 144–147.

Orton, J. Douglas, and Karl E. Weick, 1990. Loosely coupled systems: a reconceptualization. *Academy of Management Review* **15:** No. 2, 203–223.

Osborn, Alex, 1953. *Applied imagination: principles and procedures of creative thinking.* New York: Scribner's.

Osborn, Susan M., and Gloria H. Harris, 1984. Using the small group for assertive training. In Robert S. Cathcart and Larry Samovar. *Small group communication: a reader* (4th ed.). Dubuque, Iowa: Wm. C. Brown.

Osgood, Charles, 1969. Calculated de-escalation as a strategy. In D. G. Pruitt and R. C. Synder (eds.). *Theory and research on the causes of war.* Englewood Cliffs, N.J.: Prentice-Hall, pp. 213–216.

Ouchi, William, 1981. *Theory Z: how American business can meet the Japanese challenge.* Reading, Mass.: Addison-Wesley.

Parkinson, C. Northcote, 1957. *Parkinson's law: and other studies in administration.* Boston: Houghton Mifflin.

Patton, Bobby, and Kim Giffin, 1973. *Problem-solving group interaction.* New York: Harper & Row.

———, and ———, 1981. *Interpersonal communication in action* (3rd ed.). New York: Harper & Row.

Paulus, Paul B. (ed.), 1989. *Psychology of group influence* (2nd ed.). Hillsdale, N.J.: Lawrence Erlbaum Associates.

Payne, Sam, David Summers, and Thomas Stewart, 1973. Value differences across three generations. *Sociometry* **36:** 20–30.

Penley, Larry E., and Brian Hawkins, 1985. Studying interpersonal communication in organizations: A leadership application. *Academy of Management Journal* **28:** 309–326.

Petelle, John, 1964. The role of conflict in discussion. *Speaker and Gavel* **2:** 24–28.

Pettinger, Robert, 1964. *The first five minutes.* Itasca, N.Y.: Peacock.

Pfeffer, Jeffrey, 1981. *Power in organizations.* Marshfield, Mass.: Pitman.

Pfeiffer, J. William, and John Jones, 1969. *Structured experiences for human relations training.* Iowa City: University Associates.

Phillips, J. D., 1948. Report on discussion 66. *Adult Education Journal* **7:** 181–182.

Popkey, Dan, 1986. NFL football sacks Monday meetings of Boise Council, *The Idaho Statesman,* March 1, p. 1.

Psychology Today, 1970. Del Mar, Calif.: CRM Publications.

Quinn, Robert, 1973. *Job satisfaction: Is there a trend?* Washington, D.C.: United States Department of Labor.

Rarick, David, Gary F. Soldow, and Ronald S. Geizer, 1976. Self-monitoring as a mediator of conformity. *Central States Speech Journal* **27**: 267–271.

Redding, W. C., 1972. *Communication within the organization: An interpretive review of theory and research.* New York: Industrial Communication Council.

Regula, C. Robert, and James Julian, 1973. The impact of quality and frequency of task contributions on perceived ability. *Journal of Social Psychology* **89**: 112–115.

Ringwald, Barbara, Richard Mann, Robert Rosenwein, and Wilbert McKeachie, 1971. Conflict and style in the college classroom: An intimate study. *Psychology Today,* February, pp. 45–47, 76–79.

Roberts, W. Rhys, 1941. Rhetoric. In Richard McKean (ed.). *The basic works of Aristotle.* New York: Random House, pp. 1318–1451.

Robinson, F. P., 1961. *Effective study.* New York: Harper & Row.

Roethlisberger, Fritz, and William Dickson, 1939. *Management and the worker.* Cambridge, Mass.: Harvard University Press.

Rogers, Carl R., and F. J. Roethlisberger, 1952. Barriers and gateways to communication. *Harvard Business Review* **30:** 48.

Rogers, Everett, and Dilip K. Bhowmik, 1971. Homophily-heterophily: Relational concepts for communication research. In Larry Barker and Robert Kibler (eds.), *Speech communication behavior: Perspectives and principles.* Englewood Cliffs, N.J.: Prentice-Hall, pp. 206–225.

———, and F. Floyd Shoemaker, 1971. *Communication of innovations* (2nd ed.). New York: Free Press.

Rokeach, Milton, 1948. Generalized mental rigidity as a factor in ethnocentrism. *Journal of Abnormal and Social Psychology* **43**: 259–278.

———, 1954. The nature and meaning of dogmatism. *Psychological Review* **61**: 194–204.

———, 1960. *The open and closed mind.* New York: Basic Books.

———, 1968. *Beliefs, attitudes, and values.* San Francisco: Jossey-Bass.

———, 1971. Long-range experimental modifications of values, attitudes, and behavior. In William A. Hunt (ed.), *Human behavior and its control.* Cambridge, Mass.: Schenkman, pp. 93–105.

———, 1973. *The nature of human values.* New York: Free Press.

Rosenfeld, Howard, 1965. Effect of approval-seeking induction on interpersonal proximity. *Psychological Reports* **17**: 120–122.

———, 1966. Instrumental affiliative functions of facial and gestural expressions. *Journal of Personality and Social Psychology* **4**: 65–72.

Rosenfeld, Lawrence B., and Gene D. Fowler, 1976. Personality, sex, and leadership style. *Communication Monographs* **43**: 320–324.

———, and Vickie Christie, 1974. Sex and persuasibility revisited. *Western Speech* **38:** 244–253.

———, and Kenneth Frandsen, 1972. The "other" speech student: an empirical analysis of some interpersonal relations orientations of the reticent student. *Speech Teacher* **21:** 296–302.

Ross, Edward, 1920. *The principles of sociology.* New York: Century.

Ross, Raymond, 1970. *Speech communication fundamentals and practice.* Englewood Cliffs, N.J.: Prentice-Hall.

Ruben, Brent, 1972. General system theory: an approach to human communication. In Richard Budd and Brent Ruben (eds.). *Approaches to human communication.* New York: Spartan, pp. 120–144.

———, and John Y. Kim (eds.), 1975. *General systems theory and human communication.* Rochelle Park, N.J.: Hayden.

Ruch, Richard S., 1972. An analysis of the Freudian slip and errors in speech communication. *Journal of Technical Writing and Communication* **2**: 343–352.

Ruch, Richard S., and Ronald Goodman, 1983. *Image at the top: crisis and renaissance in corporate leadership*. New York: Free Press.

Runyan, Kenneth, 1973. Some interactions between personality variables and management styles. *Journal of Applied Psychology* **57:** 288–294.

Russo, N. F., 1967. Connotations of seating arrangements. *Cornell Journal of Social Relations* **2:** 37–44.

Sabatine, Frank J., 1989. Rediscovering creativity: unlearning old habits. *Mid-American Journal of Business*, Fall, **4:** 11–13.

Sattler, William, and N. Edd Miller, 1968. *Discussion and conference*. Englewood Cliffs, N.J.: Prentice-Hall.

Saunders, Carol, and Jack William Jones, 1990. Temporal sequences in information acquisition for decision making: a focus on source and medium. *The Academy of Management Review* **15:** No. 1, 29–46.

Savage, Grant T., John D. Blair, and Ritch L. Sorenson, 1989. Consider both relationships and substance when negotiating strategically. *The Academy of Management Executive* **3:** No. 1, 37–48.

Schachter, Stanley, 1951. Deviation, rejection, and communication. *Journal of Abnormal and Social Psychology* **46:** 190–207.

———, Norris Ellertson, Dorothy McBride, and Doris Gregory, 1968. An experimental study of cohesiveness and productivity. In D. Cartwright and A. Zander (eds.). *Group dynamics* (3rd ed.). New York: Harper & Row, pp. 192–198.

Scheidel, Thomas, 1970. Sex and persuasibility. *Speech Monographs* **37:** 292–387.

Schein, Edgar H., 1988. *Process consultation: its role in organization development* (Vol. I). Reading, Mass.: Addison-Wesley.

———, 1987. *Process consultation: lessons for managers and consultants* (Vol. II). Reading, Mass.: Addison-Wesley.

———, and Warren Bennis, 1965. *Personal and organizational change through group methods*. New York: Wiley.

Schelling, Thomas C., 1960. *The strategy of conflict*. Cambridge, Mass.: Harvard University Press.

Schembechler, Bo, and Mitch Albom, 1989. *Bo: life, laughs, and lessons of a college football legend*. New York: Warner Books.

Schnake, Mel E., 1990. *Human relations*. Columbus, Ohio: Merill Publishing Company.

———, and Michael Dumler, 1989. Managerial "Unleadership" behavior and the moderating effects of task scope. *The Journal of Management Systems* **1:** No. 2, 49–61.

Schneider, Frank W., and James G. Delaney, 1972. Effect of individual achievement motivation on group problem-solving efficiency. *Journal of Social Psychology* **86:** 291–298.

Schools reject longstanding medical oath, 1986. Associated Press, *The Idaho Statesman*, May 18.

Schutz, William C., 1958. *FIRO: a three-dimensional theory of interpersonal behavior*. New York: Holt, Rinehart and Winston.

———, 1967. *Joy: expanding human awareness*. New York: Grove.

———, 1971. *Here comes everybody: bodymind and encounter culture*. New York: Harper & Row.

Schweiger, David M., William R. Sandberg, and James W. Ragan, 1986. Group approaches for improving strategic decision making: a comparative analysis of dialectical inquiry, devil's advocacy and consensus. *Academy of Management Journal* **29:** 51–71.

Schweiger, David, William R. Sandberg, and Paula L. Rechner, 1989. Experimental effects of dialectical inquiry, devil's advocacy, and consensus approaches to strategic decision making. *Academy of Management Journal* **32**: 745–772.

Seeger, John A., 1983. No innate phases in group problem solving. *The Academy of Management Review* **8**: 683–689.

Seiler, John A., 1967. *Systems analysis in organizational behavior.* Homewood, Ill.: Irwin-Dorsey.

Seligmann, Jean, 1990. Variations on a theme. *Newsweek,* Winter/Spring: 38–46.

Sellers, Patricia, 1989. Getting customers to love you. *Fortune,* March 13: 38–49.

Sereno, Kenneth, and Edward Bodaken, 1975. *TRANS-PER: understanding human communication.* Boston: Houghton Mifflin.

Shapiro, Laura, 1990. Eating habits. *Newsweek,* Winter/Spring: 78–79.

Shaw, Marjorie, 1932. A comparison of individuals and small groups in the rational solution of complex problems. *American Journal of Psychology* **44**: 491–504.

Shaw, Marvin E., 1964. Communication networks. In Leonard Berkowitz (ed.). *Advances in experimental social psychology* (Vol. 1). New York: Academic Press, pp. 111–147.

———, 1981. *Group dynamics: the psychology of small group behavior* (3rd ed.). New York: McGraw-Hill.

Sheldon, William, 1940. *The varieties of human physique.* New York: Harper & Row.

———, 1942. *The varieties of temperament.* New York: Harper & Row.

———, 1954. *Atlas of man: a guide for somatotyping the adult male of all ages.* New York: Harper & Row.

Sheppard, James A., and Rex A. Wright, 1989. Individual contributions to a collective effort: an incentive analysis. *Personality and Social Psychology Bulletin* **15**: No. 2, 141–149.

Sherif, Muzafer, 1963. *The psychology of social norms.* New York: Harper & Row.

———, Carolyn Sherif, and Roger Nebergall, 1965. *Attitude and attitude change: the social judgment-involvement approach.* Philadelphia: Saunders.

Shils, Edward, 1951. The study of the primary group. In Harold Lasswell and Daniel Lerner (eds.). *The policy science.* Stanford, Calif.: Stanford University Press, pp. 44–69.

Sieburg, Evelyn, 1971. Dimensions of interpersonal response. A paper presented at the annual convention of the International Communication Association, Phoenix, April.

Simmel, George, 1955. *Conflict.* Trans. K. H. Wolff. Glencoe, Ill.: Free Press.

Simon, Herbert A., 1987. Making management decisions: the role of intuition and emotion. *The Academy of Management Executive,* February: 57–64.

Sims, Henry P., Jr., and James W. Dean, Jr., 1985. Beyond quality circles: self-managing teams. *Personnel,* pp. 25–32.

Smircich, Linda, and Charles Stubbart, 1985. Strategic management in an enacted world. *The Academy of Management Review* **10**: 724–736.

Smith, David C., 1974. WAW adds its selections to '75 model name parade. *Ward's Auto World* **10**: 13.

———, 1975. The new small Seville: Cadillac's king-size gamble. *Ward's Auto World* **11**: 23–28.

———, 1985. Team Taurus: Ford's $3-billion mid-market plunge. *Ward's Auto World,* February: pp. 26–33.

Sommer, Robert, 1959. Studies in personal space. *Sociometry* **22**: 247–260.

———, 1965. Further studies of small group ecology. *Sociometry* **28**: 337–348.

———, 1969. *Personal space: the behavioral basis of design.* Englewood Cliffs, N.J.: Prentice-Hall.

Sorenson, Ritch L., Grant T. Savage, and Elizabeth Orem, 1990. A profile of communication faculty needs in business schools and colleges. *Communication Education* **38:** 148–160.

South, E. B., 1927. Some psychological aspects of committee work. *Journal of Applied Psychology* **11:** 348–368, 437–464.

Spock, Benjamin, 1990. It's all up to us. *Newsweek,* Winter/Spring: 106–107.

Stech, Ernest, and Sharon A. Ratliffe, 1985. *Effective group communication: how to get action by working in groups.* Lincolnwood, Ill.: National Text Book Company.

Stein, Carroll, 1973. Group grope: the latest development bromide. *Personnel Journal,* January, pp. 19–26.

Steiner, Ivan D., 1972. *Group process and productivity.* New York: Academic Press.

Steinmetz, Lawrence, 1969. *Managing the marginal and unsatisfactory performer.* Reading, Mass.: Addison-Wesley.

Steinzor, B., 1950. The spatial factor in face-to-face discussion groups. *Journal of Abnormal and Social Psychology* **45:** 552–555.

Stigler, G. J., 1974. Free riders and collective action: an appendix to theories of economic regulation. *Bell Journal of Economics and Management Science* **5:** 359–365.

Stogdill, Ralph, 1948. Personal factors associated with leadership. *Journal of Psychology* **25:** 35–71.

———, 1972. Group productivity. *Organizational Behavior and Human Performance* **8:** 26–43.

———, 1974. *Handbook of leadership: a survey of theory and research.* New York: Free Press.

Stoner, J. A. F., 1961. *Comparison of individual and group decisions involving risk.* Unpublished master's thesis. Massachusetts Institute of Technology, School of Industrial Management.

Streigel, Quincalee Brown, 1975. Self-reported behavioral and attitudinal changes by participation in a women's consciousness-raising group. Paper presented at the annual convention of the Central States Speech Association, April, Kansas City, Missouri.

Strodbeck, Fred, and L. H. Hook, 1961. The social dimensions of a twelve-man jury table. *Sociometry* **24:** 397–415.

Strongman, K., and B. Champness, 1968. Dominance hierarchies and conflict in eye contact. *Acta Psychologica* **28:** 376–386.

Sturges, David L., 1988. Combined forces and computer-aided instruction small group interaction. *The Journal of Professional Studies* **12:** No. 2, 19–23.

Symington, James W., 1971. *The stately game.* New York: Macmillan.

Tannenbaum, Robert, Irving Weschler, and Fred Massarik, 1961. *Leadership and organization: a behavioral science approach.* New York: McGraw-Hill.

———, and Warren Schmidt, 1972. How to choose a leadership pattern. In Jay Lorsch and Paul Lawrence (eds.). *Managing group and intergroup relations.* Homewood, Ill.: Irwin, pp. 188–200.

Tavris, Carol, 1974. Women in China: they speak bitterness revolution. *Psychology Today,* May 7: pp. 43–49.

Teger, Allan I., and Dean G. Pruitt, 1970. Components of group risk taking. In R. Cathcart and L. Samovar (eds.). *Small group communication: a reader.* Dubuque, Iowa: Wm. C. Brown, pp. 72–81.

Terman, L., and C. Miles, 1936. *Sex and personality: studies in masculinity and femininity.* New York: McGraw-Hill.

Thayer, Lee, 1968. *Communication and communication systems.* Homewood, Ill.: Irwin.

Thelen, Herbert, and Watson Dickerman, 1949. Stereotypes and the growth of groups. *Educational Leadership* **6:** 309–316.

Thiagarajan, Sivasailam, 1988. Beyond brainstorming. *Training and Development Journal,* September: 57–60.

Thibaut, John W., and Harold H. Kelley, 1950. An experimental study of the cohesiveness of underprivileged groups. *Human Relations* **3:** 251–278.

———, and ———, 1959. *The social psychology of groups.* New York: Wiley.

———, and ———, 1986. *The social psychology of groups* (2nd ed.). New Brunswick, N.J.: Transaction Books.

Thomas, David, 1989. Teachers, students and small groups. *The Journal of Professional Studies* **12:** No. 3, 15–19.

Thomas, Evan, 1986. Growing pains at 40. *Time,* May 19: pp. 22–41.

Thompson, J. D., 1967. *Organization in action.* New York: McGraw-Hill.

Tichy, Noel M., and Mary Anne Devanna, 1986. *The transformational leader.* New York: Wiley.

Time, January 19, 1976, pp. 55–56. Groupthink.

Time, July 23, 1973, pp. 31–32. The return of the gang.

Time, January 14, 1974, p. 58. The impresario of the brain.

Time, August 3, 1981, p. 32. The trust builder.

Thornton, G., 1944. The effect of wearing glasses upon judgments of personality traits of persons seen briefly. *Journal of Applied Psychology* **28:** 203–207.

Tillman, R., Jr., 1960. Problems in review: committees on trial. *Harvard Business Review* **47:** 162–172.

Tosi, Henry L., John R. Rizzo, and Stephen J. Carroll, 1986. *Managing organizational behavior.* Marshfield, Mass.: Pitman.

Toulmin, Stephen, 1958. *The uses of argument.* Cambridge: At the University Press.

Triandis, Harry C., 1971. *Attitude and attitude change.* New York: Wiley.

Tubbs, Stewart L., 1976. The transactive nature of therapeutic communication. Paper presented at the annual convention of the Speech Communication Association, San Francisco, December.

———, 1985. Consulting teams: a methodology for teaching integrated management skills. *Organizational Behavior Teaching Review,* Fall: 52–57.

———, and John Baird, 1980. *Self-disclosure and interpersonal growth.* Columbus, Ohio: Special Press.

———, and Robert M. Carter, 1977. *Shared experiences in human communication.* Rochelle Park, N.J.: Hayden.

———, and Ruth M. Dischner, 1990. From the brink of death. *Industry Week,* May 21: 15–18.

———, and Sylvia Moss, 1974. *Human communication: an interpersonal perspective.* New York: Random House.

———, and Sylvia Moss, 1991. *Human communication* (6th ed.). New York: McGraw-Hill.

Tuckman, Bruce, 1965. Developmental sequence in small groups. *Psychological Bulletin* **63:** 384–399.

Tuddenham, R. D., 1961. The influence upon judgment of the apparent discrepancy between self and others. *Journal of Social Psychology* **53:** 69–79.

Underwood, W., 1965. Evaluation of laboratory method training. *Training Director's Journal* **5:** 34–40.

Unger, Mark, 1974. Unpublished behavioral science term paper. Flint, Mich.: General Motors Institute.

Valiquet, M. I., 1968. Individual change in a management development program. *Journal of Applied Behavioral Science* **4**: 313–326.

Varney, Glenn H., 1989. *Building productive teams*. San Francisco: Jossey-Bass.

Vegetarian graduates get paper diplomas, 1986. Associated Press, *The Idaho Statesman*, May 10: 2.

Viscott, David, 1972. *The making of a psychiatrist*. Greenwich, Conn.: Fawcett.

Von Bertalonffy, Ludwig, 1968. *General system theory*. New York: George Braziller.

Wahlers, Kathy J., and Larry L. Barker, 1973. Bralessness and nonverbal communication. *Central States Speech Journal* **24**: 222–226.

Wallach, Michael A., Nathan Kagan, and Daryl J. Bem, 1962. Group influence on individual risk taking. *Journal of Abnormal and Social Psychology* **65**: 77.

Walker, E. L., and R. W. Heynes, 1967. *An anatomy for conformity*. Belmont, Calif.: Brooks/Cole-Wadsworth.

Walsh, James P., 1989. Selectivity and selective perception: an investigation of managers' belief structures and information processing. *Academy of Management Journal* **31**: No. 4, 873–896.

Walster, E., V. Aronson, D. Abrahams, and L. Rohmann, 1966. Importance of physical attractiveness in dating behavior. *Journal of Personality and Social Psychology* **4**: 508–516.

Warschaw, T., 1980. *Winning by negotiation*. New York: McGraw-Hill.

Watson, Kathleen M., 1982. An analysis of communication patterns: a method for discriminating leader and subordinate roles. *Academy of Management Journal* **25**: 107–120.

Watzlawick, Paul, Janet Beavin, and Donald Jackson, 1967. *Pragmatics of human communication*. New York: Norton.

Weaver, Richard, 1971. Sensitivity training and effective group discussion. *Speech Teacher* **20**: 203–207.

Weick, K. E., 1979. *The social psychology of organizing*. Reading, Mass.: Addison-Wesley.

Weisinger, Hendrie, 1989. *The critical edge: how to criticize up and down your organization and make it pay-off*. Boston: Little, Brown.

Werther, William B., William A. Ruch, and Lynne McClure, 1986. *Productivity through people*. St. Paul, Minn.: West Publishing.

Whetten, David A., and Kim S. Cameron, 1984. *Developing management skills*. Glenview, Ill.: Scott, Foresman.

White, Ralph, and Ronald Lippitt, 1968. Leader behavior and member reaction in three social climates. In D. Cartwright and A. Zander (eds.). *Group dynamics* (3rd ed.). New York: Harper & Row, pp. 318–335.

Whyte, Glen, 1989. Groupthink reconsidered. *Academy of Management Review* **14**: No. 1, 40–56.

Whyte, William F., 1943. *Street corner society*. Chicago: University of Chicago Press.

———, 1955. *Money and motivation*. New York: Harper, Chapter 10.

Widgery, Robin, 1974. Sex of receiver and physical attractiveness of source as determinants of initial credibility perception. *Western Speech* **38**: 13–17.

———, and Bruce Webster, 1969. The effects of physical attractiveness upon perceived initial credibility. *Michigan Speech Journal* **4**: 9–19.

———, and Stewart L. Tubbs, 1972. Machiavellianism and religiosity as determinants of attitude change in a counterattitudinal situation. Paper presented at the annual convention of the International Communication Association, April, Atlanta.

Williams, Lena, 1989. Counter culture: despite AIDS, report finds teens voicing entitlement to sex. *Ann Arbor News*, February 27: A1, A5.

Wilmot, William, 1975. *Dyadic communication: a transactional perspective.* Reading, Mass.: Addison-Wesley.

Wilson, Paul, 1968. Perceptual distortion of height as a function of ascribed academic status. *Journal of Social Psychology* **74:** 97–102.

Wingret, Pat, and Barbara Kantrowitz, 1990. The day care generation. *Newsweek,* Winter/Spring: 87–92.

Wolfe, T., 1979. *The right stuff.* New York: Farrar, Straus & Giroux.

Wong, H., and W. Brown, 1923. Effects of surroundings upon mental work as measured by Yerkes' multiple choice method. *Journal of Comparative Psychology* **3:** 319–331.

Wood, Julia T., Gerald M. Phillips, and Douglas J. Pedersen, 1986. *Group discussion: a practical guide to participation and leadership.* New York: Harper & Row.

Wood, Robert, and Albert Bandura, 1989. Social cognition theory of organizational management. *The Academy of Management Review* **14:** No. 3, 361–383.

Woodward, Kenneth L., 1990. Young beyond their years. *Newsweek,* Winter/Spring: 54–60.

Yale, Diane, 1988. Metaphors in mediating. *Mediation Quarterly* **22:** 15–25.

Yates, Douglas, 1985. *The politics of management.* San Francisco: Jossey-Bass.

Zajonc, Robert, 1966. *Social psychology: an experimental approach.* Belmont, Calif.: Brooks/Cole.

Zalesny, Mary D., and Richard V. Farace, 1987. Traditional versus open offices: a comparison of sociotechnical, social relations, and symbolic meaning perspectives. *Academy of Management Journal* **30:** No. 2, 240–259.

Zaleznik, Abraham, 1990. The leadership gap. *Academy of Management Executive* **4:** No. 1, 7–22.

———, and David Moment, 1964. *The dynamics of interpersonal behavior.* New York: Wiley.

Zander, Alvin, 1961. Resistance to change: its analysis and prevention. In Warren Bennis, Kenneth Benne, and Robert Chin (eds.). *The planning of change.* New York: Holt, Rinehart and Winston, pp. 543–548.

Zeman, Ned, 1990. The new rules of courtship. *Newsweek,* September: 24–27.

Zenger, Todd R., and Barbara S. Lawrence, 1989. Organizational demography: the differential effects of age and tenure distributions on technical communication. *Academy of Management Journal* **32:** No. 2, 353–376.

Zimbardo, Philip, 1972. Pathology of imprisonment. *Society* **9:** 4–8.

INDEX